Corel® WebMaster Suite For Dummies®

Cheat Sheet

Knowing as much as possible about the Web server that you're going to publish your site to *before* you begin to build it can save you many exasperating hours of updating your pages — doing things right the first time is always faster than having to go back and fix them. Have your system or server administrator fill out this sheet and make sure that you keep it handy while you use all the power of WebMaster Suite to build a truly first rate Web site. Don't worry if some of these terms don't seem familiar to you, Chapter 4 details the answers to every one of the following questions.

Project: _____

Basic Issues:

What is my Web site's domain? (For example, www.mycompany.com)

My own domain _____ , ISP's domain _____

What is the root directory of my Web site?

_____

What name must I use for my home page?

_____

What hardware/operating system does the server run?

_____

What program/version server software is running?

_____

What security systems (if any) are available?

_____

    Documentation? _____

Is this site case sensitive? Yes ___, No ___

Who is the server administrator? _____

    E-mail: _____

    Phone: Day: _____   Evening: _____

If ISP, Name: _____

    Address: _____

    URL: _____

D1519131

...For Dummies: #1 Computer Book Series for Beginners

Corel® WebMaster Suite For Dummies®

Programming:

What is the CGI-BIN URL?

_____

What CGI scripts are available?

_____

_____

What is the JAVA BIN URL?

_____

What Java classes are available?

_____

_____

Are JavaBeans supported? Yes ___, No ___

What JavaBeans classes are available?

_____

_____

Are ActiveX controls supported? Yes ___, No ___

What ActiveX controls are available?

_____

_____

What server extensions are available (such as, RealAudio)?

_____

_____

_____

Support:

What support documentation is available?

_____

_____

_____

Online documentation:

_____

_____

File Transfer Protocol:

What is the URL of the FTP root?

_____

What is the FTP address of my Web root?

_____

Copyright © 1997 IDG Books Worldwide, Inc.
All rights reserved.
Cheat Sheet $2.95 value. Item 0300-6.
For more information about IDG Books,
call 1-800-762-2974.

...For Dummies: #1 Computer Book Series for Beginners

ii **Corel WebMaster Suite For Dummies** _____

COREL® WEBMASTER SUITE FOR DUMMIES®

COREL® WEBMASTER SUITE FOR DUMMIES®

by Paul Bodensiek

IDG Books Worldwide, Inc.
An International Data Group Company

Foster City, CA ♦ Chicago, IL ♦ Indianapolis, IN ♦ Southlake, TX

Corel® WebMaster Suite For Dummies®

Published by
IDG Books Worldwide, Inc.
An International Data Group Company
919 E. Hillsdale Blvd.
Suite 400
Foster City, CA 94404
www.idgbooks.com (IDG Books Worldwide Web site)
www.dummies.com (Dummies Press Web site)

Copyright © 1997 IDG Books Worldwide, Inc. All rights reserved. No part of this book, including interior design, cover design, and icons, may be reproduced or transmitted in any form, by any means (electronic, photocopying, recording, or otherwise) without the prior written permission of the publisher.

Library of Congress Catalog Card No.: 97-80752

ISBN: 0-7645-0300-6

Printed in the United States of America

10 9 8 7 6 5 4 3 2 1

1O/QZ/RS/ZX/IN

Distributed in the United States by IDG Books Worldwide, Inc.

Distributed by Macmillan Canada for Canada; by Transworld Publishers Limited in the United Kingdom; by IDG Norge Books for Norway; by IDG Sweden Books for Sweden; by Woodslane Pty. Ltd. for Australia; by Woodslane Enterprises Ltd. for New Zealand; by Longman Singapore Publishers Ltd. for Singapore, Malaysia, Thailand, and Indonesia; by Simron Pty. Ltd. for South Africa; by Toppan Company Ltd. for Japan; by Distribuidora Cuspide for Argentina; by Livraria Cultura for Brazil; by Ediciencia S.A. for Ecuador; by Addison-Wesley Publishing Company for Korea; by Ediciones ZETA S.C.R. Ltda. for Peru; by WS Computer Publishing Corporation, Inc., for the Philippines; by Unalis Corporation for Taiwan; by Contemporanea de Ediciones for Venezuela; by Computer Book & Magazine Store for Puerto Rico; by Express Computer Distributors for the Caribbean and West Indies. Authorized Sales Agent: Anthony Rudkin Associates for the Middle East and North Africa.

For general information on IDG Books Worldwide's books in the U.S., please call our Consumer Customer Service department at 800-762-2974. For reseller information, including discounts and premium sales, please call our Reseller Customer Service department at 800-434-3422.

For information on where to purchase IDG Books Worldwide's books outside the U.S., please contact our International Sales department at 415-655-3200 or fax 415-655-3295.

For information on foreign language translations, please contact our Foreign & Subsidiary Rights department at 415-655-3021 or fax 415-655-3281.

For sales inquiries and special prices for bulk quantities, please contact our Sales department at 415-655-3200 or write to the address above.

For information on using IDG Books Worldwide's books in the classroom or for ordering examination copies, please contact our Educational Sales department at 800-434-2086 or fax 817-251-8174.

For press review copies, author interviews, or other publicity information, please contact our Public Relations department at 415-655-3000 or fax 415-655-3299.

For authorization to photocopy items for corporate, personal, or educational use, please contact Copyright Clearance Center, 222 Rosewood Drive, Danvers, MA 01923, or fax 508-750-4470.

is a trademark under exclusive license to IDG Books Worldwide, Inc., from International Data Group, Inc.

About the Author

So who is this **Paul Bodensiek** person, why is he qualified to write a *...For Dummies* book about Corel WebMaster Suite, and more to the point, how the heck do you pronounce his last name?

I'll take these questions in reverse order, if for no other reason than that answering the last one first will make the answers to the first two easier to read: Bodensiek rhymes with "hide 'n' seek." Pretty easy, huh?

As to the why I'm qualified to write a book that will expose all the mysteries of Corel WebMaster Suite without weighing you down with a lot of unnecessary technical jiggery pokery, there are really two answers:

- ✔ I'm a Web publisher and have used many, many tools to create Web sites including (yetch!) coding HTML by hand. Of all the tools I've used, WebMaster Suite is by far my favorite.

- ✔ I have written, contributed to, or edited about 15 books on Web publishing, computer graphics, and computer gaming. I've also written over 100 operating and user manuals for various hardware, software, and manufacturing companies. Although this is my first *...For Dummies* book, I really enjoy making tough subjects seem easy.

And now for "Who is this Paul Bodensiek person, anyway?" Well, I'm a terribly complex and deep individual for whom a description only a couple of paragraphs in length could never do justice. To give you some information that you can really use, however, read on.

Professionally, I'm the owner of ParaGrafix, a small Web publishing, graphics, technical writing, and engineering consulting company located just outside of Providence, Rhode Island. I honed all the skills required to make ParaGrafix a go during my 12-year tenure as the entire engineering, technical service, graphics, and training departments for a small manufacturing company. During my time with that company, I also picked up 5 U.S. and over 25 foreign patents.

On the personal front, I'm lucky enough to share my home and my life with my wife, Mary, and daughter, Melissa. Both of them are great reminders of what IT is all about.

ABOUT IDG BOOKS WORLDWIDE

Welcome to the world of IDG Books Worldwide.

IDG Books Worldwide, Inc., is a subsidiary of International Data Group, the world's largest publisher of computer-related information and the leading global provider of information services on information technology. IDG was founded more than 25 years ago and now employs more than 8,500 people worldwide. IDG publishes more than 275 computer publications in over 75 countries (see listing below). More than 60 million people read one or more IDG publications each month.

Launched in 1990, IDG Books Worldwide is today the #1 publisher of best-selling computer books in the United States. We are proud to have received eight awards from the Computer Press Association in recognition of editorial excellence and three from *Computer Currents'* First Annual Readers' Choice Awards. Our best-selling *...For Dummies®* series has more than 30 million copies in print with translations in 30 languages. IDG Books Worldwide, through a joint venture with IDG's Hi-Tech Beijing, became the first U.S. publisher to publish a computer book in the People's Republic of China. In record time, IDG Books Worldwide has become the first choice for millions of readers around the world who want to learn how to better manage their businesses.

Our mission is simple: Every one of our books is designed to bring extra value and skill-building instructions to the reader. Our books are written by experts who understand and care about our readers. The knowledge base of our editorial staff comes from years of experience in publishing, education, and journalism — experience we use to produce books for the '90s. In short, we care about books, so we attract the best people. We devote special attention to details such as audience, interior design, use of icons, and illustrations. And because we use an efficient process of authoring, editing, and desktop publishing our books electronically, we can spend more time ensuring superior content and spend less time on the technicalities of making books.

You can count on our commitment to deliver high-quality books at competitive prices on topics you want to read about. At IDG Books Worldwide, we continue in the IDG tradition of delivering quality for more than 25 years. You'll find no better book on a subject than one from IDG Books Worldwide.

John Kilcullen
CEO
IDG Books Worldwide, Inc.

Steven Berkowitz
President and Publisher
IDG Books Worldwide, Inc.

Eighth Annual Computer Press Awards ≥1992

Ninth Annual Computer Press Awards ≥1993

Tenth Annual Computer Press Awards ≥1994

Eleventh Annual Computer Press Awards ≥1995

IDG Books Worldwide, Inc., is a subsidiary of International Data Group, the world's largest publisher of computer-related information and the leading global provider of information services on information technology. International Data Group publishes over 275 computer publications in over 75 countries. Sixty million people read one or more International Data Group publications each month. International Data Group's publications include: **ARGENTINA:** Buyer's Guide, Computerworld Argentina, PC World Argentina; **AUSTRALIA:** Australian Macworld, Australian PC World, Australian Reseller News, Computerworld, IT Casebook, Network World, Publish, Webmaster; **AUSTRIA:** Computerwelt Oesterreich, Networks Austria, PC Tip Austria; **BANGLADESH:** PC World Bangladesh; **BELARUS:** PC World Belarus; **BELGIUM:** Data News; **BRAZIL:** Annuário de Informática, Computerworld, Connections, Macworld, PC Player, PC World, Publish, Reseller News, Supergamepower; **BULGARIA:** Computerworld Bulgaria, Network World Bulgaria, PC & MacWorld Bulgaria; **CANADA:** CIO Canada, Client/Server World, ComputerWorld Canada, InfoWorld Canada, NetworkWorld Canada, WebWorld; **CHILE:** Computerworld Chile, PC World Chile; **COLOMBIA:** Computerworld Colombia, PC World Colombia; **COSTA RICA:** PC World Centro America; **THE CZECH AND SLOVAK REPUBLICS:** Computerworld Czechoslovakia, Macworld Czech Republic, PC World Czechoslovakia; **DENMARK:** Communications World Danmark, Computerworld Danmark, Macworld Danmark, PC World Danmark, Techworld Denmark; **DOMINICAN REPUBLIC:** PC World Republica Dominicana; **ECUADOR:** PC World Ecuador; **EGYPT:** Computerworld Middle East, PC World Middle East; **EL SALVADOR:** PC World Centro America; **FINLAND:** MikroPC, Tietoverkko, Tietoviikko; **FRANCE:** Distributique, Hebdo, Info PC, Le Monde Informatique, Macworld, Reseaux & Telecoms, WebMaster France; **GERMANY:** Computer Partner, Computerwoche, Computerwoche Extra, Computerwoche FOCUS, Global Online, Macwelt, PC Welt; **GREECE:** Amiga Computing, GamePro Greece, Multimedia World; **GUATEMALA:** PC World Centro America; **HONDURAS:** PC World Centro America; **HONG KONG:** Computerworld Hong Kong, PC World Hong Kong, Publish in Asia; **HUNGARY:** ABCD CD-ROM, Computerworld Szamitastechnika, Internetto online Magazine, PC World Hungary, PC-X Magazin Hungary; **ICELAND:** Tolvuheimur PC World Island; **INDIA:** Information Communications World, Information Systems Computerworld, PC World India, Publish in Asia; **INDONESIA:** InfoKomputer PC World, Komputek Computerworld, Publish in Asia; **IRELAND:** ComputerScope, PC Live!; **ISRAEL:** Macworld Israel, People & Computers/Computerworld; **ITALY:** Computerworld Italia, Macworld Italia, Networking Italia, PC World Italia; **JAPAN:** DTP World, Macworld Japan, Nikkei Personal Computing, OS/2 World Japan, SunWorld Japan, Windows NT World, Windows World Japan; **KENYA:** PC World East African; **KOREA:** Hi-Tech Information, Macworld Korea, PC World Korea; **MACEDONIA:** PC World Macedonia; **MALAYSIA:** Computerworld Malaysia, PC World Malaysia, Publish in Asia; **MALTA:** PC World Malta; **MEXICO:** Computerworld Mexico, PC World Mexico; **MYANMAR:** PC World Myanmar; **NETHERLANDS:** Computer! Totaal, LAN Internetworking Magazine, LAN World Buyers Guide, Macworld Netherlands, Net, WebWereld; **NEW ZEALAND:** Absolute Beginners Guide and Plain & Simple Series, Computer Buyer, Computer Industry Directory, Computerworld New Zealand, MTB, Network World, PC World New Zealand; **NICARAGUA:** PC World Centro America; **NORWAY:** Computerworld Norge, CW Rapport, Datamagasinet, Financial Rapport, Kursguide Norge, Macworld Norge, Multimediaworld Norge, PC World Ekspress Norge, PC World Nettverk, PC World Norge, PC World ProduktGuide Norge; **PAKISTAN:** Computerworld Pakistan; **PANAMA:** PC World Panama; **PEOPLE'S REPUBLIC OF CHINA:** China Computer Users, China Computerworld, China InfoWorld, China Telecom World Weekly, Computer & Communication, Electronic Design China, Electronics Today, Electronics Weekly, Game Software, PC World China, Popular Computer Week, Software Weekly, Software World, Telecom World; **PERU:** Computerworld Peru, PC World Profesional Peru, PC World SoHo Peru; **PHILIPPINES:** Click!, Computerworld Philippines, PC World Philippines, Publish in Asia; **POLAND:** Computerworld Poland, Computerworld Special Report Poland, Cyber, Macworld Poland, Networld Poland, PC World Komputer; **PORTUGAL:** Cerebro/PC World, Computerworld/Correio Informatico, Dealer World Portugal, Mac*In/PC*In Portugal, Multimedia World; **PUERTO RICO:** PC World Puerto Rico; **ROMANIA:** Computerworld Romania, PC World Romania, Telecom Romania; **RUSSIA:** Computerworld Russia, Mir PK, Publish, Seti; **SINGAPORE:** Computerworld Singapore, PC World Singapore, Publish in Asia; **SLOVENIA:** Monitor; **SOUTH AFRICA:** Computing SA, Network World SA, Software World SA; **SPAIN:** Communicaciones World España, Computerworld España, Dealer World España, Macworld España, PC World España; **SRI LANKA:** Infolink PC World; **SWEDEN:** CAP&Design, Computer Sweden, Corporate Computing Sweden, Internetworld Sweden, it.branschen, Macworld Sweden, MaxiData Sweden, MikroDatorn, Nätverk & Kommunikation, PC World Sweden, PCaktiv, Windows World Sweden; **SWITZERLAND:** Computerworld Schweiz, Macworld Schweiz, PCtip; **TAIWAN:** Computerworld Taiwan, Macworld Taiwan, NEW ViSiON/Publish, PC World Taiwan, Windows World Taiwan; **THAILAND:** Publish in Asia, Thai Computerworld; **TURKEY:** Computerworld Turkiye, Macworld Turkiye, Network World Turkiye, PC World Turkiye; **UKRAINE:** Computerworld Kiev, Multimedia World Ukraine, PC World Ukraine; **UNITED KINGDOM:** Acorn User UK, Amiga Action UK, Amiga Computing UK, Apple Talk UK, Computing, Macworld, Parents and Computers UK, PC Advisor, PC Home, PSX Pro, The WEB; **UNITED STATES:** Cable in the Classroom, CIO Magazine, Computerworld, DOS World, Federal Computer Week, GamePro Magazine, InfoWorld, I-Way, Macworld, Network World, PC Games, PC World, Publish, Video Event, THE WEB Magazine, and WebMaster; online webzines: JavaWorld, NetscapeWorld, and SunWorld Online; **URUGUAY:** InfoWorld Uruguay; **VENEZUELA:** Computerworld Venezuela, PC World Venezuela; and **VIETNAM:** PC World Vietnam. 3/24/97

Dedication

I would like to dedicate this book to Melissa. Thanks for understanding while my writing has turned the schedule around our house into absolute ruin. Now that it's over, I know life will begin to return to its normal, only slightly insane, self again.

Author's Acknowledgments

Anyone who thinks that a book just materializes from the finger tips of its author obviously hasn't written one before. A book, especially one like this, comes about through a major group effort. Sure, these are all my words, but so many people were responsible for making sure that what came from my fingers has eventually reached you.

The first person I have to thank is Ellen Camm. She guided this book from its first, simple idea ("How about a book on Corel WebMaster Suite?") all the way through to the completed outline. It wouldn't have been half the book it is without her insight and help.

Shannon Ross, my project editor, has been fantastic. She's always been there to put pressure on people I needed something from and give me a pep talk when I couldn't figure out a "handle" for a chapter. Luckily, neither of these problems happened *too* often.

My technical editor, Lee Musick, and copy editors, Jill Brummett and Tina Sims, have done a great job at making sure what I wrote is, well, readable. Many thanks.

The rest of the staff at IDG has been great. Heather Dismore, Joyce Pepple, and all the folks in production — thanks for all the help!

Thanks to Joe Hartley of Brainiac Services (www.brainiac.com) for his help in developing the pull-out sheet at the beginning of this book. Thank you to Eric Robichaud of Rhode Island Soft Systems for giving permission to put Palette Express on the CD-ROM. Thanks to Jelane Johnson and Celine Chamberlin for allowing me to put their clip art libraries on the CD.

A special thank you to all of ParaGrafix's customers, who were patient with me during the writing of this book — I'm back (at least until I head off to Australia for three weeks!).

Nancy Stevenson deserves a huge thank you for putting me in touch with Ellen Camm at exactly the right time to work on this book.

And last, but not least, thank you to Mary and Melissa. I can now be home on weekends instead of closeted in my office typing away. I've missed you both.

Publisher's Acknowledgments

We're proud of this book; please register your comments through our IDG Books Worldwide Online Registration Form located at http://my2cents.dummies.com.

Some of the people who helped bring this book to market include the following:

Acquisitions, Development, and Editorial

Project Editor: Shannon Ross

Acquisitions Editor: Ellen Camm

Media Development Manager: Joyce Pepple

Associate Permissions Editor: Heather H. Dismore

Copy Editors: Jill Brummett, Tina Sims, Brian Kramer, Tamara Castleman

Technical Editor: Lee Musick

Editorial Manager: Leah P. Cameron

Editorial Assistants: Paul E. Kuzmic, Donna Love

Production

Project Coordinator: E. Shawn Aylsworth

Layout and Graphics: Jonathon Andry, Steve Arany, Linda M. Boyer, Lou Boudreau, Drew R. Moore, Brent Savage, Janet Seib, Michael A. Sullivan

Proofreaders: Henry Lazarek, Christine Berman, Kelli Botta, Michelle Cronninger, Joel K. Draper, Janet M. Withers

Indexer: Steve Rath

Special Help

Suzanne Thomas, Associate Editor; Kyle Looper, Project Editor

General and Administrative

IDG Books Worldwide, Inc.: John Kilcullen, CEO; Steven Berkowitz, President and Publisher

IDG Books Technology Publishing: Brenda McLaughlin, Senior Vice President and Group Publisher

Dummies Technology Press and Dummies Editorial: Diane Graves Steele, Vice President and Associate Publisher; Mary Bednarek, Acquisitions and Product Development Director; Kristin A. Cocks, Editorial Director

Dummies Trade Press: Kathleen A. Welton, Vice President and Publisher; Kevin Thornton, Acquisitions Manager

IDG Books Production for Dummies Press: Beth Jenkins, Production Director; Cindy L. Phipps, Manager of Project Coordination, Production Proofreading, and Indexing; Kathie S. Schutte, Supervisor of Page Layout; Shelley Lea, Supervisor of Graphics and Design; Debbie J. Gates, Production Systems Specialist; Robert Springer, Supervisor of Proofreading; Debbie Stailey, Special Projects Coordinator; Tony Augsburger, Supervisor of Reprints and Bluelines; Leslie Popplewell, Media Archive Coordinator

Dummies Packaging and Book Design: Patti Crane, Packaging Specialist; Lance Kayser, Packaging Assistant; Kavish + Kavish, Cover Design

◆

The publisher would like to give special thanks to Patrick J. McGovern, without whom this book would not have been possible.

◆

Contents at a Glance

Cartoons at a Glance

By Rich Tennant

page 229

page 337

page 317

page 7

page 59

Fax: 508-546-7747 • **E-mail:** the5wave@tiac.net

Table of Contents

Introduction

So you want to design Web pages using Corel WebMaster Suite? You've come to the right place. The next couple hundred pages include everything you need to know about WebMaster. But you don't have to read the whole book — that's one of the great things about *Corel WebMaster Suite For Dummies.* If you just need to know how to use one command that's giving you trouble, then flip to that page; if you want to know every nitpicky little detail, then read the whole book. It's up to you.

In the last few years, having a Web site has become almost a requirement for every business. Business cards are filled with e-mail and Web site addresses. Lucrative businesses have been built around the assumption that creating a Web site is just too darned hard for the average Joe. That assumption no longer holds water.

With the introduction of WebMaster Suite, Corel makes creating an attractive, well-designed Web site possible for just about anybody. With the same strategy (more power, more utilities, more *value*) that made CorelDRAW the bestselling illustration suite, WebMaster Suite is poised to bring Web publishing to the masses.

Sure, WebMaster Suite is easy to use (almost as easy as your word processing program), but unless you've done some Web publishing before, most of the terms are gibberish. *Corel WebMaster Suite For Dummies* is your guide to getting the most out of this powerful software.

What You Can Expect from This Book

Chances are, you shelled out your hard-earned money for this book because you want to know the easiest and best ways to get results from Corel WebMaster Suite. Just about every other book on WebMaster Suite is going to fill your head with dry, technical information on URLs, DLLs, ISPs, and a bunch of other stuff that's great if your main interest in life is becoming a geek.

Corel WebMaster Suite For Dummies takes a different approach. This book is filled with down-to-earth, practical information written in the now classic *...For Dummies* style: clear writing in everyday English, without the serious "this is as tough as doing your taxes" approach.

This book shows you how to build technically perfect Web sites that'll make your geek friends drool. And, for icing on the cake, it shows you how to make your sites visually exciting, quick to load, and easy to navigate.

Even if you already know how to use WebMaster, you can find new tips and techniques in this book to make your sites great. All that good stuff Web gurus have been claiming exclusive rights to for years is now at your fingertips.

You're Smart, but You Still Need This Book

I make a couple of assumptions about you in the next few hundred pages because, well, if I didn't, most of this book would be about opening menus and copying files. That's not what you want, now is it? I didn't think so. You want to know how to put WebMaster Suite to work.

So here are the assumptions I make:

- ✔ **You're smart.** You may not know much about building Web sites, but you knew enough to buy this great book, so it's obvious to me that you're one smart cookie. And that's a good thing because, even though this book's titled *Corel WebMaster Suite For Dummies* and even though software is getting easier and easier to use, some degree of intelligence is still involved.

- ✔ **You already know how to use your computer.** You've been able to coerce your computer into doing generally what you want (believe me, even my computers don't *always* do what I want). You can use your mouse and keyboard to select menu commands, copy files, launch programs, and deal with the Windows 95 desktop.

- ✔ **You've already got WebMaster Suite, though you may not have it installed on your computer.** This assumption is important: You're not going to get a whole lot out of this book if you don't have the program or at least have access to it. If you haven't installed WebMaster Suite yet, check out Appendix A for helpful hints on making the installation go smoother.

- ✔ **You're a novice when it comes to Web publishing.** Until recently, this category included everyone out there except for a couple nerds with propeller beanies, no social life, and 3,000 empty soda bottles littering their computer rooms. You may have started trying to use WebMaster, but the differences from the programs that you're used to made you run out and buy this book.

What's This Book About?

This book's *about* 400 pages. But seriously, folks. . . .

Corel WebMaster Suite For Dummies tells you everything you need to get professional results out of WebMaster Suite and to get your site published on the World Wide Web or your corporate Intranet. WebMaster is a *suite* of programs, from DESIGNER to PhotoPaint to DATA, that you can use to design your Web pages, create or update graphics, and publish databases (plus a whole lot more).

All this information could get pretty confusing if it were lumped together, so I've broken this book down into smaller chunks that handle one aspect of the suite at a time.

Part I: Getting Up and Running

Part I gets you going with the main applications (DESIGNER and SiteManager) and introduces you to the Web Wizard that can help you set up the structure of your site in a couple of easy steps. I also give you some (in my humble opinion) great tips on how to keep your site organized so that it's easier to maintain, and there are complete instructions on how to use (and interpret) the cheat sheet at the beginning of the book.

Part II: The Nitty-Gritty

Part II gives you the down-and-dirty details on how to make WebMaster Suite work for *you.* You can find out how to add text and graphics to your pages, import information from other programs, and even incorporate sound in your Web site.

Chapter 13 even helps you do things that WebMaster Suite isn't specifically designed to do by showing you how to edit HTML code directly.

Part III: Creating Your Own Graphics

Corel WebMaster Suite isn't content to just give you the tools to incorporate existing graphics in your site. Part III shows you how to create brand new graphics using PhotoPaint, DRAW, MOVE, and WORLD. Each of these programs is a complete package that deals expertly with a different aspect of Web graphics design.

Part IV: Publishing Your Site

After you create your site, what do you do with it? Part IV details the two main ways to publish your Web site and how to list it in the major search engines so that people actually know where your site is.

Part V: The Part of Tens

The Part of Tens section gives you useful information outside the regular scope of the book. For example, Chapter 23 tells you about ten great (or at least interesting) Web sites that can help spark your creative juices.

The Appendixes

With all the software, clipart, and utilities that come with WebMaster Suite, installing it may seem a little daunting. Appendix A helps you make informed decisions about the installation and walks you through all the choices you need to make.

Appendix B outlines all the cool utilities and clipart that I include on the CD-ROM.

The Amazing Free CD Stuff!

Hey, what would a computer book be without scads of free utilities and demo software? I have to say that the CD-ROM was the hardest part of the book to put together: WebMaster Suite gives you a ton of great programs, utilities, and clipart, so finding stuff to put on the CD-ROM that wasn't just gratuitous fluff was pretty difficult.

I have succeeded, however! The tools and utilities on the CD-ROM help you make the most of your Web publishing hours. Appendix B lists everything that I include on the CD and gives you instructions on how to work the spiffy CD interface program that makes installing all this stuff a breeze.

How to Use This Book

This is a reference book, which means that you don't have to start at Chapter 1 and read every single page until you reach the appendixes. I've written this book in such a way that you can leave it on your bookshelf until you hit a point where you say, "I know I can do that" or "Why the heck did the program do that?" At that point, you can grab the book, flip to the right page (thanks to the spiffy and detailed index and table of contents) and read a quick passage that tells you exactly what the deal is.

Of course, you *can* read the book cover to cover if you want. I won't object. I wrote all these words on the assumption that every one of them would eventually be read. Perhaps the better way, though, is to give the book a quick skim to get an idea of the power of WebMaster Suite. Then as you create your Web site, you can tell yourself, "You know, I remember seeing that I could do such and such with this program." And then you can look up the exact procedure.

What Are All Those Funny Symbols?

Just like the yield sign on the side of the road, the icons placed throughout this book help you find information that's vitally important (or at least interesting).

This icon marks a tip or technique that can make your life a little easier or show you how to do something that may not be immediately obvious.

I call this the *Geek Alert* icon because it indicates something that isn't absolutely necessary to know, unless you want to get to the underlying technical information behind what you're doing. Chapter 13 is one giant Geek Alert chapter.

This icon appears beside information that you don't want to forget.

When the text talks about something tricky, where making a misstep could cause a problem, you see this icon.

One of the best places to find out things about Web publishing or to track down cool utilities is on the World Wide Web. Wherever you see this icon, you'll find a URL leading to a Web site. Don't worry, you won't have to type the URLs (unless you want to) because the CD-ROM includes a Web page that includes every URL listed in the book.

Whenever I mention a program or piece of clipart on the CD that comes with this book, this icon lets you know.

System Requirements

If you have a relatively new computer system, you can probably run WebMaster Suite without a problem. However, if your machine is getting a little long in the tooth, check out this list to make sure that your computer is up to snuff. Note that these are the requirements for running WebMaster Suite. The requirements for running the programs on this book's CD-ROM are basically the same — I list the specifics for the CD at the beginning of Appendix B.

- A PC with a 486 or better processor (The processor can be from any of the major companies including Intel, AMD, or Cyrix.)
- Microsoft Windows 95 or Windows NT 4 or later
- 16 megabytes (MB) or more of RAM
- A CD-ROM drive
- A VGA monitor and graphics card
- A mouse or other pointing device
- A connection to the Internet, either through a local Internet Service Provider (ISP) or through one of the major online services like America Online, CompuServe, or The Microsoft Network

Part I
Getting Up and Running

The 5th Wave   By Rich Tennant

HMM — NICE TREE STRUCTURE.

In this part . . .

*W*here to begin? Corel WebMaster Suite has so many programs and utilities that you're liable to be a little confused about where to start. The two main Web programs, SiteManager and DESIGNER, are the tools you use most often as you create and organize your site.

In this part, I introduce you to these two powerful programs, show you how to get them up and running, and help you to begin using them.

Chapter 1

Cooking Up a Web Page with DESIGNER

- -

- -

*B*ack in the dark, primal days of World Wide Web publishing, I began creating Web pages and sites using nothing more than Windows Notepad and a notebook full of paper printouts of so-called tutorials and instructional Web sites. It was long, painful work, during which I had to type all kinds of weird codes, such as `<a href="http://home.htm">Click Here To Go Home</A>`, and even more bizarre ones.

Then along came a couple of programs that automatically entered all the codes for me when I clicked a button on the toolbar. Quite an improvement. Of course, I still needed my notebook, now the size of *War and Peace,* sitting next to me the whole time. None of these programs was super-easy to use, because I still had to know what the codes were and how they worked before I could use them. Sure, I could have bought one of those what-you-see-is-what-you-get (WYSIWYG) Web editing programs, but they cost as much as a small car.

Then Corel started selling WebMaster Suite, a soup-to-nuts Web authoring system with the power of the expensive models at a fraction of the cost, and I've been going along swimmingly ever since.

You're not going to hire me to author your Web site, at least not after shelling out the money for Corel WebMaster Suite and this spiffy book. What this means is that you have all the power of a professional Web editing system in a form that's extremely easy to use.

So What Is a Web Page, Anyway?

Wow. You ask some hard questions. Think about something a little more familiar for a moment — your word processor. You type something, maybe import a picture, add a table, and then print out your work. What you see on your computer screen is pretty much what your printer spits out on paper.

Of course, as with most computer programs, much, much more is going on behind the scenes of your word processor. Each time you type a letter, the word processing program adds another character to your document's file. But what happens when you decide that you want to make a word bold? Sure, all *you* have to do is highlight the word and press Ctrl+B, but what happens to the *file* in which your computer stores the document?

Typically, word processors format text by inserting a code on each side of the passage. The code on the left side essentially says, "Start bold" (or whatever kind of effect you want), and the code on the right side says, "Okay, now stop bold."

A Web page works exactly the same way. Codes say, "Insert a picture here," and "When somebody clicks here, go to such-and-such Web site." See Figure 1-1 for a view of the codes hiding inside your Web page files.

A *Web browser* is a program that translates the codes on a Web page and displays the text and graphics generally the way that the person who created the page intended it to. One nice thing about browsers is that, if they don't know what a code is, they just ignore it — although this can lead to some bizarre results (see the section called "What you see isn't always what you get," later in this chapter).

Another program, in addition to a Web browser, is necessary for displaying Web pages: a *Web server.* The Web server is like a waiter, taking orders from people who visit a site. By clicking on a link or entering a URL, visitors say "I want to look at such-and-such page." The server, which runs on the same computer that stores all the pages for that site, gathers up all the files that make up the requested page and sends them to the visitor's browser. The browser interprets all the codes and reconstructs the original page. This overview of the process is very simplified, but it gives you the general idea.

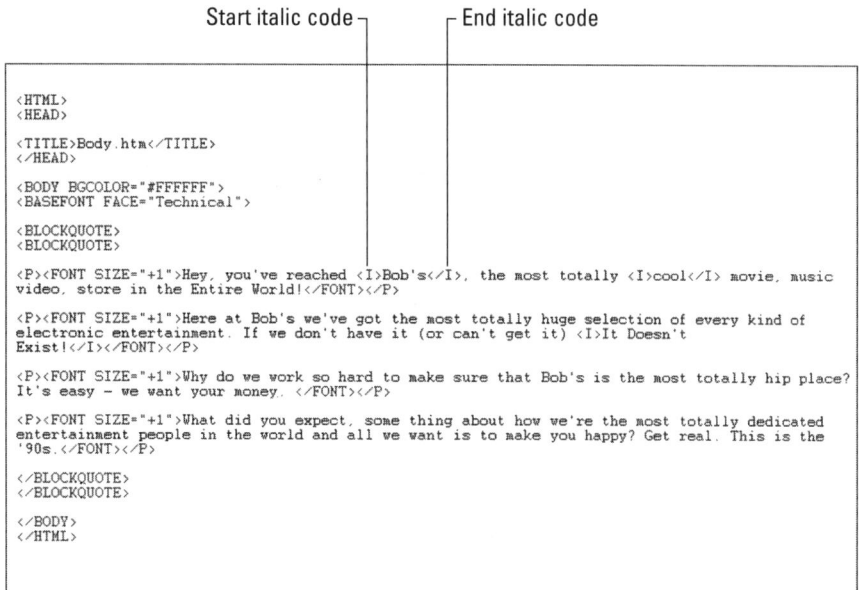

Start italic code ⌐   ⌐ End italic code

```
<HTML>
<HEAD>

<TITLE>Body.htm</TITLE>
</HEAD>

<BODY BGCOLOR="#FFFFFF">
<BASEFONT FACE="Technical">

<BLOCKQUOTE>
<BLOCKQUOTE>

<P><FONT SIZE="+1">Hey, you've reached <I>Bob's</I>, the most totally <I>cool</I> movie, music
video, store in the Entire World!</FONT></P>

<P><FONT SIZE="+1">Here at Bob's we've got the most totally huge selection of every kind of
electronic entertainment. If we don't have it (or can't get it) <I>It Doesn't
Exist!</I></FONT></P>

<P><FONT SIZE="+1">Why do we work so hard to make sure that Bob's is the most totally hip place?
It's easy — we want your money. </FONT></P>

<P><FONT SIZE="+1">What did you expect, some thing about how we're the most totally dedicated
entertainment people in the world and all we want is to make you happy? Get real. This is the
'90s.</FONT></P>

</BLOCKQUOTE>
</BLOCKQUOTE>

</BODY>
</HTML>
```

Figure 1-1:
The codes
in a Web
page.

Unpacking WebMaster Suite

With WebMaster Suite, Corel combined all the tools and programs you need
to create first-rate Web sites. The two WebMaster Suite programs you use
most in creating your site are:

- **WEB.DESIGNER** is a WYSIWYG Web page design and editing program.
  This chapter introduces DESIGNER, and Part 2 is almost totally devoted
  to putting the program through its paces.

- **WEB.SiteManager** lets you organize your site so that it's easier to
  maintain. All the files that make up your Web site (from the actual Web
  page files to your images) are shown in a Windows Explorer-type
  display. Chapter 3 shows you how to use SiteManager to ensure that
  your site runs smoothly.

In addition, Corel continues its tradition of giving you the most bang for
your buck by including a host of other programs, utilities, and clipart that
help you bring your site alive:

- **WEB.PhotoPaint** is a full-featured graphics editing program. You can
  use PhotoPaint to create the images you want to include in your
  pages — or you can edit existing images like the ones on CD-ROM #2
  to make them unique to your site. See Chapter 14 for an introduction to
  this program.

- ✔ **WEB.DRAW** is also a graphics editing program, but instead of creating bitmap images (pictures made up of a bunch of colored dots), DRAW uses lines and shapes so that you can make images any size you want — this type of image is called a *vector graphic*. Chapter 15 introduces DRAW.
- ✔ **WEB.MOVE** creates animated pictures for your Web pages. Chapter 16 shows you how to make your site come alive with different types of animated images.
- ✔ **WEB.WORLD** is an entry-level VRML (virtual reality modeling language) program that you can use to create 3-D Web pages for your visitors to explore. WORLD is detailed in Chapter 17.
- ✔ **WEB.DATA** takes information from a database and puts it in a form that can be viewed by a Web browser. Chapter 12 shows you how to use your existing databases with WEB.DATA.
- ✔ **Tons of clip art** is available on CD-ROM #2.

You can use each of these programs by itself, or you can start by running SiteManager, open a Web page in DESIGNER, and then start the other programs from DESIGNER's handy-dandy application toolbar.

The Basic Recipe

When you start your word processor, you see a blank area on the screen just waiting for you to type your business letter, memo, or note to Mom. One of the great things about DESIGNER is that it looks and feels very similar to the word processing programs that you're already familiar with: You type letters on the keyboard, and they magically appear on your computer screen — no special tricks, obscure programming codes, or secret handshakes necessary.

Starting DESIGNER

The first step to creating anything with DESIGNER is to start the program. If you followed the suggestions on-screen when you installed the program, a shortcut to DESIGNER is already waiting for you under your Start menu. It's in a folder called Corel WebMaster Suite. If you decided to put the WebMaster Suite programs in a different shortcut folder, though, you'll use that folder instead of Corel WebMaster Suite.

To start DESIGNER, just choose Start⇨Programs⇨Corel WebMaster Suite⇨ Corel.DESIGNER, and up pops a clean screen, perfect for creating Web content (see Figure 1-2). Chapter 3 shows you how to start DESIGNER through SiteManager — this is the best way when you're creating a whole Web site, but to get a feel for working with pages, go straight to DESIGNER.

Type text here

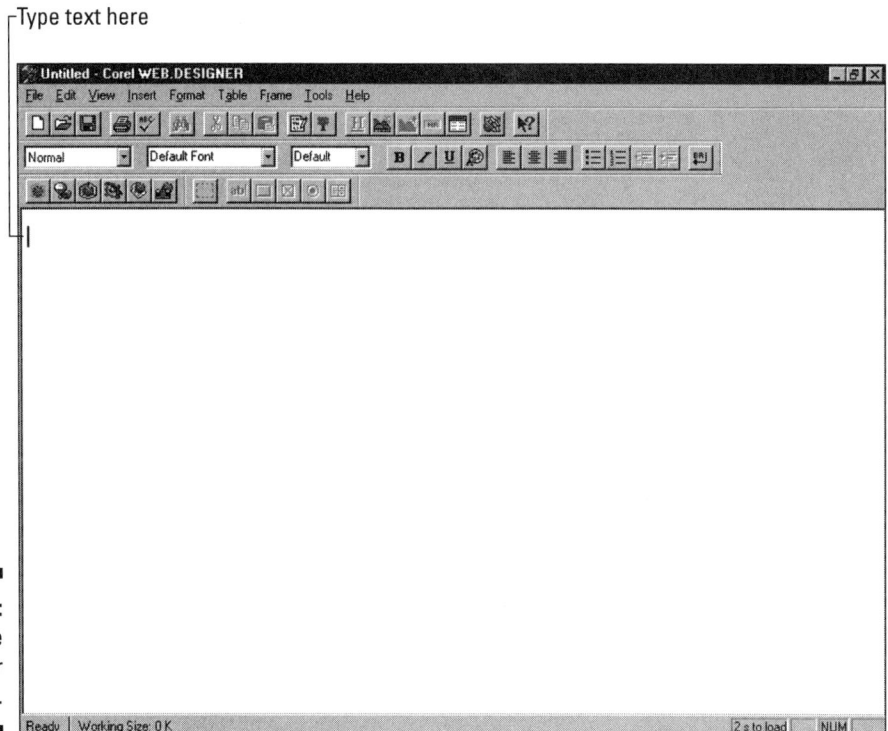

Figure 1-2:
The
Designer
window.

As soon as DESIGNER has started, you can begin typing away, adding graphics, and generally creating your Web page.

The first time you start DESIGNER (unless you happen to start it through SiteManager), a dialog box opens and asks you what your server root is. The *server root* is the folder where all the files for your Web site are located. You can either type in the full name of the folder you want to use in the Server Root text box, or click Browse and select the folder in the Select the Server Root Directory text box and click OK. When you've typed in or selected the server root folder, click the OK button to start DESIGNER. You are not locked into using this folder forever — you can change the server root folder at any time, as outlined in Chapter 3.

Create shortcuts to programs that you use all the time, like DESIGNER, and the other programs in WebMaster Suite. Doing so means that you don't have to keep navigating through the Start menu to open them. To make a shortcut, right-click the Start button, and select Open from the pop-up menu. Then double-click to open the Programs folder, and then the Corel WebMaster Suite folder. Now simply Ctrl+drag the icon of the program for which you want to create a shortcut onto your desktop, and arrange it however you please. Whenever you want to use the program, you just double-click its desktop shortcut, and the program starts.

Creating a new page

Often, when working on one page, you realize that you really want to start editing a new page.

 To start a new page when you're already in DESIGNER, simply choose File➪New or click the New button. Your old page disappears, and a blank, new page appears. If you haven't saved changes to your old page, a dialog box appears and asks, `Save changes to (old file)?`. You can click Yes to save the changes, No to discard the changes, or Cancel to forget about creating a new page.

If you elect to save the changes but have never saved your page before, the Save As dialog box opens — use the same procedure as I outline in "Saving Files in DESIGNER." If the page was previously saved, then it's just saved normally. Be very careful if you decide not to save your pages, because after you click the No button, those changes are gone forever.

Opening an existing page

Quite often, the Web page that you want to work on already exists. Perhaps it's one that you've been preparing to publish on the Web, or maybe it's already on the Web and you want to study it to see how it's put together. It could also be one of the WebMaster Suite template pages.

Opening a local page

A *local page* is one that is saved on your hard drive or on a network drive that you can access directly, without having to go through the Web. I predict that you're going to use a local page 99 percent of the times that you work with an existing Web page, whether it's one that you created or one that a colleague has made.

If you've opened a file in any Windows program, this procedure will feel eerily familiar to you.

1. **Start DESIGNER, if it isn't already running.**

 2. **Choose File➪Open or click the Open button.**

   The Open dialog box appears with some options (see Figure 1-3). The default selection is to open a local page.

3. **Click Browse.**

   A standard Windows Open dialog box opens.

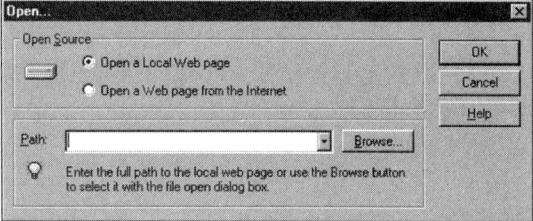

Figure 1-3:
The Open
dialog box.

4. Navigate your hard drive to locate the file you want to open.

5. Highlight the file and then click <u>O</u>pen.

You are returned to the Open dialog box.

6. Click OK to open the file.

The page opens in DESIGNER, ready for you to work with it.

Opening a page from the Web

One of the best ways to figure out all the ins and outs of Web design is to dissect someone else's work. No, this isn't cheating — haven't you ever been in an art museum and seen a student sketching a copy of a DaVinci? Same thing.

Opening a *remote* Web page (one that's located somewhere in the nether regions of cyberspace) using DESIGNER makes it easy to understand how the page is put together. When you open a remote Web page, DESIGNER actually copies the page and its graphics to your own hard drive (called *downloading*).

You can also download a Web page so that you can edit it if you don't have its files on your local hard drive. For example, a few months ago, a friend of mine asked me to do some cleanup work on her family's Web site. Using DESIGNER, I downloaded her site, made the changes, and then e-mailed her the updated files — because I don't have her password, she had to take care of actually publishing the updated files to her Web site. (Chapters 18 and 19 tell you how to publish your own Web site.)

Keep the following things in mind when you open a page from the Web:

✔ **Generally, pages are copyrighted.** This means that copying the page to your hard drive and editing it *may* be illegal. If you just want to look over the formatting in DESIGNER, and see how certain things have been done, you're probably okay. But if you publish a page that's substantially the same as someone else's (because you copied it from their site), you could be litigated.

✔ **Some pages on the Web have a lot of graphics.** Because DESIGNER puts the page in a folder under your most recently opened local page, make sure that you have enough room for the page before loading it.

✔ **You need to know the exact URL of the page you want to open.** No browse feature exists when opening pages from the Web (but check out the following tip for a way around this).

To open a page from the Web without having to memorize its URL:

1. **Start the connection to the Internet and launch the Web browser.**

2. **Find the page you want to open.**

3. **Highlight the URL (which generally appears at the top of the screen in an Address or Location box) and press Ctrl+C to copy it to the Windows Clipboard.**

4. **Switch to DESIGNER (if it's already open in the background) or start DESIGNER.**

5. **In DESIGNER, choose File⇨Open (or click the Open button) and select the radio button beside Open a Web page from the Internet.**

6. **Press Ctrl+V to paste the address into the URL text box.**

7. **Click OK.**

The Web page and all of its graphics are downloaded to my hard drive and are now displayed in DESIGNER. Now I can see exactly how the page's author created some nifty effect or formatted a particularly intricate part of the page.

Opening a WebMaster template

In addition to the Site Builder Wizard (refer to Chapter 3 for more information), Corel WebMaster Suite comes with about a kajillion premade Web pages that you can customize. These *templates* already include images, backgrounds, and all the formatting options. All you have to do is type the text that you want them to include.

Even though these pages were designed by somebody else, you don't have to worry about copyright problems — Corel has "given" these pages to you (for the price of WebMaster Suite), and you're free to use them as is or change them in any way you want.

To open a template in DESIGNER:

1. **Start DESIGNER.**

2. **Choose File⇨Templates or press Ctrl+T.**

The Open Template dialog box opens, showing you a list of all the available templates.

3. Single-click on a template file (all of which end with an .htm extension).

The window at the right of the dialog box shows a preview of the page that the selected template creates (see Figure 1-4).

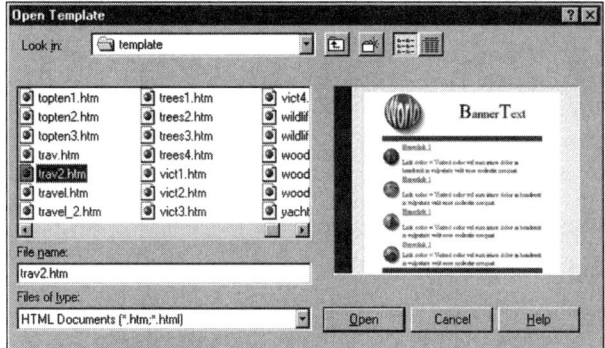

Figure 1-4: Previewing a template.

4. When you find the template you want, click Open.

The page opens in DESIGNER.

Before you can start making changes to the template, you have to save it to a new location. Check out the next section that just happens to tell you all about saving your files.

Remembering those three important words: Save, save, save

When I was writing my first computer book, I had an assistant who took care of the computer hardware around the office and ran errands for me. One day, while I was engrossed in a particularly nasty section of the book, John (his name has been changed to protect the innocent) was working on a printer that was giving us some trouble. In an attempt to unplug the printer, he grabbed the wrong plug by mistake, and unplugged my computer instead.

Because I had been so engrossed in my writing, I hadn't remembered to save what I was working on. Consequently, everything I'd done in the last three hours was lost, and I freaked. I couldn't get mad at John, though. His was an honest mistake — I was the one who didn't click the Save button. I learned an important lesson that day. Pray that *you* don't have to learn that lesson the hard way.

Because DESIGNER doesn't come with an auto-save feature like many word processors (that save files every ten minutes, so the most you lose is ten minutes of work), you have to remember to save regularly while you're creating your Web pages.

Of course, the most important reason to save your Web pages is that, well, nobody else will be able to see them if you don't! After you save your Web page files to your own hard drive, you copy those files to a Web server, which makes them available for everybody in the world to see. The names you choose for your files become their Uniform Resource Locator (URL), which refers to the Web address that visitors type into their Web browsers to go straight to this page. If your Web server is named www.bobsvideo.com and your Web page's filename is video.htm, then its URL is www.bobsvideo .com/video.htm. If you publish your site through an Internet Service Provider (ISP), then your site will probably be stored in a folder on the ISP's computer; in this case, your URL might be www.isp_domain.com/users/ bobsvideo/video.htm or something similar.

Saving files in DESIGNER

DESIGNER has three different ways for you to save a page. Which method you choose depends on how you're working with the page:

- ✔ If you've opened an existing local page and you want to save it to the same location from which it originated, all you have to do is choose File⇨Save (or press Ctrl+S or click the Save button). All of your updates are saved.

- ✔ If, however, you've started a new page or a template, extra steps are involved:

  1. **Choose File⇨Save (or File⇨Save As) or click the Save button.**

     The Save As dialog box opens.

  2. **Using standard Windows techniques, navigate to the folder you want to save the page in.**

  3. **Type a name for your file in the File name text box and then click Save.**

- ✔ You can also save the page you've been working on with a new name, so that it doesn't replace the page you originally opened. You may want to use this approach if you've formatted the page just the way you like it, and you want to use the formatting for different pages (doing so makes your Web site look consistent). To save a page with a new name, choose File⇨Save As, type a new name for your page in the File name text box, and then click Save.

Your Web site's filenames (Web pages, graphics, and any other files that you include in your site) can have any combination of letters or numbers — but never include spaces in filenames because spaces can really mess up Web server software. If you want to have a name like bob tape.htm, name the file bob_tape.htm, using the underscore in place of the space. Also, Macintosh computers can't recognize long Windows 95 filenames. If you're going to publish your site to a Macintosh-based server, make sure that all of your filenames are in the old style *eight-dot-three* format: eight letters in the name, a period, and a three-letter extension (for example, websuite.htm). Folder names should also be no longer than eight letters or numbers.

Getting back to your roots — saving your home page

Saving Web pages is a little different from saving word processing documents. With a word processing file, where you save the document makes no difference (except in how easily you can find it later). With a Web page, however, where you put the file makes a big difference in how you can work with it and other pages.

The folder in which you place the main page (or *home page*) of your Web site is the *Web root* folder (though you can name the folder whatever you'd like). You must then save all the pages and graphics for your site in this Web root folder or in one of its subfolders.

You should name your site's home page either index.htm or default.htm, depending on the type of computer to which you will ultimately be publishing it. (*Publishing* is just a fancy way of saying "copying your files to a Web server computer so that they're available to people surfing the Web.") If you'll be publishing to a Windows 95-, Windows NT-, or Macintosh-based server, you can use either name. But if you plan to publish your site on a UNIX system, you have to name your file index.htm.

You use these names for the sake of your site's visitors. If you use the appropriate name, your visitor will only have to type the site's location, not the filename. For example, if Corel had named its home page home.htm instead of index.htm, a visitor would have to type www.corel.com/home.htm into a browser, instead of just www.corel.com, to get to the Corel site.

Admiring Your Work

Earlier in this chapter, I called DESIGNER a what-you-see-is-what-you-get (WYSIWYG) Web editing program, which isn't exactly true. What you publish on the Web is always extremely close to what's displayed in the DESIGNER window, but often minor (and sometimes major) differences occur. As you design your pages, periodically preview them to make sure that what you are designing is really what you're intending.

Previewing a Web page

 To preview the way a page that you're currently working on in DESIGNER will look on your Web browser, choose Tools➪Browser Preview, press F12, or click the Browser Preview button. Your page opens in your Web browser. In Figure 1-5, you can see that the spacing in the Web browser preview is different from the spacing you see when you view the page in DESIGNER.

Unless you specify otherwise, DESIGNER uses your system's default browser to preview your Web pages. (Your *default browser* is the one that opens when you double-click an Internet shortcut, or click a URL embedded in a document.) If you have more than one browser installed on your computer, you can specify a different browser in which to preview the page; choose Tools➪Set Browser, pick a browser from the list, and then click OK.

 Because each Web browser program will display your page differently, I highly suggest that you preview your pages in a number of different browsers. At the very least, you should use Netscape Navigator and Microsoft Internet Explorer, and you may want to consider using Mosaic as well. I'd also suggest that, when possible, you use more than one version of the same browser because things change from version to version (you can't do this with Internet Explorer because each new version automatically replaces the old version).

What you see isn't always what you get

A Web browser is kind of like a piece of paper. When you write a letter in your word processing program, you print it on a sheet of paper. When you produce a Web page, you "print" it to a Web browser.

This analogy breaks down a bit, though. If a printed letter doesn't look exactly like you want it to, you tweak it a little bit, and then print it out again. You have ultimate control over what goes out of your office. You just don't have that level of control with Web pages, although it's getting better.

Web pages weren't originally intended to be the artistic beauties that some of them are. When the Web was first started, the whole notion was to make it easy to use, and not really worry about the niceties of page layout, type faces, and all the things people take for granted in a magazine. To a large degree, how a page looked was up to the person viewing it, not the person who designed it.

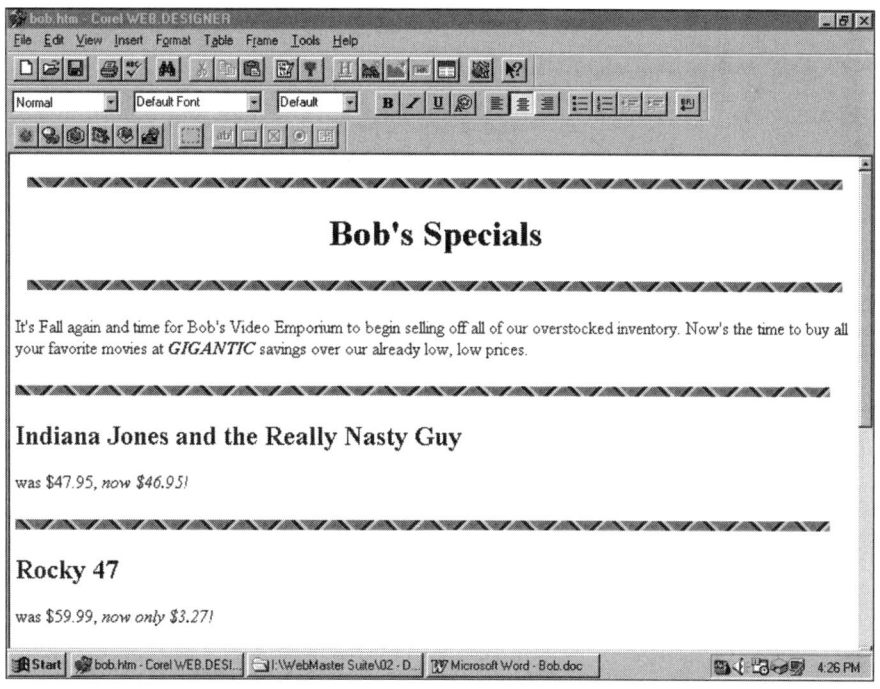

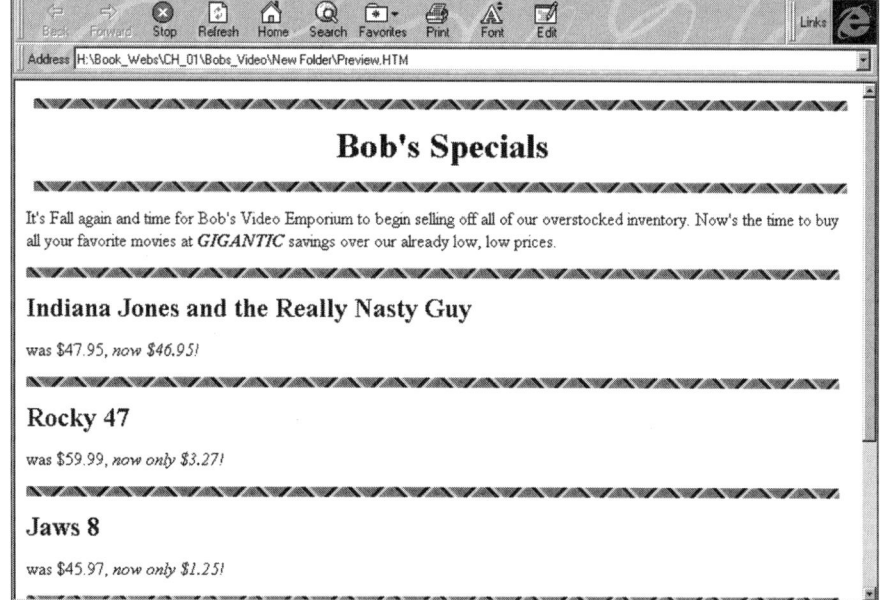

Figure 1-5:
Preview
your Web
page in a
browser
(right) to
see the
ways it
differs from
the view in
DESIGNER
(above).

As more graphic designers, and people schooled in traditional publishing, became involved in the Web, they wanted more control of their work — why spend five hours perfecting the layout of a page, when you can't be sure that your visitor will be able to see it? With changes coming fast and furious, you can always expect that a few people out there won't be viewing your pages with the latest and greatest browser, and you need to make things look right for them, too.

Check out Figure 1-6. These two shots show exactly the same Web page, but they don't look it, do they? That's because the page is being displayed in two wildly different Web browsers — Microsoft Internet Explorer Version 3.02 (above) and Mosaic Version 1.

The Mosaic version 1 browser (the bottom shot in Figure 1-9) doesn't understand the HTML codes for tables, fonts, or relative URLs. A little earlier in this chapter, I described a URL as a Web address (you know, the `www.domain.com/page.htm` thingy). A *relative URL* comes in handy when you're linking to a page that's in your own site — in this case, you ignore the `www.domain.com/` part and just include the name of the page itself. You can read more about tables in Chapter 8, fonts in Chapter 5, and relative URLs in Chapter 6.

Does this mean you can't use these codes? Not in the least. Using Mosaic version 1 in this example was a cheap shot — it's really out of date, and almost no one still uses it. It took me a couple of hours to track down someone who's still running it on his system (my timing was perfect because he'd just gotten the latest version from his ISP in the mail that morning but hadn't installed it).

The preceding example shows you the extreme. In most cases, what you'll see are slightly different interpretations of fonts and layouts.

One way around the problem of browsers not recognizing a particular HTML code is to tell people to use a certain browser to make your page look exactly the way you want it to look. Currently, this approach isn't practical if you want the maximum number of people to be able to view your site *exactly* the way you want it to be displayed. The *browser wars* are in full force, and finding visitors who have more than one browser loaded on their system is rare.

Although exact figures are impossible to come by, Netscape Navigator is still the most popular browser in the world, with Microsoft Internet Explorer gaining ground every day. Other browsers (such as Mosaic) are out there, too, but the number of people using them is minuscule.

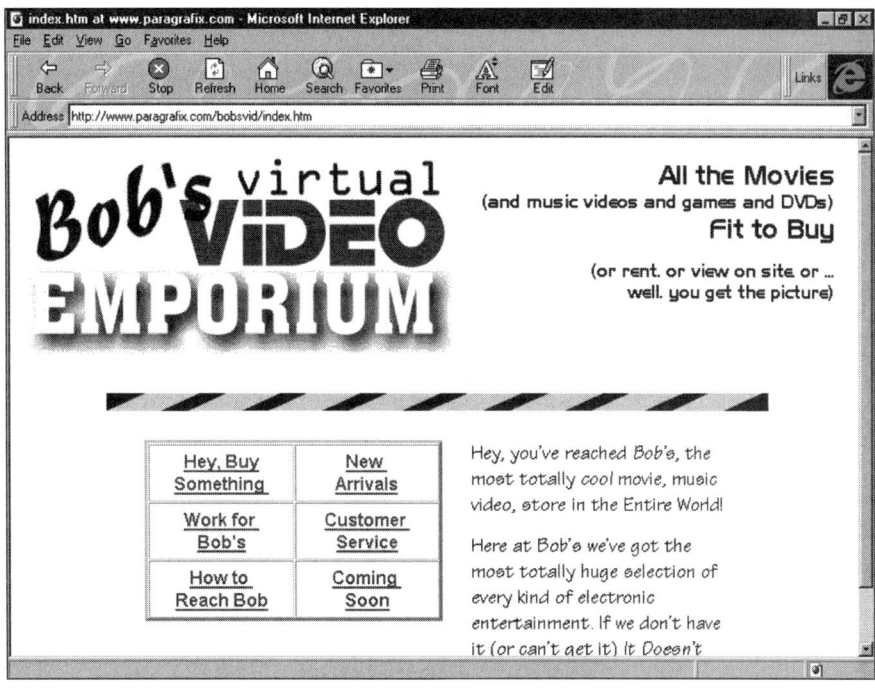

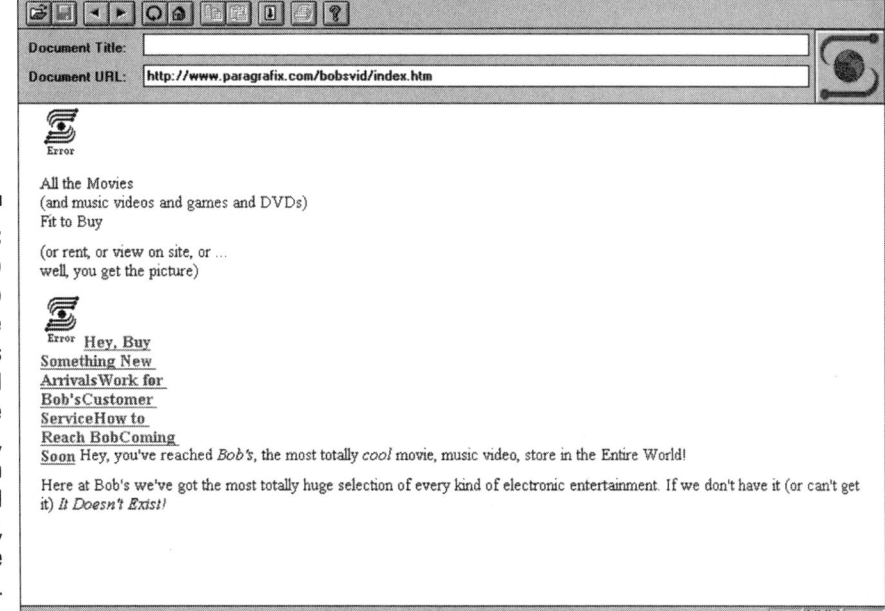

Figure 1-6:
The Web page on top looks the way it's supposed to; but the same page, viewed in an old browser, looks like a dud.

Chapter 2

We're Off to See the Wizard!

● ●

In This Chapter

▶ Using the Site Builder Wizard to create a new Web site

▶ Picking the type of Web site you want to create

▶ Deciding which style to use

▶ Viewing and editing your new Web site

● ●

*Y*ou have to complete three main tasks in order to create a new Web site:

✔ Plan and design the site.

✔ Build the site on your hard drive.

✔ Upload the site to a Web server.

One of the most daunting tasks when you're creating a new Web site has nothing to do with actually using WebMaster Suite: It's designing your site so that it's easy to navigate and has a consistent look. If you're a budding Webmaster with little or no experience, this design process can seem even more difficult.

Luckily, Corel WebMaster Suite includes a nifty Site Builder Wizard that takes the initial agony out of designing your site and building it on your hard drive. The Site Builder Wizard asks you a bunch of questions and then creates a brand-new Web site out of thin air!

The pages that Site Builder Wizard creates are pretty generic and don't include any real text, just placeholders that say something like `use this text to explain why your site exists.` You still have to type all your own text and personalize the pages by using DESIGNER. But don't worry, DESIGNER is really easy to use, and I devote most of this book to making it even easier.

Creating Your New Web Site, Wizard Style

To create a new site using the Site Builder Wizard, follow these steps. (*Note:* This run-through of the Wizard is only an example. Depending on how you answer questions along the way, the Wizard may not ask you some of the questions in the following instructions, or it may ask you ones that aren't listed.)

The tear-out Cheat Sheet at the beginning of this book lists a bunch of information that's invaluable when you're creating your site. I recommend having your system or server administrator fill out this sheet before you begin to build your site.

1. **Insert WebMaster Suite CD-ROM #2 in your CD-ROM drive.**

   You must have this disc in your CD-ROM drive before you start the Site Builder Wizard because the information that the Wizard needs to work is not copied to your hard drive when you install the program.

2. **Choose Start➪Programs➪Corel WebMaster Suite➪Corel WEB.SiteManager to start SiteManager, and then select the Create a New Site radio button in the Open dialog box.**

   Note that you may first have to click OK to close the Welcome to CorelWEB.SiteManager screen before you can view the Open dialog box.

   If you're already in SiteManager, simply choose File➪Site Builder Wizard.

3. **Click OK.**

   The Site Builder Wizard dialog box opens.

4. **Select either the index.htm or default.htm radio button to name your site's home page.**

   The name that you pick for your home page depends on the type of computer on which you ultimately publish your site. In general, if you publish on a PC-based or Macintosh server, you can use either index.htm or default.htm, but if you publish to a UNIX system, you must choose index.htm.

5. **In the Directory text box, enter the location where you want to build your site, as shown in Figure 2-1.**

   If you plan to work on only one Web site, then using the default location C:\WEBMASTR\PROGRAMS\WebSite\ is okay (the drive letter may be different if you installed WebMaster Suite on a drive other than C). On the other hand, if you're going to work on several different sites, you may want to create a new folder named something like WEBS, inside of which you can create subfolders for each site. I use this method to keep my Web sites organized. Besides, if you use the default location and then want to make another site, the default location stays the same, and you may end up overwriting all of your work by mistake.

You can also click Browse and use the Browse for Folder dialog box to locate the folder in which you want to create your new site. Just double-click a drive to display its folders. You can view the contents of these folders by double-clicking them. When you locate the folder you want to use, select it by clicking it once, and then click OK to close the Browse for Folder dialog box. The folder name now appears in the Directory text box.

If you type in the name of a folder that doesn't exist, the Wizard creates the new folder for you. This feature is handy if you use the Browse for Folder dialog box to locate a main folder, and you want to create your site in a folder inside of that folder. Just add a backslash (\) after the name of the folder in the Directory text box and then type the new folder name.

Figure 2-1:
Starting the
Site Builder
Wizard.

6. **Click Next.**

   Your CD-ROM drive spins for a moment while a little graphic asks you to be patient. Eventually, the graphic is replaced by the Site Builder Wizard dialog box, which opens again and displays several icons representing different types of Web sites the Wizard can create.

   You have 13 alternatives to choose from, ranging from a single blank page to a complete corporate site. The figures that appear in this example are based on the Company Web Site option.

7. **Select the type of site you want to create by clicking its icon once and then clicking Next.**

   The icons in the dialog box now change to display a number of styles that are available for your site.

8. Pick a style for your Web site by clicking its icon.

This option sets the appearance of your site — each style uses different images, background color, and even text color and size. The styles range from pretty funky (Wiener Dog) to fairly staid (Business 1). Your choice really depends on the image that you want your site to convey. I chose Business 2 for the figures in this example.

You can view some of the graphics from each of the styles by highlighting the style and clicking the View button. The graphics then appear in a dialog box. When you finish previewing the graphics, click the Close button to return to the Site Builder Wizard dialog box.

9. Click Finish.

The Finish button is a ruse — you're only finished with the initial portion of creating your site. The Site Builder Wizard dialog box now displays a text box asking for the banner you want displayed on your home page.

10. Type a headline for your home page in the Banner on Page text box.

A *banner* is the large text at the top of a page, similar to a banner headline in a newspaper. For the following reasons, try to keep your headline short and sweet:

- The Wizard uses graphic images to create banners, and graphics take a lot longer than text to download. A long banner increases the time it takes someone to download your page — and nobody likes to wait.

- If your banner is very long, it may end up being wider than your viewer's browser window. Unlike regular text, graphics don't automatically wrap to the next line. This *could* cause some serious confusion — just imagine if you wanted to create a banner for "The Society for Cruelty Prevention," but all that showed on-screen was "The Society for Cruelty"!

11. Click OK.

The Wizard now shows you a bunch of check boxes listing the available components for your site.

12. Select the components you want to include in your site by clicking the appropriate check boxes.

Even if you're not going to use a particular page right away, if there's a chance that you may want it later, go ahead and select it in the Site Builder Wizard. Then you can simply delete any links to these pages in your site's other pages (see Chapter 6). Planning ahead in this way ensures that all your pages maintain the same look and feel, and it also saves you from unnecessary formatting work later.

If you don't want to include a component that's already checked, you can deselect it by clicking the component to clear the check box.

The pages and components you have to choose from depend on which style of Web site you chose in Step 8.

13. Click OK.

You're not done yet. The Wizard now asks you a series of questions about the particular components that you elected to install. Of course, the questions it asks depend on which components you choose. The next section, "Stuff to Keep in Mind," explains the questions that the Site Builder Wizard is likely to ask you.

Stuff to Keep in Mind

As you answer the questions that the Site Builder Wizard keeps throwing at you, keep the following list (and Figure 2-2) handy to help you make sense of the terms that the Wizard uses. Also, program your phone's autodialer with the number of your network administrator; because each server is set up a little differently, only a system administrator can answer some of the following questions.

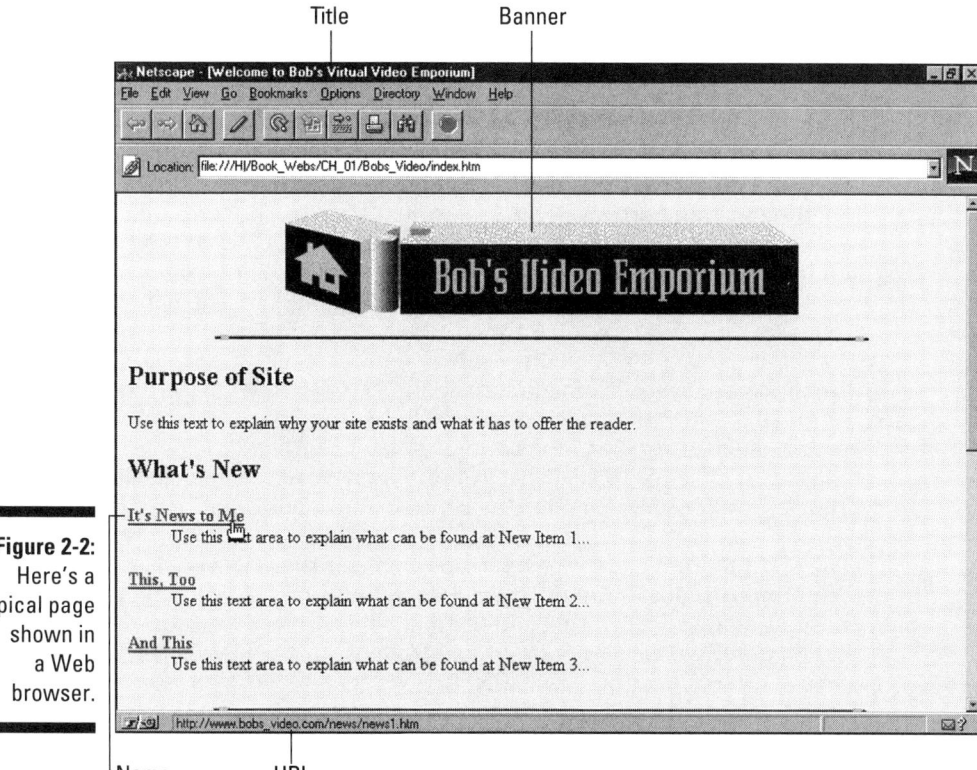

Figure 2-2:
Here's a typical page shown in a Web browser.

- ✔ **Title:** A Web page's title is the name that appears in the title bar of your visitor's browser.

- ✔ **Banner:** A banner is the large text at the top of a page, similar to a banner headline in a newspaper.

- ✔ **URL:** The abbreviation URL stands for Uniform Resource Locator, which probably doesn't help you much. A URL (pronounced *you are elle*) is a geeky term for *Web address*. When the Wizard asks you for a URL, it wants to know the address of a page to create a link to. (Chapter 6 contains everything you need to know about links.) Just enter the usual `http://www.domain.com/folder/page.htm` address that you use with your Web browser.

- ✔ **Name:** Typically, when the Wizard asks you for a name, it means the word or words that you want to use as a hyperlink to another page. (These words appear underlined on your page, indicating that your visitors can click them.)

Viewing and Editing Your Shiny New Site

When you click the last OK button, the Site Builder Wizard dialog box closes, and your hard drive and CD-ROM drive whir and click for a few minutes. Ultimately, you return to SiteManager, where you can view and edit your newly created site (see Figure 2-3).

SiteManager's view of your site may not make much sense to you right off the bat. But don't worry, after a few moments reading this book and experimenting with the program, the fog begins to clear. The time and effort you invest are well worth it — SiteManager is the most powerful tool available for maintaining, creating, and organizing your site. This section is an introduction to SiteManager. Chapter 3 gives you complete instructions on how to make SiteManager work for you.

 The first view you see of your site contains two parts. On the left side is a list of all the files that make up your site; on the right is a representation of your home page (called index.htm or default.htm) and the pages within your site that it links to. To see what your home page actually looks like, choose View⇨Browser View (or click the Browser View button or press F8).

The text that first appears on your page is just there to say, "Hey, put in something original." You don't want to publish your Wizard-created page without doing some editing and personalizing. To enable you to edit your pages, Corel WebMaster Suite provides you with a what-you-see-is-what-you-get (WYSIWYG) editor — DESIGNER. If you're familiar with word processing programs, you'll feel right at home using DESIGNER.

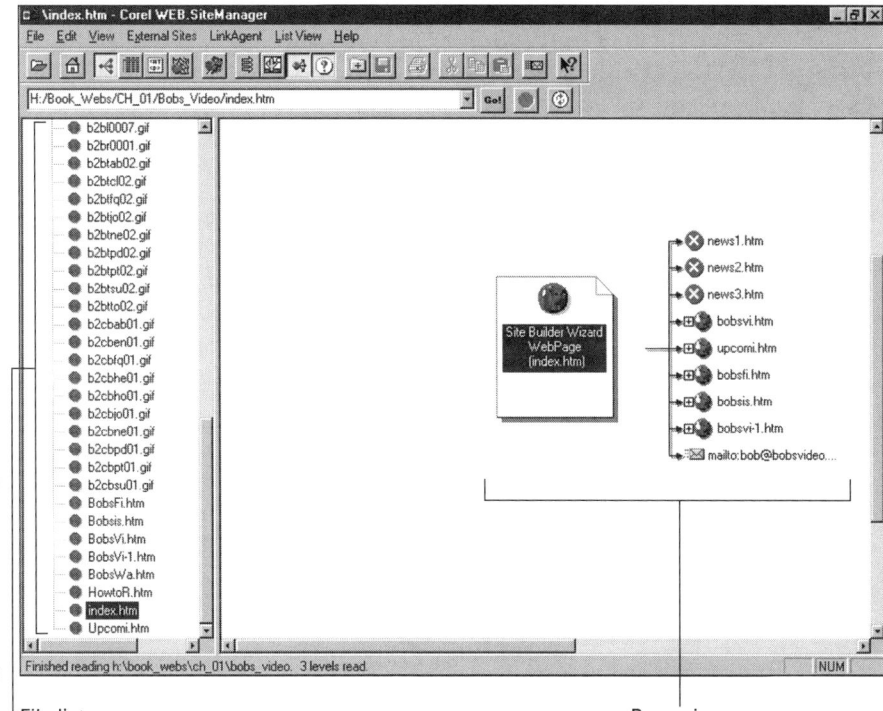

Figure 2-3:
Your new
site, as
shown in
SiteManager.

File list   Page view

 To open a page in DESIGNER, highlight a page file (a file ending in .htm) in the left-hand file window and choose View⇨Launch Editor (or click the Editor button or press Ctrl+E). You can also just double-click the page's filename. In DESIGNER, you can add new text and graphics and edit the existing text. See Chapter 1 for an introduction to DESIGNER. Part II of this book has instructions for using every aspect of DESIGNER and all the other tools to help you create a cutting-edge Web site.

When you finish editing your page, choose File⇨Exit and click Yes when the dialog box asks if you want to save your changes. If you've made changes to the links or the graphics that are included in your page, update SiteManager's view of your site by choosing File⇨Reload the Current Site. Note that when you reload your site, SiteManager switches to Page View and selects your home page (index.htm or default.htm), no matter what page or view you had selected before.

When you get your site just perfect (for now, that is, because you will always have updates and changes), you're ready to upload the entire site to a Web server. Chapters 18 and 19 show you two methods for doing this. Which method you choose depends on whether you're publishing to MicroCrafts PageDepot (using its 30-day free hosting) or to your corporate server or an Internet service provider (ISP).

After you publish your site, it's just waiting for visits (called *hits* in Web-talk). Chapter 20 shows you how to announce your site on all the major search engines so that people all over the world can find your site.

Chapter 3

Using SiteManager Before Things Get Out of Control

● ●

In This Chapter

▶ Viewing the structure of a Web site

▶ Previewing pages

▶ Moving items around in your Web site

▶ Loading Web sites from the Internet

● ●

*A*fter you use DESIGNER (the WebMaster Suite spiffy Web page editor) to create a couple of pages, add some graphics, and insert a bunch of hyperlinks, things start to get more than a little complicated. When you first began working with your site, everything seemed clear; you knew what you had to do, and you knew where every file was and what it did.

As your site gets more intricate, though, you may start asking yourself questions like, "Did I remember to update that link to my supplier's home page?" "What was the name of that page that had the information about last quarter's sales?" "Isn't the president's message page supposed to have a photograph on it?" "Is there an easier way to work with all my pages at once?"

Good news: WebMaster Suite includes SiteManager to help you keep track of all this information — and more. SiteManager looks (and works) an awful lot like Windows Explorer. With SiteManager, you can easily move files, update hyperlinks, and organize your site.

Looking at Your Site's Structure through SiteManager

One of SiteManager's most useful features is that it makes short work of visualizing the way all your Web components work together. When you first start SiteManager, it greets you with a split window (see Figure 3-1).

Site name and location   Toolbar

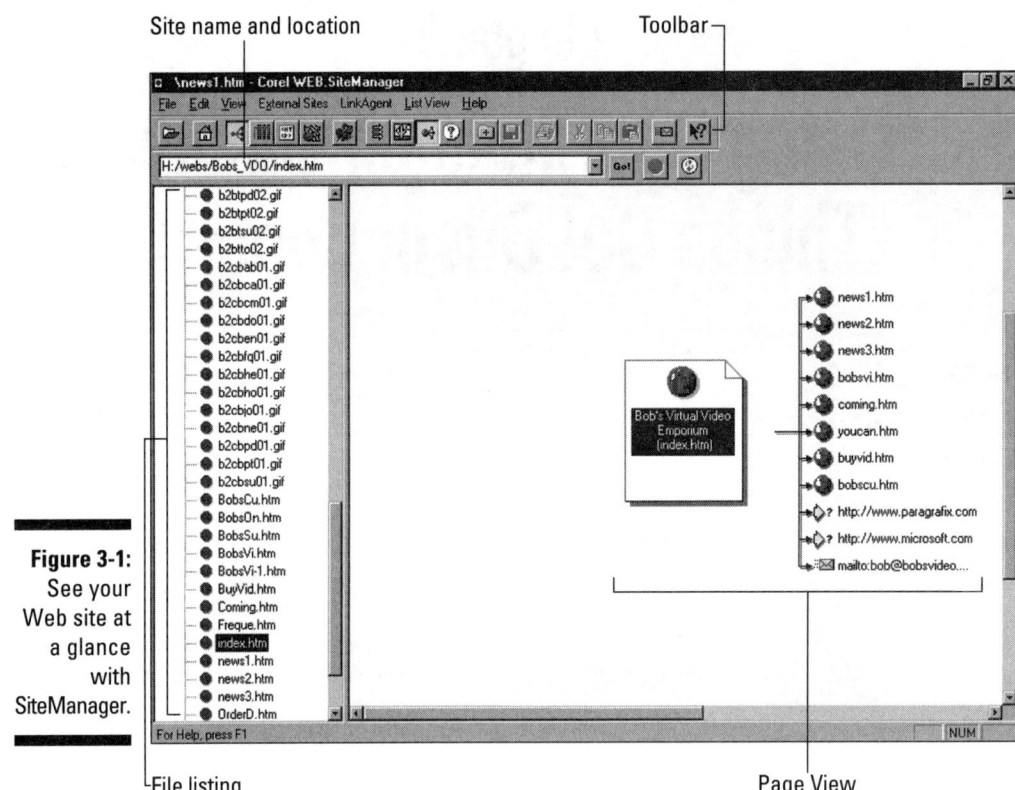

Figure 3-1:
See your
Web site at
a glance
with
SiteManager.

└─File listing   Page View

The left side of the window shows you every file in your Web site, and the right side provides a graphic representation (called *Page View*) of the links in your home page. (You can view your site in other ways besides Page View — when you select these other views, as detailed later in this chapter, they replace the Page View in the right-hand window.)

SiteManager provides a number of ways to open your site and view its structure. To start SiteManager and view your site's structure in five easy steps:

1. **Choose Start⇨Programs⇨Corel WebMaster Suite⇨Corel WEB.SiteManager.**

   SiteManager starts, and the Tip of the Day dialog box displays a timely idea for improving your productivity. (If you want to turn off the Tip of the Day feature so that it doesn't appear every time you start SiteManager, uncheck the Show This Screen When SiteManager Starts check box in the Tip of the Day dialog box.)

2. Click OK.

The Open dialog box appears, as shown in Figure 3-2.

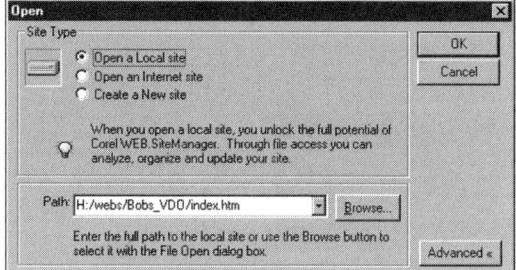

Figure 3-2:
The Open
dialog box.

3. Select the Open a Local Site radio button.

4. Type the path name of your Web site's home page in the text box.

Or you can click Browse to open a standard Windows Open dialog box, from which you can locate the home page of the site you want to open and then click Open.

5. Click OK to load your site into SiteManager.

If you're already in SiteManager and want to open and view your site, you can use any of the following shortcuts:

✔ Choose File⇨Open or click the Open button on the toolbar, and then follow Steps 3, 4, and 5 of the preceding instructions to open a local site using the Open dialog box.

✔ Choose File⇨1, 2, 3, or 4 to open one of your most recently opened sites.

✔ Select the site from the drop-down list in the toolbar, and then click the Go! button.

Sometimes, when you try to open a local site, SiteManager displays a dialog box that says `Corel WEB.SiteManager was unable to open the specified site. Please check the specified URL or file path.` *Don't Panic!* Every once in a while, the name of your home page (usually index.htm or default.htm) gets tacked onto the name of the site root in the Open dialog box, and SiteManager freaks a little. (The *site root* is the name of the folder that contains your site's home page — refer to Chapter 1 for details.) You didn't do anything wrong. The Site Root entry should read something like `c:/webroot/`. If it reads `c:/webroot/index.htm`, then you just have to fix it. Here's how:

1. Click OK to close the `Corel WEB.SiteManager was unable to open the specified site. Please check the specified URL or file path` **dialog box.**

2. Choose File⇨Open or click the Open button.

The Open dialog box appears.

3. Click the Advanced button.

The dialog box expands and displays the Advanced Options section (see Figure 3-3).

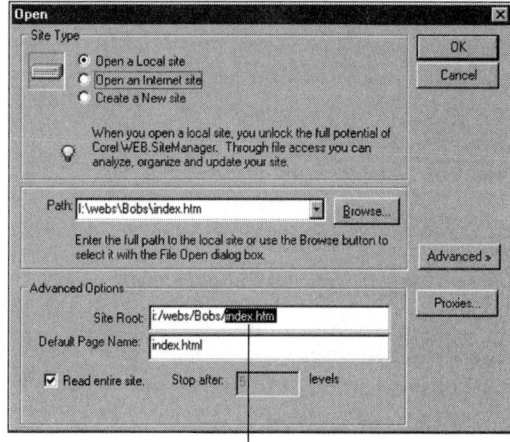

Figure 3-3:
The
Advanced
Options in
the Open
dialog box
give you
more
control over
the site
you're
loading.

Home page name included in site root name

4. Delete the name of the home page from the Site Root text box.

This name will be index.htm or default.htm.

5. Click OK.

The site opens normally.

Taking in the Page View

Picturing how pages relate to one another can be really difficult. Each page may have six, eight, or more hyperlinks to other pages, and those pages have still more links. Imagine a big tree reaching up into the sky, spreading out into more and more branches. A Web site is even more complicated because each of those branches can split and reach back to the earlier branches.

When you use SiteManager's Page View (see Figure 3-4), you can easily visualize the relationships between pages and their elements. SiteManager offers three other ways to view your site: List View, Browser View, and

Source View. Each provides a different way to visualize details about a particular page or the organization of the site as a whole. You can find out more about these other views later in this chapter, in the section called "Digging for details in other views."

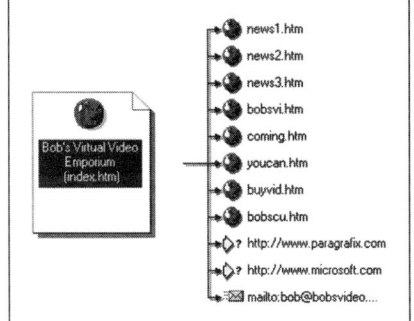

Figure 3-4:
The
SiteManager
Page View.

 When you start SiteManager, you automatically see your site in Page View. If you change to a different style view, however, you can switch back to Page View by choosing View⇨Page View, pressing F5, or clicking the Page View button on the toolbar.

The page that's currently selected in the file listing is previewed on the left. Any page that has a link *to* the current page is listed to the left of the selected page, and any links *from* the current page appear on the right (see Figure 3-5). If you want to see another page's links, you can select that page in the file listing or double-click it in the Page View. Whatever page you select becomes the big page, and you can see all the links to and from it.

Figure 3-5:
Everything
that links to
the current
page or is
linked to by
the current
page.

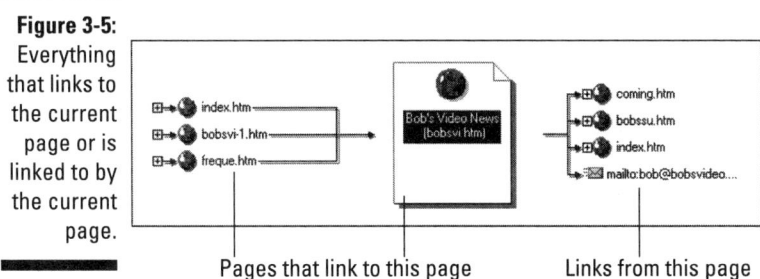

Expanding the tree

Page View starts with a single page, and shows all links directly from that page. You can expand the view to see a linked page's own links to show the trail that a visitor might make. Just click the small plus sign (+) beside that link (if no plus sign appears next to a page, then that page doesn't have any links). Note that you can only expand the links for pages inside your own Web site. If you have a link to Netscape's site, for example, no plus sign appears next to the link, even though there are links within the Netscape site (external links are represented by the big arrows).

Viewing links to images

If a page on your Web site contains images, as most will, Page View shows the images as links from the current page, just as if they were other Web pages. This approach enables you to quickly see which pages use which image files.

 To hide the filenames of pictures linked to a Web page, choose View➪Show Links to Picture Files, or click the Show Links to Pictures button in the toolbar. To view the filenames of pictures after you've hidden them, click the button again or repeat the menu selection.

Checking for duplicate links

 Web pages often have two or more links to the same page or image. For example, you may want to make absolutely sure that visitors find your online catalog, or maybe you want to show a link both as a graphic and as text. Sometimes, though, you discover that a bunch of the links are just gratuitous — making your page confusing to your visitors. To check for duplicate links, choose View➪Show Duplicate Links or click the Show Duplicate Links button.

SiteManager doesn't display duplicate links in any special way — it just shows you all your links, even if two or more of them are exactly the same (duplicates, you know).

Digging for details in other views

Page View is great for getting an overall feel for your Web site, but some-times you need more details about individual pages. The three other SiteManager views give you different sorts of information about your site and the pages that make it up. You can switch between these views at will.

Looking at List View

 To switch from Page View to List View, choose View➪List View or click the List View button in the toolbar.

List View provides a snapshot of the most important information about the pages on your Web site: their filenames, page titles, file sizes, and so on. Figure 3-6 shows a list of Web site pages in List View.

In my opinion, the most important piece of information that List View provides is the page title. Because filenames aren't always obvious, knowing the title can be helpful when you want to track down a particular page.

You can also choose what type of pages and files are shown in List View (a feature known as *filtering*). This can be great for tracking down specific files. Say, for example, that your Web server is being upgraded to handle Java, and you need to make changes to all your pages that have Java scripts. By listing just those pages, you can make short work of the updates. You don't have to look at each and every page in DESIGNER to figure out whether it contains any Java scripts.

To pick the type of files you want to view, click the List View menu and pick from the following selections:

✔ **All Files and Links:** Lists every file on your Web site, plus all your links to external sites.

✔ **All Files:** Lists every file in your Web site, but doesn't list the links to external sites.

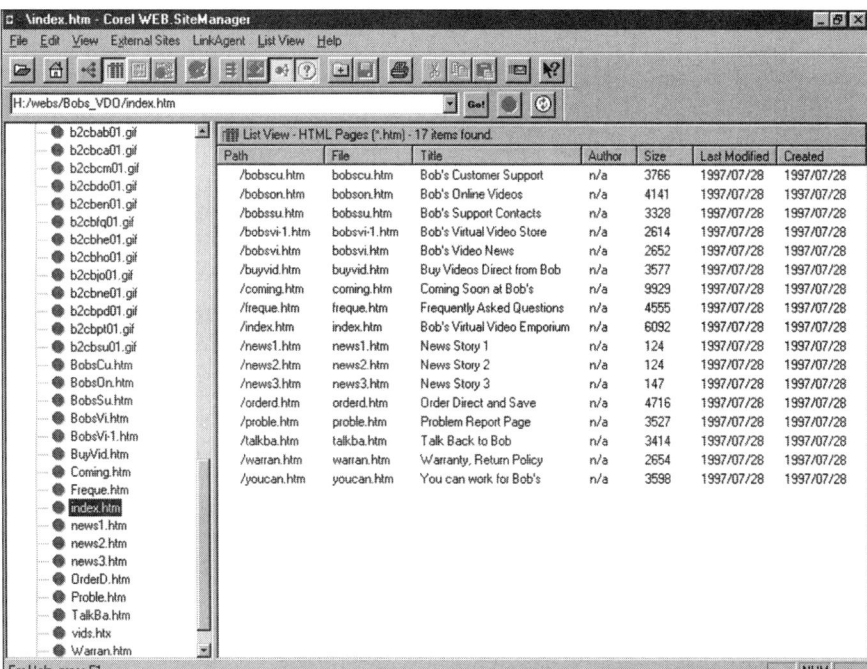

Figure 3-6:
A list of
Web site
pages in
List View.

✔ **HTML Pages:** Lists just the Web pages. Web pages are coded in Hypertext Markup Language (HTML) and are sometimes referred to as *HTML pages.*

✔ **Links to External Sites:** Shows just the external sites that your site links to.

✔ **Image Files:** Lists (surprise!) all the images used in your site.

✔ **Mailto: Links:** Lists all links that launch your visitors' e-mail programs and load in an address. This view is particularly useful if someone leaves your company or changes responsibility, and you need to update e-mail addresses.

✔ **Pages with Broken Links:** Gives you a list of pages with broken links but doesn't detail which links are broken. (A *broken link* is a hyperlink that points to a page that doesn't exist. The section "Checking links," later in this chapter, delves more deeply into broken links and how to fix them.)

✔ **Broken Links:** Lists all the actual broken links.

✔ **Orphan Files:** Lists files that aren't referenced by any other files. These may just be taking up space on your Web site for no good reason.

✔ **Pages Using Java:** Lists pages that use Java applets. (See Chapter 11 for more information on incorporating Java applets in your pages.)

✔ **Pages Using JavaScript:** Lists pages that include JavaScript scripts. (*JavaScript For Dummies,* 2nd Edition, by Emily Vander Veer and published by IDG Books Worldwide, Inc., is a great reference for adding JavaScript to your pages.)

✔ **Pages Using ActiveX:** Lists pages that incorporate ActiveX controls. (See Chapter 11 for more information on incorporating ActiveX controls in your pages.)

✔ **Pages Using VB Script:** Lists pages that include VB (Visual Basic) Script components. *VBScript For Dummies,* by John Walkenbach and published by IDG Books Worldwide., is an ideal book for figuring out the intricacies of VBScript.

✔ **Pages Using Frames:** Lists pages that use frames. (Chapter 9 explains how to create framed pages. *Hint:* It has nothing to do with hanging them on your wall.)

✔ **Pages Using Forms:** Lists pages that incorporate forms. (See Chapter 10 for more information on adding forms to your pages.)

When you first open List View, all the files are arranged alphabetically by their filenames. This is all well and good, unless, for example, you're trying to track down the oldest pages on your site so that you can update them. In this case, you want to sort the pages so that the oldest ones are at the top and the newest ones are at the bottom. To sort files by date or any other attribute, click the appropriate column heading.

Sticking with the date example for a moment: To sort the files from oldest to newest, just click the column heading last modified once. To sort from newest to oldest, click the column heading again. This same technique works for any of the columns in List View.

Browsing through Browser View

Say you've been searching through your site and you've found a bunch of Web pages that don't seem familiar. What do you do? Well, you *could* open each page in DESIGNER or your browser, but that can get really cumbersome. The easy alternative is to switch to Browser View. In Browser View, the right side of the SiteManager screen becomes a Web browser in which you can quickly view the pages that you pick from the files menu on the left (see Figure 3-7).

 To start Browser View, choose View⇨Browser View or click the Browser View button in the toolbar.

 You can also view image files in the Browser View. See Chapter 7 for more information on incorporating images into your pages.

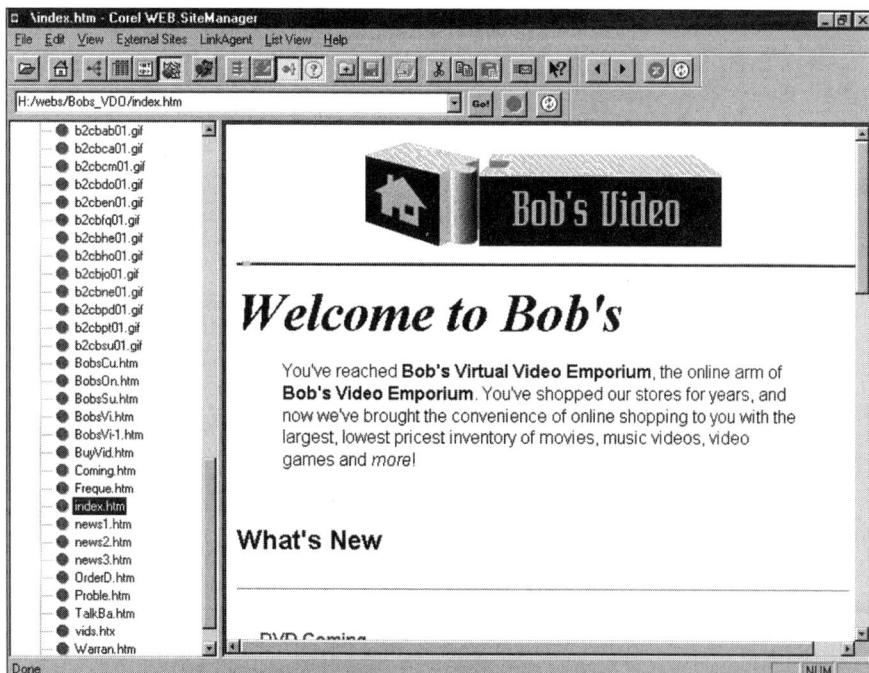

Figure 3-7:
The
Browser
View.

Switching to Source View

Source View shows the underlying technical jiggery pokery that makes a Web page work. Looking at this stuff is *not* for the squeamish. All Web pages are really just text files with gobs of codes that tell a browser how to display a page. These codes can get fairly arcane and, for some reason, are surrounded by pointy brackets, as shown in Figure 3-8.

Source View lets you look at and edit absolutely every aspect of a page. You can exercise much greater control over your page by editing the source code, but the downsides are that doing so is time-consuming, difficult, and not terribly intuitive. The main purpose of WebMaster Suite is to get as far away from editing code as possible, but sometimes dealing with source code is unavoidable. Chapter 13 goes through some of the more common tweaks and fixes that you may want to use to tune up your Web site.

To switch to Source View, choose View⇨Source View or click the Source View button in the toolbar.

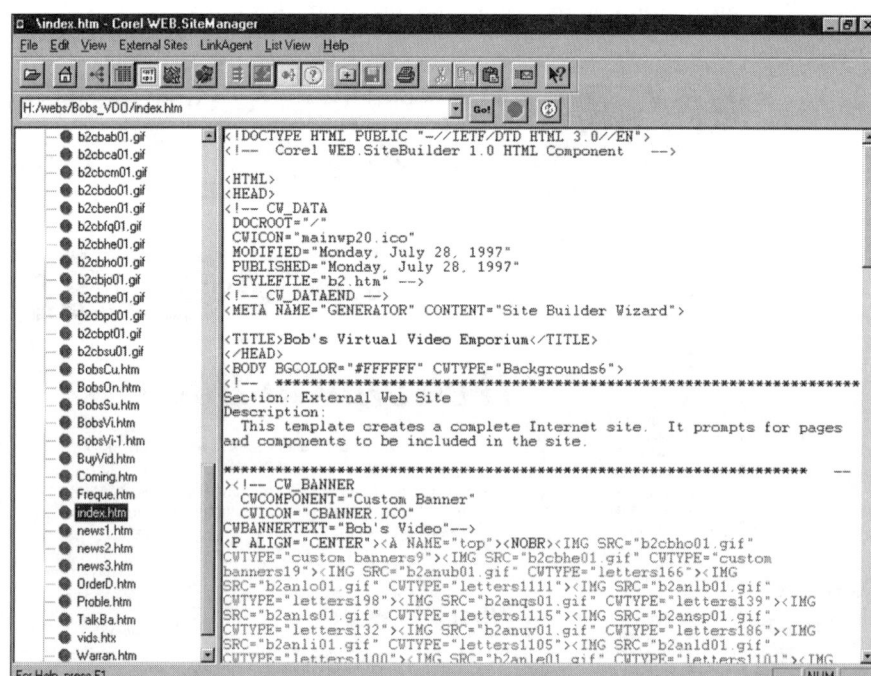

Figure 3-8:
Source
View
showing a
Web page.

Working with a Web Site in SiteManager

Oh boy! You can use SiteManager to view a site a bunch of different ways and to load a site directly from the Internet. But that stuff doesn't even begin to scratch the surface, as far as the real power of SiteManager is concerned. Organizing your site and having a central point for dealing with your site as a whole is what SiteManager is all about.

Editing files

SiteManager makes working with the individual files in your site easy. When you double-click a filename from the file list on the left, the appropriate editor starts with the appropriate file loaded into it. For example, if you double-click a Web page file, SiteManager launches DESIGNER and loads that page, so you're ready to start editing it. If you want to edit an image, just double-click its filename and SiteManager launches PhotoPaint. What could be easier?

This feature is a great time-saver: You don't have to start the appropriate editor (or even remember what program *is* the appropriate editor), access the Open dialog box, browse through your hard drive until you find the file you want to edit, and then load it. Two quick clicks, and you're ready to roll.

 When you finish editing the file, save it as you normally would and then exit the editor. If you've made changes that affect links (such as adding an image or editing a hyperlink in a Web page), press the Reload Site button to update the links shown in Page View.

You may be thinking, "Okay, SiteManager lets me move a file and keep the links intact, but *why would I want to?*" Creating new folders and moving files among them can help keep your site organized and make it easier to maintain. See Chapter 4 for a slew of tips on organizing your site.

Moving files

In the introduction, I mention that I make some assumptions in this book. One of the assumptions is that you're familiar with working with files in Windows Explorer: You know how to create folders, move and copy files, and all that sort of stuff. SiteManager gives you all the power of Explorer for dealing with the files in your Web site — plus a whole lot more.

Say, for example, that you want to move a graphic file from one folder to another. If you move the file from Windows Explorer, any page that uses that image won't know where to find it. As a result, your site's visitors will be greeted with a little icon showing where the image *should* be, but the image will not appear. But when you use SiteManager to move your files, all your links remain intact — SiteManager goes through all your page files and updates the references to the moved item.

 Adding a new folder is a little confusing. SiteManager doesn't contain a New Folder menu item the way Windows Explorer does (File⇨New⇨Folder). Instead, you have to select the folder in which you want to create a new folder, and then click the New Folder icon in the toolbar. Doing so creates an empty folder called, amazingly enough, New Folder. The name is already highlighted and just waiting for you to type a meaningful name. When you're done naming the folder, just press Enter.

You work with folders and files in SiteManager exactly the same way you work with them in Explorer:

- ✔ **When you want to move a file or folder, highlight it and drag it into another folder.** If the folder to which you move it is not visible (maybe because you have so many files that the folder is off the screen), right-click the object you want to move and then choose Cut. Then right-click the folder to which you move it and choose Paste.

- ✔ **To rename a file or folder, highlight it, click it once or press F2 (an outline appears around the name), type the new name, and then press Enter.** When you're renaming a file, make sure that you don't change its extension (the three letters after the period). If you do, you could really confuse every program that's supposed to access that file, including SiteManager, DESIGNER, and your visitors' browsers.

- ✔ **If you want to select more than one object at a time, use the old standbys: Shift+click and Ctrl+click.** To select a group of files that are all in a row, select the first file and then Shift+click the last one. Both files you clicked and all the ones in between are selected.

  To pick files that aren't right next to each other, select one file, and then press Ctrl+click subsequent files. Only the files you click are selected. To deselect a file, press Ctrl+click on the file again.

- ✔ **To delete a file or folder, highlight it and choose Edit⇨Delete, or press the Delete key.** Be sure that you really want to be rid of a file or folder before you delete it — SiteManager doesn't have an undo feature.

When you move, rename, or delete files or folders that contain links *to* other pages or are linked to *by* other pages, SiteManager sends out the Link Wizard dialog box. The Link Wizard automatically updates any links that are affected when you move, rename, or delete files. As a result, your site still works without having to do a lot of boring changes in DESIGNER. The Link Wizard also gives you the option of not updating links (although I can't imagine why you'd want to do that).

If someone else has a link (such as a bookmark, shortcut, or hyperlink on another Web page) to a page that you move or delete, that person can no longer visit your page through that link. To save your visitors from this frustration, you can instruct the Link Wizard to create a new page with the same name and location as the original one, that says either "This page has been moved" (and provides a link to the new location), or "This page has been deleted." When moving a page, select the Leave "This page has moved" messages check box. When deleting a page, check the Leave "This page has been removed" message(s) check box.

Of course, not everybody is as nice as you are. Some folks may not leave one of these friendly moved- or deleted-page messages. When a link points to a page that doesn't exist, it's called a *broken link.* The next section shows you how to find broken links on your Web site quickly and easily.

Checking links

Broken links are the bane of a Web publisher's existence. With all the changes happening out on the Web, making sure that the links on your Web site still point to the appropriate page can be a real hassle.

Broken links usually aren't a problem for links that lead to other pages within your own Web site. When you attempt to delete a page that is linked to by other pages on your site, the Link Wizard tells you that some links will be broken. You can deal with these broken links right then by leaving a message behind, or you can handle it later by removing the links from each of your pages. To make removing the links easier, click the Details button in the Link Wizard dialog box. Doing so opens a listing of all the pages that contain a link to the deleted page.

When you make links to other Web sites, however, things can get a little hairy. You don't want to spend a lot of time browsing your Web site, clicking links to other sites to make sure that they still work. SiteManager has a couple of ways to let you quickly find broken links. And after you find broken links, you can open the page or pages containing them in DESIGNER and edit or delete the links as explained in Chapter 6.

 Both of the following methods of checking links can incorrectly report broken links. I highly recommend that when you are alerted that a link is broken, you open the offending page in a browser and check the link (by clicking it) before you delete or try to change it.

Manually checking links

While you're editing your site, you can check links to external sites to make sure that they're still okay:

1. **Start SiteManager.**

   Of course, if you're already running SiteManager, you can skip this step.

2. **Connect to the Internet.**

   If you're already connected to the Internet, don't worry about this step either.

3. **Load the site containing the links that you want to check.**

4. **Select the page containing the links you want to check.**

   In Figure 3-9, all external links have a question mark next to them, which indicates that SiteManager isn't sure whether the links are okay.

Figure 3-9:
Questionable
external
links.

5. **If you're viewing your site in Page View, make sure that it's display-ing external links by choosing View⇨Show External Links or clicking the Show External Links button.**

   You can also choose List View⇨Links to External Sites to show all the external links (links to pages that aren't in your Web site but rather are in someone else's) in your site at once.

6. **Right-click the link you want to check, and choose Re-Check Link from the pop-up menu.**

   SiteManager tries to access the linked file. If it succeeds, a big arrow replaces the question mark and small arrow. If SiteManager fails, the question mark is replaced by an X. See Figure 3-10 for examples of both.

Figure 3-10:
Checked
external
links.

Broken link   Unbroken link

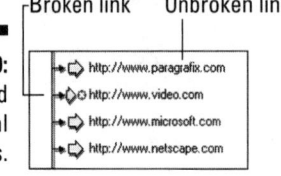

Link Agent — more trouble than it's worth?

Link Agent (available from the SiteManager menu bar) is yet a third way that you can check the links for a site. But there's a twist, instead of checking the links contained in the copy of your site that's sitting on your hard drive, Link Agent checks the links of your site *after* you publish on the Web. (Chapters 18 and 19 explain how to publish your site on the Web.)

Checking the links on your published site may sound like a great idea — you could check the links on your site and update any broken ones right then and there. Unfortunately, Link Agent just doesn't work that way.

Link Agent doesn't allow you to edit pages that are already on the Web. Instead, you have to download those pages to your own hard drive, edit them there, and then publish them back to the Web. If you do this, you run the risk of having two copies of the same page on your hard drive — one that you've updated and doesn't have any broken links, and another that you haven't updated and has (possibly) a kajillion broken links.

I suggest that you ignore Link Agent and use the two methods described in this chapter for checking your links. (Remember that if a link doesn't work from your hard drive, it won't work from your published Web site either.)

Don't forget that Web pages aren't the only type of external files that you can link to. For example, you can include pictures that are in totally different Web sites in your pages. If you're checking your links by hand, you want to have SiteManager show you links to all pictures and unrecognized files.

Checking all links

If your site includes a lot of external links, going through and checking every one of them by hand can get really tedious. Luckily, there are easier ways to check all your external links.

While your site is still located on your hard drive (before you've published it to the Web), SiteManager can validate your links two ways. (*Validate* is just an impressive-sounding way to say "check to make sure that they work.") SiteManager can check the links every time you load a site, or check them only when you want it to:

- ✔ To check all the external links at once, choose External Sites⇨Check Links to External Sites.

- ✔ To have SiteManager automatically check links every time you load a site, choose External Sites⇨Check External Links After Site Load.

Although having SiteManager always check your external links sounds like a great idea, it can be a pain if you connect to your Internet service provider through a modem. You don't want to have to remember to connect to the Web every time you start up SiteManager. Also, no matter what type of connection you have (unless you're connected with a super-speedy T1 line), if your site contains many external links, validating them can take a while. If either of these cases is true for you, I suggest that you don't have SiteManager automatically check external links when you load a site.

Chapter 4

Avoiding the "I Can Do It Right Later" Trap

. . . .

In This Chapter

▶ Deciding where to publish your site

▶ Discovering special programs available on the server

▶ Finding out who maintains the server

▶ Organizing your site for easier maintenance

. . . .

*Y*our Web site can quickly become tremendously complicated, what with all the pages, hyperlinks, Java scripts, and everything else you worked so hard to create. If you're like me, you want to jump in and get to work . . . and leave the organization for later. But you can save yourself a lot of time and effort if you do a little advanced planning.

Not All Web Servers Are Created Equal

The PC on your desk isn't the only computer involved with making your Web site available to the millions of Web surfers scattered all over the globe. When your site is ready for visitors, you must copy all its files to a computer, called a *Web server,* that's connected to the Internet. The Web server transmits your pages to anyone who wants to see them. You need to know some stuff about your Web server, and the best time to find it out is *before* you begin to build your site.

Inside the front cover of this book, I include a handy checklist or Cheat Sheet that you can ask your ISP server administrator to fill out and return to you. This checklist details all the information you need to know before you start to create your pages.

The server administrator will probably be happy to fill out this form for you. Spending a few minutes writing out the details of the server now is far better than spending hours helping you track down problems later. The following sections explain each question on the Cheat Sheet, to help you understand what the answers mean and how you can use them.

Basic issues

This section of the form asks for basic information about where your site will be located and who services it.

What is my Web site's domain?

The *domain* is the base of the Web address: the `www.whatever.com` part. As you've surfed the Web, you've probably noticed that domain names can vary a great deal. You may have seen domains like `home.netscape.com` or `www.iweb.net.au` or any one of a number of other variations. When you see a Web address at the top of your browser, everything between `http://` and the next slash (/) mark is the domain. You need to know the domain of your site so that you can give the full address to anyone who may want to visit your site.

If you're publishing your site to an Internet Service Provider (ISP), your domain may be the same as your ISP's domain. Alternatively, you may be able to pay your ISP extra money to have your own domain name that is merely "hosted" on the ISP computers.

What is the root directory of my Web site?

The *root directory* is the name of the folder in which all the files for your Web site must go.

If you operate your site through an ISP, or if you're a single publisher on a large company server, someone will likely assign you a folder in which to put all your Web materials. Your root directory name is often similar to your user name — if your username is `b_teevee`, then your folder might be something like `/~b_teevee/`. Depending on how your server is organized, the name may be a bit longer, such as `/users/b_teevee/`.

In either case, when you want to tell people how to reach your Web site, you must give them the full address. This address looks like `www.domain.com/~b_teevee/` or `www.domain.com/users/b_teevee/`.

If you don't have to put your pages in a separate folder, then your Web address is the domain name itself: `www.domain.com`, for example.

What name must I use for my home page?

Generally, the answer to this question is either index.htm or default.htm. Which answer is correct for your home page depends on the computer system and server software you're using. If you name your home page appropriately, it automatically opens in your visitors' browsers when they type your site's URL — even if they don't type the filename itself.

What hardware/operating system does the server run on?

Typically, you won't need to know what hardware (the computer itself, also called the *platform*) and operating system (such as Windows, Macintosh, or UNIX) the Web server is running. However, if you plan to purchase an add-on program for your Web site (say, an interactive database that lets visitors search for information), then you do need to know what kind of platform and operating system your server is running on before you purchase the program.

What program/version server software is used?

Again, under *normal* circumstances you don't need to know the program and version number of the Web server software. But if you're trying to debug a custom Common Gateway Interface (CGI) script, then this information comes in handy. (Fortunately for both of us, writing CGI scripts is way beyond the scope of this book.)

What security systems (if any) are available?

Security systems help you ensure that information on your site that you want kept secret really *stays* secret. For example, if you want visitors to your site to be able to place orders with credit cards, you need to have a security system that's capable of keeping unauthorized people from finding out your clients' credit card numbers. Other types of security systems ensure that only you (or someone you've given permission to) can make changes to your Web pages.

Is this site case sensitive?

If your administrator answers "yes" to this question, you must always make sure to match the exact capitalization of names when you add a hyperlink to a Web page file or when you include a picture in your page. Because DE-SIGNER takes care of entering filenames for you, case sensitivity is only a problem if you manually type HTML codes. (Manually typing HTML code is an advanced procedure for really tweaking your Web site and is outlined in Chapter 13.)

Who is the Server Administrator?

This question could have easily read, "Whom do I call if I have a problem?" The server administrator is the person who runs the Web server and makes sure that everything is operating properly. Your server administrator probably won't want to provide a home phone number, but it doesn't hurt to ask.

If ISP: name, address, URL

If you're using an ISP, then you can usually find its name, address, and URL on your service agreement or bills. But I recommend including it on the Cheat Sheet anyway so that you can have everything in one central location.

Support

Your server administrator uses this section of the form to tell you where you can find additional information when he or she is unavailable, or if you have just a small problem.

What support documentation is available?

Here, your server administrator lists any *hard copy* documentation that may be of assistance to you. Try to get copies of these documents so that you have them when you need them.

Online documentation

In many cases, documentation is available online in Web pages or downloadable document files. I recommend adding these documents to your browser's favorites list. I have a folder in my favorites directory that contains nothing but shortcuts to my ISP's documentation.

Programming

If you plan to include custom programming, such as Common Gateway Interface (CGI), Perl, Java applets or scripts, or ActiveX controls in your site, the programming information your server administrator includes in this section of the form is vital. Today, most programming is limited to creating multimedia applications (really cool animations, which I discuss in Chapters 7 and 16), but the potential exists for creating complete programs, like word processors and electronic spreadsheets, if the Web ever becomes fast enough. Incorporating these different types of Web programming systems in your site is the subject of Chapter 11.

The questions in this section of the Cheat Sheet all ask for the same information: *Is such-and-such programming option available? If any pre-made programs are already available on the server, where are they?* and *What pre-made programs are already available for me to use?*

What programming options are available?

Essentially, every server today supports CGI, Perl, Java, and ActiveX. If these features aren't available on your server, you may want to lobby the server administrator to add them. If you're using an ISP that doesn't offer support for these programming options, you should seriously consider getting a new ISP because it means that they aren't up on the latest technology and probably aren't giving you the best possible service.

At what URL are components stored?

Depending on your Web server software, you may have to place programs (also called *components*) written in CGI and Java in special folders on the server. CGI components are called *scripts,* and Java components are called *classes.* These components are usually stored in a folder called *cgi-bin* or *java-bin,* but if you plan to use these components on your site, make sure that you know where on your server to store them.

If you have the rights (this is Computerese for "if you are allowed") to add new components to the server, this part of the form contains the Web address where you can put them. More often than not, you need to send any new components to the server administrator, who will check them out. If the components you send are found to be bug- and virus-free, the administrator places them on the server for everyone to use.

What pre-made components are available for me to use?

Generally, if your Web server supports programming such as CGI, Perl, Java, and ActiveX, then it has some pre-made components for the programming language already available on the system. Pre-made components are miniprograms that you can use in your Web pages. (Before you can use these components, though, you have to know where they're located, which was answered in the previous question.)

File Transfer Protocol

When you publish your site to a Web server, you use the File Transfer Protocol (or FTP) to move all the files that make up your site from your local computer to the server. FTP defines the commands used to move files from one computer to the other. Thank goodness FTP programs are available to hide all these obnoxious commands from you and me, but figuring out *where* the files belong is still a little more involved than clicking a drive or folder icon in the Windows Explorer. You need to know ahead of time the location where your files go.

In general, this location is slightly different from your Web site's URL. The specific location depends on how your server administrator has configured the server software, but for an example, suppose that your Web site's URL is

```
http://www.domain.com/b_teevee/
```

Your FTP address may be something like this:

```
ftp://ftp.domain.com/home/b_teevee/
```

If you publish your site to the PageDepot Server using SiteManager's Publish to the Internet Wizard, you don't need to know any FTP information. PageDepot creates a new folder for you to use and hides all the nasty FTP information behind a friendly, easy-to-use Wizard. I discuss publishing your site to PageDepot in Chapter 18, and using FTP to publish to another Web server in Chapter 19.

Stay Organized with SiteManager

Organization may seem like the last thing you want to get involved with when you create a Web site. I mean, all the files are there in the Web site folder of your computer just waiting for you to pick and choose the ones you want to include in your site. But what happens when your site starts getting big, and you find yourself with a couple of hundred image files, a few dozen pages, and maybe even some sound files? Locating the exact file you want to use can become pretty difficult. SiteManager is great for creating and updating your site. But keeping your site organized is where SiteManager really shines. (Chapter 3 goes over all the mechanics of using SiteManager.)

Folders are your friends

SiteManager's List View provides approximately 1 kajillion different ways to view your site. You can choose to see just the HTML (Web page) files (as shown in Figure 4-1), just the image files, or just about any other type of file. I find, though, that the best way to see the overall structure of your site is to use Page View so that you can see all the links and how pages relate to one another.

But sometimes you just want to focus on the image files that are included in your site. When you're in Page View, as shown in Figure 4-2, you can't concentrate on the specific type of file that you're interested in: The image files are mixed together with the HTML files, any files you want available for downloading, and everything else in your site.

You can create folders and move files around in your site using the file window on the left side of SiteManager, no matter what view you currently have set in the viewing window on the right.

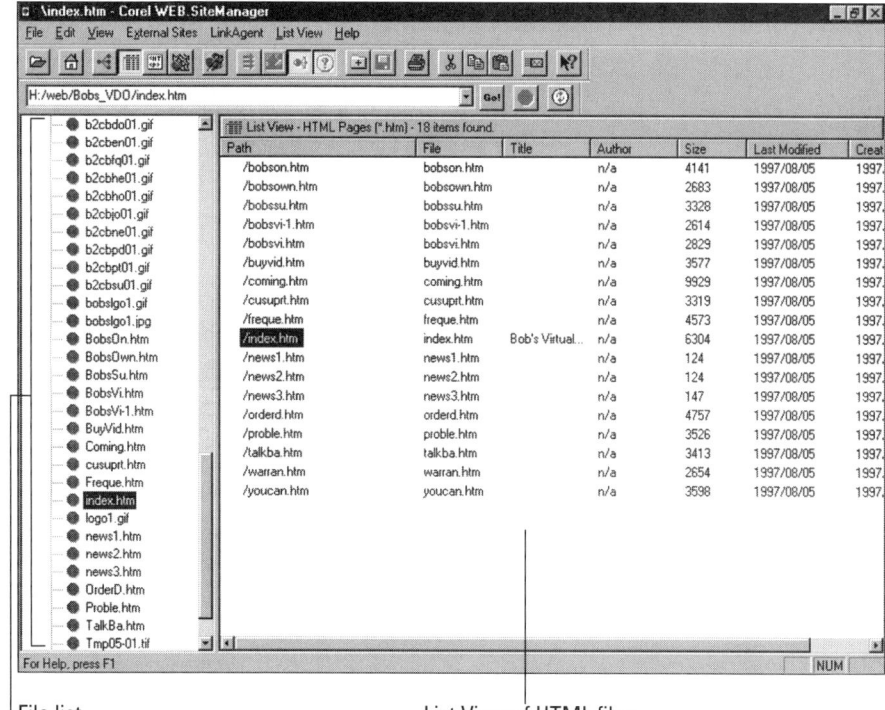

Figure 4-1:
List View
lets you
filter the
type of file
you want to
view.

File list   List View of HTML files

Exit all open copies of DESIGNER before you move files around in
SiteManager. When you move files from one folder to another, the hyperlinks
between them may change. Link Wizard takes care of updating your links,
but if DESIGNER is open with any pages loaded, saving the page after Link
Agent updates your links will overwrite the updates. Chapter 6 discusses
creating and updating links, and Chapter 3 shows you how to move files
using SiteManager and how to use Link Wizard.

Organize by file type

To keep your site organized in a way that lets you see the files you want, I
suggest creating a folder for each type of file and moving all such files into
that folder. For example, create a folder called Images to hold all your GIF
and JPG files; create another folder called FTP to hold any files you want
available for downloading, and so on.

Graphic files

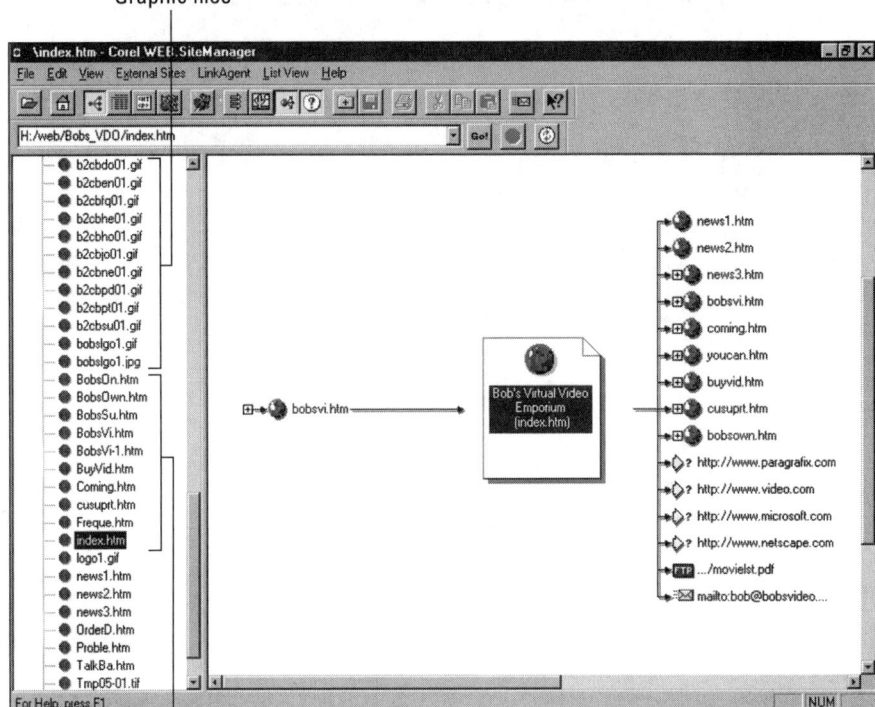

Figure 4-2:
Page View
doesn't
filter the
files.

Organize by department

If you're creating a large site, especially if you're working in an intranet
environment, you're likely to have many page files covering a range of
topics. When you're updating your site, finding the Customer Service
Department page that deals with contact personnel can be a major pain if all
of your page files are in the same folder. To make your site much easier to
keep track of, add new folders for each department or category. Organizing
by department *and* file type (as I suggest in the previous section) can really
help keep your site organized.

Use the following tips to organize the page files on your Web site.

✔ Name the main page for each department's folder index.htm or
   default.htm (whichever is appropriate for a home page on your Web
   server). Doing so ensures that people who type the URL of the department folder directly into their browsers will reach a Web page, not just
   a listing of files. Don't worry, having two pages in your site with the
   same name is fine *as long as the files aren't in the same folder.*

✔ Make a folder to hold all your departments and move each department folder into it to keep things even more organized.

✔ If a department has its own special files that should be kept separate from those of other departments (one department has its own set of graphics files that shouldn't be used by the other departments, for example), add a new folder within that department just for those files.

SiteManager starts things off

The best way to keep your site organized is to ignore DESIGNER. That may sound like bad advice, but just give me a moment. What I mean is this: Don't launch DESIGNER from the Start menu when you want to edit a page. Instead, use SiteManager as your starting off point, so you always have its powerful organizational utilities handy while you're working on your site.

To start DESIGNER from SiteManager:

1. **Start SiteManager.**

2. **Open your site.**

   You can open your site by selecting it in the Open dialog box that appears when you start SiteManager. Chapter 3 contains complete details for using SiteManager.

3. **In the file list, double-click the name of the page you want to edit.**

   DESIGNER starts automatically.

4. **When you finish editing the page, exit DESIGNER.**

   DESIGNER asks if you want to save your page. Click Yes to save your page and return to SiteManager. Chapter 1 and nearly all of Part II are devoted to using DESIGNER.

 5. **Choose File➪Reload Current Site or click the Reload Site button to update the links you made in your page.**

   SiteManager closes all your folders and selects the home page, so you have to reopen your folders. If you're planning to make changes to many pages, don't do this step until you've edited most or all of them because SiteManager can take a while to reload your site if it's very large.

Consolidating pages

When you're working on a really big site, you may find that you have a couple of pages that provide basically the same information. If you discover such overlap, consider creating one page that includes all the information from the other two, essentially combining the pages, and then delete the two original pages. By combining pages, you can save yourself a lot of time when you need to update information.

For example, if you have separate pages for contacting members of each department, you may want to consider making one larger page that lists all your contacts. Then use each department's heading on the page as a bookmark and link each department to its own bookmark (see Chapter 6 for more information about bookmarks).

If the page that would result from combining two similar pages will be really large, you're better off leaving the pages separate. Long pages may take a good deal of time for your visitors to download and force visitors to scroll through a lot of information to find what they're looking for. Remember to keep your eye on DESIGNER's download time estimate in the lower-right corner of the screen to get an idea of how long a page will take to download.

Part II
The Nitty-Gritty

The 5th Wave   By Rich Tennant

"I'm not sure I like a college whose home page has a link to The Party Zone!"

In this part . . .

DESIGNER is your number-one resource for creating and editing your Web site. With this program, you can type your text, add graphics and multimedia, create hyperlinks, and add a host of other effects to make your Web pages beautiful and functional. Part II is almost totally devoted to using DESIGNER.

In this part, I show you how to build Web pages starting from ground zero. These chapters cover every super feature that makes DESIGNER your best friend when it comes to creating Web sites. At the end of this part, I even introduce you to techniques for expanding on DESIGNER's power by editing the underlying HTML code of your pages.

Chapter 5

Words of Wisdom — Working with Text

• •

• •

*N*o matter how pretty your Web graphics are, the content and presentation of the text on your Web pages is what has the most impact on your visitors. Sure, all those fancy pictures look great, but people are most likely to visit your Web site to find out what you have to *say*.

With the ease of a word processing program, DESIGNER enables you to make your text stand out and easy to read. This chapter details all the tools that DESIGNER provides for making text formatting a breeze. For the basics of getting started in DESIGNER, refer to Chapter 1.

Putting "Pen" to "Paper"

For all intents and purposes, adding and editing text in DESIGNER is exactly the same as adding and editing text in a word processing program. If you're familiar with a word processing program (such as Word or Works), you can pretty much skip this section.

You add text to a Web page in DESIGNER simply by typing. If you want to start a new paragraph, you press Enter. To insert new text within existing text, move the I-beam mouse pointer to the point where you want the text to begin, and then click the primary mouse button. The blinking vertical bar (the *insertion point*) shows where your text will appear when you start typing. You can also move the insertion point itself, by pressing the up-, down-, left- or right-arrow keys (the *cursor keys*) on your keyboard.

Working with text in DESIGNER

Text always needs to be edited. After I completed writing this book, I had to go back and make a ton of changes based on the comments of the project editor, the copy editor, the technical editor, and Bob in accounting so that we could be sure that everything you read is absolutely accurate and conforms to the fabulously friendly *...For Dummies* style.

Highlighting text

Almost every editing task involves highlighting text, whether the text is a letter, a single word, a couple of words, or a couple of paragraphs. You can use two different approaches to highlight text in DESIGNER:

- ✔ **Keyboard:** To highlight text from the keyboard, hold down the Shift key and then press the arrow keys to define the highlight area.

  The Ctrl key is a great time-saver when highlighting text from the keyboard. If you want to highlight an entire word, move the insertion point to the beginning of the word, press and hold down the Shift and Ctrl keys, and then press the → key once. To highlight the next word press the → key again.

  You can highlight everything to the beginning or end of a paragraph by pressing and holding the Shift and Ctrl keys and then pressing the ↑ or ↓ keys. To highlight everything from the insertion point down to the end of the page, press Ctrl+Shift+End. To highlight everything from the insertion point up to the beginning of the page, press Ctrl+Shift+Home.

  To highlight everything from the insertion point to the beginning of a line, press Shift+Home. To highlight everything to the end of a line, press Shift+End.

- ✔ **Mouse:** To highlight text with your mouse, simply click the mouse pointer at the beginning of the area you want to highlight, hold down the primary mouse button, and drag. When you've highlighted everything you want, release the mouse button. For really long passages that extend past the end of the screen, click the mouse pointer at the beginning of the area you want to highlight and then use the scroll bar on the right side of the screen to move to the end of the passage that you want to highlight. Press and hold the Shift key and then click the pointer at the end of the passage.

Paragraph versus line break

One of the weird things about Web publishing is that you don't have very much control over line spacing. When you type something using your favorite word processor, you can make lines of text close together, far apart, or anything in between. There's just no easy way to do that in a Web page — this isn't a limitation of DESIGNER, it's true of Web pages no matter what program you use to create them.

The one aspect of line spacing that you *do* have control over is the space between paragraphs. Each time you want to form a new paragraph in DESIGNER, you can press Enter to insert a full line of blank space, called a *paragraph break,* between the two paragraphs.

Sometimes, however, you may want to start a new line of text immediately under the existing one, without a blank space in between. In this case, instead of pressing the Enter key alone, you press Shift+Enter to create a *line break.* Bulleted and numbered lists are automatically separated by line breaks — you can't have a paragraph break between lines of a list.

Copying text

If you want to use the same passage more than once, you can copy it from where you've already typed it, and paste it to a new location. (Later in this chapter, in the section called "Recycling text from somewhere else," I tell you how to use text from word processing programs.) To copy text:

1. **Highlight the passage you want to copy and then click the Copy icon, choose Edit⇨Copy, or press Ctrl+C.**

   A copy of the text is now in the Windows Clipboard.

2. **Place the insertion point where you want to insert the text, and then click the Paste icon, choose Edit⇨Paste, or press Ctrl+V.**

   A copy of the text is pasted in place.

Until you copy something else to the Clipboard, you can continue to insert as many copies of this text as you want simply by using the paste command. Note, however, that when you copy a new passage to the clipboard, the old text is removed. If you want to paste more copies of the original text, follow the preceding steps to copy it back to the Clipboard.

Moving text

The procedure for moving text is almost identical to the procedure for copying text. The only difference is that when you want to move text, you move (rather than copy) the original passage to the Clipboard. To move text:

1. **Highlight the passage you want to move and then click the Cut icon, choose Edit⇨Cut, or press Ctrl+X.**

   The highlighted passage disappears from your document, but a copy of it is safe and sound in the Windows Clipboard.

 2. **Place the insertion point where you want to insert the text and then click the paste icon, choose Edit⇨Paste, or press Ctrl+V.**

   DESIGNER pastes the passage in its new location.

Because the text remains in the clipboard even after you've pasted it into its new location, you can paste as many copies of the moved text as you want (until you cut or copy a new passage to the clipboard).

Deleting text

To delete text, highlight the offending passage and then choose Edit⇨Clear, or press the Delete key.

 Keep in mind that this deleted text is not placed in the clipboard, so you can't paste it somewhere else. If you want to retrieve the deleted text, choose Edit⇨Undo or press Ctrl+Z to undo the deletion. Unfortunately, you can only undo the very last thing you did — unlike many programs, DESIGNER does not allow multiple "undo's."

Recycling text from somewhere else

Odds are that some of the text you want to include in your Web page has already been typed in a word processing program. For example, a part of a memo that you want to put in an online newsletter, or a sales pitch that's going into a catalog. If you just had some way pull all that text into your Web page, you'd save time and be much happier. But wait, there is a way! (I bet you already knew that. Otherwise, I wouldn't have bothered to write this section.)

Actually, there are *two* ways to insert text from a word processing program into your Web page: by copying and pasting it, or by importing it.

Copying and pasting

One way to pull text from another application is simply to copy and paste it into your page. This method is fairly straightforward, but it has a couple of downsides. Copying and pasting text between your word processor and DESIGNER is identical to the method I describe earlier in "Copying text" in this chapter — except that you copy in your word processor and paste in DESIGNER.

✔ **All paragraph breaks become line breaks.** To restore paragraph breaks, you must place the insertion point at the end of each paragraph and then press the Delete key to combine the paragraph with the one after it. Then press Enter to create a paragraph break. Sounds easy, huh? It is if the text you've imported is fairly short. But if you have a long passage of text, the easy part is destroyed by the mind-numbing monotony of creating five billion paragraph breaks.

✔ **All formatting is lost.** This means that all the time you took making some words bold, others italic, some bigger, some smaller (and all the other ways that you've made your text look interesting) was wasted. You'll have to go through your Web page and redo it all over again.

Importing text

If you want to include a long passage of text, or one that includes a lot of character formatting, your best bet is to use Net Transit, which is included with WebMaster Suite. Net Transit makes short work of importing a word processing file and reworking it into standard Web format while maintaining the vast majority of your formatting.

Net Transit can directly import files created by Corel WordPerfect and Microsoft Word. For other word processing programs, you have to save your documents in Rich Text Format (RTF). Usually you can save RTF files by selecting Rich Text Format from the Save as Type dropdown list in the Save As dialog box — if you don't have this option in your word processor, check your documentation or help for "exporting."

To import text from a word processor file by using Net Transit:

1. **Format your word processing document using styles.**

   Styles are collections of formats that describe how a paragraph looks (bold, large type, and so on) that can be used over and over again, ensuring that your document has a consistent look. You can find information about styles in your word processing program's documentation and help file (look for, you guessed it, "style"). Using styles makes importing much easier, though Net Transit automatically makes your bold text bold, italic text italic, and so on. Net Transit doesn't, however, deal with different sized text, except in styles (as described later in these steps).

2. **Start DESIGNER.**

3. **Choose File⇨Import Word Processor File.**

   The Net Transit splash screen opens.

4. **Click Start.**

   The Conversion Wizard – Welcome dialog box opens.

5. **Click Next.**

   The Conversion Wizard – Setup Files dialog box opens (see Figure 5-1).

Word processor file

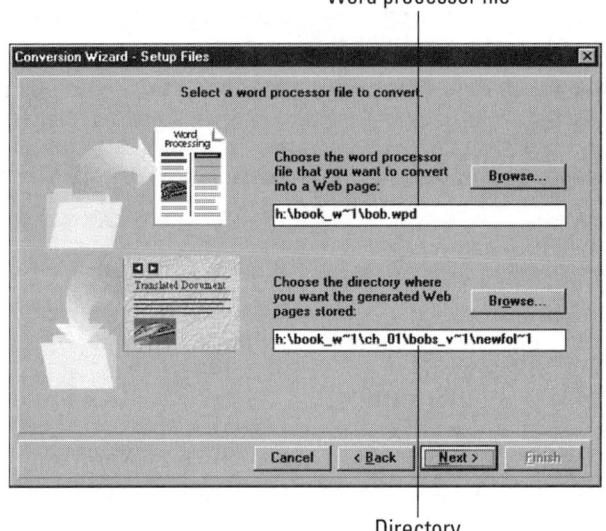

Figure 5-1:
The
Conversion
Wizard –
Setup Files
dialog box.

Directory

6. **Type the name of the file you want to import in the top text box, or click the Browse button to choose the file from a standard Windows Open dialog box.**

   Net Transit has trouble understanding long filenames and names with spaces. The program truncates a long name like `bobs_memo_9-15-97.doc` to something like `bobs_m~1.doc.` and adds a tilde (the squiggly ~ symbol) to any name with spaces, even if it's less than eight characters long. If the file you want to import has a long filename or has spaces in the name, use the Browse button to open the file instead of typing its name in the text box.

7. **Type the name of the folder in which you want the new Web file saved in the bottom text box, or press the Browse button and select from the list.**

   Note that this dialog box refers to folders as *directories* — a throwback from the bad old days of DOS.

   Even though the path listed in the text box may show long filenames for folders (if you have any), Net Transit can't understand them. If the folder you want to save your Web document in uses a long filename, click the Browse button and then click OK in the Directory Browse dialog box: The long filename in the text box is now replaced with the "short" filename equivalent. If you want to save your Web page in a different folder, click the browse button to open the Directory Browse dialog box, locate the different directory, and then click OK.

8. **Click Next to open the Convert dialog box.**

9. **Select either the Basic Conversion or the Custom Conversion radio button.**

   A basic conversion just does simple text conversions, with no fancy formatting. A custom conversion lets you add a background image, navigation buttons (to help your visitors move around your page and site), and separators (horizontal lines that break up your page), based on your existing formatting.

10. **Click Next if you selected Custom Conversion or Finish if you selected Basic Conversion.**

    One of two things occurs at this point:

    • If you selected Basic Conversion, the word processing file is converted to a Web page, saved, and loaded in DESIGNER. You're done — you can ignore the remaining steps. Figure 5-2 shows a word processing document that has been imported using the Basic Conversion option.

    • If you selected Custom Conversion, the Overview dialog box opens. Continue on with the remaining steps.

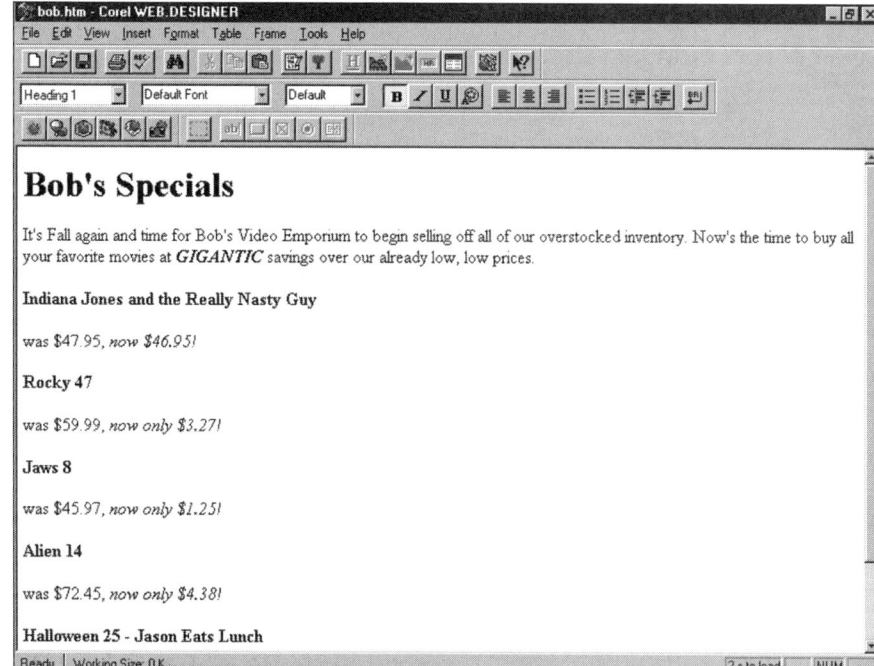

Figure 5-2:
A word processing document converted using the Basic option.

11. **Click Next.**

    A dialog box opens that shows some of the parts of a page that you can specify.

12. **Click Next to open the Background dialog box.**

13. **Select your background.**

    A *background* is similar to wallpaper in the Windows desktop.

    - If you don't want a background in your page, deselect the Add a Background to the Web Pages check box so that no check mark appears.

    - If you want to use a picture for your page's background, select the Pattern radio button and select an image from the drop-down list. When you select an image, a preview appears in the window on the left side of the dialog box.

    - If you want to use a color for your page background, select the Color radio button, click the Color button and select a color from the Color dialog box that opens. Click the OK button to close the Color dialog box.

14. **Click Next to open the Heading 1 dialog box.**

15. **Select the word processing style that you want to use as the highest level heading.**

    This style is represented in your Web page as the Heading 1 style. It is a large, bold type that is typically used for the banner at the top of the page or for any other text that you want to really stand out. "Formatting with style," later in this chapter, covers styles in more detail.

16. **Select the type of separator you want to accompany the Heading 1 text.**

    The separator may be a simple horizontal line (called a *rule*), or it may be a graphic. A separator can be above, below, or both above and below the text.

17. **Select how the Heading 1 text and any separator is aligned.**

    Choose from Left or Center by clicking the Left or Center radio button (left is the default).

18. **Click Next to open the Heading 2 dialog box.**

19. **Make the same selections for the second level heading and then click Next to open the Split file dialog box.**

20. **If you want to break up the document into a number of pages, check the Split the word processor file into multiple pages check box.**

    If the word processing document you are importing is very long, choose to break the DESIGNER document into multiple pages.

- If you decide to break up the file, you have the option of breaking it at each instance of a Heading 1 or Heading 2.

- If you decide to break the file, click Next to open the Navigation Buttons dialog box. Select the style of buttons you want to use to let your visitors move from one page of the document to the next.

21. Click Next to open the Finish Conversion dialog box.

22. Click Finish.

Net Transit completes the conversion process, saves your new Web page, and displays it in DESIGNER. See Figure 5-3, which is the same document that was shown in Figure 5-2 after being converted using the custom options.

If you want to include the information that's been imported using Net Transit in an existing page, follow the preceding instructions, and then copy and paste the information into the existing page.

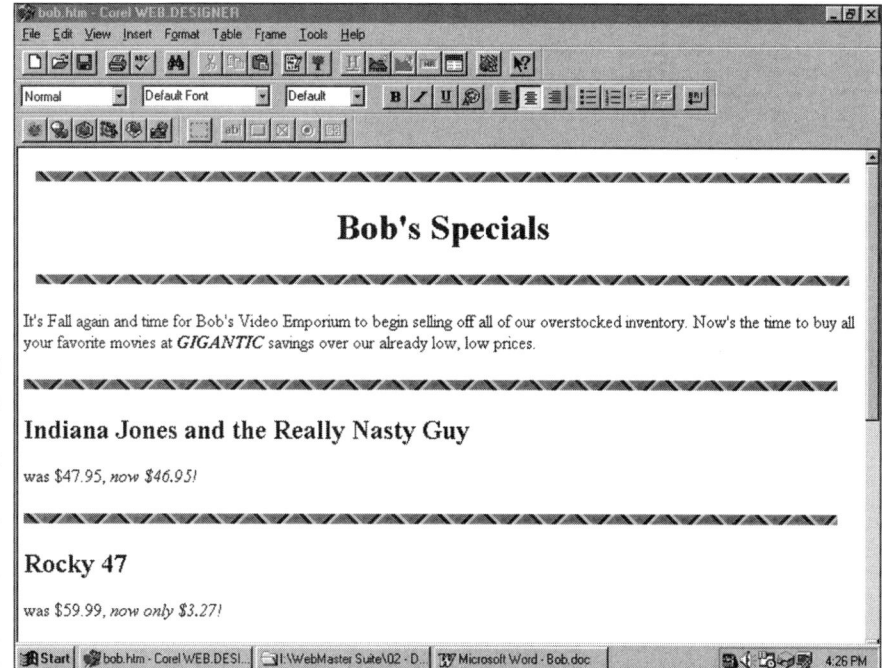

Figure 5-3: The same document as shown in Figure 5-2, converted using the custom options.

Formatting Your Words to Look as Exciting as They Sound

Web browsers can display text with all the formatting options that you're used to: bold, italic, underlined, even different typefaces. Using this formatting effectively can make your Web pages look professional without requiring an awful lot of work on your part.

Formatting is a great tool, but the best formatting advice is not to go overboard. Too much formatting can lead to pages that are difficult to read, and can drive your Web site visitors away. Use formatting to enhance what you're saying, but don't let the formatting overpower the statement.

Formatting text in DESIGNER is easy. You can highlight the existing letter, word, or words you want to format, and then select the appropriate Format button from the toolbar, as shown in Figure 5-4. Or you can choose a format and then start typing; whatever you type appears in the format you chose.

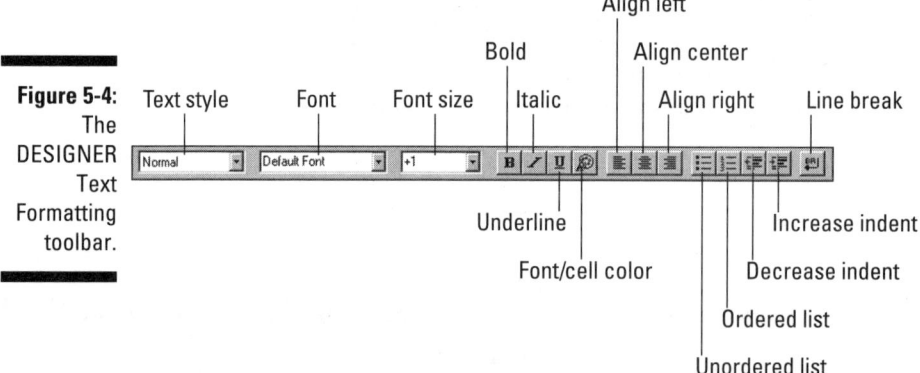

Figure 5-4: The DESIGNER Text Formatting toolbar.

You can tell when text has been formatted a certain way (aside from the obvious — that it looks bold on your computer screen) by looking at the toolbar. When the selected text uses a format, the toolbar button for that format looks as though it's pressed in.

To remove formatting from text, highlight the text and then click the toolbar button representing that format so that the button no longer appears pressed in.

The bold and the beautiful

When you start to type in DESIGNER, your text looks like standard, everyday text: It's not bold, it's not italic, it's just there. If you're writing strict prose, plain old text may be just fine. But imagine how different reading this book would be if I didn't use bold and italic text occasionally (and sometimes even underlines!).

When you're working with the typeface that Web browsers use by default, the bold and italic fonts are always available. However, if you specify a typeface — as I describe later in this chapter, in the section called "Put on a happy (type)face" — the formatting effects you can use may be limited. The Technical typeface, for example, can be italic, but not bold or bold-italic.

To format text in DESIGNER:

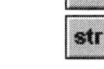

- ✔ **Bold:** Click the Bold button or press Ctrl+B.
- ✔ **Italic:** Click the Italic button or press Ctrl+I.
- ✔ **Underline:** Click the Underline button or press Ctrl+U.
- ✔ **Strikethrough:** Click the Strikethrough button, which appears on the Style toolbar. To display the Style toolbar, choose <u>V</u>iew⇨<u>S</u>tyle Toolbar.

Try to avoid using the underline format. Hyperlinks are generally indicated by underlined text, so using this format on other words can be confusing to your visitors.

Bigger is better (sometimes)

You're probably used to setting the size of your typeface by selecting a font size expressed in *points*. In word processing programs, you can set the font size to nearly any number of points you want, but most people use the 10-point or 12-point size for ordinary text. (Although my daughter uses 16-point type for school reports so that she doesn't have to write as much to fill the required number of pages.)

Just to throw a wrench in the works, Web pages only give you seven type sizes to choose from — and these sizes don't relate to any particular point size. You can blame this arrangement on the fact that the Web was invented by a bunch of scientists, not graphic artists. (Not that I have anything against scientists, mind you. I was a physics major before I switched to engineering.)

The seven type sizes available for Web pages are numbered, amazingly enough, 1 through 7. Size 1 is really teeny, and size 7 is pretty big, as shown in Figure 5-5. Although having only seven type sizes may seem like a hardship, it really isn't — after a while, you hardly notice the limitation.

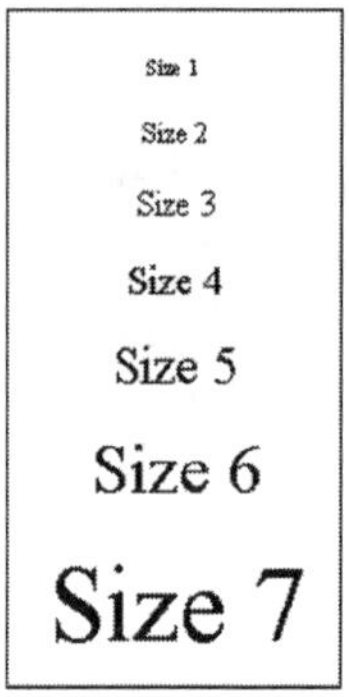

Figure 5-5:
The seven
Web type
sizes.

Size 1
Size 2
Size 3
Size 4
Size 5
Size 6
Size 7

Type size only gets tricky when you use relative type sizes; fortunately, relative type sizes are nearly extinct. By default (that is, unless you change it), text in a Web page is size 3.

Put on a happy (type) face

Typefaces are wonderful things — I love them. You can find a different typeface for just about every mood, from the fun-loving Staccato to the formal Caslon. Until recently, Web designers had only a meager selection of typefaces from which to choose, if they had any choice at all. But the day when you can use any typeface in a Web page is drawing closer.

The default typeface on a Web page is Times New Roman, or one of its variations (such as Times or TmsRmn). There are two ways to change the typeface displayed on your Web page: One way is under your control, and the other is under your visitors' control.

The following three sections explain how you can choose different typefaces for the text on your Web pages. The people browsing your Web site can usually choose to display default text in a typeface other than Times (for example, by changing the default typeface in their browser's Preferences dialog box). Their changes only affect the default typeface, though. Any typeface that you specify still comes through as you intended it to.

Changing the typeface

Changing the typeface on your Web page is very straightforward:

1. **Highlight the text you want to change.**

2. **Click the down button in the Font drop-down list on the toolbar.**

   A list of typefaces installed on your computer appears, as shown in Figure 5-6.

3. **Select the typeface.**

   The text you highlighted is changed to the new typeface.

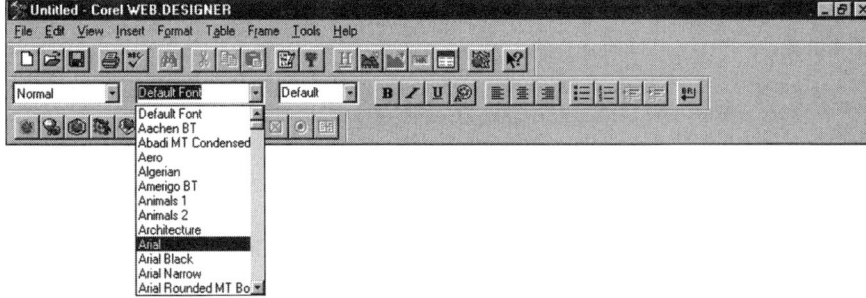

Figure 5-6:
The Font drop-down list.

Step 2 contains the important phrase: *installed on your computer.* Every typeface that's installed on your computer is stored in a file in your Fonts folder. If you don't have a file for a particular typeface in that folder, your computer won't display or print it. This goes for your Web site visitors' computers as well. You may design a great-looking page, enhanced by your use of a particular typeface, but if the person visiting your site doesn't have that typeface loaded, the effect is lost.

WebMaster Suite comes with 500 different typefaces (although some of these are just font variations, such as bold, italic, or bold-italic, of the same typeface). You may think, "No sweat. I'll just put all these typefaces on my Web site for people to download and install on their systems. That way, they can see my page just the way I see it." But this approach has two problems:

✔ **The typefaces that come with WebMaster Suite are copyrighted.** You are licensed to use them when creating artwork (for example, in PhotoPaint or Draw) but distributing the typeface files themselves is illegal.

✔ **The WebMaster typefaces only work on PC-compatible computers, running Windows 3.1 or later.** These restrictions leave people viewing your site on Macintosh, UNIX, Sun, and other computers out in the cold.

Although this may seem boring, you're best off if you limit yourself to three typefaces: Arial, Times New Roman, and Courier New. All these typefaces, or very close facsimiles, are available on most computers. In Chapter 13, I outline a technique for ensuring that your page displays pretty darn close to the way you design it, no matter what computer system it's displayed on. (Unless another system has exactly the same font you used when designing your page it can never look *precisely* the same.)

Remember that the graphics files you display on your Web pages can contain whatever typefaces you want. Images are the perfect way to incorporate a different typeface into your page.

Adding typefaces to your system

When you installed WebMaster Suite, you were given the option to install a bunch of typefaces. Whichever ones you chose were copied directly to your Fonts folder and were ready to use. But chances are that you didn't install *all* the typefaces during that first installation.

If you want to add other typefaces, the process is simple:

1. **Insert Corel WebMaster Suite CD 1 in your CD-ROM drive.**

   Note that this CD-ROM contains a program called Autorun that will attempt to start the WebMaster Suite installation routine. You don't need the install program just to add typefaces, so you want to stop Autorun dead in its tracks. The easiest way to do this (and it works great for any CD-ROM with Autorun) is to press both Shift keys (left and right) as soon as you put the CD-ROM in the drive, and hold the keys down until the "busy" light on the drive stops blinking. Note that the light may stop blinking for a moment and then resume for a few seconds — you want to make sure that you hold the keys down until the second batch of blinking stops.

   If you miss the Shift keys and get the installation dialog box, don't worry, just click on Exit.

2. **Start the Windows Control Panel by choosing Start⇨Settings⇨Control Panel.**

3. **Double-click on the Fonts folder shortcut.**

   The Fonts folder (which looks like a regular Windows file folder) opens.

4. **Choose File⇨Install New Font to open the Add Fonts dialog box.**

5. **Select your CD-ROM drive in the Drives drop-down list.**

6. **Double-click on the Fonts folder in the Folders list.**

7. **Double-click on the TTF folder in the Folders list.**

8. **Open the folder with the first letter of the typeface(s) you want to install.**

   The first 30 pages of the WebMaster Suite Clipart book list, in alphabetical order, all the typefaces and variations that are included with the program. When the folder opens, you may have to wait a few moments before you can see all the typeface names from the CD, so be patient.

9. **Select the typeface(s) you want from the List of fonts listing.**

   You can select multiple typefaces by using the standard Ctrl+click and Shift+click combinations. Ctrl+click lets you pick individual files that are not right next to each other, and Shift+click picks the first and last file you click, as well as all of the files in between.

10. **Click OK.**

    The files are copied to your Fonts folder. If you selected a typeface that already exists on your computer, a dialog box opens and displays the message `The (X) font is already installed.` Just click OK to continue installing any other typefaces you selected.

That blinking is driving me crazy!

One other text format is at your disposal: blinking text. Just as its name suggests, blinking text, well, blinks on and off. I've put blinking text in its own section, because it's gotten kind of a bad rap, and I want to warn you to use it at your own risk. Here are two reasons to be careful when using blinking text:

- ✔ Only Netscape browsers can display blinking text.

- ✔ For some reason that I've never quite figured out, many of the old-time Web surfers really hate blinking text. Although it's unlikely to happen, you may get *spammed* (that is, sent huge quantities of harassing e-mail) by really militant Web users. Because of its bad reputation, blinking text is rarely used anymore.

That said, here's how to format text so that it blinks: Highlight the text in DESIGNER and then choose Format⇨Blinking Text.

Formatting with style

In addition to formatting one letter or word at a time, you can format your Web pages a paragraph at a time by applying styles. Styles can be a real time-saver when you want to give your site a consistent look, because each paragraph that you format with a particular style looks the same.

In all cases, except pre-formatted text, you can also add any of the font changes outlined in this chapter to whole paragraphs. Keep in mind that if you break a paragraph using a line break instead of a paragraph break, both sections retain the same paragraph format.

Most paragraph formats are available through the Paragraph Styles drop-down list, shown in Figure 5-7.

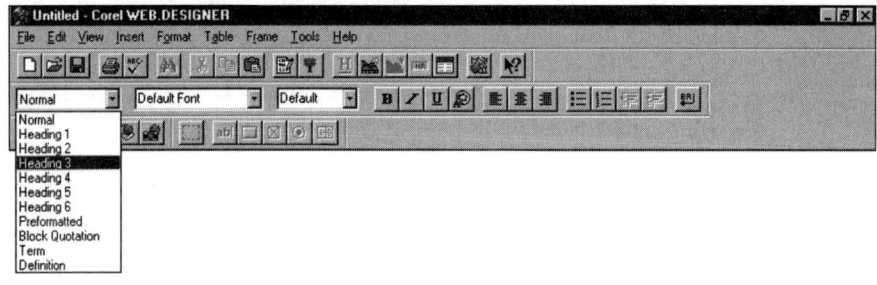

Figure 5-7:
The
Paragraph
Styles drop-
down list.

Headings

Try to imagine how tough reading this book would be if it had no headings. Text would run on endlessly, with no clues about what goes with what. Instead, this book uses a bunch of different levels of headings to break down information from very general to very specific.

As I write this book, I use particular styles to tell the printers what the headings look like, because these different levels of headings won't do *you* any good if you can't tell them apart.

Web pages can have headings, too, as shown in Figure 5-8. Up to six levels of headings are available.

To make a paragraph into a heading:

1. **Click the cursor anywhere within the paragraph you want to format.**

2. **Click the down arrow next to the paragraph format drop-down list.**

   A list of available formats appears.

3. **Select the heading level you want to use (Heading 1 through Heading 6).**

   The entire paragraph is changed to the heading style you selected.

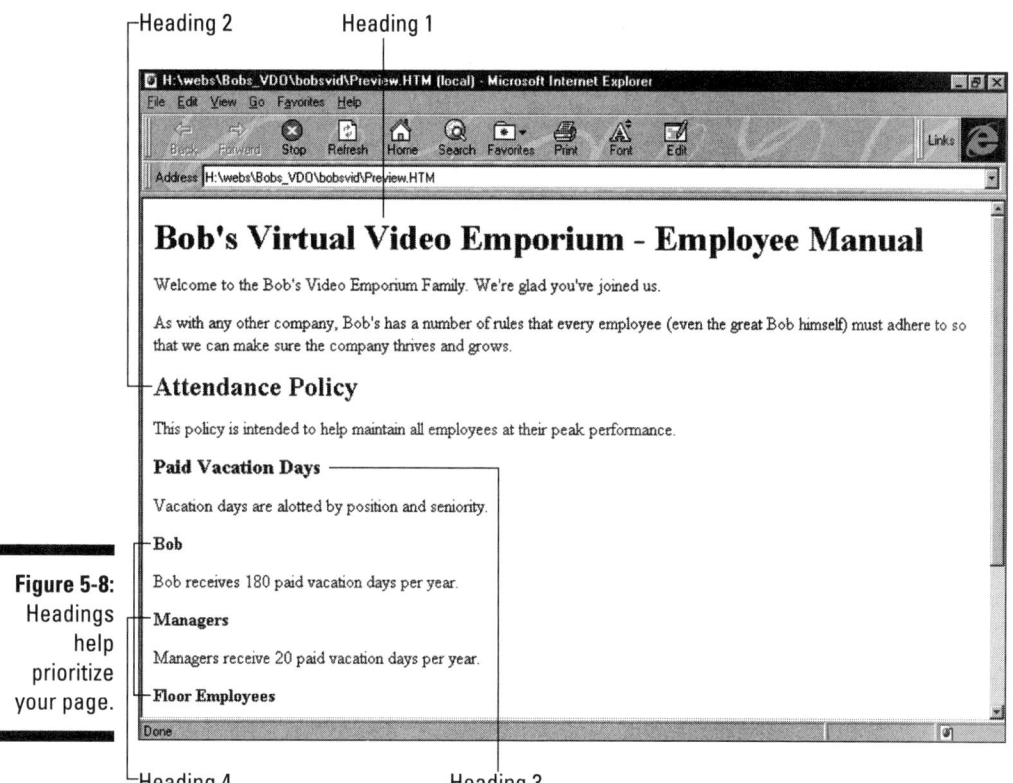

Heading 2　　　　Heading 1

Heading 4　　　　　　　Heading 3

Figure 5-8:
Headings
help
prioritize
your page.

Four or more levels of headings can actually make it more difficult to understand what you're trying to get across. If you find yourself using more than three levels of headings, you may want to reorganize your information a little, so you break up sections that use more levels, and drop the number of heading levels. Level one headings are ideal to use for page banners. In that case, you can go to a level 4 heading and still maintain ease of reading.

Indented text

You can indent text to make it easier to read. Unlike what you may be used to, indenting text doesn't just indent from the left. Rather, it indents from both the left and the right, as shown in Figure 5-9.

To indent text, highlight the paragraphs you want to indent and then choose Format➪Increase Indent or click the Increase Indent button in the toolbar. You can do this more than once to move the text ever closer to the center of the screen.

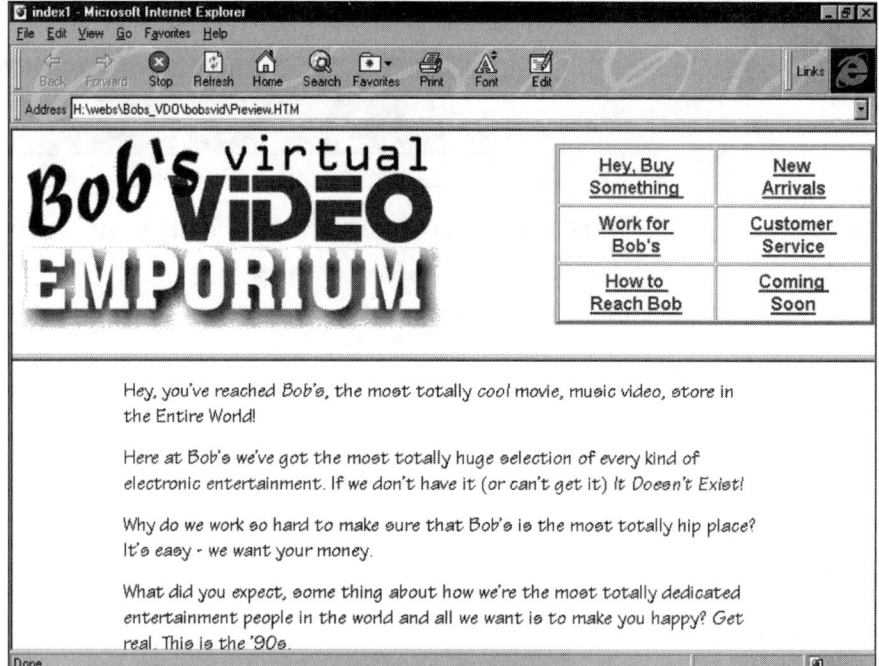

Figure 5-9:
The bottom
frame
includes
indented
text.

 To remove an indent, or reduce the amount if you indented more than once, highlight the paragraphs from which you want to remove an indent and then choose Format⇨Decrease Indent or click the Decrease Indent button in the toolbar. If the selected text isn't already indented, choosing this command won't have any effect.

 The *block quotation* style is basically a single level of indented text. Deep down in the HTML code of your Web page (which I talk about in more detail in Chapter 13) indented text uses the `<BLOCKQUOTE>` code. When you repeatedly indent text, you add another instance of the code. I believe that the block quotation format is included in the Type Style drop-down list as a kind of a transition for those Web designers who are familiar with the format.

Ordered lists

Lists are an important and easy way to help organize the information in your Web page. The two types of lists are officially called *ordered* and *unordered*, but most normal people call them *numbered lists* and *bulleted lists*. (Bullets are those little dots next to a list — in this book, I use check marks instead of dots.)

Ordered (numbered) lists are great for expressing procedures and other groups of text that have numbers associated with them. You may want to use an ordered list to outline a procedure to request extended leave, as shown in Figure 5-10, or to show how to bake a cake.

DESIGNER enables you to create an ordered list in two ways. Which method you choose depends on whether the text you want in the list is already typed or not. (The following steps are an example of an ordered list.)

To create an ordered list when you have not yet typed in the text:

1. **Choose Format⇨Ordered List or click the Ordered List button in the toolbar.**

2. **Type the information you want in the list.**

3. **Press Enter at the end of each line to create a new numbered item.**

   You can press Shift+Enter to create a line break instead of a paragraph break. Doing so keeps information under the same numbered item.

4. **Press Enter twice when you finish typing the last item and are ready to exit the list.**

   The insertion point returns to the left margin, and you're ready to begin typing "normal" text again.

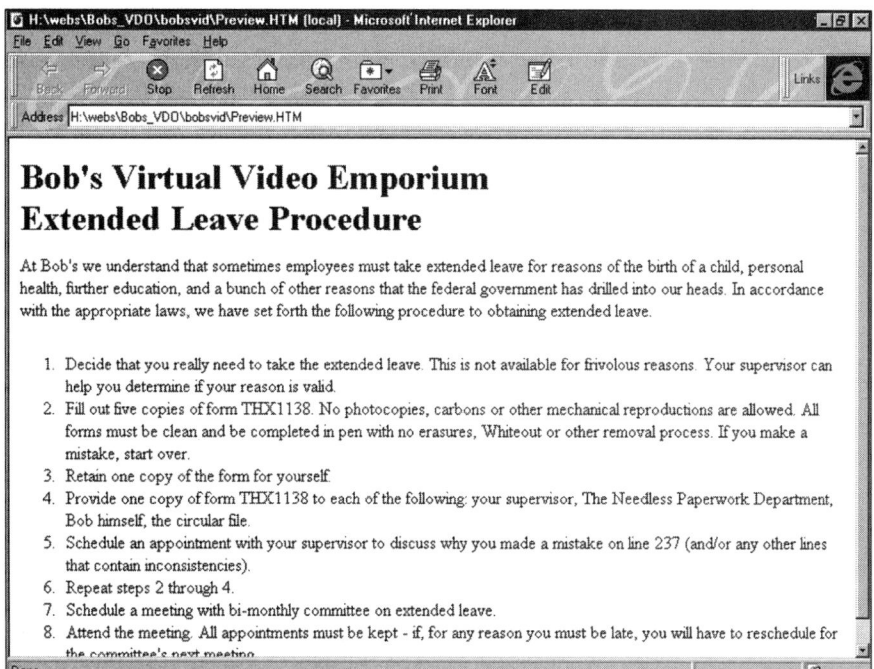

Figure 5-10: A numbered list.

If you already have a bunch of paragraphs that you want to change into an ordered list, follow these steps:

1. **Highlight at least a portion of each paragraph that you want to include in the list.**

   You don't have to include the entire paragraph when you select it. As long as you select a portion of each paragraph, the format is applied to the entire paragraph.

2. **Choose Format⇨Ordered List or click the Ordered List button in the toolbar.**

   The text is formatted into a nice list, complete with numbers and indenting, to make it easy to read.

Unordered lists

You probably know unordered lists as *bulleted lists.* Eggheads call these lists *unordered* because, unlike numbered steps, they present information in no particular order. See Figure 5-11.

You can choose between two methods for creating an unordered list, depending on whether the text you want in the list is already typed or not.

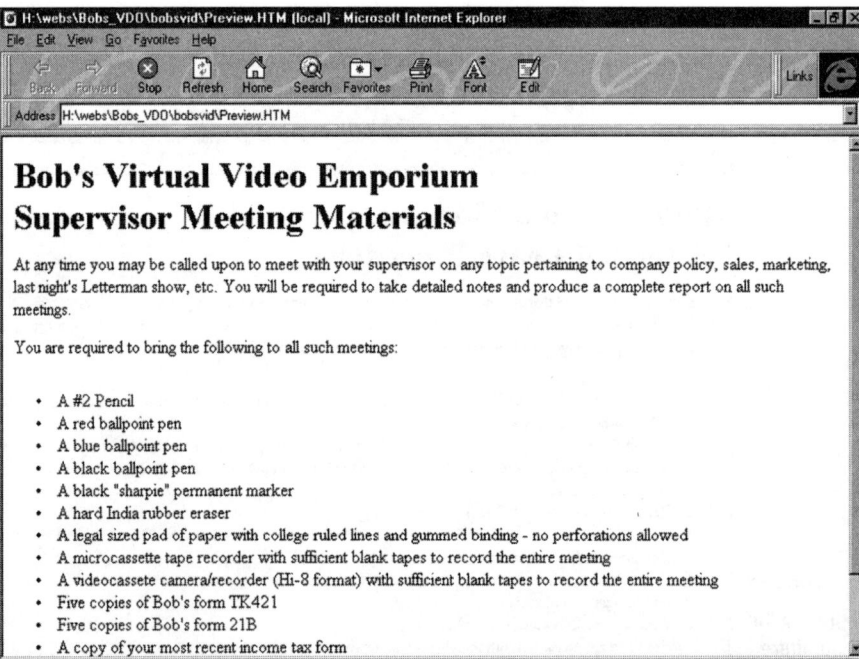

Figure 5-11:
A bulleted
(unordered)
list.

To create an unordered list if you haven't yet typed the text:

1. **Choose Format⇨Unordered List or click the Unordered List button in the toolbar.**

2. **Type in the information you want in the list.**

3. **Press Enter at the end of each line to create a new bulleted item.**

   Or press Shift+Enter to create a line break instead of a paragraph break, keeping the information under the same bulleted item.

4. **Press Enter twice when you finish typing the last item and are ready to exit the list.**

   The insertion point returns to the left margin, and you're ready to begin typing "normal" text again.

If you already have a bunch of paragraphs, and you want to turn them into an ordered list, follow these steps:

1. **Select (highlight) at least a portion of each paragraph that you want included in the list.**

2. **Choose Format⇨Unordered List or click the Unordered List button in the toolbar.**

   The text is formatted into a list, complete with bullets and indenting, to make it easy to read.

List levels

You may sometimes have information in a list that you want to include as part of one of the list items. Figures 5-12 and 5-13 show an ordered and unordered list, respectively. The information in these lists makes more sense when you add levels.

When you want to change the level of some items in a list on your Web page:

1. **In DESIGNER, highlight the list items containing the information whose level on the hierarchy you want to change.**

2. **Choose Format⇨Increase Indent.**

   The paragraphs are moved to the right.

Note: Creating a new level in an ordered list starts a new set of numbers (beginning with 1). After the indented portion, the rest of the first-level lines resume in the original numbering sequence. The indented portion of an unordered list gets a new style of bullet, to help distinguish the different levels of the list.

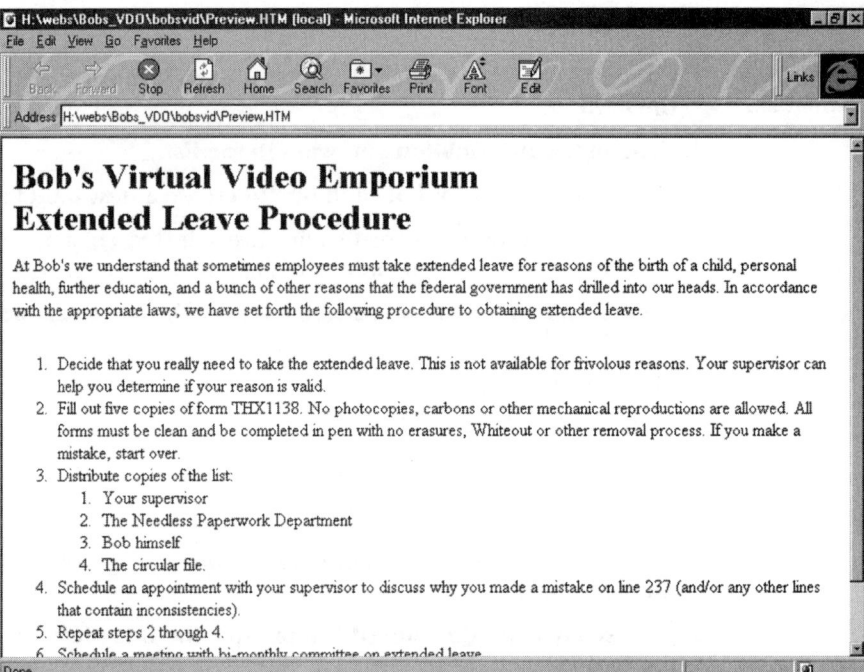

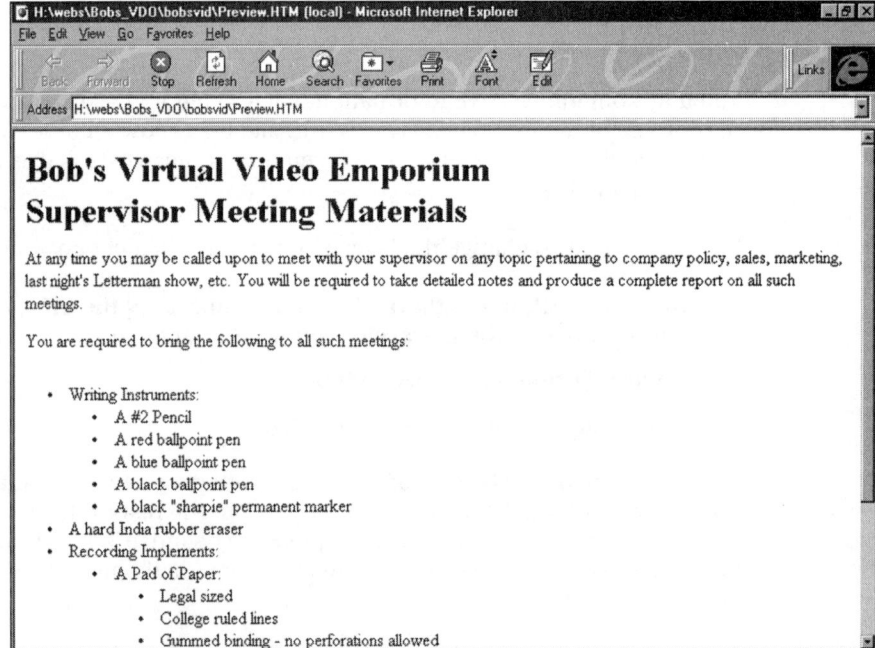

Preformatted text

For some reason, the powers that be decided that browers should ignore multiple spaces. No matter how many times you press the spacebar, you still get only one space between letters. There's only one exception to those rules: when you format text using the Preformatted Text option.

The Preformatted Text option makes your text appear exactly the way you type it in — every space and every line break remains intact. If you put five spaces between two words of preformatted text, visitors to your page see those five spaces on their browsers. And the lines of preformatted text you type will never wrap to the next line automatically; you must press Enter to start a new line. In short, using Preformatted Text option is a major change from how you normally type text in DESIGNER.

Keep these things in mind if you plan to use the Preformatted Text option:

- Preformatted text always appears in a fixed-width typeface. This typeface is typically Courier, although your visitors may change the typeface that their browsers use. Note that even though you can change the typeface of preformatted text in DESIGNER, browsers ignore the typeface you chose.

- You can format preformatted text using any of the options mentioned earlier in this chapter in the section entitled "The bold and the beautiful" (bold, italic, underline, and strikethrough).

Text on the Go: Creating Words That Move

A *marquee* is a block of text that moves across your screen, kind of like the big sign in Times Square in New York City.

Note: *Marquee* is a Microsoft Internet Explorer-only format. If your visitors use Netscape Navigator or some other browser, they may not see the text at all, or the text may not move.

Adding a marquee to your Web page is easy:

1. **Place the cursor at the beginning of a blank line.**

   Or, to turn existing text into a marquee, place your cursor at the beginning of the line containing the text.

2. **Choose Insert➪Marquee.**

   The Marquee Properties dialog box appears, as shown in Figure 5-14.

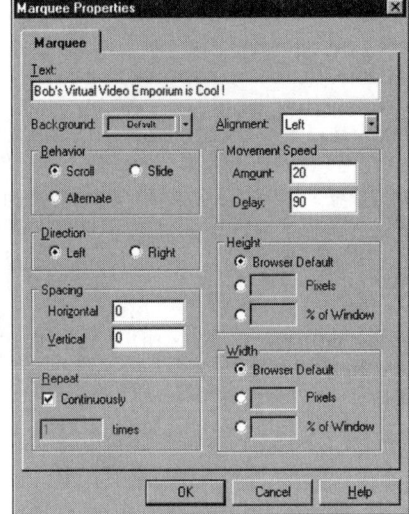

Figure 5-14:
The
Marquee
Properties
dialog box.

3. **Type the text that you want to include in the Text text box.**

4. **Click the Background button to specify a color for the marquee box.**

   You can pick a color from the Background drop-down list (the default leaves the color the same as your page's background color). You can also customize a color: Click Custom, and make adjustments in the Color dialog box, shown in Figure 5-15.

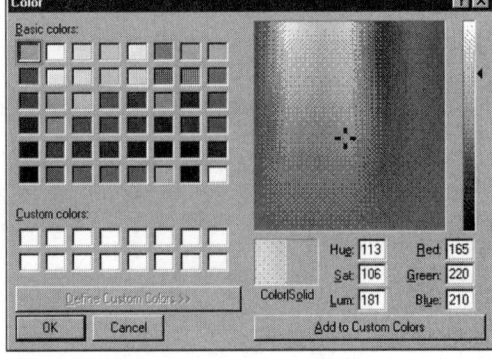

Figure 5-15:
Create a
custom
color
for your
marquee
background.

5. **If you want to control the width of the marquee, select the Pixels radio button in the Width area of the dialog box and enter a number to specify the width of the marquee in pixels.**

   If you leave the default setting, the marquee is the full width of the browser window. Alternatively, you can select the % of Window radio button and specify the width of the marquee as a percentage of the overall page width.

   Note that changing the width of the marquee does not change the size of the text, just the area in which the text moves around.

6. **If you want to control the height of the marquee, select the Pixels radio button in the Height area of the dialog box and enter a number to specify the height of the marquee in pixels.**

   If you leave the default setting, the marquee is the height of one line of text. Alternatively, you can select the % of Window radio button and specify the marquee height as a percentage of the overall page height. You're better off specifying the height in pixels, though, because if you specify the size as a percentage, someone viewing your site can change the size of the browser window, making it so small that the percentage size is smaller than the text, rendering your eloquent verbiage unreadable.

   Changing the height of the marquee has no affect on the text inside of it. Personally, I'd just ignore this option and leave the default.

7. **Pick a behavior for the marquee text from the three options in the Behavior section of the dialog box.**

   Behavior controls how the text in the marquee moves.

   - **Scroll:** This option, which is the default, causes the text to move from right to left. When all the text in the marquee and has scrolled off to the left, the marquee repeats itself.

   - **Slide:** This option causes the text to enter from the right until the first letter reaches the left edge of the marquee. Then the text stops. If you use this option, make sure that your text is shorter than the marquee, or else the end of the text will be cut off.

   - **Alternate:** This option causes the text to bounce from one side of the marquee to the other. Adding a single space at the beginning and end of the text is a good way to keep the text from hitting the edge of the marquee — it just looks better.

8. **Pick a direction for the marquee text to move in the Direction area of the dialog box.**

   Except for the Alternate behavior option (set in Step 7), specifying a direction determines which way the text in the marquee moves.

   • **Left:** This default option causes the marquee text to move from right to left. For easy-to-read text, I recommend this option.

   • **Right:** This option causes the marquee text to move from left to right. Choosing this option has no effect if you have set the behavior to alternate.

9. **Deselect the Continuously check box in the Repeat area of the dialog box and then specify the number of times you want the text to move through the marquee.**

   When the text stops moving, it comes to rest with the first letter of the text along the left edge of the marquee (or the last letter along the right edge, if the text was moving right).

   If you want the text to keep moving the entire time that viewers look at your Web page, skip this step.

10. **Specify the speed at which the text moves in the Movement Speed area of the dialog box.**

    • **Amount:** Indicates the distance the marquee text moves, in pixels. The default is 6 pixels.

    • **Delay:** Indicates, in thousandths of a second, how long the marquee waits before scrolling the text again. The default of 90 means that the text moves 11 times a second.

11. **Indicate the way that the marquee aligns with text in the same line.**

    • **Left:** This default option places the marquee to the left of the text. If the text is longer than the rest of the line, it wraps around below the marquee.

    • **Bottom:** This option aligns the bottom of the marquee text with the bottom of a capital letter in the first line of the paragraph text.

    • **Center:** This option vertically centers the marquee and paragraph text (so they line up exactly, if they are the same size).

    • **Right:** This option aligns the marquee with the right margin, and forces the paragraph text to wrap around the marquee. This option does not work in Microsoft Internet Explorer version 3.0.

    • **Top:** This option aligns the top of the marquee with the top of the paragraph text.

12. Click OK.

A dashed outline appears around your text. When you preview the page in a browser, the text moves across the screen.

Is That Really How You Spell "Weclome"?

I remember working on word problems in a grade-school math class and the cruel math teacher took off points when I spelled *Pythagorean* wrong. My argument was that it was math class, not English (or language arts, as they call it these days), so I shouldn't have to worry about spelling.

My math teacher said that spelling was important, and that I would be happy that someone pushed me into good spelling before I reached the business world, where people are judged by the quality of their spelling. I always hated this argument — and now programs like DESIGNER are vindicating me.

 Making sure that your Web pages contain correct spelling is easy, thanks to the handy-dandy spell checker. To proofread your page, choose Tools⇨ Spelling Check, press F7, or click the Spell Check button. If DESIGNER doesn't recognize some words on your page, the Spell Check dialog box opens.

Just because Spell Check doesn't know the word, it's not necessarily wrong: The word may be an abbreviation, a technical term, a proper name, or just one that's not very common. When Spell Check gives you a suspect word, you have some options:

- ✔ **Change the word to one that Spell Check suggests.** Highlight the replacement word in the Suggestions list, and click Change to change this specific misspelling, or Change All to change the word every time Spell Check finds it.

- ✔ **Ignore the word because you know that it's spelled correctly (or any other reason you may have to ignore it).** Just click Ignore. If you know that the word will come up again, you can click Ignore All to tell Spell Check to ignore the word every time it encounters it in the current document.

- ✔ **Add the word to Spell Check.** If you know that the word is spelled correctly, and you're going to use it fairly often, click Add to Personal to add the word to the Spell Check list of known words.

Spelling checkers are not terribly bright. They can't tell the difference between *to, too,* and *two,* and they don't notice when you type one word instead of the other. After you run the spell checker, it's a good idea to double-check your work for these kinds of spelling errors. Keep your eyes out for common such mistakes such as *there* versus *they're* and *their,* and *well* versus *we'll.*

Working with Lines

A section about horizontal lines, also called *rules,* may seem out of place in a chapter that deals with formatting text. That isn't really the case, though. Horizontal rules help you to break up information into sections. Horizontal rules work very well with headings, and you can format them to match the style of almost any page.

Different browsers show rules differently. Figure 5-16 shows different styles of horizontal lines both in Microsoft Internet Explorer and in Netscape Navigator. The difference is mainly in shading — if your page background is white, part of a shaded horizontal rule gets lost in Internet Explorer.

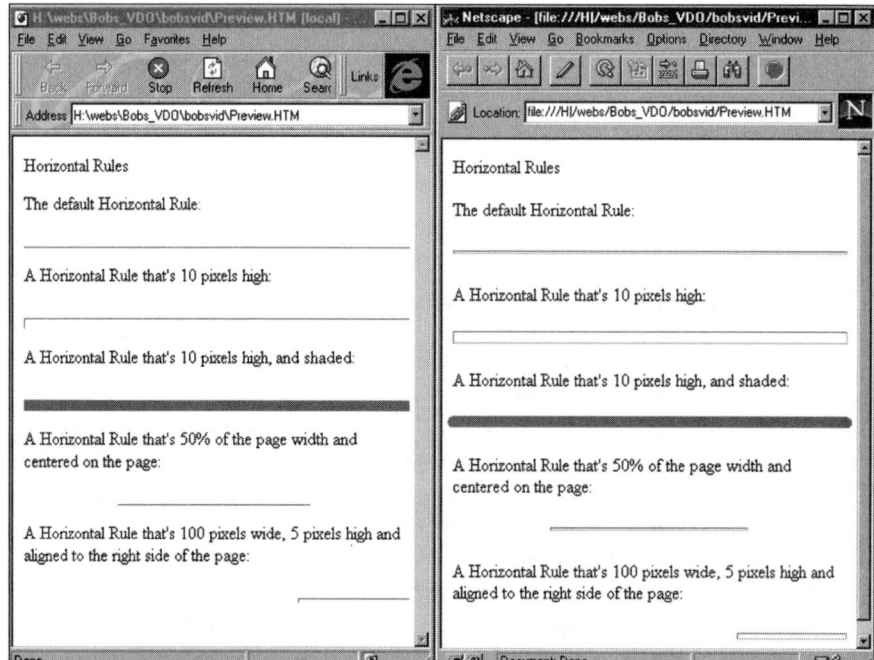

Figure 5-16:
A few examples of horizontal lines.

Adding a horizontal rule is easy. Place the cursor just above where you want the line to appear, and then choose Insert⇨Horizontal Rule or click the Insert Horizontal Rule button. A thin line runs the width of the page, right under where the cursor was. If you want a horizontal rule to appear directly under a paragraph, place the cursor at the end of the paragraph before inserting the rule.

To format a horizontal rule:

1. **Double-click the line.**

   The Horizontal Rule Properties dialog box opens.

2. **Select the radio button next to Pixels in the Height section, and specify a new height in pixels in the text box.**

3. **Select the radio button next to Pixels or % of Page Width in the Width section, and specify a custom width.**

   If you select % of Page Width, the width of the line (that is, its length from left to right) is specified as a percentage of the width of your browser window in which it's being viewed.

   If you select Pixels, the width of the line always exactly the same, no matter what the size of the browser window in which it's being viewed.

4. **Click one of the options in the Alignment section.**

   For most browsers, the default is to align the line to the left edge of the browser screen.

   - **Left:** Forces the line to the left edge of the screen.

   - **Center:** Places the line in the middle of the browser screen.

   - **Right:** Moves the line all the way to the right edge of the screen.

5. **Select Browser Default or Unshaded in the Shading section.**

6. **Click Apply to view your changes before committing to them.**

   If you want to tweak the line a little more, make any other changes you want.

7. **Click OK to accept your changes.**

Chapter 6

It's a Bird, It's a Plane . . .
It's Hyperlink!

- -

In This Chapter

▶ Adding hyperlinks to a page

▶ Organizing pages with bookmarks

▶ Formatting hyperlinks

▶ Repairing broken hyperlinks

▶ Removing hyperlinks

- -

*I*f the World Wide Web contained only one Web page, this chapter would be unnecessary. Actually this whole book would be unnecessary, because nobody would be using the Web, and you wouldn't have any reason to produce Web pages. Luckily, more than one Web page exists. As the late Carl Sagan might have said, there are "millions and millions" of them.

Getting from one page to another is possible thanks to hyperlinks. You click a link, and your browser instantly takes you to a new page (okay, with some delay for downloading). Aside from pretty Web graphics, links are what made the Web take control of the Internet.

These days, the term *Internet* refers to the physical backbone (the big data cables and computers that link computers together) of the World Wide Web. Back before the Web, the Internet meant both the backbone of the huge network and the insanely difficult text-based method of finding and retrieving information — which, by the way, did not have the benefit of graphics *or* hyperlinks.

Hyperwhat?

Hyper*link*. That's short for *hypertext links* (also known simply as *links*). A link works exactly the same way as the Favorites menu in Internet Explorer. The Web address (also known as the URL) is stored in the page code, just waiting for users to access it. When users click the link, their browsers use the address to figure out where to look for information. Then the browser sends a message to the server at that address, saying, in effect, "Send me this page." If all goes well, the server honors the request.

When you view a Web page, you're likely to see two types of links: text links and graphic links. As the names imply, a *text link* is a word or words that you click, and a *graphic link* is a picture that you click. Creating text or graphic links may sound a little intimidating, but don't worry. DESIGNER makes adding hyperlinks to your pages a snap.

Adding Hyperlinks to Your Web Page

Back in the *bad old days* of the Web, designers who wanted hyperlinks on their Web pages had to type them in by hand, including all sorts of nasty Hypertext Markup Language (HTML) codes. They had no way to browse around and just drop Web page addresses into a page.

That's all changed now. With DESIGNER, adding a hyperlink is simply a matter of following these steps:

1. **Select the text or graphic you want to use as a link.**

 2. **Click the HyperLink button to open the HyperLink Properties dialog box.**

3. **Tell DESIGNER where you want the link to connect to and close the dialog box.**

    This location can be a page within your own site or a page far out in the nether regions of the Web. Either way, when visitors click the link, their browsers know exactly where to look.

When you create text hyperlinks, always keep in mind what it is you're linking to. Make sure that the text of the hyperlink really describes what the link leads to. For example, a link that just says <u>click here</u> really doesn't give your visitor much to go on. A more informative link might say <u>See the latest in high-tech watercraft</u>.

 Hyperlink text usually stands out on a page — it's what your visitors' eyes are drawn to. Make the text interesting so that it entices people to visit whatever you've linked to.

Creating local links

Links that lead to other parts of the same Web site are called *local links*. Local links are what binds a Web site together. Without these links, your Web site would be no easier to navigate than the Web as a whole.

Turning a word or phrase into a local hyperlink is easy:

1. **In DESIGNER, highlight the word, phrase, or graphic you want to turn into a hyperlink.**

   The Hyperlink button is no longer grayed.

   If you just want to turn a single word into a link, double-click the word, and DESIGNER automatically highlights the entire word. If you want to use multiple words as a link, highlight all the words as a whole, rather than each word individually. Unlinked spaces between words make it hard to understand what's being linked to and also make clicking the link difficult. You can even highlight text and a picture, all at the same time.

 2. **Choose Format⇨HyperLink or click the HyperLink button.**

   The HyperLink Properties dialog box appears and displays the Link to URL tab, as shown in Figure 6-1.

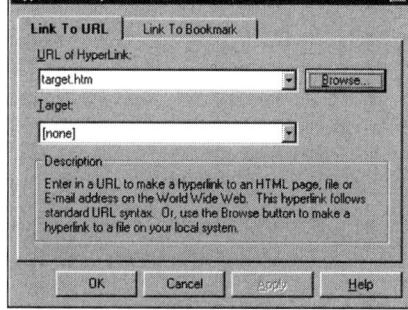

Figure 6-1:
The
HyperLink
Properties
dialog box.

3. **Click the Browse button.**

   The Select File dialog box opens. This is exactly the same as the Open File dialog box you're used to dealing with when you open a file in your word processor. The only difference is its name, and the fact that it's looking for .htm or .html files, instead of .doc or .wpd files.

4. Navigate through the list of files on your site and highlight the filename of the page you want to link to.

Make sure that the page is within your Web site, and not merely on the same hard drive. Your Web site contains only the files listed inside your Web root folder (see Figure 6-2). If you try to link a page that's on your hard drive but outside your Web site, DESIGNER copies the page file into your Web root folder, but *not* the images or any other files that the page may need (such as Java classes, ActiveX controls, and so on).

In the Web site

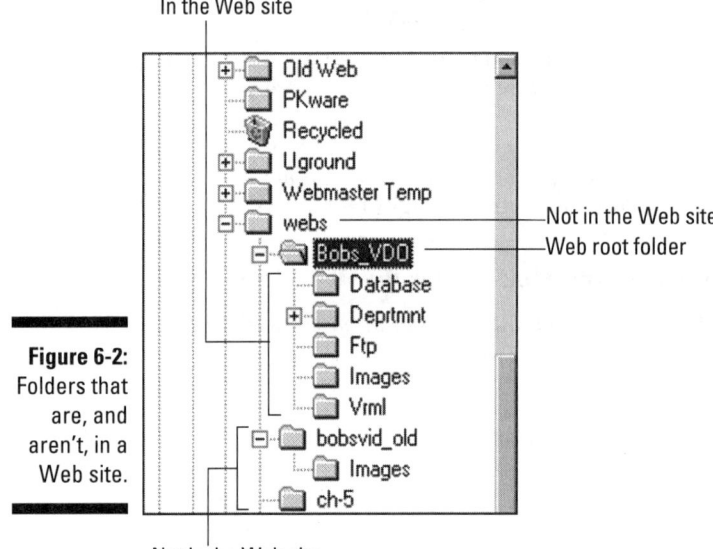

Figure 6-2:
Folders that are, and aren't, in a Web site.

— Not in the Web site
— Web root folder

Not in the Web site

5. Click <u>O</u>pen.

The Select File dialog box closes, and the URL of the HyperLink text box now contains the name of the page you're linking to. Other information (which I explain in the upcoming sidebar "Are relative URLs brother and sister?") may appear before the name.

6. Click OK.

The HyperLink Properties dialog box closes, and your text or image is now a hyperlink.

The word or phrase now appears in a blue, underlined font, indicating that it is a hyperlink. If you made a link out of an image, the image looks exactly the same as it did before, but don't worry: It's a hyperlink. The standard used to be that all image links had a blue box around them, but few people still follow that convention because it makes your graphics look really dorky.

Creating an external link

If a *local link* connects from one page to another page that's in the same Web site, then it only makes sense that an *external link* connects a page to one that's *not* in the same Web. Believe it or not, that's exactly what an external link is. (For once, those people created a name that makes sense, as opposed to cryptic terms like Uniform Resource Locator.)

To add an external link to your page:

1. **In DESIGNER, highlight the word, phrase, or graphic you want to turn into a hyperlink.**

   The Hyperlink button is no longer grayed.

 2. **Choose Format↪HyperLink or click the HyperLink button.**

   The HyperLink Properties dialog box appears, with the Link to URL tab active.

3. **Type the Web address (URL) of the page you want to link to in the URL of HyperLink text box.**

   You must enter the *complete* Web address, such as `http://www.domain .com/page.htm`. If you just type `page.htm` or `www.domain.com/ page.htm`, your visitors' browsers assume that the page is local and tries to get the page from your Web server instead of from the computer that really contains the page. If a page with the same name isn't present on your Web server, your visitors see the dreaded `404 file not found` error on a blank Web page.

   Because I'm lazy, I don't like to type information if I don't have to — especially long URLs in which one wrong letter means the hyperlink won't work. To avoid this headache, I recommend using your browser to navigate to the site you want to link to, selecting the URL in your browser's Location or Address box, and pressing Ctrl+C to copy it. Then you can switch to DESIGNER and complete the Hyperlink Properties dialog box simply by pressing Ctrl+V to paste the URL.

4. **Click OK.**

   The dialog box closes, and the text or image is now an external hyperlink.

You can also link to other Internet files and services (such as WAIS, Gopher, newsgroups, and so on). For a description of these services and how to use them, refer to Chapters 11, 20, and 21 in John and Margy Levine's *The Internet For Dummies* (IDG Books Worldwide, Inc.).

Are relative URLs brother and sister?

The names *relative* and *absolute* tell a lot about these two kinds of URLs.

✔ A *relative URL* is one in which the address is given in relation to the current page. Say you're talking about an apartment. Its relative address may be something like, "three doors down the hall from mine, on the left." If your friend Bob tried to use this address for his apartment across town, he would arrive at a totally different apartment (three doors down the hall on the left from *his*).

✔ An *absolute URL* is one in which the address tells you exactly where the page is, irrespective of where the current page is.

For a house, the absolute address may be "1600 Pennsylvania Avenue, Washington DC 20500, USA." No two houses have exactly the same address, and the same is true with absolute URLs.

With the ease of creating hyperlinks in DESIGNER, you almost never have to worry about whether a hyperlink uses a relative or absolute URL. Someday, though, you're going to have to track down trouble in a link, and that's when the difference comes into play. (See the upcoming section, "The Hyperlink Repair Shop," for more information.)

Inserting Bookmarks in Your Pages

With a name like *bookmark,* you may think that this device marks the location of a page in your Web site so that your visitors can find it easily. Well, you're almost right. Instead, a bookmark marks a location *within* a page that visitors can link to.

For example, if you have a long page that lists information about three different topics, you can save your visitors from having to scroll through the entire page by bookmarking the heading for each topic and putting a link to each bookmark at the top of the page. You can also make a link to a bookmark in another page so that your visitors can go straight to the information they're interested in without seeing the rest of the page.

Don't confuse this kind of bookmark with the bookmarks that Netscape Navigator uses. Netscape bookmarks are equivalent to Microsoft Internet Explorer's Favorites and America OnLine's Favorite Places — a shortcut that you can save in your browser to make it easier to get back to a particular Web page. Looks like the CCNS (Committee in Charge of Naming Stuff) is trying to keep you on your toes again.

Adding bookmarks

The process for adding a bookmark is similar to creating other effects in DESIGNER:

1. **Highlight the word or picture that you want to use as a bookmark.**

   If you just want to turn a single word into a bookmark, double-click the word, and DESIGNER automatically highlights the entire word. You can even highlight text and a picture, all at the same time.

2. **Choose Format⇨Bookmark.**

   The Bookmark dialog box appears, as shown in Figure 6-3.

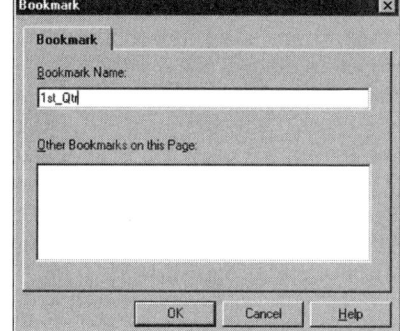

Figure 6-3:
The
Bookmark
dialog box.

3. **Type a name for the bookmark in the Bookmark Name text box.**

   Remember that you're going to reference this bookmark in the future to make links to it (otherwise, you wouldn't bother making a bookmark in the first place). Therefore, try to give it a name that makes sense to you and will be easily recognizable when you create the link.

   Don't include any spaces in the name. Bookmark names that contain spaces are unrecognizable to most server software, rendering links to the bookmark useless. Notice that the bookmark in Figure 6-3 uses an underline (_) in place of spaces, to help keep the name readable.

4. **Click OK.**

   The Bookmark dialog box closes, and you return to DESIGNER. If you highlighted text to be used as a bookmark, it is now colored red. If you highlighted a graphic, it will look exactly the same as it did before, but it is, indeed, a bookmark.

You can now use the bookmark as the target of a hyperlink, from the current page, another page in your site, or even someone's page elsewhere on the Web.

Bookmarks don't appear in color when your page is viewed in a browser. DESIGNER uses color only to help you identify where you added a bookmark. If you don't want to see bookmarks in color while you're in DESIGNER, choose View➪Bookmarks to remove the check mark from the Bookmarks option under the View menu.

Linking to bookmarks

Creating a link to a bookmark is very similar to creating one that points to an entire page. The only difference is that when you create a link to a bookmark, you also have to specify the name of the bookmark.

A bookmark in the same page

When creating a bookmark within the current page, DESIGNER ignores any part of the URL for that page and uses only information about the bookmark itself. This way, your visitors' browsers simply skip to the appropriate place in the page, without reloading the whole page.

Older browsers (more than about 18 months old) don't recognize bookmarks that don't include the page name in the link. (Really old browsers don't even recognize relative URLs, and only respond to complete URLs.) If some of your visitors are using older browsers and say they can't use your bookmarks, you do have the option of updating the links to include the URL of the current page; Chapter 13 explains how.

To add a link to a bookmark in the same page:

1. **Highlight the word, phrase, or graphic you want to turn into a hyperlink.**

   The Hyperlink button is no longer grayed.

 2. **Choose Format➪HyperLink, or click the HyperLink button.**

   The HyperLink Properties dialog box appears and displays the Link to URL tab.

3. **Click the Link to Bookmark tab.**

   The Link to Bookmark tab opens.

4. **Click the down arrow next to the Bookmarks drop-down list.**

   You now see a list of every bookmark in the current page, like the one shown Figure 6-4.

5. **Select a bookmark from the list.**

   You may have to scroll down through the list if you have several bookmarks.

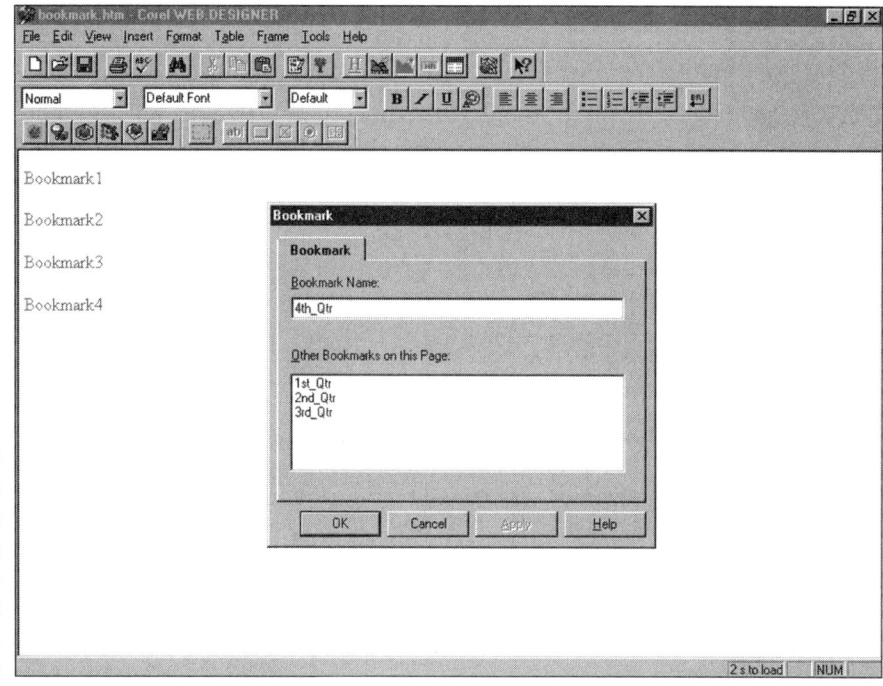

6. Click OK.

The HyperLink Properties dialog box closes. Your text or image is now a hyperlink to a bookmark.

The word or phrase now appears in blue and is underlined, indicating that it is a hyperlink.

A bookmark in a local page

Creating a bookmark to a location on a different page of your Web site is a little different:

1. In DESIGNER, highlight the word, phrase, or graphic you want to turn into a hyperlink.

The Hyperlink button is no longer grayed.

 2. Choose Format⇨HyperLink or click the HyperLink button.

The HyperLink Properties dialog box appears and displays the Link to URL tab.

3. Click Browse.

The Select File dialog box appears.

4. Navigate through the list of files on your site and highlight the filename of the page you want to link to.

Make sure that the page you select is within your Web site, and not merely on the same hard drive. Your Web site contains only the files listed inside your Web root folder.

5. Click O̲pen.

The Select File dialog box closes, and the name of the page you're linking to now appears in the URL of HyperLink text box.

6. Add a pound sign (#) followed by the name of the desired bookmark after the page name in the U̲RL of Hyperlink text box, as shown in Figure 6-5.

The pound sign tells your visitors' browsers, "Hey, the name after this is a bookmark." Don't include any spaces between the name of the Web page, the pound sign, and the name of the bookmark. Also, depending on the computer system on which you will eventually publish, you may need to make sure that the bookmark name has exactly the same capitalization as it does in the page you're linking to.

Bookmark

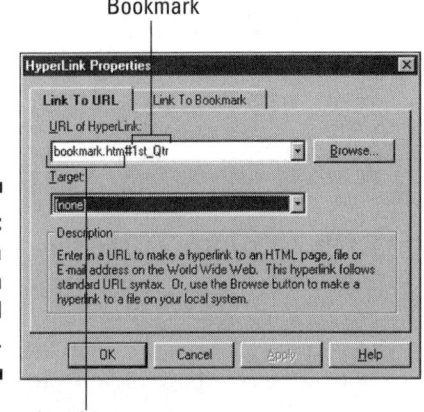

Figure 6-5:
A link to a
bookmark in
a local
page.

Local page

7. Click OK.

The HyperLink Properties dialog box closes, and your text or image is now a hyperlink to a bookmark in the local page.

If you don't type the bookmark name exactly as it appears in the referenced page, your link won't work. If you want to avoid typing errors, do the following:

1. **Start SiteManager and load your site.**

2. **Double-click the page that you want to create the link in.**

   DESIGNER opens and loads this page.

3. **Press Alt+Tab or select SiteManager from the taskbar to switch back to SiteManager.**

4. **Double-click the page that you want to link to.**

   A new copy of DESIGNER opens and loads this page.

5. **Double-click the bookmark you want to link to.**

   The Bookmark properties dialog box opens, and the current bookmark is highlighted in the Bookmark Name text box.

6. **Press Ctrl+C to copy the name to the clipboard.**

7. **While holding down the Alt key, press Tab repeatedly to switch to the other copy of DESIGNER, or select the other copy from the task bar.**

8. **Highlight the word, phrase, or graphic you want to turn into a hyperlink.**

9. **Choose Format⇨HyperLink, or click the HyperLink button.**

   The HyperLink Properties dialog box appears.

10. **Click the Browse button.**

    The Select File dialog box opens.

11. **Navigate through the list of files on your site and highlight the filename of the page you want to link to.**

12. **Click Open.**

    The Select File dialog box closes, and the name of the page you're linking to now appears in the URL of HyperLink text box.

13. **Type a pound sign (#) after the page name.**

14. **Press Ctrl+V to paste the bookmark name after the pound sign.**

    Make sure that there are no spaces between the page name, the pound sign, and the bookmark name. If any spaces exist, the link will not work.

15. **Click OK.**

    The HyperLink Properties dialog box closes and you can rest assured that you have not made a typing error, because the name of the hyperlink is exactly the same as it is in the file you're linking to.

16. **Close the copy of DESIGNER that contains the bookmark.**

A bookmark in an external page

Creating a link to a bookmark in an external page is very similar to creating a regular external link.

1. **In DESIGNER, highlight the word, phrase, or graphic you want to turn into a hyperlink.**

   The Hyperlink button is no longer grayed.

   If you just want to turn a single word into a link, double-click the word, and DESIGNER automatically highlights the entire word.

 2. **Choose Format⇨HyperLink, or click the HyperLink button.**

   The HyperLink Properties dialog box appears.

3. **Type the address (URL) of the page you want to link to.**

   This Web address has to be *complete,* including the bookmark, such as `http://www.domain.com/page.htm#bookmark`.

 To save time and avoid making errors in entering the URL, you can switch to your browser, surf to the page you want to link to, and click on the bookmark to move to the appropriate part of the page. Next, select the site's URL in your browser's Location or Address box (it shows the `#bookmark` part in addition to the standard URL) and press Ctrl+C to copy it. Then switch to DESIGNER and complete the Hyperlink Properties dialog box by pressing Ctrl+V to paste the URL.

4. **Click OK.**

   The text or image is now an external hyperlink.

Coloring Your World

Color can be very important in a Web page. Selecting the proper color for the different types of text can improve or destroy the readability or your pages. If you use text colors that don't show up well against the background, all your text will be hard to see.

Choose contrasting colors for your background and text so that they are easier to read. If you have a very dark background, use light-colored text, and vice versa. The most readable pages have black text on a white background or white text on a black background. On a medical note, you may want to avoid using red with green for your background and text colors. The most common form of color-blindness makes red and green indistinguishable, so color-blind visitors to your site won't be able to read what you've written.

If you've done your job well and created a compelling Web site, people will want to print your pages in addition to just viewing them on their computer screens. To ensure that printouts of your pages are easy to read, avoid using very light colors for text. Light-colored text is not legible when the page is printed, because background wallpaper and colors do not print.

This section details how to change the text and background colors for your page. You modify all these attributes through the Page Properties dialog box. You can adjust the colors of the following five items:

- ✔ **Background Color:** The main, underlying color of the browser window. In most browsers, the default background color is a light gray.

- ✔ **Regular Text:** The normal text that appears on your Web page — text that is not a link of any type. The default color for regular text is black.

- ✔ **Normal Links:** Text links that lead to pages that the viewer has not yet visited. The default color for normal links is dark blue.

- ✔ **Visited Links:** Text links that lead to pages that the viewer has already visited. The default color for visited links is pinkish.

- ✔ **Active Links/Bookmarks:** A link is active during the time that the viewer is actually clicking it. This is a Netscape Web extension; Microsoft Internet Explorer doesn't use a different color to signify active links. Note that Bookmarks appear in color only while you are editing your pages in DESIGNER — not when viewed through a browser. By default, this color is red.

To change the default background color or default text and link colors:

1. **Choose File➪Page Properties.**

   The Page Properties dialog box appears.

2. **Click the button of the item whose color you want to change.**

   A list of standard colors appears.

3. **Select the color you want to use.**

   The list closes, and the color you chose is displayed in the item's button face.

   Alternatively, you can click Custom, create a new color in the Color dialog box, and then click OK.

4. **Change any other colors you want in the same way.**

5. **Click OK.**

   DESIGNER updates your page to show all the new colors you picked. Of course, because you're using an editor not a browser, you won't be able to see visited links or active links change colors.

Be aware that changing the default text colors in this dialog box does not affect any text color that you have changed through the Font/Cell Color button on the toolbar (see Chapter 5 for information on using the Font/Cell Color button).

The Hyperlink Repair Shop

Broken local links mean that people who visit your site can no longer get to the appropriate page or graphic by clicking links. A number of things can cause your links to stop working. Perhaps the most common cause of broken local links is using Windows Explorer instead of SiteManager to move a page or a graphic in your site. When you use Windows Explorer to move files, the Link Wizard can't catch and correct the changing links.

You can control these broken links by never, ever moving files around your site except through SiteManager, as detailed in Chapter 3. Using SiteManager to move your files doesn't guarantee that you'll never have a broken local link, but it does make their occurrence extremely unlikely.

You can't control links to external pages. Other people move their pages and sites with reckless abandon. You have to be vigilant to ensure that your links to their pages remain intact.

The worst time to find out about broken links is when someone visits your site, tries a link, and gets nothing but a server error message saying that the page doesn't exist. This can hurt your credibility and make your site look cheap. The trick is to find broken links before your visitors do. Chapter 3 tells you how to use SiteManager to find broken links in your site.

Fixing broken links

So what can you do about broken links? Why, fix them, of course.

Even after your site has already been published, don't ever stop checking for broken links. If you find a link that's broken, fix it as outlined in the next few sections and then publish your updates as described in Chapters 18 and 19.

Checking your local links

Follow these steps to track down and fix broken local links while you're building or updating your site:

1. **Start SiteManager and load your site.**

2. **Choose List View⇨Pages with Broken Links.**

   You see a list of all pages that contain broken *local* links, as shown in Figure 6-6. Broken external links are not shown in this view.

3. **Double-click the name of one of the pages.**

   The page is highlighted in the file listings in the left window. If the page resides in a folder inside the Web root, that folder opens to display the file. The right window in SiteManager changes to Page View so that you can quickly see which link is broken, as shown in Figure 6-7.

4. **Double-click the page name in the file list in the left window.**

    DESIGNER starts and automatically loads your page. If your page has a lot of links and you want to be sure to work with the right one, click the resize botton to resize both program windows so that you can see the broken link in SiteManager while you're editing the page in DESIGNER (see Figure 6-8). If the programs are maximized, you have to click the Restore buttons in their title bars to shrink the windows before you can resize them.

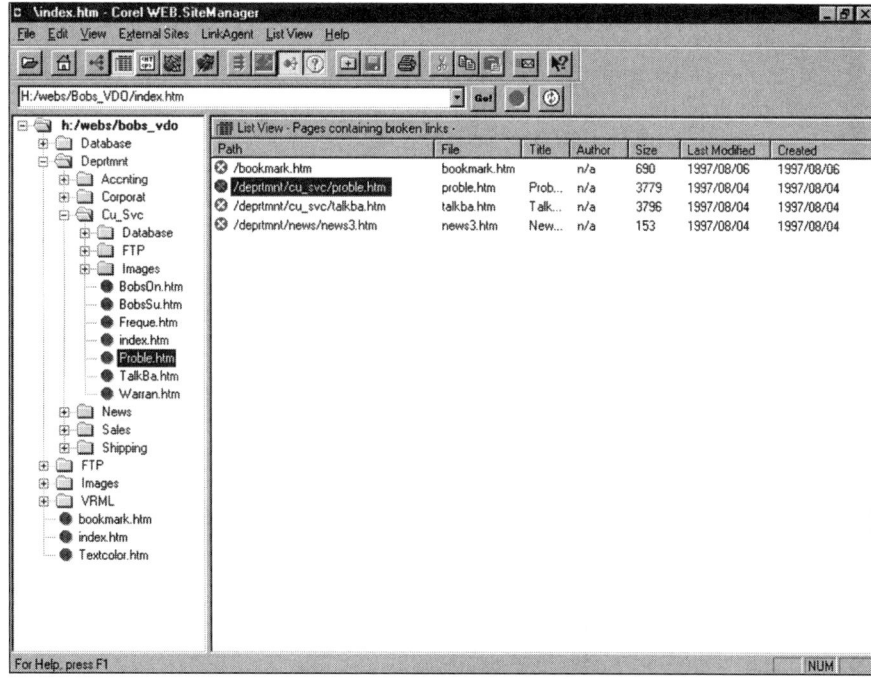

Figure 6-6:
A list of pages with broken local links.

Broken link

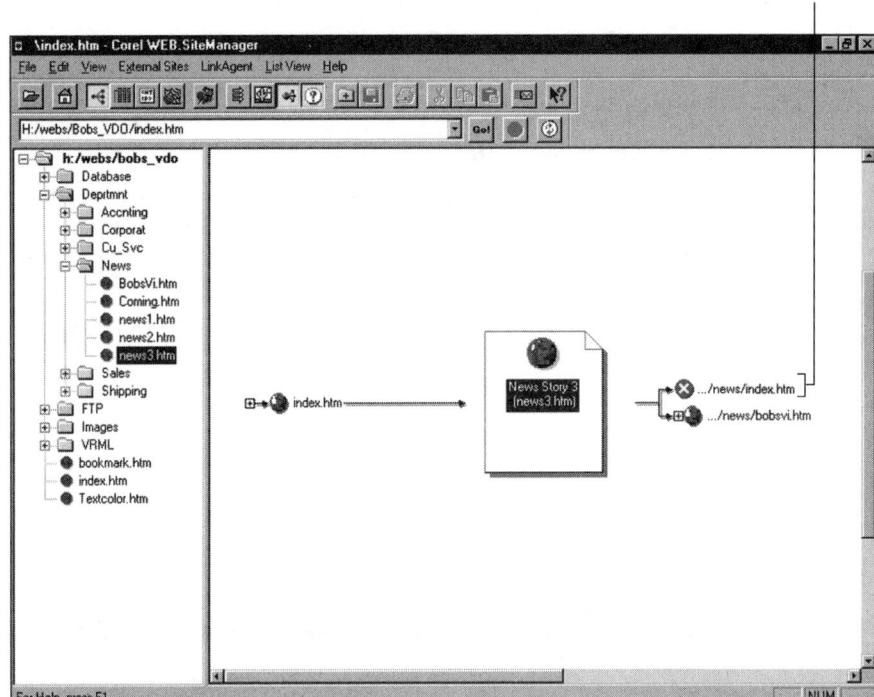

Figure 6-7:
A broken
link in
Page View.

5. Find the link that is reported as broken.

Usually, the file list shows links in the order they appear on the page.
Also, if you have named your links well (or if the graphic obviously has
to do with the intended subject of the link), you should be able to spot
the broken link fairly easily, without having to check too many links.

6. Double-click the text or graphic link that you suspect is broken.

If the link is a text link, the HyperLink Properties dialog box appears. If
it's an image link, the Image Properties dialog box opens for an image
link with the General tab selected — click the Link to URL tab to display
the hyperlink information.

Check the URL of the link in the URL of HyperLink text box. If the URL
matches the one that SiteManager shows as broken, then you've found
the broken link; if not, close the dialog box and double-click on a
different link.

Do not highlight the hyperlink text or graphic and then click the
Hyperlink button or choose Format⇨HyperLink. Doing so may delete
the hyperlink.

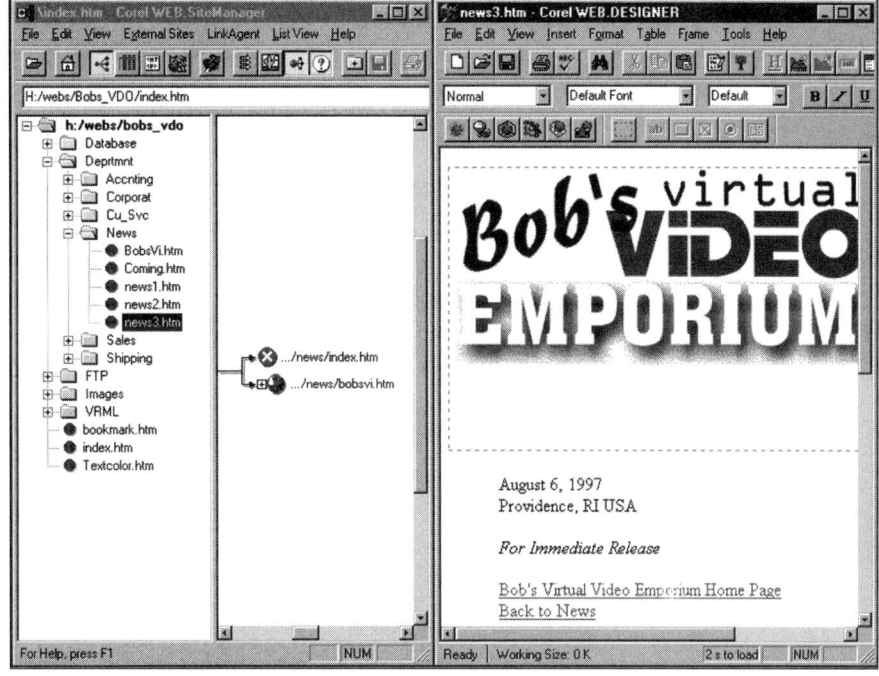

Figure 6-8:
View both
programs to
find the
broken link
more easily.

7. Fix the URL in the URL of HyperLink text box.

• If the page has been deleted or no longer exists in your site, press
Delete to erase the URL.

• If the page has been moved, click the Browse button, navigate
through your site to find the file for the page, highlight the file,
and then click Open.

8. Click OK.

The HyperLink Properties dialog box closes.

9. Choose File⇨Save to save the update.

10. Close DESIGNER.

11. Choose File⇨Reload Current Site.

The changes you just made take effect, and SiteManager is up-to-date.

**12. Repeat Steps 1–11 as many times as necessary to fix all your broken
local links.**

Checking your external links

Note that any e-mail addresses that you've made links to do not get checked. You'll have to check these by trying them yourself.

To check for broken external links:

1. **Start your connection to the Internet.**
2. **Start SiteManager and load your site.**

   If your site is already loaded in SiteManager, don't worry; connecting to the Internet first isn't important.

3. **Choose External Sites⇨Check Links to External Sites.**

   SiteManager searches the Web to make sure that the pages that your links connect to still exist. If any broken links are found, a dialog box appears, asking if you want to view the results of the search.

4. **Click Yes to switch to List View and see the list of links to external sites.**

   The window on the right displays a list of all of your site's links to external sites (see Figure 6-9).

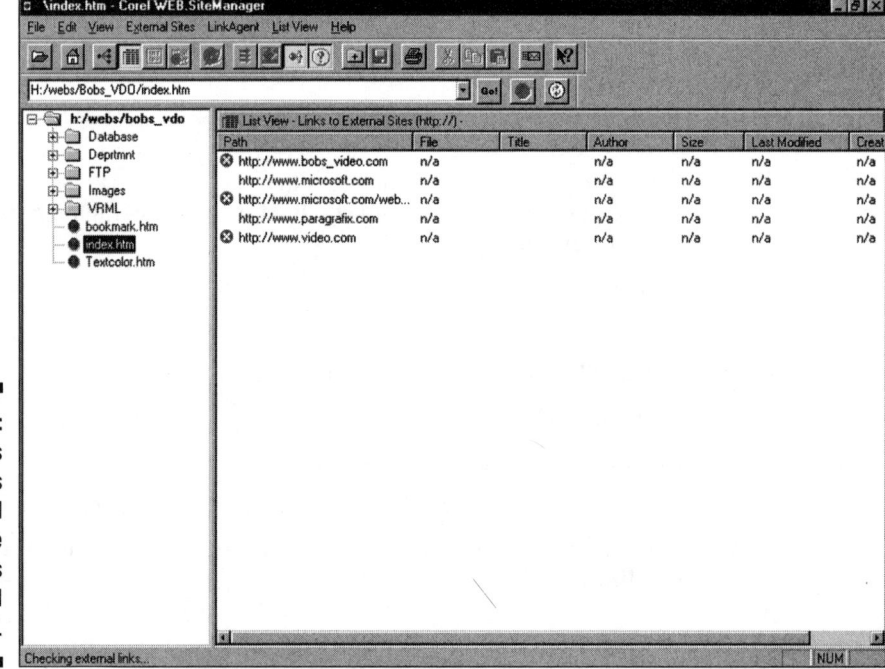

Figure 6-9:
List View's list of links to external sites. The broken links are marked with an X.

5. Double-click one of the broken links.

The right window changes to Page View and shows all the pages that contain the broken link, as shown in Figure 6-10.

Local page containing broken link

Broken link

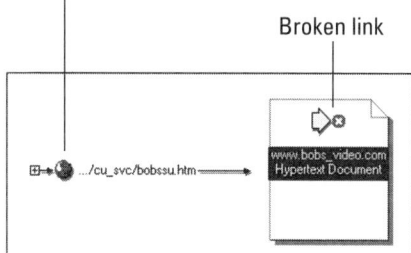

Figure 6-10:
This page
contains a
broken link.

...cu_svc/bobssu.htm

www.bobs_video.com
Hypertext Document

6. Double-click an icon representing a local page that contains a broken link.

The page is highlighted in the file listing in the left window. If it is contained in a folder inside the Web root, the folder opens to display the file.

7. Double-click the page's name in the file list in the left window.

DESIGNER starts and automatically loads your page.

8. Follow Steps 5–12 in the instructions contained in the previous section, "Checking your local links," to repair the broken links.

Making the actual link repairs is identical, no matter whether the link is local or external.

Keeping links to your site up-to-date

Don't forget that other people aren't the only culprits when it comes to breaking links. You can cause links to be broken when you move or delete pages. The whole point of having a Web site is so that other folks can visit it, and if links to your site are broken, nobody will be able to find the moved or deleted pages.

To make sure that links *to* your site always remain intact:

> ✔ E-mail people whom you know have made links to your site to inform them of the changes you've made and give them alternate URLs.

> ✔ When moving or deleting pages using SiteManager, have Link Wizard leave a `This page has moved` or a `This page has been removed` message. Doing so ensures that people who visit your site using links from other sites won't be greeted by the dreaded `404` error, telling them that the page can't be found.

Removing Hyperlinks and Bookmarks

You want to remove hyperlinks when the page or site that they link to no longer exists, or when their content has changed so much that you no longer want to link to them. You may also want to remove bookmarks if you're reorganizing your page and find that you no longer need them.

To remove a bookmark or hyperlink entirely (the text and graphic used as the bookmark and the bookmark itself), highlight the entire text or graphic of the bookmark or hyperlink and then press Delete.

To remove a bookmark but leave the text or graphic intact:

1. **Highlight the entire text or graphic containing the bookmark.**

2. **Choose Format⇨Bookmark.**

   A dialog box appears, stating that you are about to remove the bookmark.

3. **Click Yes.**

To remove a hyperlink but leave the text or graphic intact:

1. **Highlight the entire text or graphic containing the hyperlink.**

 2. **Choose Format⇨HyperLink, or click the HyperLink button.**

   A dialog box appears, stating that you are about to remove the hyperlink.

3. **Click Yes.**

Chapter 7

A Picture Is Worth a Thousand Words

*W*hat would a Web page be without graphics? It would be a dull, listless expanse of words, like the text-based Internet it replaced. No matter how interesting a site is, if it doesn't have eye-catching pictures, it's not going to get the hits. This chapter shows you how to add pictures to your Web pages, use them as hyperlinks, and discover the tricks necessary to keep your pages loading quickly.

Bitmaps, GIFs, and JPEGs — Oh, My!

This section is a primer on the two types of images that you can include in your Web page — GIF and JPG (also called JPEG) graphics. Here, I introduce what bitmaps are and what differences exist between GIF and JPG images.

If you're not planning on becoming a virtual Van Gogh, you can pretty much skip this section and jump right to the next section, "Making Your Web Page 'Picture Perfect.'" If you're using clipart images (like the ones supplied on WebMaster Suite CD #2) or pictures supplied to you by someone else (such as your company's art department), the only thing you *really* need to know about image files is that the only ones you can use in your Web pages end in .gif or .jpg.

What the heck is a bitmap?

All Web images are bitmaps. A *bitmap* image is just a bunch of dots (called *pixels*) that are arranged to make a picture. Why it's called a bitmap, I'll never know — but then why do you park in a driveway and drive on a parkway?

An easy way to think of a bitmap is to picture an old LiteBrite toy. Up close, the pictures you created by sticking colored pegs into the lighted screen looked pretty bad, but if you stood back a few yards, you could actually see a decent picture. Each plastic peg in a LiteBrite image is like a pixel in a bitmap. If you look closely at an image on your computer screen, you can actually pick out the individual pixels, as shown in Figure 7-1.

Figure 7-1:
This close-up shows *pixels,* the individual dots that make up a computer image.

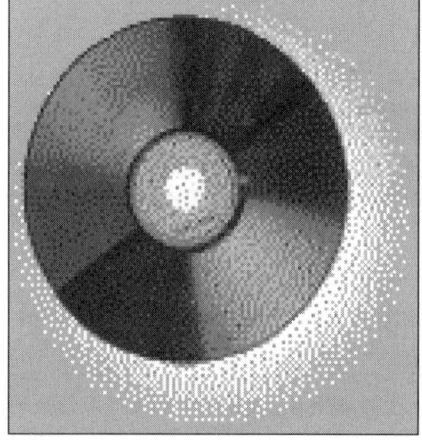

You say "jif," I say "gif" — let's call the whole thing off

The first thing you need to know about Web graphics is something called a *format.* A format is a way to store a picture so that a browser knows how to put it together on the computer screen. Hundreds of computer graphics formats are out there, including GIF, TIF, JPG, PCX, and CPT. Some of these are specific to a type of computer, whereas others are *open standards,* meaning that the same image can be displayed on any computer.

GIF (which stands for *Graphic Interchange Format*) is pronounced with either a hard G, as in *gag* or a J sound (like the peanut butter). JPG (which stands for *Joint Photographic Experts Group*) is pronounced *jay-peg.* This information isn't really important, but it can make you sound impressive, if you flaunt it when discussing the Web development project with your boss.

The main difference between GIF and JPG is the number of colors that an image can have in each format. Whereas a GIF image can have only up to 256 different colors (also called 8-bit or palleted), a JPG image (also called a 24-bit, or TrueColor image) can have up to 16 *million* different colors. You probably would never use all 16 million different colors in one image — an image with 16 million pixels is about 52 times the area of a computer screen! You do, however, have the choice to use any of these colors.

If you want to edit TrueColor images (such as JPG), make sure that your computer is set to HiColor or TrueColor. To do this, right-click the desktop and select Properties. Then click the Settings tab and set the Color palette drop-down list to HiColor (16-bit) or TrueColor (24-bit). You may have to restart your computer before the change takes effect. (Note that if you have only 1 megabyte of RAM in your video card, you will only be able to set your screen resolution to 640 x 480 pixels for 24-bit, and 800 x 600 pixels for 16-bit.) Of course you won't see exactly the correct colors if you're viewing a 24-bit image and your display is set for 16-bit, but the differences are slight.

Compression — putting your JPG files on a diet

Although you may be excited about all the colors that you can use in a JPG image, remember one thing: A JPG file (the file stored on the computer hard drive) can be up to four times larger than a corresponding GIF file. This means that it takes up to three times longer to transmit to the person viewing your page.

To counter this problem, you can *compress* JPG images by different amounts so that they take up less hard drive space and transmit more easily. The trade-off is that, with very high compression (a very small file size), a JPG image can look pretty nasty — see Figure 7-2 for an example. The funky pattern in the right picture is caused by errors introduced during compression. If the picture doesn't have a lot of solid colors, then this error doesn't show as much. (GIF images are compressed, too, but they use a technique called *lossless compression,* so they never get messed up. However, you can't make image files as small by using lossless compression.)

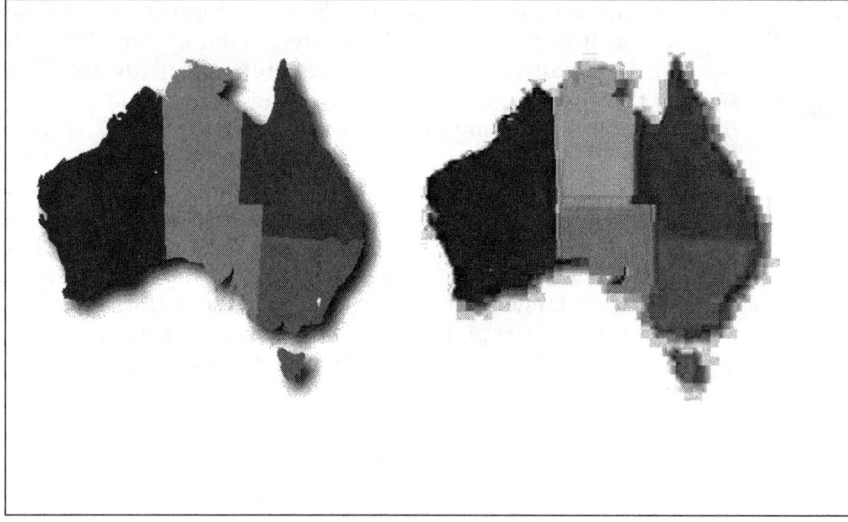

The redeeming qualities of GIF images

You knew there had to be a reason why people use GIF images on the Web, even though JPGs seem to have the advantage of better color depth. Actually, there are two reasons:

- **Animation:** You can create animation by stringing GIF images together in a single file. The result is similar to the old-style flip books that you may have played with as a child (either that, or I'm showing my age). These animations aren't broadcast quality (meaning that you wouldn't use them on broadcast television), but they can make excellent animated logos and other effects on your Web pages. GIF animations are similar to the spinning globe in the Internet Explorer title bar and the shooting star in the Netscape Navigator title bar. In Chapters 15 and 16, you can discover how to create and edit GIF animations.

- **Transparency:** You can choose *invisible* as one of your the colors in your GIF image, so the background of the Web page shows through it. This perception of *transparency* can provide some great effects and make your images more versatile. For example, if you have pages with a number of different background colors or images (see the upcoming section, "Dressing Up Your Page with a Background"), you can use the same image without it looking strange, *if* you set the background to transparent, as illustrated in Figure 7-3. Chapter 14 contains the nitty-gritty steps for creating transparent GIFs. (GIFs that contain a transparent color are called *transparent GIFs,* even though the image itself isn't transparent, just one of its colors.)

You can't eat off a color table

One odd thing about 256-color images is how the computer decides *which* 256 colors to display. Each GIF picture includes a *color table* that identifies the colors used. The computer displaying the image looks at this table, decides how to make each color, and displays the image.

You can run into trouble, though, when your page is displayed on a computer that can only produce 256 colors at a time, and you have two images, each with a totally different color table. This throws the computer for a loop, as it tries to figure out a decent match between the two different color tables. The computer has to make a best guess on displaying the images, sometimes with disastrous results.

This is a hard concept to understand. Instead of 256 colors, think of two images that each use two colors and a computer that can only display two colors. Say the first image uses red and yellow, and the second image uses red and blue. Because the computer can only display two colors, it can't make both of these images look right; the red looks okay in both images, but either the yellow or the blue (or both) will look wrong. The same thing happens with 256 colors, and the effect can be pretty weird.

The way to get around this problem is to make sure that all your images use the *same* color table, and one that's *Web-friendly* (also called *browser-safe*). There are two Web-friendly color tables: Netscape and Internet Explorer. Chapter 14 has instructions on how to update your images to these color tables.

Note: If you design 256-color images on a computer set for 16- or 24-bit display, you don't see a problem if images don't share a color table, but your Web site visitors will.

Thankfully, TrueColor images like JPG don't use color tables and so are immune to this problem.

Figure 7-3:
The two versions of this GIF on the left are transparent; the two on the right are normal.

What all this discussion of the differences between GIF and JPG images boils down to is this:

> ✔ **Use GIF images for logos and information graphics.** Usually, logos don't have many different colors, so the smaller number of colors available in GIFs doesn't really hurt them.
>
> ✔ **Use GIF images for photographs that don't need a lot of detail or that have large areas of solid color.** Due to their compression scheme, JPG images tend to make solid colors *muddy,* like the image on the right in Figure 7-2.
>
> ✔ **Use GIF images for short animations, or images in which you want the background to show through.**

Making Your Web Page "Picture Perfect"

Adding graphics to your Web page is really easy. Tweaking, aligning, and working with them later is only *slightly* less easy, but never fear: DESIGNER makes handling graphics a breeze . . . *and* you have this whole chapter to help you handle Web graphics like a pro.

If you're not a great artist (or if you just don't feel like spending the time creating images for your Web site), you can probably find existing graphics that meet your needs. Check out all the clipart images on WebMaster Suite CD#2 and the collection that's included on the CD that comes with this book.

Adding graphics

Graphics are great. Without them, the Internet would never have taken the world by storm. But you don't want to go overboard with graphics on your Web page. Think about that site you visited last week — the one that seemed to take forever to load because it had dozens of huge pictures popping up. That designer didn't use restraint, and he or she paid for it: You left the site in frustration . . . probably even before it finished loading. *Don't let this happen to your site.*

Use only the images you really need, make them relatively small, and use the correct format. (The first section of this chapter, "Bitmaps, GIFs, and JPEGs — Oh, My!," discusses the various graphics formats.)

To add an image to your Web page:

> 1. **Start DESIGNER and load the page in which you want to include an image.**

2. Place the cursor where you want the image to be.

 3. Click the Insert Image button, or choose Insert⇨Image.

The Image Properties dialog box appears, as shown in Figure 7-4.

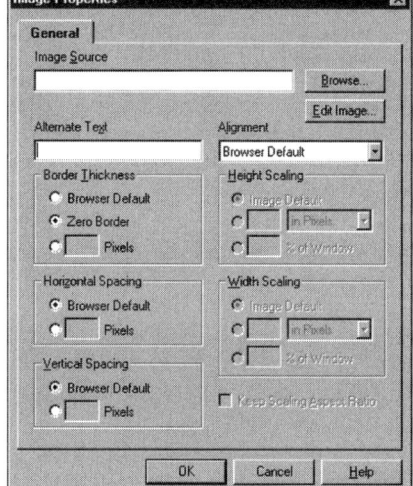

Figure 7-4:
Insert and
alter
images
using the
Image
Properties
dialog box.

4. Click the Browse button.

The Select Image Source dialog box appears.

5. Locate and highlight the image you want to use, and then click Open.

If the image isn't already in your Web site (for example, if it's on WebMaster Suite CD #2, which includes all the WebMaster Suite clipart), a dialog box opens and tells you that DESIGNER is going to copy the file to your Web site. Click OK to open the Save Picture dialog box. Click Save to save the image inside of your Web root folder (see Chapter 3 if you need a refresher on root folders).

5. Click OK.

Tada! The dialog box closes, you return to DESIGNER, and your image appears on your page.

Here are a few of things to keep in mind when inserting images:

✔ **Adding an image to a Web page only adds a *pointer* that tells the browser "I want you to display this picture."** If you use the same image more than once in a page or Web site, your visitor's browser downloads the image only once, and then displays it in all the different places you've specified. Whenever possible, reuse images throughout your Web site to cut down on transmission time.

✔ **As you add more and more images to your page, keep an eye on the load timer at the lower-left corner of the screen.** This number is an estimate of how long a user viewing your site with a 14.4 Kbps modem will have to wait for your page to load. There's no absolute rule for determining whether a page takes too long to load, but remember that if you wouldn't wait that long for a page, then you can't expect anyone else to, either. (If you're publishing to an intranet, instead of the Internet, you don't have to worry about the number of images on your page, because intranets are usually lightning fast.)

✔ **Sometimes when you choose a JPG image, DESIGNER displays a small box indicating the position of the picture, instead of showing the picture itself.** You haven't done anything wrong! Choose Tools➪Browser Preview to prove to yourself that the image is really there.

Aligning images

You can do a lot with the graphics on your Web page, but not as much as you can do with them in a word processor. You can't drag them around the page, have text wrap around them automatically, or anything like that. By default, graphics are plunked down right where you placed the cursor. If the cursor is in the middle of a line of text, that's where the image will be displayed. Period.

You can change the alignment between the text and graphic very easily, using the Image Properties dialog box. You simply double-click the image to open the dialog box, and then select the alignment option you want to use. Figure 7-5 shows the different options for aligning images.

Alignment isn't exact. If you really want control over the placement of text and graphics, see Chapter 9 for more information.

You can make text wrap around an image by placing the text in the middle of the line and setting its alignment to either left or right.

Really spaced out graphics

If you notice that your page is getting crowded (maybe text is so close to an image that you can't read it, for example), or you simply want more control over the page appearance, you can change the spacing around your graphics. See Figure 7-6 for an example of text that has been spaced away from a graphic.

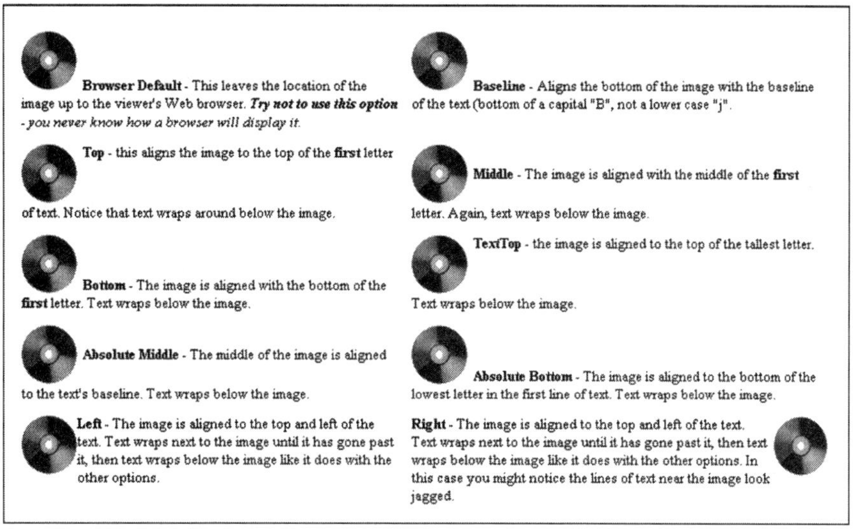

Browser Default - This leaves the location of the image up to the viewer's Web browser. *Try not to use this option - you never know how a browser will display it.*

Top - this aligns the image to the top of the **first** letter of text. Notice that text wraps around below the image.

Bottom - The image is aligned with the bottom of the **first** letter. Text wraps below the image.

Absolute Middle - The middle of the image is aligned to the text's baseline. Text wraps below the image.

Left - The image is aligned to the top and left of the text. Text wraps next to the image until it has gone past it, then text wraps below the image like it does with the other options.

Baseline - Aligns the bottom of the image with the baseline of the text (bottom of a capital "B", not a lower case "j".

Middle - The image is aligned with the middle of the **first** letter. Again, text wraps below the image.

TextTop - the image is aligned to the top of the tallest letter. Text wraps below the image.

Absolute Bottom - The image is aligned to the bottom of the lowest letter in the first line of text. Text wraps below the image.

Right - The image is aligned to the top and left of the text. Text wraps next to the image until it has gone past it, then text wraps below the image like it does with the other options. In this case you might notice the lines of text near the image look jagged.

Figure 7-5: Your options for aligning text and graphics.

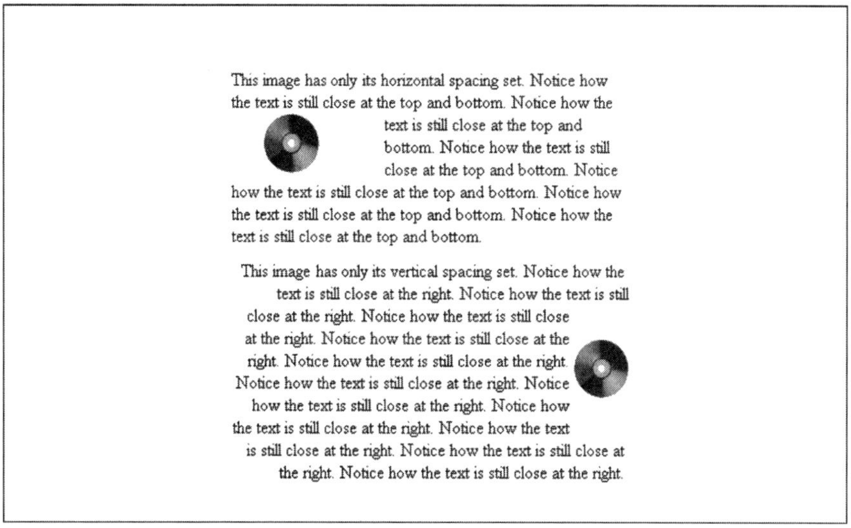

This image has only its horizontal spacing set. Notice how the text is still close at the top and bottom. Notice how the text is still close at the top and bottom. Notice how the text is still close at the top and bottom. Notice how the text is still close at the top and bottom. Notice how the text is still close at the top and bottom. Notice how the text is still close at the top and bottom.

This image has only its vertical spacing set. Notice how the text is still close at the right. Notice how the text is still close at the right. Notice how the text is still close at the right. Notice how the text is still close at the right. Notice how the text is still close at the right. Notice how the text is still close at the right. Notice how the text is still close at the right. Notice how the text is still close at the right. Notice how the text is still close at the right. Notice how the text is still close at the right.

Figure 7-6: The spacing of these two images is set to 30 pixels.

To change the spacing around an image:

1. Double-click the image, or choose Edit⇨Properties.

The Image Properties dialog box appears. This is the same Image Properties dialog box as shown in Figure 7-4.

2. Select the pixels radio button under Horizontal Spacing, Vertical Spacing, or both.

The small text box next to the radio button turns white to indicate that it is now active.

3. Type the spacing, in pixels, that you want around the image.

The number of pixels you use depends on how much space you want around your graphics.

4. Click OK.

The dialog box closes, and the text around your image shifts by the amount you specified.

An image as text

Images, especially big ones, take a while to load. Many people don't want to be slowed down by pictures on the Web. If they want to just get on the Web, get some information, and then get off again, they can tell their browsers to ignore graphics, and just show the text. Most browsers can display text in place of an image, if the person who designed the Web page was nice enough to include text (known as alternate text) for the graphic.

Another reason to include alternate text is so that people know what image is loading. If an image is especially large, your visitors may hit the Cancel button on their browsers, unless your alternate text entices them to wait for it — maybe something along the lines of This image shows you how to win a million dollars. Make your alternate text interesting, and make sure that your images are worth the wait (don't tell people that the image will show them how to win a million dollars if it won't).

To add alternate text:

1. Double-click the image, or choose Edit⇨Properties.

The Image Properties dialog box appears.

2. Type the text you want in the Alternate Text text box.

Unless your image is very large, keep your alternate text short; otherwise, it will get cut off. Alternate text doesn't wrap, and appears only within the area where the image would be, if it were displayed.

3. Click OK to close the dialog box.

Turning a Single Picture into Many Links

In Chapter 6, I discuss using text and graphics as hyperlinks. If you really want to go overboard, you can have each letter of a word link to a different Web page. You can do the same *sort* of thing with a graphic.

Say, for example, that you have five sales territories and you want people to be able to click an image of the appropriate territory to find the sales office nearest them. Using a standard image link, you'd need five separate pictures, one for each territory, and your visitors would have to click one of the five to pick the territory.

Wouldn't it be nicer if you could show the entire map and have each *section* link to a different sales territory? Using an *image map,* you can specify different areas *within the same graphic* as different links, as shown in Figure 7-7. Is that cool, or what? An *image map* is a list of the different Web pages that your image links to, and the location on your image a visitor clicks to use each link.

In the bad old days of Web publishing, creating an image map was extremely difficult. You had to . . . well, you really don't want me to explain this. I'll just say that it involved a lot of mind-numbing work.

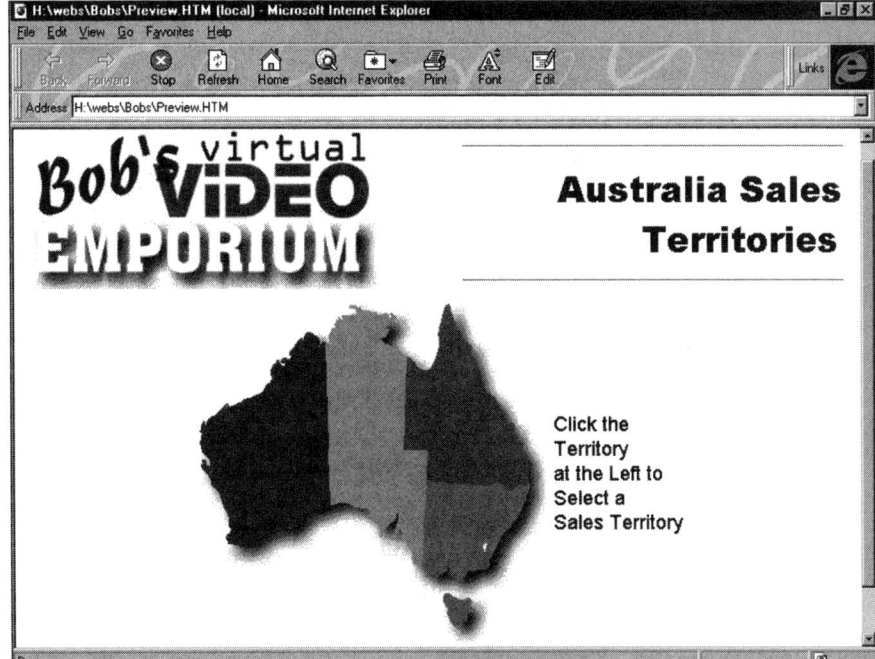

Figure 7-7:
Each area
in the single
image links
to a
different
territory.

WebMaster Suite provides you a bunch of easy methods for creating image maps. In this section, I detail how to create an image map in DESIGNER. Chapter 14 shows you how to create image maps in PhotoPaint, and Chapter 15 shows you how to create them in DRAW.

 To turn a graphic on your Web page into an image map, select the image and click the Image Map Editor button in the toolbar to open the Image Map Editor. The Image Map Editor, pictured in Figure 7-8, is a small dialog box that shows a close-up view of your graphic and provides the tools you need to create the image map.

You have to define every area of a picture that you want to be *clickable,* and you must associate the destination of the link with that area. You define these areas (called *elements*) by using the three shape tools:

✔ **The rectangle tool:** Makes rectangular elements

✔ **The circle tool:** Makes circular elements

✔ **The polygon tool:** Makes irregularly shaped elements (the perfect tool for working with images like the map shown in Figure 7-8)

┌Rectangle tool

Picker

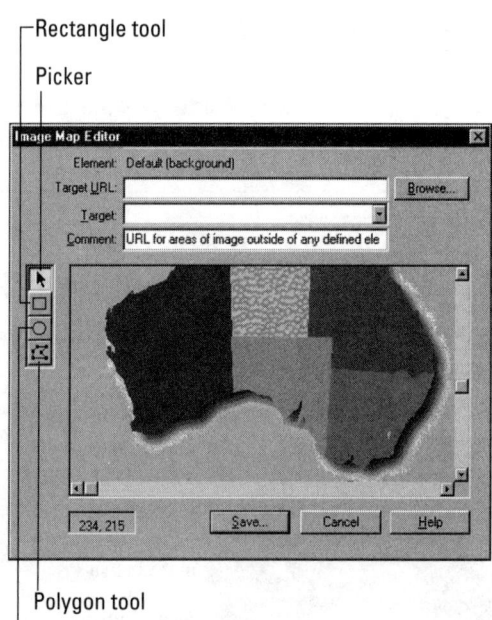

Figure 7-8:
The Image
Map Editor.

Polygon tool

└Circle tool

Client- and server-side image maps

Image maps come in two flavors: *client-side* and *server-side.* As the names imply, a server-side image map does its thing on your Web server and routes pages to your visitor. A client-side image map works in your visitor's browser (the client application) and sends a request for a page back to the server, just like a normal link.

To create an element in your image map:

1. **Open the Image Map Editor, as outlined in the preceding steps.**

2. **Select the tool you want to use.**

3. **Use the scroll bars to display the area of the image that you want to map.**

   If you can't get the entire area you want to map into the small display window, you can create two smaller elements that butt up against each other, instead of one large element.

4. **Define the portion of the element that you want to serve as a link.**

   The way you define the area depends on which of the three tools you use:

   - **Rectangle:** Click where you want one of the corners of the rectangular area to be, and drag a box that covers the area you want. When you're done, release the mouse button.

   - **Circle:** Click the center of the circular area you want to define, and drag the circle outward. When the circle is the right size, release the mouse button.

   - **Polygon:** Click a starting point, and then continue to click other points around the outline of your desired element. Keep clicking points until you've defined the shape you want. When you finish, click the first point to close the element. (You can also double-click your final point, rather than single-clicking the starting point again — the element closes automatically.)

5. **Tell the Image Map Editor what page you want this element to link to.**

   If the page you want to link to is on another Web site, type its URL in the Target URL text box. If the page you want to link to is on your own site, click Browse and select a local page.

6. **If you're using frames, select the frame in which you want the linked page to open from the Target drop-down list; otherwise, just leave this item blank.**

   See Chapter 9 to find out about frames.

7. Type information about the link in the Comment text box.

This information helps you identify the link if you come back to edit the image map later.

8. Click Save.

The Save Image Map File As dialog box appears.

9. Type a name for the file and then click Save.

This step saves the server-side image map file. If you opened the editor by clicking on the Image Map Editor button in the toolbar, you're all done. Otherwise, the Image Properties dialog box reappears.

10. Click OK.

The image looks exactly the same as it did before. But when you select the image, the name of the image map appears in the status bar at the bottom of your screen.

Here are tips for creating image map elements:

- ✔ If elements are far apart on the image, provide a little bit of *slop* around the areas where you want people to click. Making the element a little bigger than the area that represents it makes the link easier for your visitors to click.

- ✔ If the elements are very close together, leave a little bit of space between them, so that your visitors don't get confused.

- ✔ Don't overlap elements. Doing so can really freak out some browsers.

- ✔ If you make a mistake, don't worry. Select the picker tool (see Figure 7-12), click the element you don't want, and then press Delete. The unwanted element is gone.

- ✔ If you make an element the wrong size, you have to delete it and start over again. You can't resize elements after you've created them.

- ✔ Your Web server may require that all server-side image map files be stored in one location. If it does, ask your server administrator for this location. You need to copy this file separately to the appropriate location, and update the URL listed in the Server Side Image Map URL text box in the Image Map tab of the Image Properties dialog box (is that a mouthful, or what!).

- ✔ If you ever edit the image in an old image-editing program that doesn't support client-side image maps, beware that the image map information you added will be stripped from your pictures. Of course, if you always use PhotoPaint, you never have to worry about this!

Once you've created an image map, you're not stuck with it. You can also use Image Map Editor to make changes to existing image maps.

Dressing Up Your Page with a Background

These days, you can make Web pages that look almost as nice as the pages of a glossy, high-priced magazine. You can use different typefaces, add graphics, and have a fair amount of control over your layout. You can even do things that a magazine can't do, like adding animation, sound, and hyperlinks.

One important way to make your pages look professional and high-class is to alter their backgrounds. A *background* is nothing more than a color or graphic that you use as a, well, a background for your page. See Chapter 6, for information about adding a background color to your Web page.

Background images can enhance your page, and make its layout look far more interesting than it is, without a heck of a lot of work. Just as you can to many wallpaper images that you may use to make your Windows 95 desktop look nicer, you can *tile* background images. That is, you can use a small image that your visitors' browsers copy all over the screen, like bathroom tile.

To add a background image to your page:

1. **Open your page in DESIGNER.**

2. **Choose File⇨Page Properties.**

   The Page Properties dialog box appears.

3. **Type the name and path of the image you want to use in the Background Image Source text box, or click Browse.**

   If you typed the name of the image, click OK to return to DESIGNER. Your image is loaded into the page and tiled — you're done!

   If you clicked the Browse button, the Select Image Source dialog box appears, showing you the Webmastr/designer/template/back folder, which contains a bunch of backgrounds that you can use on your page. You can pick one of the 136 background images from this folder, or browse to WebMaster Suite CD #2, and look through its collection of other backgrounds (you can find a list of all the CD backgrounds in the WebMaster Suite clipart book).

4. **Select the image you want to use, click Open, and then click OK.**

   The Select Image Source and Page Properties dialog boxes close, and the image is loaded and tiled into your page.

Background tiles don't have to be square, but they do have to be rectangular, just like any other bitmap. You'll probably use or run across two types of background tiles while you're surfing the Web:

✔ **Square tiles:** An image is tiled all over your page to give it a texture.

✔ **Tall or wide tiles:** These backgrounds are specially created to break up a page, or to add a festive border. You can use tables or indenting to format your pages, and then add these types of borders to create a very impressive-looking page. (See Chapter 8 for information about formatting your page with tables.) Figures 7-9 and 7-10 show examples of these types of background tiles.

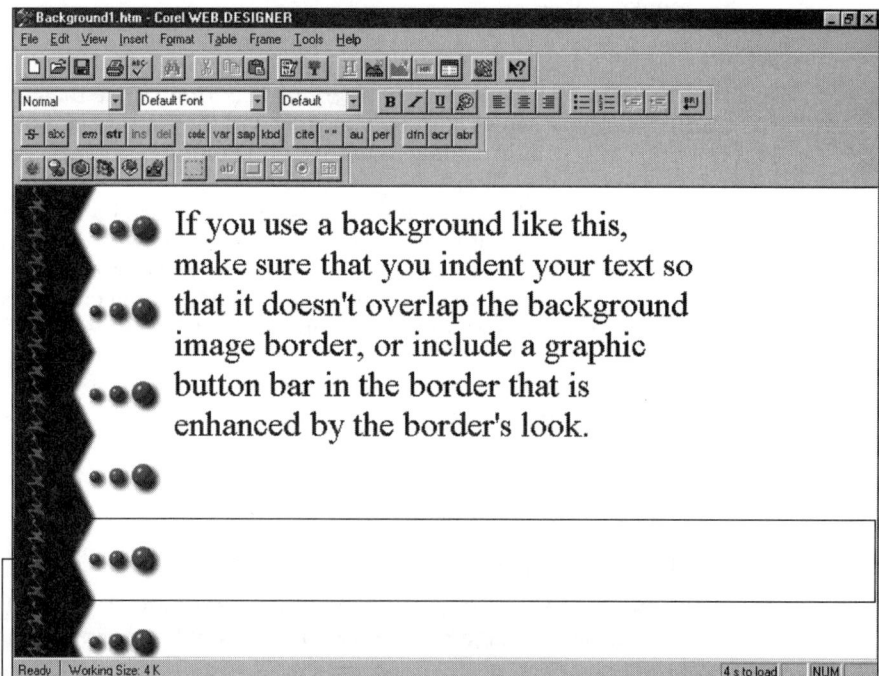

Figure 7-9:
A horizontal
(wide)
background
tile.

A single tile

Backgrounds are meant for the background

Here are some hints for keeping background images from overwhelming your pages:

- ✔ **KISS (Keep It Simple Stupid).** Very intricate backgrounds can make it almost impossible for your visitors to read the text on your page.

- ✔ **Use backgrounds with colors that contrast with your text.** If you use a light background, use dark text; if you use light text, use a dark background. (Beware, though, that if you use light-colored text, your

visitors may not be able to read your text if they print it out.)

- ✔ **Don't expect your text and graphics to line up on top of your background image on the browser the same way they do in DESIGNER.** You can spend hours making a page line up perfectly, but when your visitors view it on a different browser than the one you used for previewing, or on a different type of computer, they may see a page that looks like gibberish.

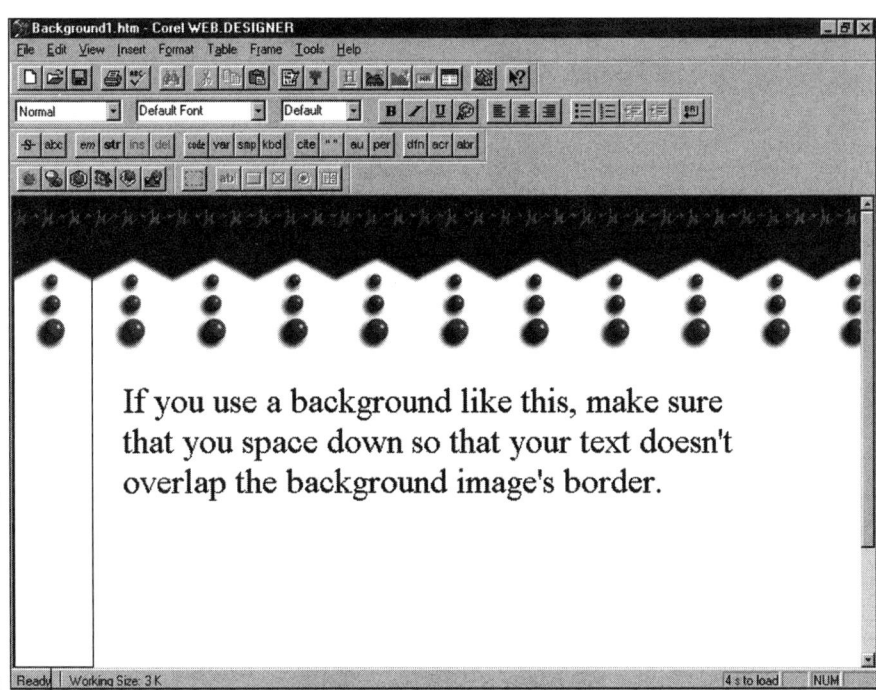

Figure 7-10:
A vertical
(tall)
background
tile.

A single tile

Chapter 8

Table That Idea

*I*f you want to write a bunch of numbers down by hand, you may use a piece of graph paper or ledger paper to keep things neat. If you want to show these numbers on a Web page, you're kind of stuck because Web pages don't have a graph or grid — or do they?

They do, otherwise I wouldn't have brought this up. Web pages have a built-in grid called a *table,* and just like its paper counterpart, you can use it to make your numbers look nice and neat. Tables have three main components: rows, columns, and cells. Rows and columns are pretty self-explanatory, but you may not be familiar with the third term. *Cells* are the individual boxes created by the intersection of a row and a column.

Tables can do much more than keep rows of numbers straight; you can use tables to keep a tight rein on your Web pages' layout. Tables are one of the most useful formatting tools around, and I give you a bunch of tips for using them to their greatest potential at the end of this chapter in the section called "Columns Aren't Just for Greece Anymore."

As with all the most useful Web page items, tables aren't supported by very old browsers. Instead of a clean table, browser-impaired visitors (in these politically correct times, such people are *not* called out-of-date-vestiges-of-the-Web's-prehistory) see everything on your page mushed together in a totally incomprehensible jumble. If you want to plan for every contingency, you may want to create a second page in which you set up your tabular information using the Preformatted Text option, which is explained in Chapter 5.

Many more options for formatting tables are available than appear in this chapter. I don't discuss these options here because you can't directly access them using the DESIGNER menus and dialog boxes. Instead, you enter these options directly into your page's HTML code. The options aren't necessary, and you can make good use of tables without them. If you really want to tweak your tables, check out Chapter 13.

Building a Table

Back in the dark ages of coding Web pages by hand, setting up even a simple table took a long time. But creating a table with DESIGNER is a breeze. Explaining all the options you can use to customize a table and make it look just the way you want will take a few pages, though.

Here's all you have to do to build a new table in a Web page:

1. Start DESIGNER and load an existing page or create a new one.

2. Place the cursor where you want your table to be.

 3. Choose Table⇨Insert Table or click the Table button.

Up pops the Table Properties dialog box, as shown in Figure 8-1.

Figure 8-1:
The Table
Properties
dialog box.

4. In the Rows and Columns text boxes, enter the number of rows and columns that you want your table to have.

Note that the Rows and Columns text boxes each initially contain a value of 2. However, you can replace these values with whatever number of rows and columns you want your table to have.

5. Click OK.

The dialog box closes, and a bunch of dashed lines show up on your page showing the rows and columns of your table (see Figure 8-2).

The dashed lines you see when you create a table in DESIGNER are just there to help you edit your page. They do not appear when your page is viewed in a browser. If you want outlines around your cells, see "Border size," later in this chapter.

That's it! You now have a table on your page. Now you can start filling in information, which is what the next section of this chapter just happens to be about.

You can adjust all the overall table formatting options I discuss later in this chapter (border size, cell padding, table width, and so on) while you insert your table. You don't have to create a table first and then make each of these adjustments later.

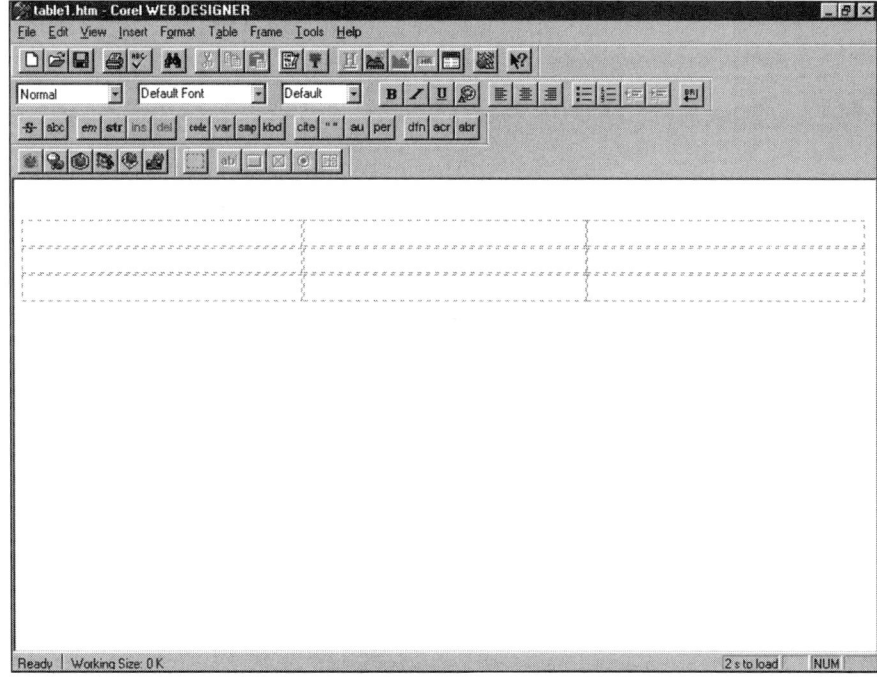

Figure 8-2:
A blank
three-row
by three-
column
table,
shown in
DESIGNER.

Setting the Table: Filling in Cells

This is the smallest part of this chapter. After all, what can I say about filling in a table? You just click a cell and put something in it. What you put in the cell is up to you: You can include text, graphics, form fields, and (as I discuss at the end of the chapter) other tables. Adding text, graphics, and form fields in a table is exactly the same as adding them anywhere else on your Web page — I discuss adding text in Chapter 5, graphics in Chapter 7, and form fields in Chapter 10.

If you've worked with tables in another Windows program, moving around in a DESIGNER table will be old hat:

- ✔ Press Tab to move your cursor to the right (or to the beginning of the next row, when you reach the last cell in a row).

- ✔ Press Shift+Tab to move left and up, when you reach the first cell of a row.

- ✔ You can also use the cursor keys (←, →, ↑, ↓) to move among cells. Note, however, that when use a cursor key, you don't always end up in the cell directly above, below, or next to the one you started in.

One thing *is* a little different from your word processor: When you reach the last cell of a table in DESIGNER, pressing Tab again doesn't automatically insert a new row. To find out how to add more cells to an existing table, check out "Adding and Deleting Cells, Rows, and Columns" later in this chapter.

(Table) Space: The Final Frontier

Well, you must have more options for controlling how a table looks, other than deciding how much text or graphics to add. This section deals with overall table formatting options that give you a large measure of control over how your table appears in a browser.

Border size

To make your table easier to read, you can add an outline, or *border,* around your table. To add a border to your table:

1. Click the cursor inside any cell within the table.

2. Choose Table⇨Table Properties.

The Table Properties dialog box opens (refer to Figure 8-1).

3. Set the border width.

Type a number in the Border Size text box or use the up and down arrows to increase or decrease the width. Border size is specified in pixels.

4. Click OK.

The dialog box closes, and your table now has a border around it with the width you specified. The border *between* the cells remains thin, no matter what you set the border width to.

If a cell is empty, the border defining the cell doesn't appear when the table is viewed in a browser (see the top table in Figure 8-3). Empty cells aren't a problem if your table doesn't have a border, because then no cells have borders around them. But when your table does have a border, an empty cell can look odd. A simple way around this problem is to include a small, totally transparent GIF (graphic file) in the cell. I like to use a tiny 1-x-1-pixel transparent GIF, so that I can be sure that it won't have any effect on the rest of the table (see the bottom table in Figure 8-3).

Overall table width

By default, a table takes up the entire width of a browser page. This can look very silly if you just have a couple of numbers or letters in each cell, leaving you with a huge table that's mostly empty space. Fortunately, you can change the overall width of the table.

Figure 8-3: These two tables are identical, except for small Transparent GIFs used as place-holders in the bottom table.

Table with nothing in some cells

This cell has text	This cell has text	
	This cell has text	This cell has text
This cell has text		

Table with 1x1 Transparent GIFs in "empty" cells

This cell has text	This cell has text	
	This cell has text	This cell has text
This cell has text		

You can specify table width two different ways: in pixels or as a percentage of the browser window width. Both methods have advantages, and which one you choose depends on what you're doing with your table. The pixel method is ideal if you're using tables to format your entire page. The percentage method ensures that your visitors don't have to do much if any side-to-side scrolling through your page.

To specify the width of a table:

1. **Click the cursor inside any cell within the table.**

2. **Choose Table⇨Table Properties.**

   The Table Properties dialog box opens (refer to Figure 8-1).

3. **Select the appropriate radio button to set the width method as Pixel or Percent.**

4. **Set the table width in the Specify Width text box.**

   You can either type a number or use the up and down arrows to increase or decrease the width.

   You can also just deselect the Specify Width check box and let your visitors' browsers do what they will with your table. I don't recommend doing this, because you can never be really sure what will happen.

5. **Click OK.**

   The dialog box closes, and your table now appears in whatever width you set for it.

Table alignment

If you adjust the width of a table, it automatically realigns with the left edge of the browser window. But you may prefer to have the table centered on the page or aligned with the page's right edge.

The easiest way to align a table is to click the Align Left, Align Center, or Align Right buttons in the DESIGNER toolbar. You must select the *entire* table before you click one of these buttons; otherwise, only the text in the selected cell gets aligned. To select the entire table, click inside any cell in the table and then choose Table⇨Select Table.

However, if you use the Align buttons in the toolbar, text won't be able to wrap around the table the way it can around an image. (For more information on wrapping text around an image, see Chapter 7.) If you want your text to wrap around your table, perform the following steps:

1. **Select a cell within your table.**

2. **Choose Table⇨Table Properties.**

   The Table Properties dialog box opens (refer to Figure 8-1).

3. **Select an option from the Alignment drop-down list.**

   The options are Default, Left, Right, and Center. The Left and Right options allow the rest of your page's text to wrap around the table.

4. **Click OK.**

   The dialog box closes, and your table now appears with whatever alignment you set.

Cell space

This section has nothing to do with the size of prison cells. No, this section deals with the spacing in and around the cells of a table.

Tables can sometimes get crowded and difficult to read — especially if each cell is totally packed with text or graphics. You can add space inside and around each cell to make the table easier to read.

The two types of spacing that cells can have are called *cell padding* and *cell spacing:*

 ✔ **Cell Padding:** Adds space within a cell and moves the borders away from the text

 ✔ **Cell Spacing:** Adds width to the borders between cells of a table

Figure 8-4 shows three tables — the top table has no cell spacing or padding specified (the default), the middle table has a cell padding of 10 pixels, and the bottom table has a cell spacing of 10 pixels.

To change the cell spacing or cell padding:

1. **Click the cursor inside any cell in your table.**

2. **Choose Table⇨Table Properties.**

   The Table Properties dialog box opens (refer to Figure 8-1).

3. **Type the amount (in pixels) of Cell Padding or Cell Spacing in the appropriate text box.**

   If you want to, you can set both cell padding and cell spacing at the same time.

10-pixel padding

A default table.	There is no space between cells.	Or space within cells.
A default table.	There is no space between cells.	Or space within cells.
A default table.	There is no space between cells.	Or space within cells.

A spaced-out table.	Cell padding is set to 10 pixels.	The text is easier to read.
A spaced-out table.	Cell padding is set to 10 pixels.	The text is easier to read.
A spaced-out table.	Cell padding is set to 10 pixels.	The text is easier to read.

A spaced-out table.	Cell spacing is set to 10 pixels.	The text is easier to read.
A spaced-out table.	Cell spacing is set to 10 pixels.	The text is easier to read.
A spaced-out table.	Cell spacing is set to 10 pixels.	The text is easier to read.

10-pixel spacing

   4. Click OK.

   The dialog box closes, and your table now appears, using whatever
   alignment you set.

   Note: When you don't specify any cell spacing or cell padding, the browser
   default is used, even though the Table Properties dialog box says that the
   values are set to zero. Chapter 13 has information about setting the cell
   padding and spacing to zero (and other really useful table tweaks) by
   directly editing your page's HTML file.

Formatting Cells

   In addition to formatting your table as a whole, you can also format individual cells within the table.

Column width

   Setting the column width may not seem like it should be included in a
   section about cells, but the width of a cell is what determines a column's
   width. When you set the width for a single cell, all the other cells in that
   column become that same width.

Your tables may not look exactly correct when you view them in DESIGNER. Remember to always preview your tables in a browser to see how they'll *really* look to your visitors.

To set the column width:

1. **Select a cell in the column.**

2. **Choose Table⇨Cell Properties.**

   The Cell Properties dialog box appears.

3. **Select the Specify Width check box.**

   The text box and radio buttons in the Minimum Width section of the dialog box are no longer grayed.

4. **Select in Pixel or in Percent.**

   Selecting in Pixel sets the width for the column in pixels. Selecting in Percent sets the width as a percentage of the table.

5. **Type the desired width in the Specify Width text box.**

6. **Click OK.**

   The dialog box closes, and your column is now the width you specified (see Figure 8-5).

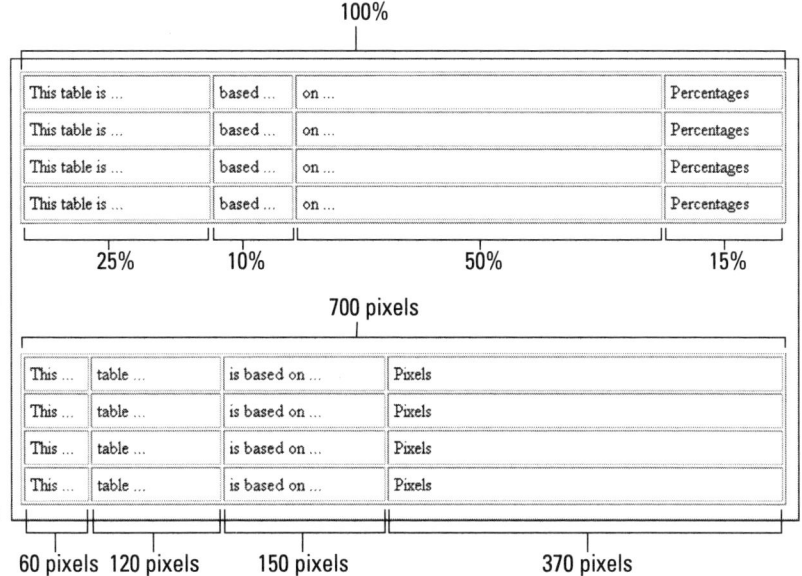

Figure 8-5: Column widths, based on percentages and pixels.

Cell widths are not set in stone. The numbers that you type as the widths are the *minimum* widths for the cells. The columns may become wider than you intend, if you don't set widths for all the columns, or if the widths don't add up to the width of the whole table.

To make sure that columns remain the way you want:

✔ Set the widths of all of the columns.

✔ When your table width is set as a percentage, use a percentage for your cell widths. If the table is set in pixels, use pixels.

✔ Always set your cell widths in the top row of your table. Although technically it doesn't make a difference what cell in the column you use, always using the same cells makes it easier for you to make changes later. For example, if you keep changing a cell width, but the column remains the same, you probably set the width in a different cell.

✔ When using percentages, remember that your column widths should total 100 percent, not the percentage width that you set for your entire table. For example, if your table width is 80 percent of the browser width, you still want your column widths to add up to 100 percent, not 80 percent.

Make sure that all your column widths add up to 100 percent or less when you're working with percentages, and the actual table width 700 or less when working by pixels. If, for example, you have column widths that add up to 105 percent, some browsers (especially new ones) can freak out and really mess up the way your page looks.

Aligning text in a cell

Tables are two-dimensional: They have a width *and* a height. Sometimes, when the text or graphic in a cell is much larger than that of surrounding cells, the way things line up can be confusing. Changing the alignment of the text in the table can make the text easier to understand. The two tables in Figure 8-6 illustrate this point: In the top table, the text is at its default alignment; in the bottom table, the text has been aligned to be more readable.

You can align text both vertically and horizontally within a cell, depending on your requirements. To align the text in individual cells:

1. Select the cell that you want to format.

You only need to place the cursor inside the cell. You don't have to select the entire contents of the cell.

	Daily Rental Rates	Total Revenues (not including the really awful month we had in August when everybody was at the beach and not renting movies)
Fiscal Year 1996	$1.97	$47,094,197.01
Fiscal Year 1995	$0.57	$150.68

	Daily Rental Rates	Total Revenues (not including the really awful month we had in August when everybody was at the beach and not renting movies)
Fiscal Year 1996	$1.97	$47,094,197.01
Fiscal Year 1995	$0.57	$150.68

Figure 8-6:
How the total revenues compare is not immediately obvious in the top table.

2. **Choose Table⇨Cell Properties.**

   The Cell Properties dialog box appears. You can also right-click in the cell and select Cell Properties from the pop-up menu.

3. **Choose your alignment option from the appropriate drop-down list.**

   - For horizontal alignment, your choices are Left (the default setting), Center, and Right.

   - For vertical alignment, your choices are Top, Middle (the default setting), and Bottom.

4. **Click OK.**

   The dialog box closes, and the text is aligned within the cell as you designated.

If you want to horizontally align a couple of cells at a time, you can select the cells by clicking and dragging through all the cells you want to align, and then clicking the Left-, Right- or Center-alignment buttons in the toolbar. Alternatively, if you want to align an entire row, column, or perhaps the whole table, you can pick these groups easily, as follows:

✔ **To pick a complete row:** Click any cell in that row and then choose Table⇨Select Row.

✔ **To pick an entire column:** Click any cell in that column and then choose Table⇨Select Column.

✔ **To select the whole table:** Click in any cell within the table and choose Table⇨Select Table.

Cells that span

Cells can be wider than one column or taller than one row. In Web-page lingo, these cells *span* the row or column, kinda the way a bridge spans a river. Figure 8-7 shows an example of a table with cells that span both rows and columns. You create spanning cells by *merging* together cells in a row or column, so that they end up as one big cell that takes up the same space as all the originals.

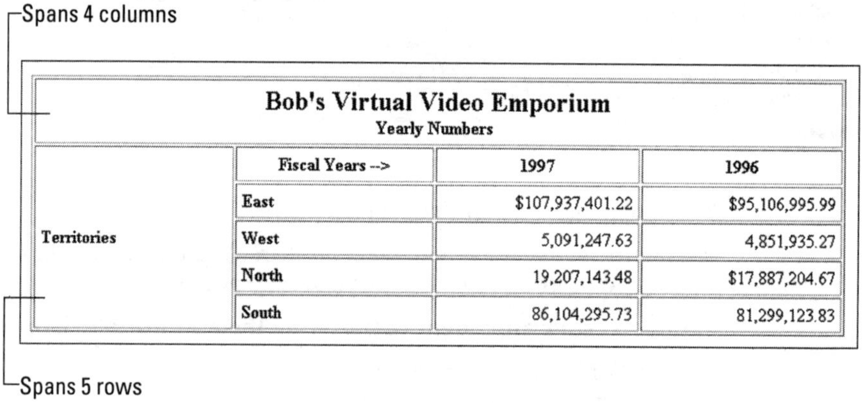

┌Spans 4 columns

Bob's Virtual Video Emporium Yearly Numbers			
	Fiscal Years -->	1997	1996
	East	$107,937,401.22	$95,106,995.99
Territories	West	5,091,247.63	4,851,935.27
	North	19,207,143.48	$17,887,204.67
	South	86,104,295.73	81,299,123.83

Figure 8-7: A table that uses spanning cells.

└Spans 5 rows

To create a cell that spans rows or columns:

1. **Create a normal table.**

2. **Highlight the cells you want to merge together.**

   Highlight cells in a single column or row or a block of adjacent cells. To do this, you click one cell and drag through the rest of the cells that you want to merge. All the cells now have small highlights in them. Note that if the cells you want to merge have text in them, the text will run together in the newly merged cell.

3. **Choose Table⇨Merge Cells.**

   The cells combine together into one block.

You can also create a spanning cell by setting the number of columns or rows you want the cell to span in the Cell Properties dialog box. However, this method can really change the layout of your table, as shown in Figure 8-8. All the tables in this figure started out with the same layout; I only changed the spanning properties of the upper-left cell.

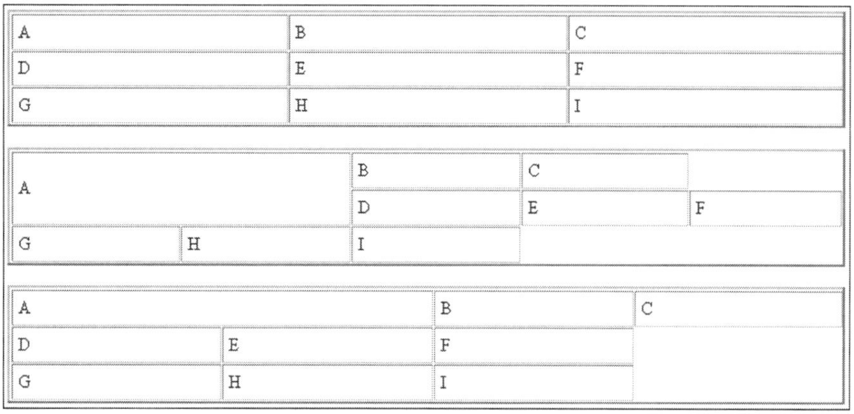

A		B		C	
D		E		F	
G		H		I	

A			B	C	
			D	E	F
G		H	I		

A			B		C
D		E		F	
G		H		I	

Figure 8-8: The spanning cells in the bottom two tables have forced the other cells out of alignment.

If you want to split a cell apart into a bunch of individual cells:

1. Select the spanning cell you want to break apart.

2. Choose Table⇨Split Cells.

The Split Cell dialog box appears.

3. Select the appropriate check box to tell whether you want the cell broken apart horizontally or vertically.

These selections may seem a little backwards: Splitting a cell horizontally creates new cells one on top of the other, and splitting vertically creates new cells next to the other.

4. Click OK.

The dialog box closes, and your cell is split apart.

You can also split apart a cell that doesn't span any rows or columns. In this case, you create new spanning cells in the row or column that the cell is in. When you split a non-spanning cell, you can specify how many new cells you want to split into, unlike a spanning cell, which can only split into the number of rows or columns that it spans.

Adding and Deleting Cells, Rows, and Columns

If you find that you've made your table too small or too big, you can quickly add or delete cells, rows, and columns to get it up to snuff. To add a cell:

1. Select the cell to the left of where you want to insert the new cell.

2. Choose Table⇨Insert Cell.

A new cell appears to the right of the cell you just selected, and the cursor is now in your new cell.

Note: Adding a cell increases the number of cells in the row, and may throw off your layout. To alleviate the problem, you make the cells in the row or column affected by the new cell into a spanning cell. Just add 1 to the Rows Spanned or Columns Spanned numbers in the Cell Properties dialog box.

To add a row:

1. Select a cell above or below where you want the new row.

2. Choose Table⇨Insert Rows/Columns.

The Insert Rows/Columns dialog box appears with the Insert Rows check box selected.

3. Type the number of new rows you want to add in the Number of Rows text box.

4. Click the Above selection or Below selection radio button to determine the location of the new row.

5. Click OK.

The dialog box closes, and the new row appears in your table, just waiting for you to fill it.

To add a column:

1. Select a cell to the right or left of where you want the new column.

2. Choose Table⇨Insert Rows/Columns.

The Insert Rows/Columns dialog box appears.

3. Select the Insert Columns check box.

The Rows area becomes gray and inactive, and the Columns area is no longer grayed.

4. Type the number of new columns you want to add in the Number of Columns text box.

5. Click the Left of selection or Right selection radio button to determine the location of the new row.

6. Click OK.

The dialog box closes, and the new column appears in your table.

To delete a cell, just select the cell and choose Table⇨Delete Cell. To delete a row or column, select a cell within the row or column you want to delete, and choose Table⇨Delete Row or Table⇨Delete Column.

Creating the Amazing Technicolor Table

Offsetting headings and certain information in your table is much easier if you use color. Color attracts the eye much more than bold or italics do. You can change the color of a single cell, row, column, or even the entire table.

To specify a color for a cell, row, column, or the whole table:

1. Select the cell, row, or column in your table, or select the entire table.

If you select a single cell, you must select the entire cell or else the color that you specify will only affect text that's highlighted. To select an entire cell, click within the cell and choose Table⇨Select Cell.

 2. Click the Font/Cell color button in the toolbar.

A drop-down list of standard colors appears.

3. Select a color from the list or click Custom Color.

- If you choose a color from the list, your selection now appears in that color.

- If you elect to generate a custom color, the Color dialog box appears. Create your color — by picking from the large color window or by entering values for red, green, and blue or for hue, saturation, and luminance — and click OK. Your selection now appears in that color.

 Make sure that the color you generate is contained in the palette your GIF images use. Chapter 7 contains a tip for generating colors that are appropriate to the palette you're using.

Tables within Tables within Tables. . . .

As you get more experienced at using tables to format your pages, you may find that you just can't get things to line up the way you want — especially if you're using cells that span rows. As the spanning cell grows, so do the cells that it spans — and that can throw your alignment off (see Figure 8-9).

Using a table that has only two columns and inserting a new table into the left column, you can format these buttons separately from the main table (see Figure 8-10). This process is called *nesting tables,* because one table is nested inside another.

 The inner table in Figure 8-10 has been hand-formatted (using techniques outlined in Chapter 13) to make the images bump up against each other.

These buttons would look better bumped up against one another.

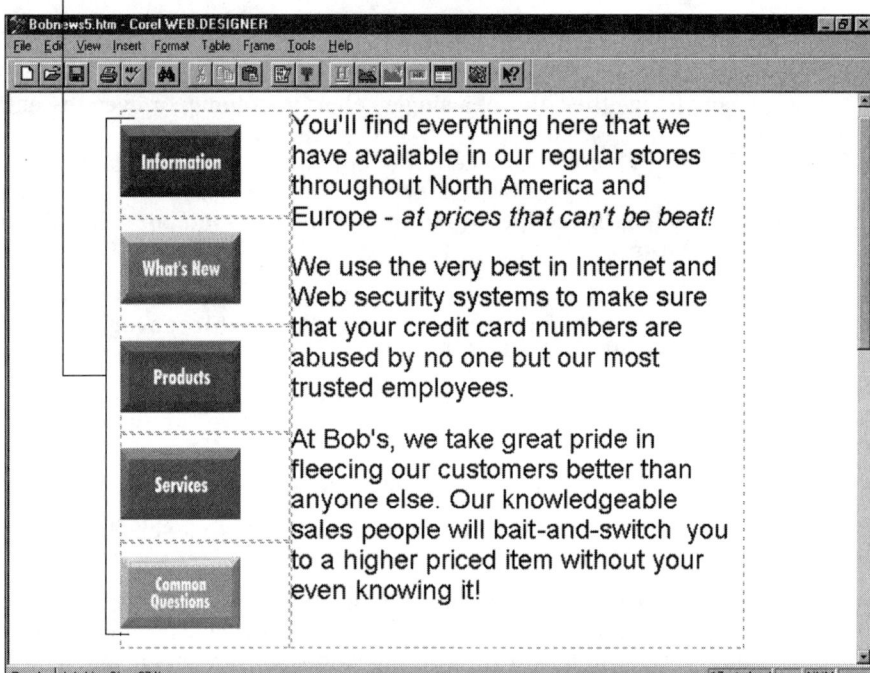

Figure 8-9:
The right
spanning
cell has
forced
apart the
buttons on
the left.

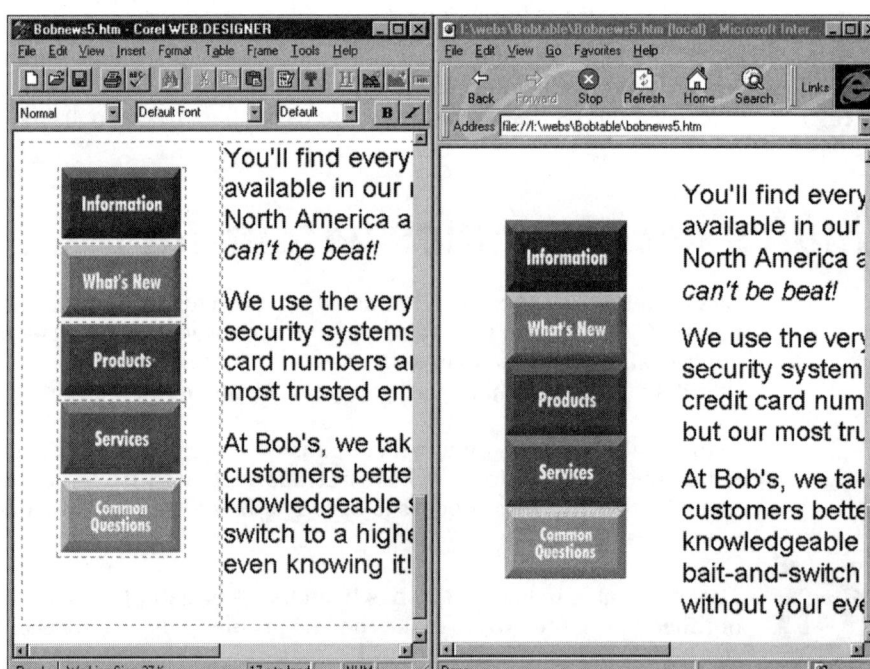

Figure 8-10:
The buttons
are
contained
in a single
table with
five cells.

Adding a nested table is easy. The only difference between creating a nested table and a normal one is where you place the cursor. When you create a normal table, you place the cursor in a blank area of your page. When you create a nested table, you place the cursor inside an existing cell.

To add a nested table:

1. **Create a table.**
2. **Select the cell in which you want to add a table.**
3. **Choose Table⇨Insert Table.**

   The Table Properties dialog box opens (refer to Figure 8-1).

4. **Type the properties that you want the nested table to have.**
5. **Click OK.**

   The dialog box closes, and you have one table nested inside another.

Columns Aren't Just for Greece Anymore

You've read newspapers and magazines — go ahead, admit it. Nearly all publications use columns to help break up stories and reduce the distance a reader's eyes have to travel to reach the next line. A long line of text is more difficult to read than a relatively short one. (I say *relatively short* because a column that is too skinny becomes difficult to read. How can you create multiple columns in your Web pages? By using tables.)

Tables are, in my humble opinion, the most useful formatting tool available to you as a Web page designer. This section shows you how to use tables to your advantage so that you can really take control of your Web page designs. You won't find any specific instructions or hard-and-fast rules here (that's what the rest of this chapter is for). Instead, the goal of this section is to spark your imagination.

Creating columns is one of the most valuable uses of tables. Figure 8-11 shows a fairly basic use of tables to create a page layout. Notice that the top table ensures that the logo and banner text line up properly, and the bottom table creates two columns containing stories. Neither table uses borders, which helps them look more like newspaper and magazine columns — although I did add a color to the center column of the bottom table to make a break between the two stories.

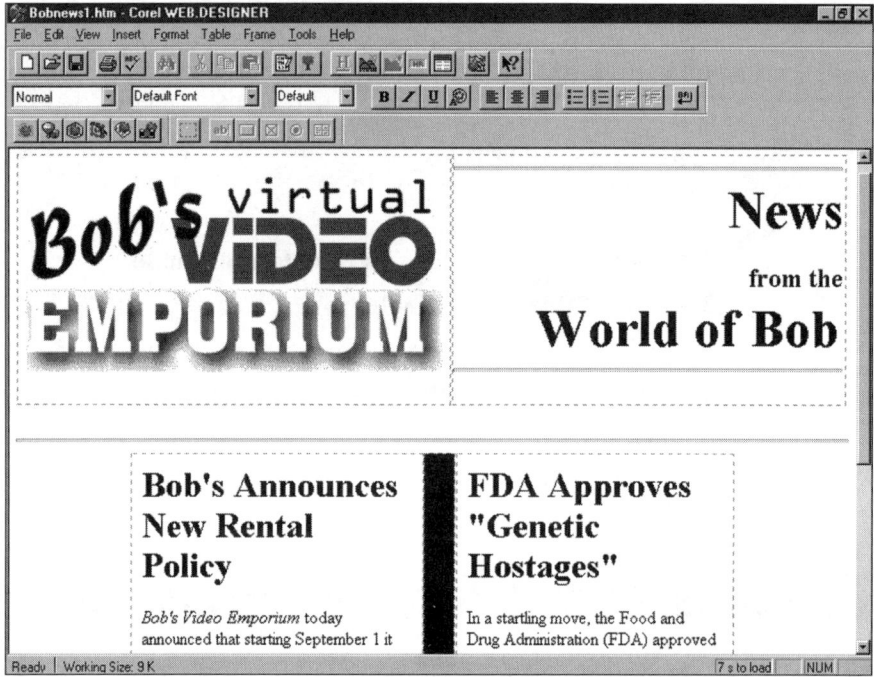

Figure 8-11:
Dashed
lines show
the two
tables in
this page.

Here are the technical specs on the columns shown in these figures:

- The top table is made up of two columns in one row. I inserted Bob's logo in the left cell, and the text with horizontal rules above and below it in the right. I formatted the left cell with left horizontal alignment and middle vertical alignment. I set the right cell for right horizontal alignment and top vertical alignment. I made no width adjustments to either cell.

- The bottom table contains three columns, and is set to 75 percent width and center alignment with 10-pixel cell padding. The two outside columns are 49 percent wide, and the middle column is only 2 percent wide. (Remember that the columns need to add up to 100 percent, not 75 percent.) Both outside columns are formatted for left horizontal alignment and top vertical alignment. I colored the middle column to create a vertical line between the stories.

Cell spanning is an effective way to create headlines and figures that stretch across multiple columns of text. Figure 8-12 shows an example of each.

Figure 8-12:
This
DESIGNER
view shows
spanning
cells
containing
graphics
and text.

Use a table to create a button bar. Adding graphic or text hyperlinks in separate cells of a single-row table ensures that the cells stay lined up and don't wrap around in your visitors' browsers.

Chapter 9

I Frame, I Saw, I Conquered

• •

• •

I've said this about tables, I've said it about image maps, and now I'm saying it about frames: Frames are the most useful and powerful design tool at your disposal.

I'm not being wishy-washy or anything like that. All three tools are amazingly powerful and useful. (And when you combine them, you can make some really kickin' Web sites!)

And a Frame Is . . . ?

Frames split the browsing window into a bunch of mini-browsers that enable visitors to view multiple pages on your site at once. You can format each frame differently, have each display different information, or use them as navigation aids for your visitors. Frames can also save you time while you're producing your site, because if you have an item that you want to show up on your Web site *all the time,* you can put it in a frame that doesn't change. That way, you don't have to place it in every page of your site. Figure 9-1 shows a framed page (also called a *frame set*).

The power of frames doesn't come solely from their ability to help you lay out a page (you can use tables for that!), nor from their ability to show more than one page at a time. No, the truly cool thing about frames is that they provide you with new ways to present your page.

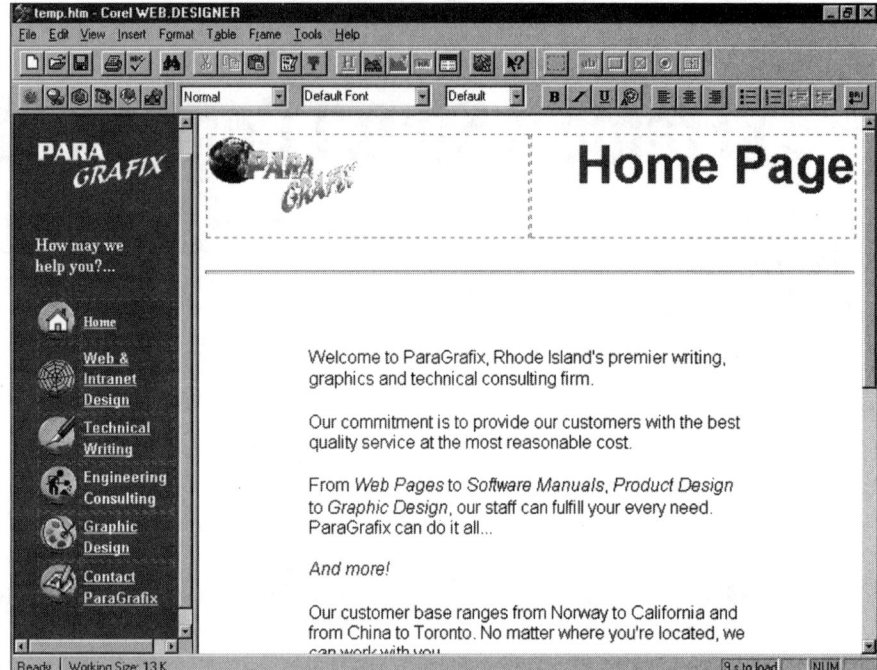

Figure 9-1:
A typical
framed
page.

Frame sets are made up of two parts: The *main page* defines your frame set (how big your frames are and where they're located), and the *subpages* show the information you actually want to display. Each subpage is actually a completely independent Web page — there's nothing special about subpages; you can create them exactly the same way you create any other Web page.

One of the most useful things about frame sets is that they allow your links to work independently of the frame that they're in. You can have a table of contents in one frame, where clicking an entry changes what page you see in a larger frame. You can also have the table of contents page change to show more entries. The choice is yours.

Working with frames may sound complicated, but DESIGNER makes it just as easy as editing any other Web page. Even if you're a novice Webmaster, you won't find anything difficult or complicated about working with frames. After you read the tips and techniques in this chapter, you'll be churning out framed sites like a pro.

At the risk of sounding like a computer nerd, you may want to familiarize yourself with some frame terminology (see Figure 9-2):

Row frame

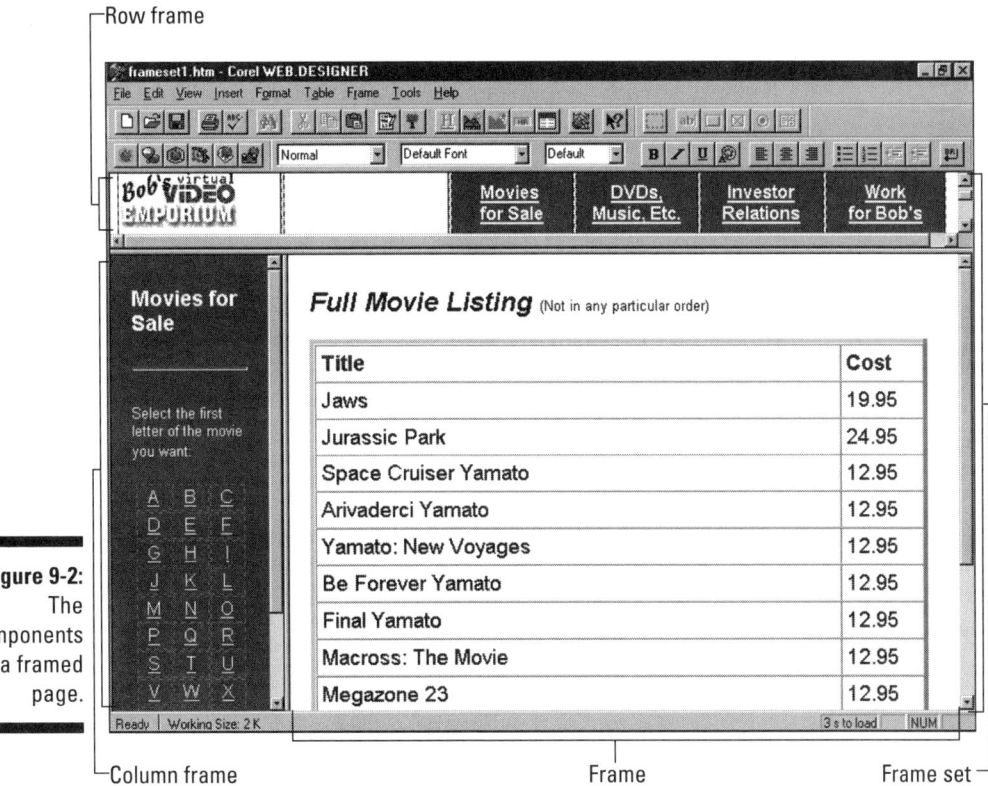

Figure 9-2: The components of a framed page.

Column frame   Frame   Frame set

- ✔ **Frame:** The area inside a framed page that displays a Web page.

- ✔ **Frame set:** A group of pages arranged in a frame. This also refers to the HTML page that you use to define the layout of the frames.

- ✔ **Column frame:** A vertical frame — one of two or more frames side by side.

- ✔ **Row frame:** A horizontal frame — one of two or more frames arranged one on top of the other.

As with all of the best Web innovations, frames are not supported by older browsers. Luckily, you can find ways around this roadblock (for example, in the section, "The Frameless Page").

The Frames Wizard Is Your Friend

The Frames Wizard makes creating a framed page a straightforward affair. Just start the Wizard, answer a couple of quick questions, click OK, and start editing.

1. **Start DESIGNER and select Start a New Web Page With Frames from the Welcome screen.**

   If you're already working in DESIGNER, choose File⇨New with Frames.

   The Frames Wizard dialog box appears.

2. **Type a name for your main page in the Filename of Frame Layout Document text box.**

   Unfortunately, this text box doesn't give you any help in naming your file. Type in your name using the normal Web-page filing conventions outlined in Chapter 1 — that is, don't include spaces and add the .htm extension to the end.

3. **Click Next.**

   The Wizard dialog box now displays a list of premade frame sets (see Figure 9-3).

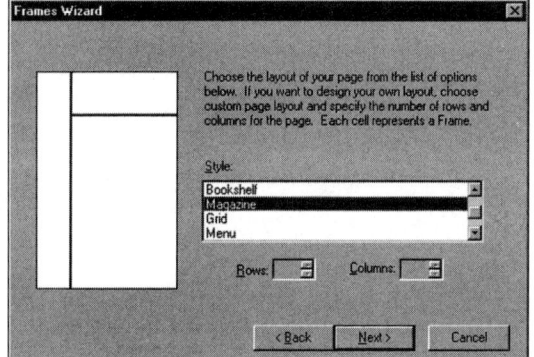

Figure 9-3:
Select a
frame style.

4. **Choose a layout style for your frames.**

   You can choose from one of eight layouts or create a custom grid with as many rows and columns as you want. If you choose to make a custom grid, set the number of rows and columns in the aptly named Rows and Columns text boxes. Whatever choice you make (including custom settings) is displayed in the preview window in the left side of the dialog box.

5. **Click Next.**

   The dialog box now displays a preview of your frame-set layout and two radio buttons.

6. Select the Next or Finish radio button.

- If you want more control over the setup of your page, or if you have some existing pages you want to include as frames, select the Next radio button and then click Next. A preview of your page appears (see Figure 9-4). Now continue on with the remaining steps.

- If you want the Wizard to create new, blank pages for you to fill, select the Finish radio button and then click Finish (when you select the Finish radio button, the Next button changes to Finish). You're done! Your framed page appears in DESIGNER, ready for you to begin adding and editing information. Note that you'll have to enter some information about your frame set when you return to DESIGNER. You can find out how to do this in the section, "Naming frames," later in this chapter.

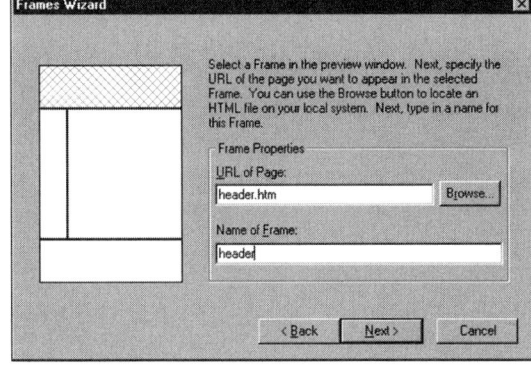

Figure 9-4:
A preview
of your
framed
page.

7. Click a frame in the preview window and specify information about it in the Frame Properties section.

- Supply a Web page filename in the URL of Page text box. The page you specify here is the actual Web page that will be displayed in this frame of your frame set. If you enter the name of a page that doesn't exist in your Web root folder (the folder that contains your Web site's home page), then a new page with that name is created in a new folder called frameset# (where the pound sign is replaced by 1, 2, 3, and so on, depending on how many frame sets you've created in your site). If, however, you want to include an existing page in this frame, type its filename or click Browse and locate the page in your site.

- Name the frame itself in the Name of Frame text box. Because each frame is like a minibrowser and can display different Web pages, each frame needs a name that's independent of the filename that's originally displayed in it. Each frame name is required when you link between pages, which is explained in the next section "Hyperlinks and Frames."

8. **Repeat Step 7 for each frame shown in the preview window.**

   The Wizard generally includes a table of contents frame called, by default, index.htm. If you've named your framed page index.htm (so you can use it as your default page), make sure that you specify a different filename for the table of contents frame. Otherwise, the results can be really messy! I suggest naming it toc.htm (for Table Of Contents).

9. **Click <u>N</u>ext.**

   The Wizard again displays a preview of your frame set, except this time, you see a bunch of radio buttons, check boxes, and text boxes that you can use to specify more information about your individual frames.

10. **Click a frame in the preview window and specify more information about it.**

    - **<u>S</u>crolling:** Determines whether you want scroll bars in the frame. By default, this option is set to Auto, which means that if the information in the frame is too large to show at once, scroll bars automatically appear. Yes and No force the page to have, or not have, scroll bars. If you choose No, and the frame is too small to show all the information at once, your visitors won't be able to scroll to see the entire contents of the frame.

    - **Bo<u>r</u>der:** Adds a small, raised-looking border between each frame. This option controls all the frames in your page, no matter which frame happens to be highlighted in the preview window. You can't make a border between some frames and not others.

    - **Resi<u>z</u>able:** Means that your visitors can drag your frame borders and make individual frames larger or smaller.

    - **Margin <u>H</u>eight and Margin <u>W</u>idth:** Lets you form a blank border inside a frame to prevent your page from getting too cluttered (not all browsers can handle margins, so be careful when using them).

    If you don't know what to choose for an option to set, just leave it. You can return and set all these options later, as described in "Formatting Your Frames," later in this chapter.

11. **Click <u>F</u>inish.**

    The dialog box closes, and your new, framed page appears in DESIGNER, ready for you to add information. If you used existing pages for each frame, you're all done!

Hyperlinks and Frames

Hyperlinks in framed pages work just the way they do in a normal page — to a point. When you click a link in a frame, the page you want appears just as it normally would, but *where* it appears is another matter.

You have complete control over where a new page appears in your framed page. You can display it in the frame you just clicked, or in another frame altogether. You can remove all the frames and have the page appear in the browser all by itself, or you can even start a whole new copy of your visitor's browser and display the page there.

Figure 9-5 shows a frame-based page that uses two different sets of links to let visitors pick the information they want to see.

Linking is where naming your frames comes into play. Any named frame can be the *target* of a hyperlink. The only thing you have to do is specify which frame you want to use as you create the hyperlink. You specify the target frame in the Target drop-down lists of the HyperLink Properties dialog box and Image Map Editor dialog box — these options are the same in both dialog boxes. The Target list contains all the named frames in your frame set, along with these special targets:

Links to Table of Contents frame

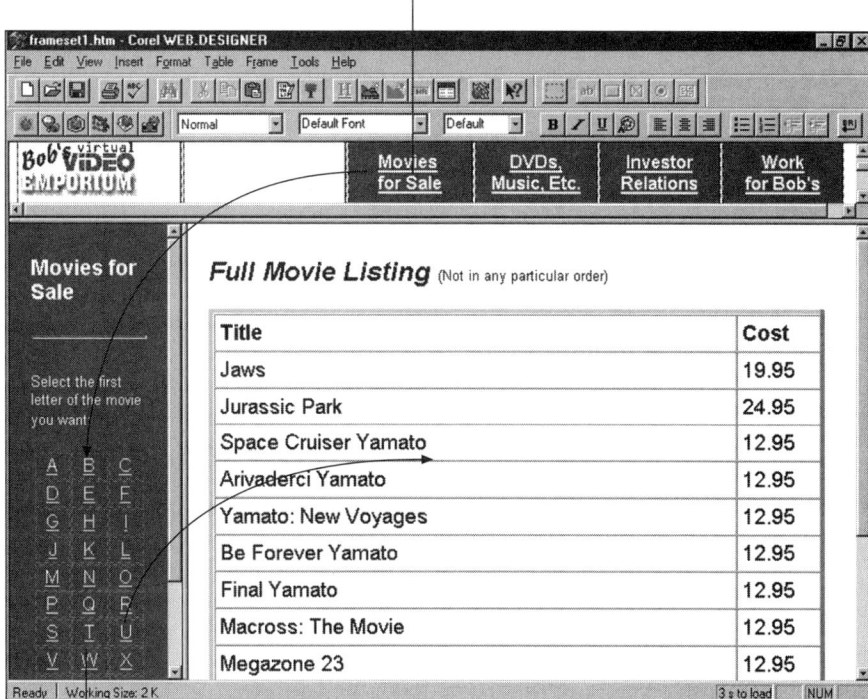

Figure 9-5:
A page
being
edited in
DESIGNER.

Links to body frame

✔ **_blank:** Opens a second copy of your visitor's browser for displaying the linked page. I suggest that you don't use this option as each new browser that your visitors open reduces their computers' performance and can make them frustrated with your site.

✔ **_parent:** When you use nested frames, use this target in links inside the inner page, so that the linked page fills the entire parent frame.

One neat thing about framed pages is that you can display framed pages *inside* another frame. This concept is very similar to the nested tables, discussed in Chapter 8. The frame holding the page is called the *parent frame.* Using nested frames gives you a great deal of control over the layout and usability of the site.

✔ **_self:** The linked page opens in the same frame as the link. (If you don't specify a target frame, this happens anyway.)

✔ **_top:** The linked page replaces the whole frame set. If you're linking to an external Web page (one that's not inside your own Web site) you generally want to use this option.

If you can't remember the name of a frame, right-click anywhere inside the frame and select Properties from the pop-up menu. The Frame Properties dialog box appears and displays the name for you.

Formatting Your Frames

After you create a frame set, you're ready to fill it with text and graphics, and to format it so that it looks and acts just the way you want it to — all the same stuff you do with a regular page. This section details the main formatting options you have for your framed page.

Changing the page that's loaded in a frame

As you update and change your site, you may want to change the page that's automatically loaded in a frame. To do so, follow these steps:

1. **Click inside the frame you want to change.**

2. **Choose Frame⇨Properties.**

   The Frame Properties dialog box appears.

3. **Type the filename of the page you want to edit in the URL of Page text box.**

   You can also click Browse and select the page from a standard Windows file open dialog box.

4. **Click OK.**

The dialog box closes, and the page you selected is now displayed in the frame.

Naming frames

You name frames so that your visitors' browsers can identify them when they are trying to load information into a frame. If you don't have any frame names, any link that your visitors click displays the new page in the same frame where they clicked, rather than in its own frame. This result isn't necessarily bad, but it does crimp your style.

If you went through the full Frames Wizard and didn't click Finish midway through, you were asked to name each frame in your page. If you did stop midway through the steps or if you didn't avail yourself of the opportunity, here's your chance to name your frames:

1. **Start DESIGNER and load the frame set whose frames you want to name.**

2. **Click anywhere within the frame you want to name.**

3. **Choose Frame⇨Properties.**

The Frame Properties dialog box appears.

4. **Type a name for the frame in the Name of Frame text box.**

Name the frame something memorable. When you create hyperlinks that lead to this frame, you need to recognize the name of the frame. For example, say you have a page with three frames: one that acts like a heading, another that acts like a table of contents, and a third one that contains the main body text. You may want to name these frames header, contents, and body, or any other name that you find easy to remember.

5. **Click OK.**

The dialog box closes, and you return to DESIGNER. Your page *looks* exactly the same, but now that you've named your frame, you can add a link using this frame as a target.

Resizing frames

The size you want a frame to be depends primarily on what you're putting in it. Say you have a table of contents frame that just provides the major categories of your Web site. This frame may be fairly small. Your main body frame, however, may be fairly large. You can tweak the sizes of your frames a number of ways.

You can set your frame size from the Frame Properties dialog box:

1. **Click anywhere within the frame you want to resize.**

2. **Choose Frame⇨Properties.**

   The Frame Properties dialog box appears.

3. **Click the Custom radio button.**

   The text box next to it and the in Pixels and in Percent radio buttons are no longer grayed.

4. **Select the in Pixels or the in Percent radio button.**

   This choice determines whether you specify the height or width of your frame in pixels or as a percentage of the window's height or width.

5. **Type the size you want for your frame in the Custom text box.**

6. **Click OK.**

   The dialog box closes, and your frame becomes the size you specified.

You can also resize a frame by simply grabbing the frame border and dragging it to the new size. By default, frame size is set as a percent of the browser's window, but if you want to drag your frame to an exact size regardless of the size of the browser window, open the frame properties dialog box and click the in Pixels radio button. Now, when you drag the border, you set the exact frame size.

"Borders? We don't need no stinkin' borders."

Borders define the edges of your frames. But, as with tables, you may not want to have borders around your frames so that your frame set has a more unified look. Unlike tables, however, frames automatically have borders; so if you don't want borders around them, you have to remove them yourself.

To remove the border from your frames, open the Frame Properties dialog box and deselect the Border check box. If you decide that you want the border back, just return to the Frame Properties dialog box and reselect the Border check box.

Note: WebMaster's frame formatting options use Netscape Navigator HTML codes. Microsoft Internet Explorer uses slightly different HTML codes to format the borders around frames, so removing the borders by using the Frame Properties dialog box has no effect when the frame set is viewed with Internet Explorer. To remove the borders for folks viewing your page in Internet Explorer, you have to do some old-fashioned hand coding. Chapter 13 shows you how to add the necessary codes to remove borders.

The Frameless Page

As I noted at the beginning of this chapter, not all browsers support frames. You have two options for letting people who use one of these dinosaurs see your site:

- ✔ Create a second Web site that doesn't include frames at all.

- ✔ Create your body pages so that they look okay in either a frame-enabled or frame-challenged browser. To do so, you must include all the same links in your pages that visitors could use if they were viewing the site with frames. (This option can often be the easier of the two.)

Browsers that can't deal with frames probably can't deal with tables, image maps, and all the other high-tech stuff you've included in your site, either. If you create a frameless site just for folks with these old-time browsers, consider leaving these other elements out as well.

Hidden in your main frame page is a page that is only visible to people who don't have frame-capable browsers — the No Frames Page. People who visit your page with frames-capable browsers don't see this page at all, but a technologically challenged visitor does. This page helps your browser-challenged visitors by allowing them access to the page, even though they don't have frame capabilities. This page is also great for people who reach your site from a link because you can include a link to your nonframe site.

You may be asking "Why would I want to create a second frameless site or format all the pages in my site so that they will work even if they're not displayed in a frame?" Good question. The answer is really straightforward: The No Frames Page is only a single page, not an entire site. If you just let the No Frames Page be available for your browser-impaired visitors, their access to your site is going to be severly limited.

To edit the No Frames Page:

1. **Open your framed page in DESIGNER.**

2. **Choose View⇨No Frames Page.**

   A page opens in DESIGNER. If you haven't edited the page before, the message `This web browser does not support frames` appears. (The next time you open the View menu, the No Frames Page item isn't checked.)

3. **Edit the page as you normally would.**

   Remember that you can't add frames to this page. After all, that's the whole point.

4. When you finish editing your No Frames Page, choose <u>V</u>iew⇨ No Frames Page again.

Doing so closes the No Frames Page and returns you to your framed page.

Not everybody who has a frame-capable browser wants to view your site with frames — as I note earlier in this chapter, a site with frames also generally has other advanced Web features that take longer to download. Often, your visitors will want to view your site quickly without taking advantages of these advanced features. An easy way to give people the option of which version of your site they want to visit is to make your home page (default.htm, or index.htm) a small introduction to your site with two hyper-links: one leading to the framed version, and the other leading to the version with no frames. Two things to keep in mind if you decide to go this route:

✔ Include a link that takes visitors from your framed site to your home page. Include this link somewhere in one of the frames that opens with your frame set. This is important in case someone arrives at the framed page via a link from somewhere else, and not via your home page.

  Make sure that this link loads the new page in the main browser window, not in a frame. Otherwise, you've defeated the purpose of having a frameless version of your site. The section "Hyperlinks and Frames," earlier in this chapter, explains how to do this.

✔ Include a link to your nonframe site in the No Frames Page or make the No Frames Page a duplicate of the nonframe home page. Doing so ensures that visitors using browsers that can't recognize frames can still reach your nonframed site, even if they happen to use a link to your framed page.

You need to keep both versions of your site updated because you want to give all visitors access to the same up-to-date information.

Adding and Deleting Frames

After you create a framed page, you're not stuck with the layout you origi-nally created. If you need more frames, or if you want to get rid of some, DESIGNER is at your service.

You can add a frame in three different ways: Add a column frame, add a row frame, or split a frame. Which method you use depends on what you want to do.

✔ Adding a row frame creates two horizontal frames, of which the bottom is new.

✔ Adding a column frame creates two vertical frames, of which the right one is new.

✔ Splitting a frame creates a row or column frame, depending on where the cursor is when you split it. If the cursor is in a column frame, you get a new column frame. If it's in a row frame, you get a new row frame.

To add a row frame:

1. Click inside the frame where you want to add a frame.

2. Choose Frame➪Insert Row Frame.

The current frame shrinks to half its height, and a new frame appears directly below it.

To add a column frame:

1. Click inside the frame where you want to add a frame.

2. Choose Frame➪Insert Column Frame.

The current frame shrinks to half its width, and a new frame appears directly to its right.

To split a frame:

1. Click inside the frame you want to split.

2. Choose Frame➪Split Frame.

Depending on where you clicked, a new row or column frame is added. If you split a column frame, you now have *two* column frames. If you split a row frame, you now have *two* row frames.

If you have a page with no frames and you want to split it into two frames, you must create a new framed page that incorporates your original page. Before you do this, rename your existing page. (You can rename the page by saving it with a new filename using the File➪Save As command in DESIGNER, or by renaming the file in SiteManager.) If you use SiteManager to rename the file, as explained in Chapter 3, *don't let Link Wizard update any links;* otherwise, any pages that you want to link to the framed page now links to the unframed page.) Now, create a new page with frames, using the page's old name. Any links to the old page now go to your new framed page. Also include the old page's new filename as one of the frames so that it will automatically appear in that frame.

To delete a frame:

1. Click inside the frame you want to delete.

2. Choose Frame⇨Delete Frame.

The frame is gone. If it was a column frame, the frames next to it expand to take up the lost space. If it was a row frame, the frames above and/or below it expand to take up the space it vacated.

Chapter 10

Forms and Functions

● ●

In This Chapter

▶ Creating an Internet form

▶ Adding buttons, text fields, and menus to a form

▶ Getting information from a form

▶ Making your form look good

● ●

*O*nline ordering, guest lists, service requests — you can handle all these and more on your Web pages. Nearly every other section of this book deals with how to provide information to your site's visitors, but this chapter shows you how to get information from them.

Forming an Understanding of Forms

As the name implies, a *form* is a part of a page where your visitors fill in information (see Figure 10-1). What your site does with the information is up to you. If you used a search engine (such as Yahoo! or Lycos), you've used a form.

Typically, when visitors use a form, they input information or make selections from menus and then click a Submit button. The information is then sent to a program called a Common Gateway Interface (CGI) script, for processing. The CGI may create and send an e-mail message or look up information in a database and display the results. The uses for forms are almost endless.

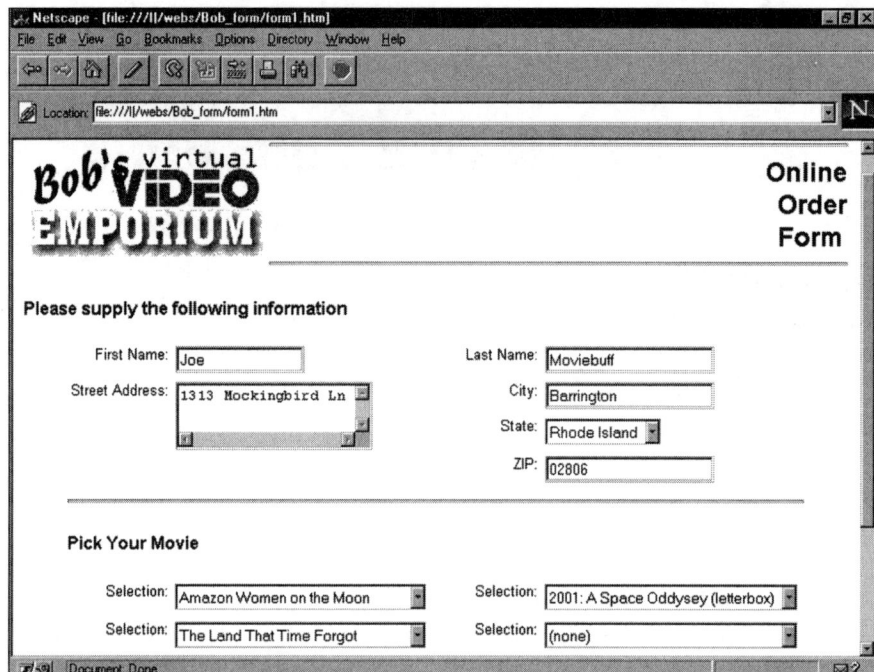

Figure 10-1:
A typical
Internet
form.

What to Do with All That Information

After a visitor to your Web site fills out all the text boxes, clicks the check boxes and radio buttons, and makes selections from lists and menus, what the heck do you do with all the information? You let a program — specifically, CGI script — deal with the information for you.

You have to know what kind of information the CGI script needs from your form before you can put the form together. After all, you wouldn't start to build a bridge before you knew how far it had to go, would you?

One of the shortcomings of WebMaster Suite is that it doesn't come with any premade CGI scripts that you can use on your Web site (with a few exceptions, which I list in the sidebar "PageDepot does your scripting for you"). This dearth of CGI scripts isn't Corel's fault, though. Scripts are generally machine-specific, and so many types of computers are running Web server software, that to include CGI scripts would make things pretty confusing.

Your Internet service provider (ISP) or Webmaster may talk about Perl instead of CGI. Perl is a standardized form of CGI that a great number of different types of computers can understand. As long as you know what the script needs from your form, you really don't have to know whether it's a CGI or Perl script.

You have four options when you want to include forms in your pages:

- ✔ **Write CGI scripts yourself.** Avoid this option, if at all possible — that is, unless you enjoy programming and don't mind driving yourself crazy.

- ✔ **Hire someone else to create custom CGI scripts for you.** This is an excellent option, but pricey.

- ✔ **Use the CGI scripts that are already loaded on your server.** If you sent your ISP or Webmaster the tear-out Cheat Sheet at the beginning of this book before you began working on your site, you should already know what scripts your server has available. If you didn't, now is a great time to send it. Chapter 4 details all the questions that are asked on this form.

- ✔ **Ask your ISP or Webmaster to copy some CGI scripts from the Web and install them on the server.** Using copied scripts is usually your best option, unless you need something really customized. Tons of Web sites have premade CGI scripts that do just about anything you could possibly want. You just have to talk your Webmaster or ISP administrator into copying these files to your server's CGI bin directory.

A ton of people have written CGI scripts and made them available for little or no charge to anyone who visits their sites. One of these people, Matt Wright, has created a whole slew of great (and free!) CGI scripts that you can use, assuming that your server administrator agrees to add them to your server. One of Matt's CGI scripts that I think you'll find particularly useful is FormMail. FormMail takes the contents of a form and e-mails it to you — this is a quick and easy way to get information from your site's visitors. Point your browser to `www.worldwidemart.com/scripts` to see Matt's collection.

After you know what CGI script you'll be using, you can get down to business. Usually, you receive a little technical manual with the script, explaining all the form fields you can use and how you can use them. Unfortunately, these manuals almost always list the specifications for a field in raw HTML code. Like this:

```
<INPUT TYPE="field_type" NAME="field_name">
```

What the heck are you supposed to do with this stuff? The name inside the quotations is the name that you have to give your text box, check box, and so on. The type is the type of form field that you use.

If a field has any restrictions (for example, a text box can't have a maximum length of more than 30 characters), the specifications tell you so.

PageDepot does your scripting for you

PageDepot is a company that makes its money by storing your Web pages for a fee and making them available over the Web (called *hosting*). If you publish your site to PageDepot (see Chapter 18 for more information), you're at a slight advantage. PageDepot supplies a couple of premade forms that link straight to their CGI scripts. You can choose from an e-mail form, a guest book, or a site search.

After you add a PageDepot form to your page and uploaded it to your site, PageDepot automatically creates any extras that your site may need. For example, if you select a guest book, it creates the actual guest book that your visitors' comments go into. You don't have to do any of the insanely difficult programming yourself.

To include any of these features in your site:

1. **Place the cursor where you want the PageDepot form.**

2. **Choose Insert➪CGI Script.**

   The Insert CGI Script dialog box appears.

3. **Select the PageDepot Script radio button.**

   Almost everything in the dialog box is grayed — your choices are very limited.

4. **Click OK.**

   The PageDepot Scripts dialog box appears.

5. **Select the type of form you want.**

   Choose from Email, Guest Book, or Site Search.

6. **Click OK.**

   The form is inserted into your page.

7. **Format the form.**

   You can change the layout, typefaces, and so on, but do not change the names or add or delete any of the form fields; otherwise, the form won't work!

8. **Upload, or update, your site.**

   You're all done.

Creating a Form

WebMaster Suite makes creating a form extremely easy. All you have to do is make a *container* for your form, and then add the items that your visitors will use. Each individual item in your form (each bullet, text field, and so on) is called a form *field*.

Making a form

The first step in making a form is to add a container to your page to hold the form. No, this container isn't a plastic jug that you stick all your form fields into and shove on the top shelf of the fridge — a *form container* defines the location on your page where you can place form fields. Even though, while you're editing your form in DESIGNER, the form container looks like a dashed outline, your visitors won't see the outline or even be aware that a container is there at all.

Creating the form container is really just like pulling out a piece of paper to create a form by hand. To add a form container to your page:

1. Start DESIGNER and load an existing page or create a new one.

2. Place the cursor where you want to make your form.

3. Choose Insert⇨Form or click the Insert Form button on the Forms toolbar.

The Form Properties dialog box appears (see Figure 10-2). If the Forms toolbar doesn't show up on your screen, display it by choosing View⇨Forms Toolbar.

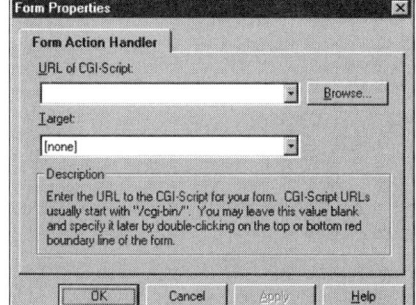

Figure 10-2: The Form Properties dialog box.

4. Type the location and name of the CGI script that will handle your form's data in the URL of CGI-Script text box.

The CGI script is described in the earlier section, "What to Do with All That Information." If you don't know the name and location of the CGI script, leave this blank, and you can change it later.

5. If you're using frames, pick the target frame for the confirmation page from the Target drop-down list.

This choice determines which frame of your frame set displays the confirmation page.

6. Click OK.

A dashed red rectangle appears in your page. This rectangle is the form container (see Figure 10-3). Every form field (button, text field, and so on) that you add to your form goes in this container.

Form container

Figure 10-3:
The Form
container
holds all
your form
fields.

If you want to go back and change the CGI script or the target frame for your confirmation page:

1. Double-click the top or bottom dashed line.

The Form Properties dialog box appears. (Note that double-clicking the form container outline is the *only* way to open this dialog box.)

2. Make your changes to the existing settings.

3. Click OK.

Filling out a form

Now that you have a form container, what do you do with it? You fill it, of course. The next few sections tell how to add form fields.

Remember that your visitors won't know what to do with a form field unless you tell them. Make sure that you include some text around each form field that tells the visitors what the field for, what kind of data you expect them to put in it, and whether they have to deal with this field at all.

You don't have a lot of control over how your visitors' browsers display your form. To help keep your form looking neat and orderly, I suggest that you put your form fields in the cells of a table and follow the advice I give in the Chapter 8 section, "Columns Aren't Just for Greece Anymore."

Adding text fields

Text fields are where you get most of your information in a form: your visitors' names, where they live, what problems they're having, why they are wearing bell-bottom pants, that sort of thing. As the name implies, text fields require that your visitors type some text.

Not all text fields are alike, however. And each different style has its own particular uses (see Figure 10-4):

- ✔ **Single Line:** As the name implies, this field provides just a single line in which your visitors can type.

- ✔ **Multi Line:** This is getting too easy. Obviously a multiline text field gives your visitors more room to type information.

- ✔ **Password Field:** You knew the simplicity had to end. Yes, a password field is where your visitors type a password, but it's also where they type any other information that's confidential, such as a credit card number.

Beware that a password field does not encrypt data. It just masks your visitors' input from prying eyes in the same room. You need to add security measures outside of your form. The tear-out Cheat Sheet at the beginning of this book includes a space for your server administrator to list basic information about the security systems available to you. For more information about these systems, contact your ISP or Webmaster.

Single-line text field   Multiline text field   Password field

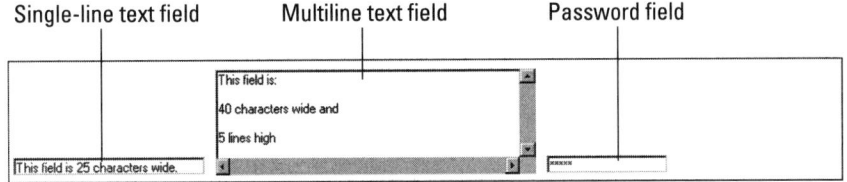

Figure 10-4:
The three
types of text
fields.

To add any one of the text fields:

1. Place the cursor where you want the text field to go.

Remember that a text field can only be placed inside a form container (the red outline).

2. Choose Insert⇨Form Field⇨Text Field.

A default sized text field appears.

3. Double-click the text box or choose Edit⇨Properties.

The Text Field Properties dialog box appears.

4. Type a name for the field in the Name dialog box.

The field name can't include any spaces, and it must correspond to a name in the CGI script that will handle the form's input. There's more about CGI scripts in the earlier section, "What to Do with All That Information."

5. Click the appropriate radio button to pick the type of text field you want.

You can choose from a single line, multiline, or password text field in the Type area.

6. Specify the size of the text box in the Size area.

This area changes according to the type of text field you picked in Step 5. You don't have to specify any values here. If you don't, your visitors' browsers use their default values. Because default values can vary from browser to browser, I suggest setting the values so that you retain control over the look of your form.

- **Single Line:** Set the Field Width and Maximum Length, both of which state the size in number of characters (letters or numbers). So, setting Field Width to 10 means that the text field will be as wide as 10 letters. Unfortunately, this approach isn't very exact because each letter is a different width, but it's a weird Web thing. The Maximum Length setting specifies how many total characters your visitors can type into the field. When they reach the maximum number, they can't type any more text into the field.

- **Multi Line:** Field Width remains (and works exactly the same), but Maximum Length is replaced with Number of Lines. The Number of Lines setting specifies the number of visible lines that are available to type in. Your visitors can type as much as they want, though, and the scroll bars on the side and bottom of the field let them view all that they have written.

- **Password Field:** The Field Width and Maximum Length settings are available and work the same as they did for a Single Line text field.

7. Type an initial value for the field.

This step is optional, but including an initial value for a field can make the form easier to work with. The initial value text automatically appears in the text box when your visitors first get to the page. You might include what you think will be the most common response; for example, if your site has to do with medical equipment, you might have the initial value for a field named occupation be Physician.

8. Click OK.

The dialog box closes, and the text field is updated to reflect the changes you've made.

To go back and make changes to your text field, follow Steps 3 through 8 above.

What's on the menu?

Lists and menus work together to give your visitors a range of stuff to choose from. This is ideal when you don't want them to go off on a wild tangent as they try and explain what they want. If it's not on the list you give, tough! These are their choices (see Figure 10-5).

Figure 10-5:
Two different types of lists: Menu field (on the left) and list box (on the right).

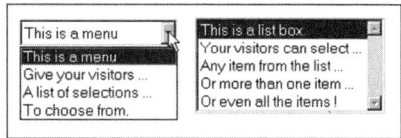

You've probably used lists and menus hundreds of times in the process of creating Web pages with WebMaster Suite. The menus and lists that you create in your forms work exactly the same way as those you use in programs like DESIGNER.

To add a list or a menu to your form:

1. Place the cursor where you want the list or menu field to go.

Remember that you can only place a list or menu field inside a form container (the red outline).

2. Choose Insert⇨Form Field⇨List/Menu or click the List/Menu button in the Forms toolbar.

A small menu field appears.

3. Double-click the menu box.

The List Properties dialog box appears.

4. **Type a name for the field in the Name text box.**

   This name can't include any spaces and must correspond to the one in the CGI script that will handle the form's input.

5. **Select the appropriate radio button to pick the type of field you want to create.**

   If you select List Box, the Height text box and Allow Multiple Selections check box become active:

   • **Height:** Lets you specify how many selections are initially visible to your visitors. If you set the height smaller than the number of items you include (see the next step), then your visitors can use the scroll bars to see more selections.

   • **Allow Multiple Selections:** Enables your visitors to select more than one item from the list. To select more than one item, they use the standard Shift+click or Ctrl+click combinations (you may want to mention these commands in text around the list). Make sure that your CGI script can handle more than one selection before you use this option.

6. **Click the Add button to create the contents for your list or menu.**

   The Add Item dialog box appears. Repeat Steps 6 through 10 for each item you want to appear in the menu or list.

7. **Type the text that you want your visitors to see for this item in the Item Label text box.**

   This text becomes the options that your visitors can choose from. For example, if this field gives your visitors a choice of states to choose from for their address, you enter the name of each state here.

   You may want to add a none item in your contents list and make it the initially selected item.

8. **Type the value that should be sent to the CGI script in the Value text box.**

   Using the state example again, if you don't want the full name of the state to be sent to the CGI script, you can set the value to its standard abbreviation (such as RI for Rhode Island).

9. **If you want this item to be the default selection, check the Initially Selected check box.**

   In a menu, you can only set one item as initially selected. In a list, however, you can have as many items as you want, as long as your CGI script can handle multiple pieces of information from this field. To include multiple items in your list, select the Allow Multiple Selections check box in the List Properties dialog box.

10. Click OK.

You return to the List Properties dialog box, and the item you just entered now appears in the Contents list box.

11. Click OK.

The List Properties dialog box closes, and you return to DESIGNER.

To modify the contents of your list or menu after you've created it, follow Steps 3 through 8 above.

Adding check boxes

Check boxes enable your visitors to choose from a bunch of different options by clicking the box or boxes of the item they want. You can create a group of check boxes that all have the same name, but that contain different values so that checking different check boxes sends different information to the same CGI script item (the name of each check box in the group must correspond to the name of the CGI script item).

Keep in mind that your visitors can select more than one check box in a group at a time. If you want to give your visitors a bunch of unique choices, you may want to consider radio buttons, instead (see the next section, "Adding radio buttons").

Sometimes, you want to have only a single check box. For example, if you have a mailing list, you can have a single check box that your visitors check if they want to be added to the list.

To add a check box:

1. Place the cursor where you want the check box to go.

Remember that a check box can only be placed inside a form container (the red outline).

 2. Choose Insert⇨Form Field⇨Check Box or click the Check Box button in the Forms toolbar.

A check box appears in your form container.

3. Double-click the check box.

The Check Box Properties dialog box appears (see Figure 10-6).

4. Type a name for the field in the Name text box.

This name has to correspond to one in the CGI script that will handle the form's input. The name can't include any spaces.

5. Click the appropriate radio button to set whether you want this check box to be checked or unchecked when your visitors load the page.

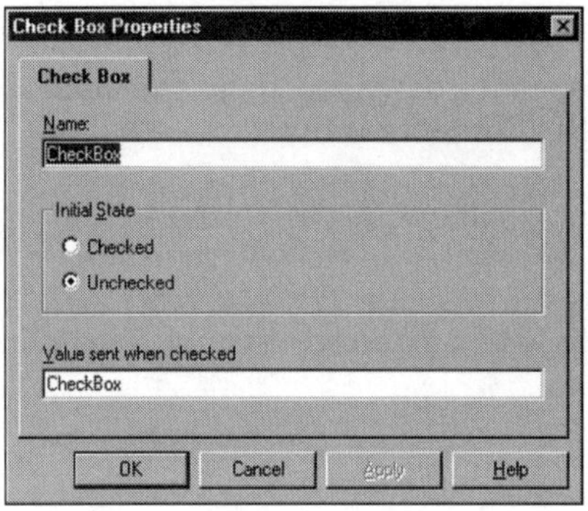

Figure 10-6:
The Check
Box
Properties
dialog box.

6. **Type a value for the check box in the Value sent when checked text box.**

   This is the data that's going to be sent to your CGI script when your visitor clicks the Submit button (see "Adding buttons," later in this chapter), and it can be anything that makes sense. For example, if you have a selection of movies that your visitors can pick from, instead of having the values be movies titles, they can be the catalog numbers.

7. **Click OK.**

8. **Add some descriptive text next to the check box so that your visitors know what the check box is for.**

As I mentioned at the beginning of this bit about check boxes, you usually want to have groups of check boxes that have the same name. Well, you don't really want to go through those seven steps to add every new check box to the group, now do you? I didn't think so. The easiest way to make a group of check boxes is to

1. **Highlight a check box that you've already formatted with the proper name.**

2. **Press Ctrl+C.**

   This copies the check box to the clipboard.

3. **Place the cursor where you want the new check box in the same group to go.**

4. **Press Ctrl+V.**

   This pastes a copy of the check box into position. You can add as many check boxes as you want by doing this.

5. Change the value of the check box.

Now that your check boxes are in position, you want to change the value of each check box so that each one sends unique information to the CGI script. Just double-click the check box to open the Check Box Properties dialog box, make whatever changes you want, and click OK.

Adding radio buttons

Radio button is probably the most oddly descriptive name in all of Webdom, when you think about it. Radio buttons are like the buttons on your car radio that each store a specific station. You can only select one of them at a time, just like a Web radio button. (I think, though, that the round shape goes back to radios from 20 years ago, not the modern square buttons you usually see on radios — but let's not quibble.)

What can you do with radio buttons? The short answer is *anything you want.* The long answer is *anything you want,* like offering a choice of two different payment options, specifying what kind of feedback a visitor wants, or asking the mundane yes-or-no question (see Figure 10-7).

Figure 10-7:
Some typical radio buttons.

How would you rate this movie?

- ○ ***** Wow! It was the best thing since sliced bread!
- ○ **** Excellent. I'd recommend it to my friends.
- ○ *** Pretty good. Definitely worth seeing in the theater.
- ◉ ** OK. If it's on HBO I might see it.
- ○ * Pretty bad. I'd only watch it if nothing else were on.
- ○ (0) Awful. Wild horses couldn't make me watch this again.

If you just want to have a single option, like click here if you want to be on our mailing list, use a check box instead of a radio button. If you only provide a single radio button, your visitors can't deselect it after it has been selected.

To add a radio button:

1. Place the cursor where you want the radio button to go.

Remember that a radio button can only be placed inside a form container (the red outline).

 2. Choose Insert⇨Form Field⇨Radio Button or click the Radio Button icon in the Forms toolbar.

A radio button appears in your form container.

3. Double-click the radio button.

The Radio Button Properties dialog box appears (see Figure 10-8).

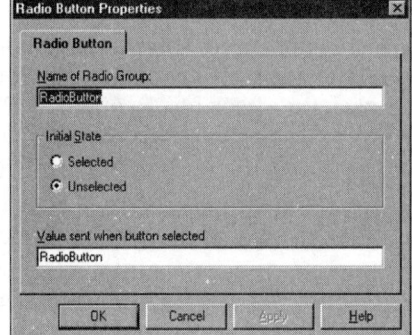

Figure 10-8:
The Radio
Button
Properties
dialog box.

4. **Type a name for the field in the <u>N</u>ame dialog box.**

   This name has to correspond to one in the CGI script that will handle the form's input. The name can't include any spaces.

5. **Click the appropriate radio button to set whether you want the radio button you're creating to be selected or unselected when your visitors load the page.**

   Because this is a radio button, the visitor can select only one button in the group. Also, you don't have to have any of the buttons in the group initially selected — that's up to you.

6. **Type a value for the radio button in the <u>V</u>alue sent when button selected text box.**

   This is the data that will be sent to your CGI script when your visitor clicks the Submit button (more about this in a couple of sections). This value doesn't have to be the text that's next to the button. For example, if you're giving your visitors a payment option (cash, check, Visa, MasterCard, Amex, and so on), each radio button's value can be a short code, rather than the whole word (such as CA, CH, V, MC, AX).

7. **Click OK.**

8. **Add descriptive text next to the button so that your visitors know what the button is for.**

You want to make groups of radio buttons that share the same name. Otherwise, you're defeating their purpose. You can go through all the preceding steps to add a radio button, change its name, and all that stuff. But to make life easier, follow the same instructions I give for creating multiple check boxes earlier in this chapter in "Adding check boxes."

Adding buttons

Now you've completed your form. All the text boxes, radio buttons, lists, and menus are just as you want them. Only two things are missing. Your visitors need to be able to say, "Okay, I'm done filling out the form. Take all my info." They also need a way to say, "Oops! I made a mistake. Let me clear this form."

Both are handled by buttons — specifically, the Submit and Reset buttons. If you think these are tough to add, you're totally wrong. If it were difficult, it wouldn't be DESIGNER.

To add a Submit or Reset button (typically, you want to add one of each):

1. **Place the cursor where you want the button to go.**

   Remember that a button can only be placed inside a form container (the red outline).

 2. **Choose Insert⇨Form Field⇨Button or click the Button icon in the Forms toolbar.**

   A button appears in your form container.

3. **Double-click the button.**

   The Button Properties dialog box appears (see Figure 10-9).

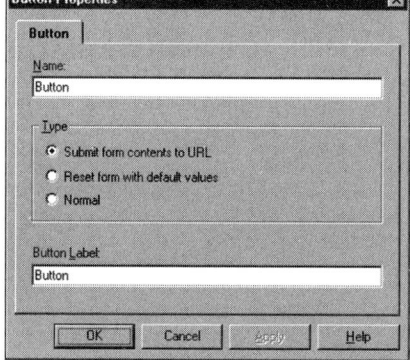

Figure 10-9:
The Button
Properties
dialog box.

4. **Type a name for the button in the Name text box.**

5. **Select the type of button that you want this one to be.**

   Choose either Submit form contents to URL or Reset form with default values — a Submit and a Reset button, respectively.

6. Type the text you want to appear on the face of the button in the Button Label text box.

Note that the size of the button depends on the text you enter as the label — the longer the text, the bigger the button.

7. Click OK.

The dialog box closes, and your button is set.

Chapter 11

Putting the Multi Back in Multimedia

For all the graphical excitement you can add to your Web pages, you may still be missing something. You want sound, motion, and maybe a trip to Europe.

People who like to debate such things had a heyday arguing over what exactly constitutes multimedia. Here's my own real-world definition: I call multimedia *any combination* of different styles of computer information. This can include sound, text, still graphics, and animation.

What does multimedia mean to you? In a nutshell, putting multimedia on your Web site means that you can include any of those things in your pages. Taken literally, my definition means that any of your Web pages that include still images are multimedia pages. But you want more multiplicity in your multimedia, right? Read on to discover how you can add sound, animation, and even nifty Java and ActiveX features to your Web site.

No More Sound of Silence

Maybe the simplest way to spice up your Web site with multimedia is to add a little music or other sound to greet your visitors.

There are two main types of sound that you can include in your Web pages: digitized sounds files and Musical Instrument Digital Interface files (or MIDI, pronounced "mid-ee"). These two types of files store music very differently:

✔ Digitized sounds — files with extensions such as .wav (pronounced "wave"), .aiff, .au, and .snd — are actual sounds that are recorded and stored on the computer so that they sound exactly like the original.

✔ MIDI files on the other hand, *simulate* music by storing the notes that are supposed to be played. The computer that plays back the sounds takes the MIDI file and uses virtual instruments stored in the sound card to create the sound that you or your visitors hear.

Each type of sound file has its own benefits: Digitized sounds produce richer, more realistic sounds, and MIDI music files are *much* smaller than their digitized counterparts. Which type of file you want to use in your Web site depends on what you want the sound to do.

Digitized files can quickly become huge and slow the speed at which your pages download. At the lowest-quality setting, a digitized file uses about 10 kilobytes per second. Using a stereo sound doubles the size of the file. If you use digitized sounds on your Web site, be sure to keep them short.

Adding sounds for Internet Explorer visitors

I just said that adding a little sound to your Web page is about the easiest way to add multimedia to your Web page, and now you're going to make me prove it, aren't you? Well, I take your challenge. The following instructions show just how easy it is to add sound to your page that plays as soon as the browser loads your page.

There's only one downside to this quick-and-dirty method: The sound only plays for visitors using Microsoft Internet Explorer — folks visiting your Web site with Netscape Navigator or another browser hear only the whir of their own computers. The next section, called "Embedding a sound," shows you how to add sound to your page that anyone with any browser can hear.

To add a background sound that only Internet Explorer visitors can hear:

1. **Open your Web page in DESIGNER as described in Chapter 1.**

2. **Choose File⇨Page Properties.**

   The Page Properties dialog box appears.

3. **Click the Browse button next to the Background Sound text box.**

   The Select a sound file dialog box appears.

4. **Select the type of sound file you want to include from the Files of type drop-down list.**

   Usually, you want to include either WAV or MIDI files.

5. **Select the sound file you want to use.**

   You may have to use the Look in drop-down list to select a drive and open folders to locate the file you want.

   You can preview (or would that be prehear?) a sound by selecting it and clicking the Play Sound File button.

6. **Click Open.**

   The Select a sound file dialog box closes, and the Page Properties dialog box reappears.

7. **Set how many times you want your sound to repeat in the Loop text box.**

   If you want the sound to repeat continuously until your visitor moves to a different Web page, check the Infinite check box.

   If you use a sound file that's a spoken greeting or any other sound that might make your visitors crazy after listening to it for a few minutes, don't check the Infinite check box.

8. **Click OK.**

   The Page Properties dialog box closes, and your sound is now a part of your Web page — ready to bring joy and happiness to all who visit your site.

   If you select a file from outside your Web site, DESIGNER informs you that it will copy that file into the Web folder. Click OK.

See? I didn't lie when I said it was easy, did I?

Embedding a sound

If you want to add a background sound that works with both Internet Explorer and Netscape Navigator, you have to embed the sound. Embedding a sound is just as easy as adding a background sound for Internet Explorer visitors. The only difference is that pages with embedded sounds display a control panel and your sound file is linked to your page, but the link is "clicked" as soon as someone loads the page.

To embed a sound file in your page:

1. **Open your Web page in DESIGNER as described in Chapter 1.**

2. Choose Insert⇨Embedded File.

The Embedded File Properties dialog box appears, as shown in Figure 11-1.

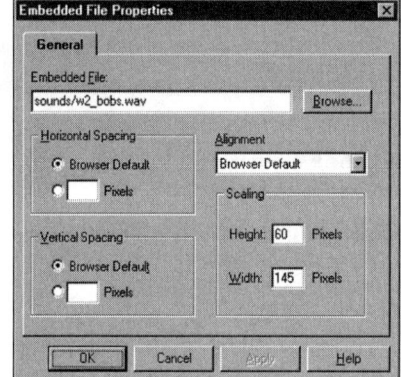

3. Type the filename and path of the sound file you want to embed in the Embedded File text box or click Browse to locate the file you want from the Select File dialog box.

You can insert a number of types of the sound files (.wav, .midi, .aiff, .au, and .snd), but WAV and MIDI are the most common.

4. Click OK to close the Embedded File Properties dialog box.

A small control panel appears on your Web page. If you stop now and don't follow the next set of instructions, your visitors can use this control panel to start and stop the sound file.

Depending on the type of file you embedded and the plug-ins that your visitors have installed (see "Plug-Ins," later in this chapter), they may see something different in their browsers. Because these controls can look different depending on your visitors' computers, don't count on them as design elements.

You can remove the control panel from your page to make the embedded sound indistinguishable (to your visitors) from the background sound that's available to Internet Explorer users — but that requires a little mucking about in the HTML source file for your Web page. The next section, "Sending your embedded sound to the background," explains how to edit the code for your embedded sound.

Sending your embedded sound to the background

Embedding a sound is easy, but now comes the interesting part: updating your HTML code to hide the sound control and turn your sound file into a little beasty that plays on its own.

Chapter 13 provides the instructions for changing HTML codes within your Web pages. The code that tells a browser to play your sound file looks like:

```
<EMBED SRC="filename" WIDTH="145" HEIGHT="60">
```

Note that the filename and path of your sound will replace "filename" in the preceding line of code.

To hide the small sound control panel and start the sound as soon as your page is loaded, insert the following text (including the quotation marks) to this line, right before the greater-than sign (>):

```
HIDDEN="true" AUTOSTART="true" LOOP="n"
```

The line should now read:

```
<EMBED SRC="filename" WIDTH="145" HEIGHT="60"
             HIDDEN="true"AUTOSTART="true" LOOP="n">
```

If you want the sound to repeat, change the n after LOOP to one of the following:

- ✓ **A number:** Replace the n with the number of times you want the sound to repeat when visitors view your page with Netscape Navigator. Unfortunately, this control tells Internet Explorer to repeat the sound forever (the same effect as TRUE, which I explain next).

- ✓ **The word** TRUE: This makes the sound continue repeating until your visitors move on to another page.

You can find a bunch of WAV and MIDI files on the WebMaster Suite CD#2. The majority of these files are in the \Webworld\Sounds\Wav, and \Webworld\Sounds\Midi folders. Others are in individual folders within the \Webworld\Samples folder.

Major download time alert! All the recorded music formats I previously mention (that is, everything except MIDI files) are huge bandwidth hogs. Some of the sound files on CD #2 are over $1^1/_4$ megabytes! I don't know about you, but I wouldn't wait the 15 minutes or so for the music to download even if the Web site were really fantastic. Keep your recorded sound files short and make them worth the wait.

Beyond GIF Animations: Video Rocks

Chapter 16 introduces MOVE, the animation program that comes with WebMaster Suite. With MOVE, you can create *GIF animations:* spiffy little GIF images that seem to move by changing the image that's displayed every few one-hundredths of a second. These little images look nice and can add simple spice to your Web pages, but to really make your Web pages come alive with motion, you need motion *and* sound. You need *video*.

Video files come in many different forms, including Apple QuickTime Movies (.mov), Microsoft Video for Windows (.avi), Motion Picture Expert Group (.mpg, also called MPEG or "Em-Peg"), and Macromedia Director Movies (.dir). Fortunately, the vast majority of computers out there can display QuickTime and Video for Windows (also just called *AVI*) movies, so you're best off sticking with these formats when you add video to your Web pages. Another good thing about these file types is that you can open them in PhotoPaint, which I discuss in the section, "Linked video: saving your visitors from 'hourglass hell, later in this chapter.

Embedded video brings Web pages to life

How your visitors view an embedded video file depends on what browser they're using. In Microsoft Internet Explorer, the video has a little toolbar at the bottom that lets your visitors control playback. Netscape Navigator just shows the first frame, and your visitors have to click the video to make it play (see Figure 11-2).

To embed a video file in your Web page, follow the same instructions detailed earlier in this chapter in "Embedding a sound," except use your video's file name in place of a sound file.

Because Internet Explorer adds a control panel below your video, the video image is squished in that browser. Adding 33 pixels to the height (for example, replacing 200 with 233) "unsquishes" your video in Internet Explorer. Luckily, this change has no effect on the Netscape Navigator display.

An image of two film reels appears on your page to show where your video will go.

If you edit the code that embeds a video in your Web page by adding `AUTOSTART="true"`, the video plays as soon as your visitors load your Web page. Note that the code for an embedded animation is identical to that for an embedded sound, so all the instructions (except for the exact command to add) are exactly the same as those explained in the section, "Sending your embedded sound to the background." Editing HTML code is fairly technical stuff, but if you have a strong stomach, you can read more about it in Chapter 13.

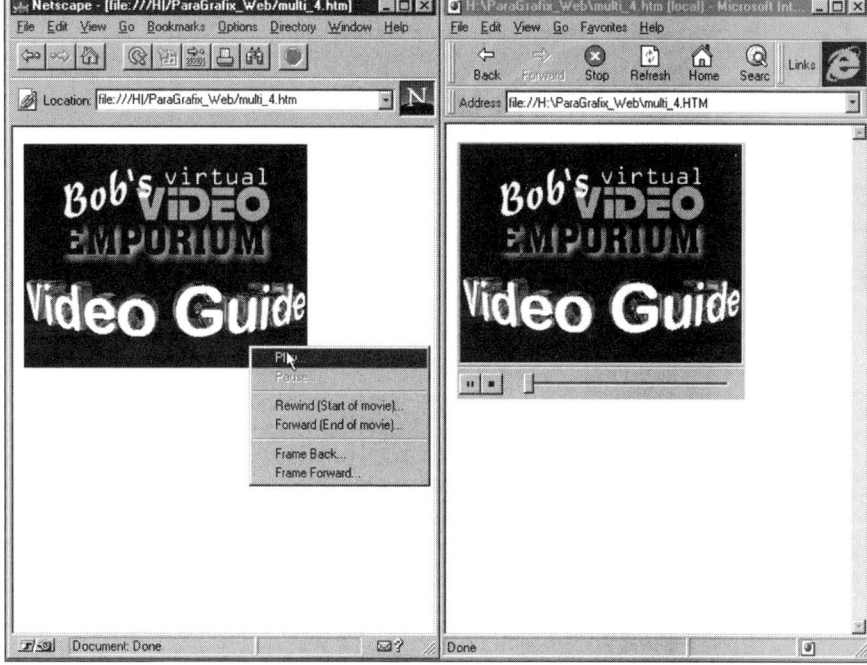

Figure 11-2:
The embedded video controls your viewers see depend on what browser they use.

Linked video: saving your visitors from "hourglass hell"

Video is huge. I don't mean that video is really popular (though it is) — I mean that video files are gigantic. If you thought digitized sound files were large, video files just blow them away. Remember that video files generally contain pictures *and* sound. If you greet your unsuspecting Web visitors with a page containing an embedded video file, you're just asking for complete elimination of repeat business and word-of-mouth advertising. What *should* you do if you want video on your Web site? You basically have two options:

- ✔ Make all the links to the page containing the video read `Warning:` `Huge video file on the page that opens when you click` `this link,` or words to that effect. Chapter 6 explains how to create links between Web pages.

- ✔ Create a link to the video, instead of embedding it in a page. Proper Web etiquette requires that you announce the size of a really big linked file. This gives your visitors advance warning that they'll have enough time to get their cars Simonized while they're waiting for the video to download.

 One way to make sure that your visitors will want to take the time to download the video your page links to is to give them a sneak preview. Use PhotoPaint to turn a single image (called a *frame*) of the video into an image link that leads to the complete video.

You Don't Have to Grind Coffee to Get Java

After *multimedia,* the next buzzwords to be bandied about computer circles were *Internet* and *World Wide Web.* Now comes *Java.* Java was touted as the technology that would crush Microsoft's grip on personal computing and turn every single inhabitant of Planet Earth into a Web surfing, information-absorbing technophile within the year. Java has fallen somewhat short of this promise, but it does let you do some interesting things with your Web page, such as adding really intricate animations and even "real" programs, like word processors.

And Java is . . . ?

So what the heck is Java, anyway? At its most basic, Java is a computer language — like the one used to make the word processing program that I'm writing this book on (or even the browser that you use to surf the Web).

But what sets Java apart from other programming languages is the fact that it's *platform independent,* meaning that it runs equally well on a Windows-based PC, for example, as on a Macintosh. Thus, Java *applets* (mini-applications) can run on any computer, as long as the Web browser understands Java. And because every modern browser understands Java, the only people who can't run Java applets are people who are unable to use any other cool Web stuff you've created (like frames and tables). Lucky for you, these people are a minuscule (and diminishing) minority.

The upshot of all this is that although some platforms can't display, say, .avi videos without a plug-in, *any* computer with a Java-capable browser can display a Java animation. Using Java virtually ensures that your programs and animations work on anyone's computer. The downside to Java applets is that they tend to take a while to download, so you have to decide whether the benefit of the applet is worth the extra time it takes your visitors to download your Web pages.

An applet a day . . .

So you've decided to take the plunge and add an applet or two to your Web site? In this section, you find out how to add an applet to your Web page and set up its parameters.

Showing you how to write the applet itself would take far more room than this chapter. In fact, it would require a whole book. And there just happens to be an excellent one on the topic, called *Java For Dummies* by Aaron E. Walsh (IDG Books Worldwide, Inc.). If you're interested in finding out more about Java, I highly recommend this book.

If you would rather let someone else do all the dirty work, RJHM van der Bergh's home page at `www.nedernet.nl/~rvdb/java.html`, and ET Applets at `www.entanke.se/`, contain excellent directories of free and shareware Java applets. The applets in these directories let you enhance your Web page with real-time clocks, links that display different images when your visitors click on them, and even a couple of games that your visitors can play.

To add an applet to your Web page:

1. **Find out what parameters (names and values) the applet requires.**

   This information is very important. If the applet that you're inserting requires information from you (like the name of an image file or the height of Mount Everest), you want to have the information on hand before you start this procedure. This information is usually available in the documentation created by whoever made the applet — if you downloaded the applet from the Web, you should receive the documentation along with the applet file.

2. **Start DESIGNER and load the page to which you want to add the applet.**

3. **Place the cursor where you want to add the applet.**

   Generally, applets work with graphics. But if you're inserting an applet that controls, say, the text in the status bar at the bottom of the browser, then where you place the cursor doesn't matter.

4. **Choose Insert⇨Applet.**

   The Applet Properties dialog box appears.

5. **Type the filename and path of the applet in the Applet Class text box.**

   Or you can click Browse and locate the applet using the Select Class File dialog box. As you complete this step, keep the following in mind:

   • If the applet is located on a different computer that your viewers access via the Web, you have to enter its URL, and you won't be able to use the Select Class File dialog box. Most applets just don't work if they're not on your local computer. Unless the applet's documentation specifically says that it can work when the applet file is on another computer, assume that the file needs to be on yours.

- If you browse to a class file that's located outside your Web site, DESIGNER attempts to copy the file to your Web site. As I note earlier, you're best off copying the class file into your Web page folder.

6. Type the location of the applet in the Code<u>b</u>ase text box.

I know this step seems redundant, but that's the way it is. What you're putting in this text box is everything from the last step, *except* for the name of the class file. If the class file is in the same folder as your HTML file, leave this text box blank.

7. Set the size of the applet in the Height and <u>W</u>idth text boxes.

If you don't know these values or if the applet doesn't show up on a browser, ignore these boxes.

8. Click the Parameters tab of the Applet Properties dialog box.

The list of applet parameters now appears. Unfortunately, the list is empty until you fill it in with parameters. Figure 11-3 shows the parameters for a specific applet.

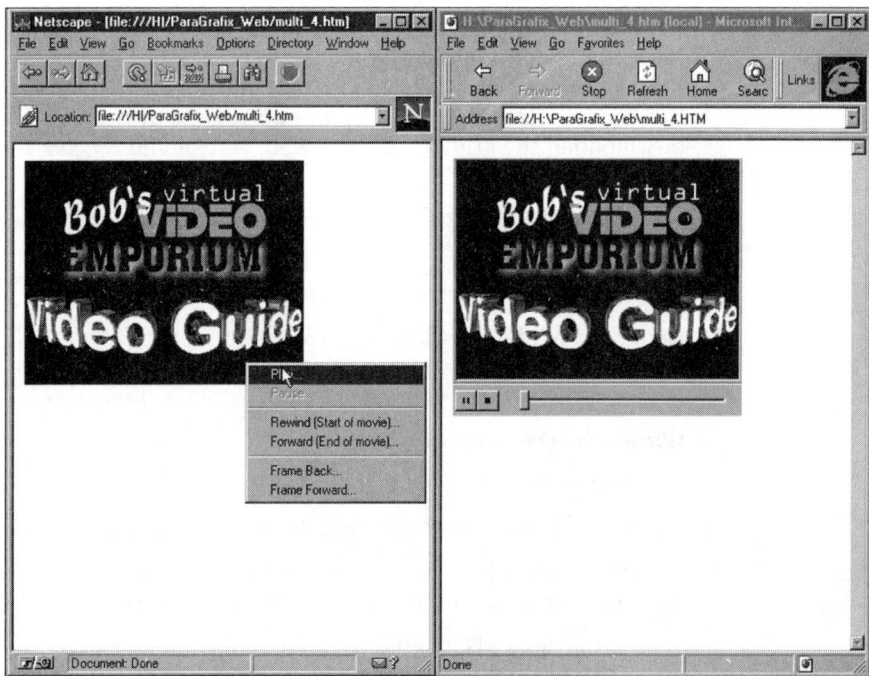

Figure 11-3:
You need
to know
what the
parameters
are before
you can
add them.

9. **Type a parameter name and value in the Name and Value text boxes, and then click the Add button.**

   This is where the information you collected in Step 1 comes in. You need to know the name of each parameter and what its value should be. If your applet is well documented, this information is readily available.

   Just repeat Step 8 for all the parameters that the applet requires.

10. **Click OK.**

    A rectangle with a big J appears on your Web page. This J only appears while you're editing your page in DESIGNER. It will be replaced with the actual applet when your page is viewed through a browser.

11. **Save your page and preview it using a browser.**

    Congratulations! You just added a Java applet to your Web page.

Activating ActiveX

ActiveX is Microsoft's answer to Java. Like Java, ActiveX provides generally small programs (called *controls,* not applets) that you add to your Web pages to enhance your site. ActiveX is based in large part on Microsoft's successful Visual Basic programming system.

Using ActiveX controls has its plusses and minuses compared to using Java applets:

- ✔ **Plus:** People only have to download ActiveX controls the first time they visit your site; after that, their local hard drive saves a copy of the control. By contrast, people have to download the same Java applet every time they visit your Web site.

- ✔ **Plus:** ActiveX has the 900-pound gorilla of software design and marketing (Microsoft) behind it. Java was created and its standards are maintained by the relatively minuscule Sun Microsystems. (Some may see the Microsoft connection as a minus. But me, I don't care where it comes from, I just want software that works.)

- ✔ **Minus:** ActiveX controls run best through Microsoft Internet Explorer, whereas Java applets are almost totally computer and browser independent. ActiveX controls can work *reasonably* well on Netscape Navigator, if your visitors have the appropriate plug-in. You can find out more about plug-ins in the next section, called "Plug-Ins."

You don't want to write your own ActiveX controls? I can't say that I blame you. ActiveX.com at `www.activex.com`, has a great library of ActiveX controls, and `http://browserwatch.internet.com/activex.html` lists a ton of controls and provides links to download them. Microsoft's ActiveX area at `www.microsoft.com/activeplatform/compgal.asp` lists ActiveX control galleries, where you can find even more lists of components. Most of these controls are free (or relatively free) to use, but some may require you to purchase them (particularly the ones available in the Microsoft ActiveX area).

The extension `.asp` at the end of the Microsoft URL stands for *Active Server Page*. This is a super high-tech version of HTML code. It's not anything you really have to be concerned about, but I didn't want you to be confused by the name. And besides, it's another one of those great-to-drop-around-the-water-cooler phrases.

To insert an ActiveX control:

1. **Find out what parameters (names and values) the ActiveX control requires.**

   Taking care of this step first is very important. If the control requires information from you, you'll want to have it on hand before you get going. This information is usually available in the control's documenta-tion — typically in a readme file that came with the control. You also need to know the location of the control's file.

2. **Start DESIGNER and load the page to which you want to add the control.**

3. **If necessary, install the control on your system.**

   Follow the control creator's instructions (you should receive these at the same time you get the control).

4. **Place the cursor where you want to add the ActiveX control.**

   Where you place the cursor doesn't really matter if you're adding a control that won't be visible in your visitors' browsers, such as a control that plays a sound file.

5. **Choose Insert⇨ActiveX.**

   The ActiveX Control Tags dialog box appears, as shown in Figure 11-4.

6. **Select the ActiveX control from the Control drop-down list.**

   If you didn't properly install the control on your system, the name does not appear here. In this case, you must close the dialog box by clicking Cancel, exit DESIGNER, and then attempt to reinstall the control before starting these steps over again.

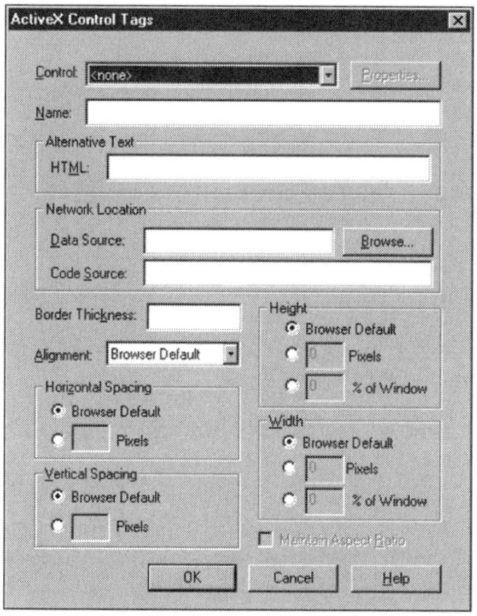

Figure 11-4:
Specify the
parameters
for your
ActiveX
control
in this
dialog box.

7. Click Properties.

The ActiveX Control Properties dialog box appears. If your control has any size options, you can easily set them here. Just drag the scaling handles (the eight black boxes) that appear around the control.

8. Click the Property Pages button and set the appearance parameters for the control.

The Properties For dialog box appears. The parameters are interactive and depend on the control being added. This dialog box may remain open while you're setting other options. Any changes you make are instantly visible in the preview of the control in the ActiveX Control Properties dialog box. If these parameters are not available, the Property Pages button is gray and inactive, and you cannot open the Properties For dialog box.

9. Click Edit Properties and set the control parameters.

The Edit Properties dialog box appears. You can set each parameter for the control here. Just select the parameter from the list and then type or select its value from the drop-down list above it. How you set these parameters depends on the control and what you're doing with it.

This is where the information you collected in Step 1 comes in handy. If no parameters need to be set, the Edit Properties button is gray and inactive.

10. Click OK to close the Edit Properties dialog box.

11. Click OK to close the ActiveX Control Properties dialog box.

You return to the ActiveX Control Tags dialog box.

12. If your control works with a form, type the field name in the <u>N</u>ame text box.

Your form uses this name to refer to the control. Chapter 10 tells all about working with Internet forms.

13. In the HT<u>M</u>L text box, type the text you want to appear if a browser can't display the control.

This text appears if, for example, someone running Netscape Navigator visits your Web page.

14. Specify the ActiveX control's URL in the <u>D</u>ata Source text box.

This URL must not contain the actual name of the control, just the URL of the folder it's contained in.

If the control is located in your Web site, you can use the Browse feature to locate it. After you locate the control and click Open, you have to remove the name of your hard drive, any information before your Web root, and the name of the control from the Data Source text box.

15. If your control requires an external file source, include that file's name and URL in the Code <u>S</u>ource text box.

16. In the bottom half of the ActiveX Control Tags dialog box, define the appearance specifications for your control.

The text boxes and radio buttons below the Network Location section of the dialog box work exactly the same way that they do for image files. For more information on these appearance controls, see Chapter 7.

17. Click OK.

The ActiveX Control Tags dialog box closes, and the control appears on your Web page. Depending on the control you picked, it may appear in DESIGNER as a big X or a display of the actual control. Either way, when you view your page through a browser, it will look fine.

Plug-Ins

While surfing the Web, you may come across a link that says something like `Corel CMX Viewer Required to View this File`. This message means that the embedded or linked file is in Corel CMX format and can't be viewed directly by a Web browser. As someone visiting the page, you need the CMX Viewer to be able view the file.

The CMX viewer is known as a *plug-in.* Netscape created the plug-in system to enhance its browser and make it possible to include all sorts of images, word processing documents, and even multimedia systems in Web pages — even though HTML doesn't support these items.

You can include files that require plug-ins on your Web pages as well. Doing so gives you greater flexibility to add all sorts of exotic files that aren't directly supported by Web browsers. Check with the maker of the software whose format the file uses to find out if a plug-in is available. In the previous example, Corel makes a plug-in for its CMX file format (you can create CMX files using DRAW, which is detailed in Chapter 15).

To include files that require plug-ins in your Web page, just create a link to or embed the file.

If you embed the file (using the same procedure outlined earlier in this chapter in "Embedding a sound"), a small image of an electrical plug appears on your Web page. This image only appears in DESIGNER — your visitors see the file as you intend it.

Be nice! If you embed or add a link to a file that needs a plug-in program in order to be viewed, add a link to the home page for that plug-in. That way, your visitors can easily download the application they need.

Chapter 12

Publishing a Database on Your Web Site

Corel WEB.DATA (DATA for short) has a very simple-looking interface (see Figure 12-1): nine buttons lined up in a nice, neat column, just waiting to publish your company's database on the Web. Behind the simple facade, however, lies a wonderfully sophisticated system for bringing your database to life on the Web.

Unfortunately, with all this sophistication comes a user interface that's not wonderfully intuitive. This chapter helps you get past the arcane terminology peppered throughout DATA and publish your databases with the least muss and fuss.

DATA is a *linear program*. That is, you have to do one action before you can proceed to another. Each of the actions necessary to publish a database is represented by a button in the column on the left side of the DATA window. Starting at the top of the button bar, you click each button in turn and work with the particular dialog box that opens. This chapter is arranged in the order of the actions that you take to publish a database. When you finish one section of this chapter, proceed to the next section to find out what you need to do next.

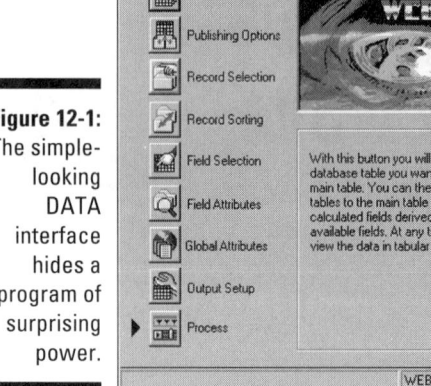

Figure 12-1:
The simple-looking DATA interface hides a program of surprising power.

Before you begin to publish a database, you need to know how it was put together (what field names were used, for example). If you're not the person who created the database, search the author out so that you can find out how it was created. Finding this information beforehand can save you a lot of trouble when you're trying to set all the options that DATA uses to publish your database.

The Recipe for DATA Success

Word processors save in *document* files, computer aided design (CAD) programs save in *drawing* files, and database programs save in, well, *data-base* files. These names seem to make sense, but for some reason, DATA saves its information in *recipe* files.

Though the connection isn't immediately obvious, *recipe* is a good name for the file that defines how you publish your database to the Web. Just as a food recipe contains a list of ingredients and all the instructions for preparing the dish, a DATA recipe lists all the databases and their fields that you use and contains the instructions for formatting your final publication the way you want it.

Starting DATA

As always, WebMaster Suite gives you a couple of ways to open DATA. Which one you choose depends on how you plan to publish your database (the section called "Publish or perish," later in this chapter, tells more about using these options):

✔ If you plan to publish your database to a new Web page, choose Start⇨Programs⇨Corel WebMaster Suite⇨Accessories⇨Corel WEB.DATA.

 ✔ If you plan to publish your database directly to an existing Web page, open the page in DESIGNER and then click the WEB.DATA button in the Applications toolbar.

Opening an existing recipe

If you've already created a recipe, you can open it up to modify it or to update an existing Web page's published database. Saving a recipe is explained in the next section, appropriately named "Saving your recipes." To open an existing recipe file:

1. **Start DATA.**

   The previous section, "Starting DATA," details the various ways to start DATA.

 2. **Choose File⇨Open, press Ctrl+O, or click the Open button on the toolbar.**

   The Open dialog box appears.

3. **Locate your recipe file and select it in the main file list.**

   Select a drive from the Look in drop-down list and double-click folders in the main file list to open them. Click the filename once to highlight the file you want.

4. **Click Open.**

   The Open dialog box closes, and your recipe loads into DATA.

Saving your recipes

After you set up your recipe exactly the way you want it (as outlined later in this chapter in "Your Database, Your Way" and "Outstanding in the Field"), save your recipe so that you can use it later to publish your database or update your published database.

To save a recipe that has already been saved (that is, one that already has a name), just choose File⇨Save or click the Save button in the top toolbar. If you're saving a new recipe or want to save your recipe under a different name:

1. **Choose File⇨Save As, or, if this is the first time you are saving the recipe, you can choose File⇨Save.**

   The Save As dialog box appears.

2. **Locate the folder where you want to save your recipe.**

   Select a drive from the Look in drop-down list and double-click folders in the main file list to open them.

 To make your life a little easier, I suggest that you save your recipe file in your Web site folder. That way, you know exactly where it is when you need it. Because DATA defaults to saving your recipes in the Recipe folder, you can save some time in navigating your hard drive by setting your Web site folder as the default folder. To do this, choose Tools⇨ Options and type the path of your Web site folder in the Recipe Files text box.

3. **Type a name for your recipe in the File name text box.**

   You can choose any name you want. The limitations on Web filenames don't apply to a recipe file because it will never be accessed on the Web.

4. **Click Save.**

   The Save As dialog box closes, and your recipe is saved.

Your Database, Your Way

The database that you use is really the heart of your recipe. Without a database to publish, you need not go further. As a matter of fact, you *can't* do anything else. Unless you already selected a database, every button, other than the Select Database button (the top button in the column), is grayed and inactive.

This section shows you how to select a database and set its basic publishing options. The upcoming section "Outstanding in the Field" details how to select particular information.

Selecting a database

To select a database to publish:

1. **Click the Select Database button.**

   The Select Database dialog box appears.

2. **Click Browse.**

   The Select Database File dialog box appears.

3. **Select the type of database file you want from the Files of type drop-down list.**

   All the standard database formats are supported by DATA, in addition to Microsoft Excel, Lotus 1-2-3 spreadsheets, and delimited text files. (*Delimited text files* are plain text files that use tabs or commas to set fields apart.)

4. **Locate the database file you want to use.**

   Select a drive from the Look in drop-down list and double-click folders in the main file list to open them.

5. **Select your database file in the main file list.**

   Click the file once to highlight it.

6. **Click Open.**

   The Select Database File dialog box closes, and you return to the Select Database dialog box. The name and location of the database file you selected now appear in the Main Table text box.

   If you selected a database that uses a number of tables (which basically act as subdatabases), the Select Table dialog box opens. Choose the table you want to publish and then click OK to return to the Select Database dialog box.

   You can click Display now to view a tabular form of your database to make sure that it's the database you meant to select.

7. **Click OK.**

   The Select Database dialog box closes, and you return to the main WEB.DATA window. Now, however, the Publishing Options button is no longer gray, indicating that it is active. Because all the other buttons are still gray, you know that you have to set up your publishing options before you can do anything else. These options provide basic control over how your database is displayed — for example, is your data in a table or is each record listed individually. Lucky for you, the next section, "Publish or perish," shows you exactly how to set these options.

Publish or perish

How you publish your database has a lot to do with what you plan to do with it. You most likely want to publish a table or list form of your database, like the one shown in Figure 12-2.

You can publish the same database many different ways. Figure 12-3 shows links to different pages that all started with the same database. By using different sorting options (detailed later in this chapter in "Sorting records"), you can add much of the flexibility of an interactive database without having to work with more sophisticated, difficult, and expensive programs.

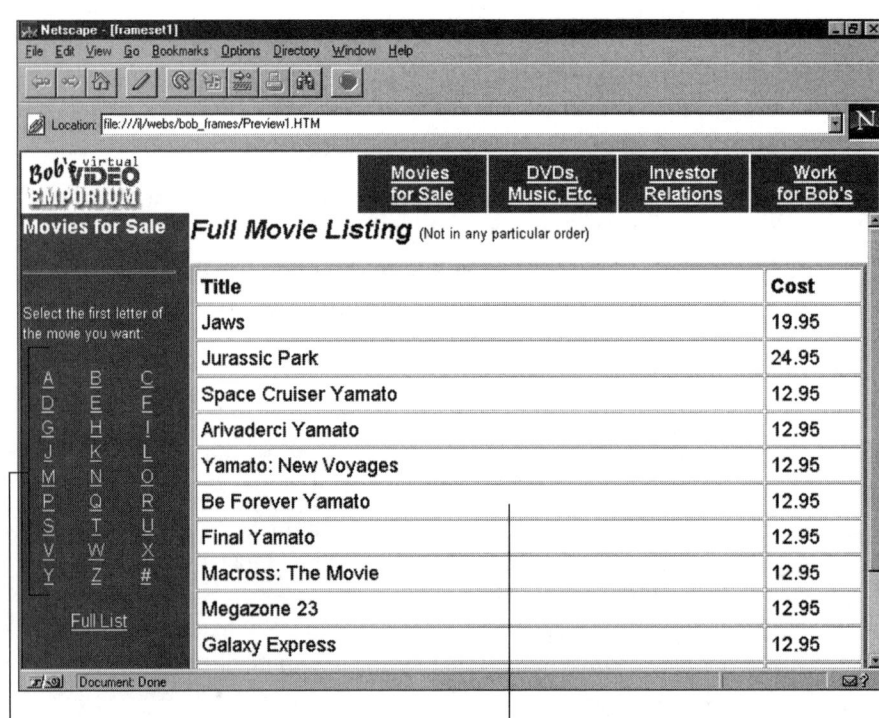

Figure 12-2:
A simple table database.

└─Links to other databases   A single database

To set your publishing options:

1. Click the Publishing Options button in the vertical toolbar.

The Publishing Options dialog box appears (see Figure 12-3).

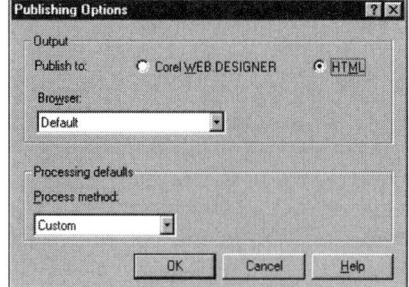

Figure 12-3:
In the
Publishing
Options
dialog box,
specify how
you plan to
publish your
database.

2. **Select where you want to publish your database in the Output section.**

   If you started DATA through DESIGNER, you have no option here. DATA automatically publishes directly to your currently opened page in DESIGNER. If you started DATA directly from the Start menu, you can select Corel DESIGNER or HTML.

   - **If you elect to publish to DESIGNER:** When you process your recipe (as described later in this chapter in "Publishing Your Database"), DESIGNER starts automatically, and a new page containing your database appears, ready to be edited.

   - **If you elect to publish to an HTML page:** The page is saved in your current Web site (the most recent Web site you opened in SiteManager). To edit the page, start DESIGNER and load the page.

     DATA can create a Web page that uses HTML code specific to certain browsers to aid in formatting. I suggest, however, that you leave the Browser setting at Default, rather than pick a specific browser. Doing so gives you the most flexibility later.

3. **Select how you want your database to appear from the Process method drop-down list.**

   I suggest that you pick the Custom or Table option.

   - **Custom:** Creates a format where your database information is listed on the page. Creating a custom format requires some work on your part.

   - **Table:** Formats your information in a standard Internet table (as described in Chapter 8).

   - **View, Chart, and Analyzer:** Creates Java applets to include in your page. These applets add complexity to your page and greatly increase its download time. You can generally achieve results just as effective by using the graphic output features of your database program, and then including the graphic in your page. View, Chart, and Analyzer are of limited utility because they only work with databases that are relatively simple (one text field and any number of numerical fields in each record).

- **Make Dictionary:** Is used only with a two-column database that is designed to control the actions of another database.

4. **Click OK.**

The Publishing Options dialog box closes and you return to the WEB.DATA window. Notice that all the buttons down to Field Selection are now active. The blackdtriangle next to Field Selection means that you must select the fields to be included in your published database; the others choices (Record Selection and Record Sorting) are optional.

You are not locked into either of these decisions. If you decide later that you want to change the process method or where you will publish your database, click the Publishing Options button, make your changes, and then click OK. A dialog box opens and asks whether you want to retain your formatting. Simply click Yes, and your changes are made.

Outstanding in the Field

Records and fields are what your databases are all about. They are what provide the database information and make it useful. If a database isn't broken into records, and records into fields, the information is a useless mishmash of text, with no way to figure out what it means.

DATA gives you the tools to work with your database information so that it becomes recognizable and organized. This section details the tools for organizing and sorting your database.

Records

Records are the first major breakdown of information in your database. Each record holds all the information about a particular subject. Each individual piece of information is contained in a separate field.

Selecting records

Some databases can be awfully large. Publishing every record in the database can make for a really big Web page that's difficult for your visitors to view. If you only want to publish a certain portion of your database, you can filter out records based on the information in certain fields.

This selection process involves what are called *Boolean operators* (greater than, less than, equal to, and so on). If you're publishing a list of employees, for example, you may use these operators to publish only those employees who have been working for a company *greater than* one year.

If you want to publish *all* your records, you can skip the selection process outlined in this section. Otherwise, to select a subset of records to include in your published database:

1. **Start DATA.**

   Before you can select records, you have to select a database (as explained earlier in this chapter, in "Selecting a database") and set your publishing options (see "Publish or perish"). If you've previously saved a recipe in which you've done this, you can open that recipe.

2. **Click the Record Selection button.**

   The Record Selection dialog box, shown in Figure 12-4, appears.

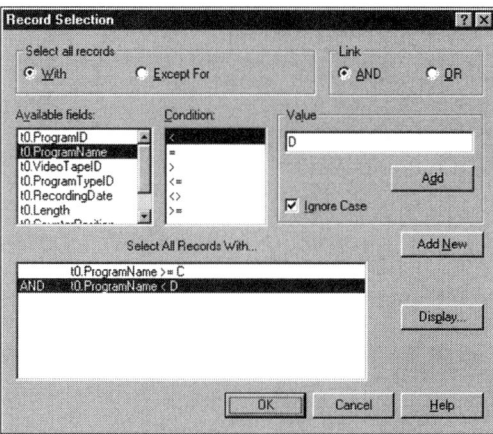

Figure 12-4:
The options selected here tell DESIGNER to publish only those records whose ProgramName field starts with C.

3. **In the A̲vailable fields list, double-click the field that you want to use to determine which records to select.**

   The field's name appears in the Select All Records With list, along with the default selection settings. Notice that these settings correspond to the highlighted option under Condition and the word NULL under Value. *NULL* means that you haven't specified how you want to work with this field yet.

4. Select the operator for your selection from the Condition list.

The operator appears after the field name that you selected:

< means *less than*

= means *equal*

> means *greater than*

<= means *less than or equal to*

<> means *not equal to*

>= means *greater than or equal to*

These operators tell DATA how to filter out records based on the value (which is set in the next step). For example, if a field of employee names is *less than* a value of D, then only employees whose names begin with A, B, or C will be selected. The options selected in Figure 12-6 tell DESIGNER to publish only those records whose ProgramName field starts with C.

5. Type a value for the operator to work with in the Value text box.

This is the letter, word, phrase, or number that you want your selection to be based on. For example, if you want all names less than D, then **D** is the value that you enter here.

If the field you select deals with text, you type a letter. If it deals with numbers, you type a number.

Selecting the Ignore Case check box tells DATA to disregard capitalization. For example, when you select this option, DATA treats the word *BOB* the same as *Bob* or *bob*. Records matching any of these versions of the word are selected so you don't have to enter separate selections for each type of capitalization.

6. Click Add.

The value you typed in the Value text box now replaces NULL in the Select All Records With list.

7. If you want to add more options for selecting fields, double-click another field name, repeat Steps 4, 5, and 6, and then go on to Step 8; if not, skip to Step 9.

You can include as many field options as you want. You can also specify multiple options for the same field, as shown in Figure 12-6. After you've performed Step 8, you can add even more options by double-clicking another field name.

8. Select AND or OR in the Link area of the dialog box.

This choice determines how the new field selection interacts with the previous one.

- **AND:** Specifies that a record must meet both conditions in order to be selected.

- **OR:** Specifies that a record will be included as long as it meets either of the specified conditions. For example, if you have a field called Color, you can have DATA select all those records where the value equals Blue and then have it select all records where the value equals Red. If you choose AND to connect these conditions, no records will be selected because the color can't be both blue *and* red.

9. Click OK.

The Record Selection dialog box closes, and you return to the WEB.DATA window. If you want, you can save your recipe at this point or continue on to sort your records as detailed in the next section, "Sorting records."

To delete a selection criterion, click the Record Selection button to open the Record Selection dialog box. Then highlight the line that you no longer want in the Select All Records With list and press Delete. Click OK to close the dialog box.

Sorting records

In general, the records in a database file appear in the order they were entered, which may not be terribly useful. Usually, you want to sort the records in your database alphabetically or numerically, according to a specified field. For example, you might want to sort a database of movies alphabetically by movie title or numerically by the year the movie was made.

To sort your database:

1. Click the Record Sorting button in the DATA toolbar.

The Select Sort Fields dialog box appears (see Figure 12-5).

Figure 12-5:
You can choose any field by which to sort your database.

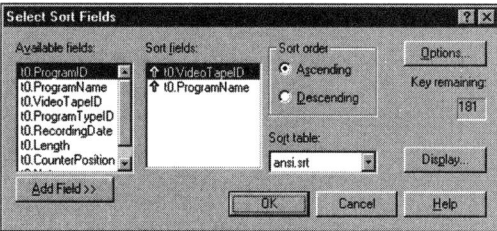

2. Double-click the field you want to sort on in the A̲vailable Fields list.

The field name is copied to the Sort fields list.

3. Select the order in which you want to sort the data.

- **A̲scending:** Puts data in order from lowest to highest: A, B, C, or 1, 2, 3

- **D̲escending:** Puts data in order from highest to lowest: C, B, A, or 3, 2, 1

4. Select another field to sort on (refer to Step 2), and set its order (refer to Step 3), or click OK.

If you click OK, the Select Sort Fields dialog box closes, and you return to the WEB.DATA window. If you want, you can save your recipe at this point or continue on to the fields to be published, as detailed in the next section, "Selecting fields."

When you add another field by which to sort, the database is sorted twice. Using the phonebook example again, names are sorted by last name *and then* by first name, so that all people with the same last name are listed in order by their first name.

Selecting fields

Some databases are huge, containing tens or even hundreds of different fields. You probably won't be interested in publishing all that data at once. Luckily, DATA allows you to publish only those fields that you're really interested in and ignore the others.

To select the fields you want to include in your published database:

1. Start DATA.

Before you can select fields, you have to choose a database (as explained earlier in "Selecting a database") and set your publishing options (see "Publish or perish"). Selecting and sorting fields are optional. If you've previously saved a recipe in which you've done this, you can open that recipe.

2. Click the Field Selection button.

The Field Selection dialog box appears.

3. Click a field that you want to include in your published database in the A̲vailable list and then click Add field(s).

The field is copied to the Selected list. You can add as many fields as you want. Also, you can process many fields at a time by using the standard Shift+click and Ctrl+click combinations to select fields.

4. Click OK.

The Field Selection dialog box closes.

Putting your fields in order

When your database is published, the fields appear in the same order that you selected them in the preceding steps. You can change this order if you want to. Note that changing the order here does not affect your original database at all. To change the order of the fields:

1. Click the Field Selection button in the DATA toolbar.

The Field Selection dialog box appears.

2. Right-click the field in the Selected list that you want to move.

A pop-up menu appears.

3. Select Cut.

The field disappears from the list.

4. Select the field above or below which you want the cut field to appear.

5. Right-click the selected field.

The pop-up menu appears, only this time the Paste Above and Paste Below options are active.

6. Select either Paste Above or Paste Below from the pop-up menu.

Which one you select depends on where you want to insert the removed field. After you make your selection, the field is inserted in the location you picked.

7. Move other fields, as outlined in the preceding steps, or click OK.

If you click OK, the Field Selection dialog box closes, and you return to the WEB.DATA window.

Grouping records together

Sometimes, several of your records may have the same information in a particular field (maybe you have a bunch of movies on the same tape so you have multiple entries with the same tape number). In this case, you can use this field as a heading for a group of records. To add a heading:

1. Click the Field Selection button in the DATA toolbar.

The Field Selection dialog box appears.

2. Click the Insert Above button in the Heading Blocks section.

A box labeled h1: Heading Level 1 appears in the window to the right of the dialog box (see Figure 12-6). The Selected list now only shows those fields that are in the heading. Right now none are shown because you haven't added any.

Newly inserted heading level ⌐

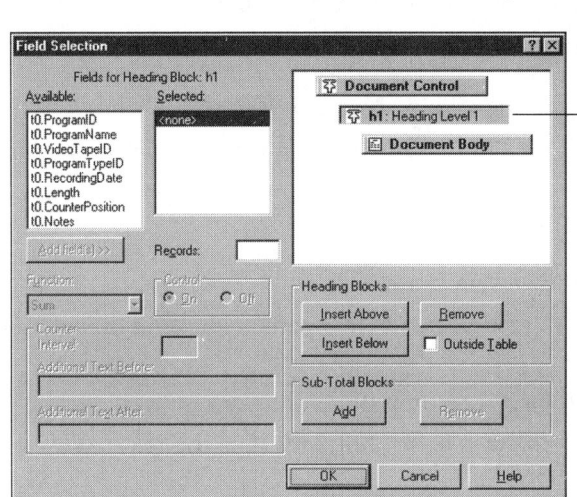

Figure 12-6:
Heading
levels
let you
organize
your
database.

3. Select a field to use in the heading from the Available list and then click Add field.

The field appears in the Selected list.

4. Click OK.

The Field Selection dialog box closes, and you return to the WEB.DATA window. Figures 12-7 shows the same database with headings in table format.

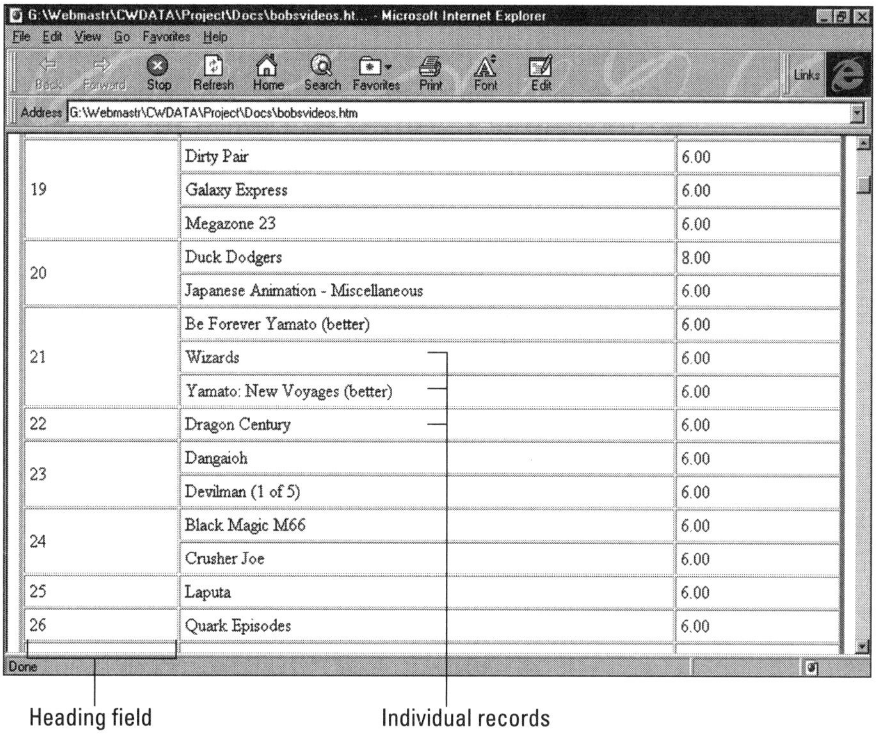
G:\Webmastr\CWDATA\Project\Docs\bobsvideos.ht... - Microsoft Internet Explorer
File Edit View Go Favorites Help
Back Forward Stop Refresh Home Search Favorites Print Font Edit
Links
Address G:\Webmastr\CWDATA\Project\Docs\bobsvideos.htm
Dirty Pair 6.00
19 Galaxy Express 6.00
Megazone 23 6.00
Duck Dodgers 8.00
20 Japanese Animation - Miscellaneous 6.00
Be Forever Yamato (better) 6.00
21 Wizards 6.00
Yamato: New Voyages (better) 6.00
22 Dragon Century 6.00
Dangaioh 6.00
23 Devilman (1 of 5) 6.00
Black Magic M66 6.00
24 Crusher Joe 6.00
25 Laputa 6.00
26 Quark Episodes 6.00
Done
Heading field
Individual records

Figure 12-7: A table format database using fields.

Publishing Your Database

This is what it's all about — publishing your database to a new HTML page or as part of an existing page in DESIGNER, so that you can make it available on the Web. Keep in mind that you can't publish your database until you complete the minimum operations:

- Select a database (see "Selecting a database")
- Set your publishing options (see "Publish or perish")
- Select the fields to be published (see "Selecting fields")
- Set up your output (required only if you're publishing directly to an HTML file, see "Formatting That Data")

If you're publishing your data to a new HTML page (as opposed to adding it to an existing Web page in DESIGNER), the first thing you need to do to prepare for publishing your database is set the filename for the new page. To do this:

1. Click the Output Setup button in the DATA toolbar.

The Output Setup dialog box appears.

2. Type the name and location of the Web page file you want to create in the Output file text box or click Browse to locate the file.

3. Select the drive in which you want to create your Web page from the Save in drop-down list.

4. Double-click folders in the main list window to open the folder you want.

5. Type the name of the Web page file you want to create in the File name text box.

6. Click Save.

The Select Output File dialog box closes, and you return to the Output Setup dialog box.

7. Click OK.

The Output Setup dialog box closes, and you return to the main WEB.DATA window.

When you're ready to publish your database:

 1. Click Process in the DATA toolbar.

Two Processing dialog boxes appear: one showing the progress of analyzing your database, and the other showing the progress of saving your HTML data. Then the Processing Output dialog box appears.

2. Press the button for the option you're interested in.

You have three of the following four options:

- **View in Text Editor:** This option is available only if you're publishing directly to an HTML file.

- **Publish to WEB.DESIGNER:** This option is available only if you're publishing to DESIGNER. If you select this option, the WEB.DATA window closes.

- **Preview in Browser:** This button opens your Web browser and shows you what database you've been working with.

- **Close:** This option returns you to the WEB.DATA window.

You're all done! You can close DATA (unless you published to DESIGNER, in which case DATA closes automatically, and DESIGNER starts) or work on another database.

One important thing to keep in mind is that DATA never changes your original database. When you publish your database, all the information that you specify in your recipe is copied to the Web page that you're creating. Because your Web page is not directly linked to your database, as your database changes, your Web page remains the same. When you want to update your Web page with new database information, simply open your recipe in DATA and publish it again. If you originally published your database to an existing page in DESIGNER, you have to delete the originally published database information before you republish it.

Using the Tutorial: DATA Does More

This chapter has barely scratched the surface of the power of DATA. As I mentioned at the beginning of this chapter, DATA is an amazingly sophisticated program behind it's simple facade. From integrating graphics to creating Java-based tables and charts, you can do much more with DATA. To really put it through its paces would require almost an entire book devoted to the subject.

Even the Corel WEB.DATA Tutorial (in my opinion, the best piece of documentation that comes with WebMaster Suite because of its attention to detail and comprehensiveness) merely hints at some of the WEB.DATA power. This tutorial is an excellent place to start your journey toward using DATA to its highest potential.

To start the tutorial:

   1. **In DATA, choose Help⇨Tutorial.**

   The Help Topics: Corel WEB.DATA Tutorial dialog box opens.

   2. **Double-click the second item, Lessons for publishing to the World Wide Web.**

   A list of three lessons appears.

   3. **Double-click Lesson 2: Creating a table-based online catalog.**

   The Corel WEB.DATA Tutorial dialog box opens, as shown in Figure 12-8. By the way, most of the information in Lesson 1 of the tutorial is covered in this chapter.

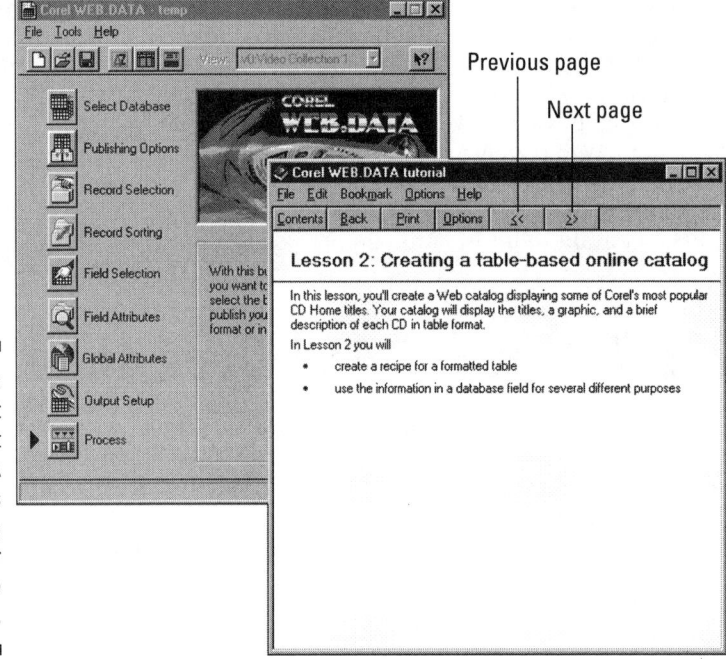

Previous page

Next page

Figure 12-8:
Find out
more about
DATA
and its
publishing
power
using the
tutorial.

4. **Click the Next Page button to begin the lesson.**

The Contents page appears.

5. **Click Creating a new Corel DATA recipe file.**

The lesson page appears. Follow the instructions on the screen to interact with and learn more about WEB.DATA.

Chapter 13

Under the Hood: Tuning Up Your Web Site

*T*rue what-you-see-is-what-you-get (WYSIWYG) simplicity still doesn't exist in a relatively low-priced Web design program (even one with the power of WebMaster Suite). Sometimes (especially when you work with frames and tables), you have to pop the hood and get your hands dirty to really tweak your Web site. You perform these tweaks by making small changes to the Hypertext Markup Language (HTML) code that DESIGNER creates — this is the code Web browsers use to display your pages.

In this chapter, I talk about some of the more common tune-ups that you may want to perform on your frames, tables, text, and graphics. I also talk about editing your data files, bypassing DESIGNER.

Warning: Geek Information Ahead! If you're an adventurous soul, dying to know what hidden secrets lie beneath the DESIGNER friendly facade — or you can't seem to do something you know is possible — keep reading. Otherwise, ignore this chapter. This is advanced stuff that isn't absolutely necessary to know.

Editing HTML Code

This whole chapter is based on one thing: editing the Hypertext Markup Language (HTML) codes to existing pages. Don't worry — this procedure isn't outrageously complicated. This first section shows how to edit the codes themselves, and the following sections show what codes to actually edit.

What are HTML codes?

As I mention in Chapter 1, HTML codes tell a browser what to do. For example, the HTML codes <B> and </B> tell a browser to make any text in between them bold.

Browsers don't display these codes but rather use them to display your Web pages just the way you want. The brackets (< and >) are what set HTML codes apart from all the text that you type into your Web pages. The slash mark (/) tells browsers that this is an ending code. Codes that have a beginning and end are called *containers,* because everything that is contained between them gets formatted.

Some codes are a little more complicated than a single letter. The code for adding an image, for example, includes the name of the image, its location, and some formatting options. Images don't have any ending code. Here's an example of an image code:

```
<IMG SRC="images/bobslgo2.gif">
```

IMG tells the browser that the code is an image file. SRC indicates the filename and path of the image. Most HTML codes are relatively easy to figure out when you look at them. It's trying to remember the correct codes to type that's given rise to editing programs like WebMaster Suite.

Viewing HTML code

The folks at Corel knew that a lot of people would want to edit HTML code, so they made this code very easy to get to. They included a menu item in DESIGNER that leads to a bare-bones HTML text editor. They also included a Source View in SiteManager that lets you edit your HTML code and also offers advantages like color-coded text and a search-and-replace feature.

Figure 13-1 shows a Web page displayed in the DESIGNER HTML editor. In Figure 13-2, the page's HTML code is displayed in the SiteManager Source View.

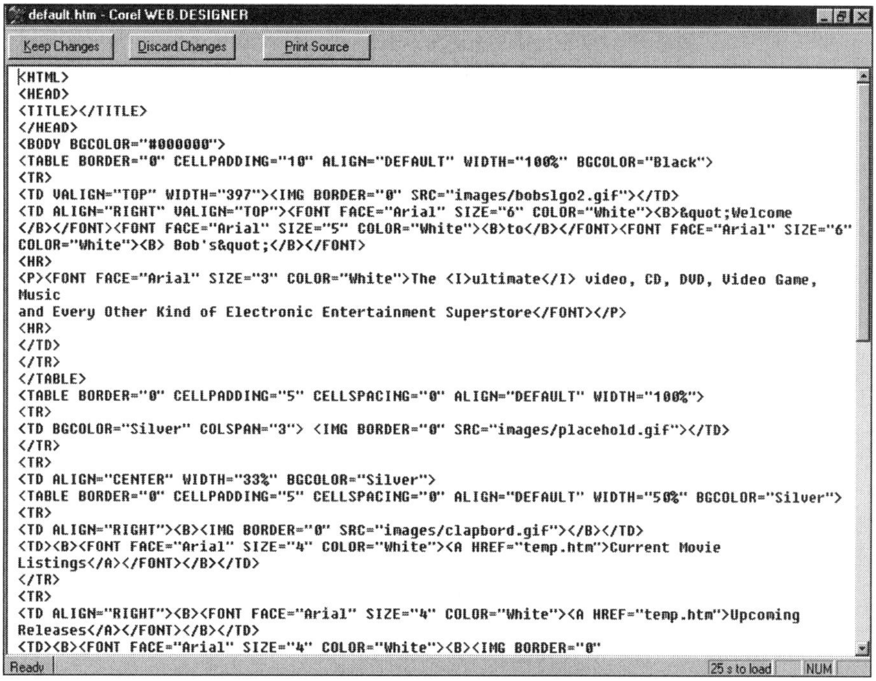

Figure 13-1:
The page's
HTML code,
shown in
DESIGNER
Source
View.

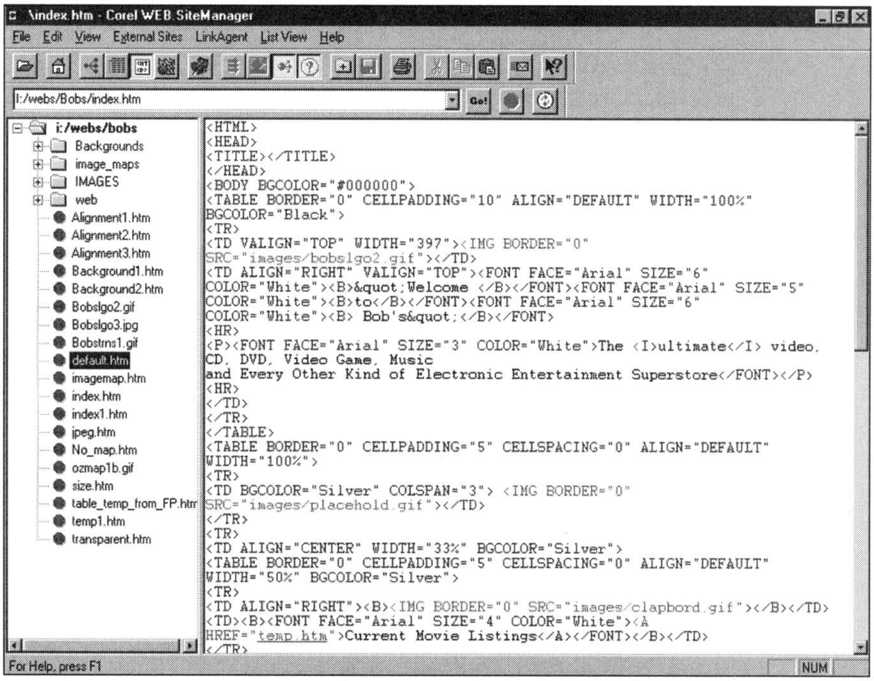

Figure 13-2:
The same
page's
HTML code,
shown in
SiteManager
Source
View.

When you're using DESIGNER, you can open its HTML text editor by choosing View⇨Document Source. The window changes to show the HTML code. (This procedure is a little different if you're working with frames, but I explain the differences in "Tweaking Frame Borders," later in this chapter.)

 To display SiteManager Source View, highlight the page you want to display and then choose View⇨Source View or press F7.

Whether you edit code through SiteManager or DESIGNER really depends on what you're doing with your Web site at the time:

Editing codes

After you display a page's source code in the DESIGNER editor or in SiteManager Source View, editing the code itself is easy. You simply make the changes necessary to get the results you want (as explained in the rest of this chapter) and then save your work.

To save your edits to the source code:

✔ **In the DESIGNER HTML editor:** Click the Keep Changes button.

 ✔ **In SiteManager Source View:** After you make changes to the code, the Save button becomes active, and you can simply click it to save your changes.

You aren't stuck with the changes you make to the source code. If, for example, you happen to make a mistake, you can discard the changes by following these steps:

✔ **In the DESIGNER HTML editor:** Click the Discard Changes button.

✔ **In SiteManager Source View:** Click any other file in the file listing to the left. When a dialog box opens and asks whether you want to save changes, click No.

Finding stuff in Source View

Just from looking at the figures at the beginning of this chapter, you can see that HTML code can get pretty confusing. Luckily, you can let your computer search and replace text and HTML codes when you use Source View in SiteManager.

Combing a page with the Find feature

If you're looking for a specific code within a Web page, you can use the Find feature built into SiteManager's Source View. The SiteManager Find feature works like the one you use in your word processor:

1. **Start Source View.**

2. **Choose Edit⇨Find or press Ctrl+F.**

   The Find dialog box opens.

3. **Type the text you want to search for in the Find text box.**

4. **Set the options for your search.**

   - **Match whole word only:** Select this option when you want to find the word only when it appears independently.

   - **Match case:** Select this option if you want to ensure that you only get words with the same capitalization as what you typed.

   - **Search Display Text Only:** Select this option if you just want to check the text that appears on your page.

5. **Click Find Next.**

   If the item you're looking for exists in your Web page, the first instance of it is highlighted.

6. **Click Cancel to end your search or click Find Next again to seek out the next instance of the item.**

   When you click Cancel, the dialog box closes, but the results of your search remain highlighted. You can make any changes you want to the page. Then, if you want to repeat the search for the same text, choose Edit⇨Find Next or press F3. The next instance of the text is highlighted.

Global Find works much like the regular Find, except that it isn't limited to the page that you're displaying. You can select a number of files to search or have Global Find search your entire Web site for some text. To search some or all the pages in your site, choose Edit⇨Global Find to open the Find dialog box. This dialog box is exactly the same as the standard Find dialog box, except that you have the option of searching all the page files in your Web or only specific ones that you select. Keep the following tips in mind when performing a global search:

- ✔ If you want to search only some pages, highlight them in the file list to the left before you start your search. You can use the standard Shift+click and Ctrl+click methods to select files. When the Find dialog box opens, click the Selected Files radio button.

- ✔ When Find finishes searching your site for the text you entered in the Find dialog box, it displays a list of files containing the text in the appropriately named Files Containing dialog box. To view a specific file, double-click its filename in the list — the file is now displayed with the first instance of the text highlighted, and the standard Find dialog box opens.

  - You can search for another instance in the same file by clicking Fine Next, or you can click Cancel to return to the list of files.

- If you want to edit the file that opens, click Cancel in the Find dialog box and then click Done in the Files Containing dialog box.

- To view another file with the text you entered, click Cancel in the Find dialog box to return to the Files Containing dialog box. Then double-click another file in the list.

Replacing what you find

Sometimes, you don't just want to *find* some specific text or code in your Web page (or your entire site), but you know exactly what you want to *replace* it with. Perhaps you consistently misspelled a name, or you changed an image that you want to use. The Replace and Global Replace features of SiteManager make this process extremely easy.

Follow these quick tips for using the search-and-replace feature with HTML codes that define your pages (in other words, everything except the text that appears on your pages):

✔ Don't select the Match case check box because you can't be absolutely certain of the capitalization of any filenames.

✔ Don't select the Search Display Text Only. HTML code isn't display text!

To replace text in a single file:

1. **Select the file in the file listing to the left.**

2. **Choose <u>V</u>iew⇨<u>S</u>ource View.**

3. **Choose <u>E</u>dit⇨<u>R</u>eplace or press Ctrl+R.**

   The Replace dialog box appears.

4. **In the Find text box, type the text you want to replace.**

5. **In the Replace with text box, type the text you want to insert in place of the Find text.**

If you are typing filenames (such as image or sound files) and will be publishing your Web site to a UNIX computer, make absolutely certain that the text you type in the Replace with text box is capitalized exactly the same as the filename because UNIX is case sensitive.

6. **Select the search options.**

   These options are the same as for the Find feature. (See the earlier section, "Combining a page with the Find feature," earlier in this chapter.)

7. **Click the <u>R</u>eplace button.**

   The Replace dialog box appears, and the first instance of the text you typed is highlighted.

8. Click the <u>Y</u>es, <u>N</u>o, or Yes to <u>A</u>ll button as appropriate.

- **<u>Y</u>es:** Replaces the highlighted text with the text you typed into the Replace with text box and then highlights the next instance of the text. You now have the same choice to make for this word.

- **<u>N</u>o:** Leaves the highlighted text alone. The next instance of the text is highlighted, and you now have the same choice to make for this word.

- **Yes to <u>A</u>ll:** Changes every instance in the page and closes the dialog box.

9. Click <u>C</u>lose when you're done replacing, unless you clicked Yes to <u>A</u>ll.

Global Replace works very similarly to the standard replace but lets you search any or all your Web's pages for the text you want to change. Before you use Global Replace, you may want to review the options for Global Find outlined in the earlier section, "Combing a page with the Find feature."

To pick and choose what replacements to make with Global Replace:

1. Highlight a page and click Edit File.

The page appears in Source view, the first instance of the word is highlighted, and the Replace dialog box appears.

2. Click one of the following buttons, as appropriate.

- **<u>Y</u>es:** Replaces the highlighted text with the text you typed into the Replace with text box and then highlights the next instance of the text. You now have the same choice to make for this word.

- **<u>N</u>o:** Leaves the highlighted text alone. The next instance of the text is highlighted. You now have the same choice to make for this word.

- **Yes to <u>A</u>ll:** Changes every instance in the page and closes the dialog box.

- **<u>C</u>ancel:** Closes the Replace dialog box and reopens the Files Containing dialog box. The file you were working on now has a check mark next to it indicating that you've already worked with that file.

When all your changes have been made, the Continue with Next File dialog box appears (unless you clicked Cancel).

3. Make sure that the Save changes to this file before continuing check box is selected.

If this check box is not selected, then your changes will not be saved.

4. Click <u>Y</u>es.

Your changes are saved, and the next page appears. Repeat these steps for all your Web pages.

To make all the replacements at one time:

1. Click <u>R</u>eplace All.

A dialog box appears, asking if you want to back up your files before proceeding.

2. Click Yes.

All the listed files are backed up, all the replacements are made, and the Files Containing dialog box reappears. Now all the filenames have check marks next to them, indicating that they've been updated.

3. Click <u>D</u>one.

The Files Containing dialog box closes, and all your files have been updated.

Tweaking Text and Graphics

The WebMaster Suite support for text and graphics is fantastic. You can do almost anything with either of them — almost. In this section, I show you a few extra tricks to help you display your text exactly the way you want it to be and to speed up the view time for your graphics.

Specifying more than one typeface

As I mention in Chapter 5, your best bet is to stick with the standard Windows typefaces Arial and Times New Roman. Unfortunately, this approach doesn't help when the person viewing your Web page is running a Macintosh, which usually doesn't include either of those typefaces. Here's an easy way to get around this problem: Specify two typefaces instead of just one.

On other computer systems, the typeface Helvetica is extremely similar to Arial, and Times is almost identical to Times New Roman. What you need to do is tell your visitors' browsers, "Hey, use Arial if you're a Windows computer and use Helvetica if you're anything else." (In the case of Times New Roman, you'd tell the other browsers to use Times.) I bring this topic up in this chapter because you can't do it by using the standard editing techniques in DESIGNER. You have to attack the HTML code directly.

When a typeface is specified in HTML code, it reads:

```
<FONT FACE="...">
```

Inside the quotation marks is the name of the typeface. So, for example, if the text appears in Times New Roman typeface, the HTML code reads as follows:

```
<FONT FACE="TIMES NEW ROMAN">
```

But how do you tell the browser that it has a choice of typefaces to display? Just add a comma followed by the name of the other typeface inside the quotes, like the following examples:

```
<FONT FACE="TIMES NEW ROMAN,TIMES">
```

```
<FONT FACE="ARIAL,HELVETICA">
```

Now for the bad news: You have to make this change every place that you specify a typeface. Even for a relatively short page, this can be extremely obnoxious to change by hand. For an entire Web site with tens, or even hundreds of pages, this task would be a nightmare. Sounds like a job for Global Replace!

Here are a couple of things to keep in mind when you use the Global Replace dialog box to update your typefaces:

- ✔ In the Find text box, make sure that you include the quotation marks before and after the typeface. Type **"ARIAL"** and **"TIMES NEW RO- MAN"** — quotation marks and all. Doing so ensures that you don't end up with something later on like "ARIAL,HELVETICA,HELVETICA,- HELVETICA" if you update your Web site a couple of times.

- ✔ Type both names in the Replace with text box, including the comma and quotation marks.

- ✔ Don't check the Match whole word only check box. Otherwise you have to type in **FACE="ARIAL">** instead of just **"ARIAL"** — which increases your chances of making a typo.

Adding a low resolution image

Sometimes, you just have to include an image that takes a long time to download. There is a way to do this without driving your visitors crazy: Have their browsers display a lower-resolution version of the image that appears quickly, while the full version is downloading.

The first thing you have to do is create the low-resolution, low-color-depth version of your image. What you want to do is create an image that's one-half the size of the original and uses 256 colors. To do this, follow the instructions in Chapter 14. (I've seen this technique shrink images to less than one one-hundredth of the original's size, reducing a five-minute download to just *three seconds!*)

Be sure to save the resampled image with a new filename; otherwise, you will delete your original image! I suggest that you add "lowres" to the name of the new image. So if your original image is `filename.jpg`, you might name the new image `filenamelowres.jpg`. This addition helps you tell the two images apart.

Now you have to tell your visitors' browsers how to use that image to provide a quickly displayed image that holds your visitors' attention while the high-resolution image is downloading:

Locate the HTML tag that inserts the image you're interested in. (This is an excellent place to use the find feature and look for the image's file name.)

The HTML tag looks like:

```
<IMG BORDER="0" SRC="your.file.name.JPG" HEIGHT="700"
          WIDTH="525">
```

Add the following HTML code (including the quotation marks) after the closing quotes:

```
LOWSRC="your.new.image's.name.JPG"
```

Now when a visitor views your site, the low-resolution image loads quickly and gradually is replaced by the high-resolution image as it downloads.

Making Forms More Functional

You can do great things with forms in your Web pages. With a little tweaking, you can add new functions and even graphical buttons. Chapter 10 provides more information about incorporating forms in your Web pages.

Hidden fields

After a visitor fills out a form on your Web page, a Common Gateway Interface Script (CGI) takes the information and does something with it — it may e-mail the information to you, add the visitor's information to a database, or enter an order in an online store system. Many CGI scripts let you add special controls to them by incorporating hidden fields — a *hidden field* is just like any other field that you have in your form, except that your visitors can't see it and can't change its information. For example, you may be able to specify an e-mail address to which the form is sent.

Because DESIGNER doesn't support hidden fields, you have to add them directly into the HTML code. Figure 13-3 shows a simple form in Source View.

Your CGI script documentation has the exact format for the hidden field, but in general you type a new line similar to:

```
<INPUT TYPE="HIDDEN" NAME="required.name"
              VALUE="something">
```

You can type this text anywhere within the form (that is, anywhere between the codes <FORM...> and </FORM>).

Note that when you use DESIGNER to view and edit a form that includes hidden fields, the fields are visible (see Figure 13-4). Don't worry, though, they will be hidden again when the page is viewed in a browser. It's a good idea to format your page (with tables, typefaces, and so on) before you add hidden fields because you can't really see the formatting in DESIGNER otherwise.

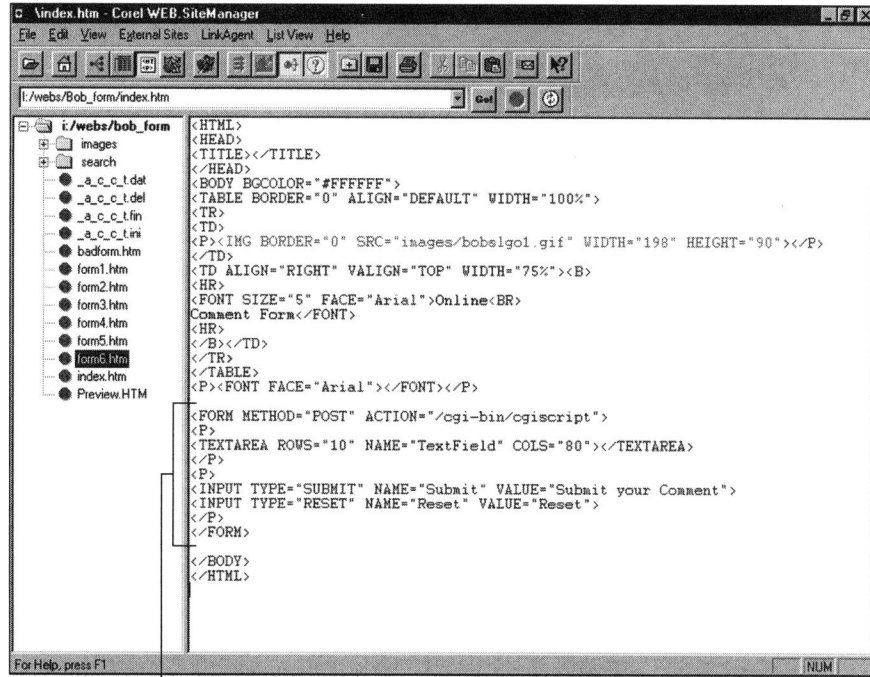

Figure 13-3:
The HTML
code for a
simple form,
shown in
Source
View.

Form code

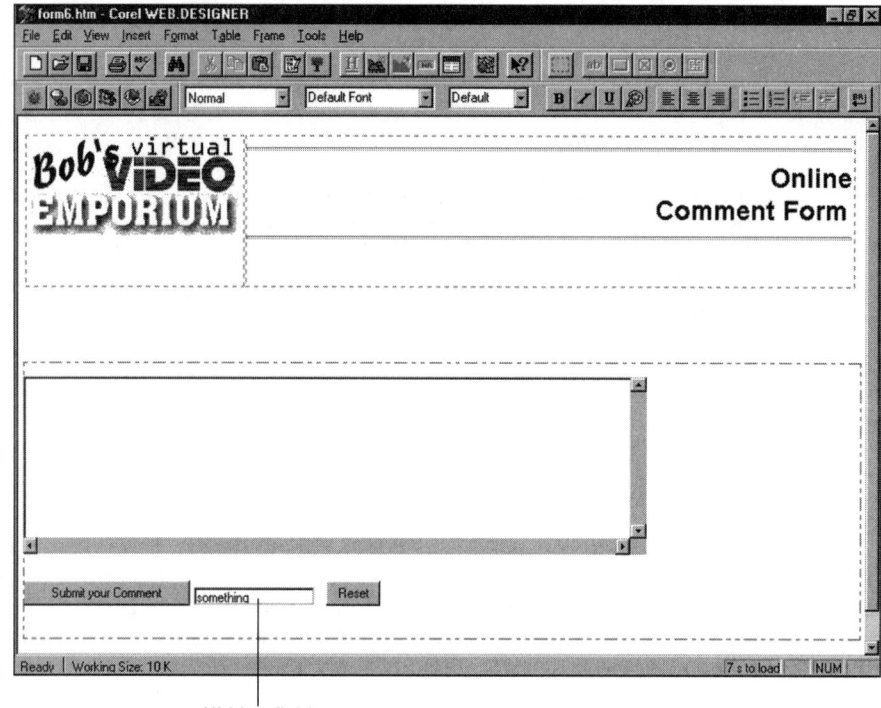

Hidden field

Creating graphical form buttons

Using really simple codes, you can make your forms look much better. The easiest way to add a graphical form button is to add a regular Submit or Reset button (refer to Chapter 10). Then you can edit the HTML code so that each button displays an image instead of the usual text. Code for a standard Submit button looks like this:

```
<INPUT TYPE="SUBMIT" NAME="Submit" VALUE="Submit">
```

All you need to do is change the code a little bit so that it looks like this:

```
<INPUT TYPE="IMAGE" SRC="your.image's.name" NAME="Submit"
         VALUE="image.name.without.path">
```

If you're posting your Web site to a UNIX computer, make sure that you get the capitalization of your filename correct because UNIX is case sensitive.

Enlivening Tables

Tables can be pretty boring affairs. Don't get me wrong, they're great for laying out your Web page, but when you put together a table where you can actually see the borders, one table looks pretty much like another. But if you're sneaky about tinkering with the source code, you can find ways to jazz up your tables and make them things of beauty.

Before you begin to edit table code, you need to know the parts of the table code. Every table has the same format in HTML code, as shown in Table 13-1.

Table 13-1	Universal HTML Table Codes
Code	*What It Means*
<TABLE>	Start a table
<TR>	Start a row
<TD>	Here comes some stuff to put in a cell
(The stuff you want to show up in the cell goes here.)	
</TD>	That's the end of the stuff that goes in that cell
</TR>	End this row
</TABLE>	End this table

In essence, these codes are all that make a table a table. You can have a bunch of cells in a row, in which case, you see more <TD>...</TD> groups. You can have a bunch of rows in a table, in which case, you see more <TR>...</TR> groups. The <TABLE>, <TR>, and <TD> tags may also have some codes within them that specify things about them, such as instructions for cell width, background color, and other things. But Table 13-1 represents the basic structure.

Row height

The Cell Properties dialog box lets you know that you can make a cell and the whole column it's in a certain width. But you may not know that you can also specify the cell height and the height of the whole row it's in. To specify the row height, you just add the code HEIGHT="#" to one of the row's cell tags (the <TD> tag). Replace the pound sign (#) with the number of pixels high you want the row to be. For example, to create a row that's 75 pixels high, you make one of its cells read:

```
<TD HEIGHT="75"> ... </TD>
```

These tags may contain other modifiers that control color, but all you really need to be concerned about is adding the height modifier.

No cell spacing

Making your cells butt right up against each other doesn't really involve a lot of HTML editing, just a bit of persistence.

When you use tables to format your Web page, you usually want to use cell colors as borders or color accents. When you try to tell DESIGNER that you don't want any space between the cells, however, you end up getting a bunch of cells with spaces between them.

These spaces appear between your cells because when you set the Cell Spacing to zero, instead of saying "Hey, don't put any space between these cells," you were telling DESIGNER to remove the CELLSPACING code from the `<TABLE>` tag. The easiest way to fix this problem and get rid of the extra spacing is as follows:

1. **Click anywhere in the table and then choose Table⇨Table Properties.**

   The Table Properties dialog box appears.

2. **Set Cell Spacing to 1.**

   I know this step sounds screwy considering that you don't want *any* cell spacing, but bear with me a minute.

3. **Click OK.**

4. **Choose View⇨Document Source.**

   The Source View of your HTML page appears.

5. **Replace the "1" in the tag** `<TABLE CELLSPACING="1">` **with** `"0"`.

   This value forces the cells together.

6. **Click Keep Changes.**

   Although your page doesn't look any different in DESIGNER, when you preview your page, you see a big difference.

Border colors and background images

The codes noted in this section are Microsoft Internet Explorer-only — Netscape Navigator does not understand them. Always preview your Web page in both Explorer and Navigator to make sure that it doesn't look too screwy when your colors and background image don't show up. All the codes noted in this section are added to the `<TABLE>` tag that defines your table.

You can even add a background image behind your table's text and borders. If the image is small, it will tile just like the background image for an entire page. (See Chapter 7 for more information about backgrounds.) To add an image behind your table, include this code:

```
BACKGROUND="your.image.name.and.location"
```

The standard light gray and dark gray for table borders can get fairly boring. You can change the border colors very easily by adding the following two codes:

```
BORDERCOLORDARK="color"
BORDERCOLORLIGHT="color"
```

DARK is the color for the right and bottom edges of the table border, and LIGHT is the color for the border's top and left edges. In place of the word color, put in whatever color you want the border to be. You have a nearly endless list of colors to choose from: blue, red, green, teal, yellow, purple, cyan, black, aqua.

Tweaking Frame Borders

In Chapter 9, I note that Microsoft uses a couple of different codes to remove frame borders from the codes that Netscape and DESIGNER use. To have a frame without any border when viewed with Internet Explorer, you have to add a couple of quick codes to your frame set HTML.

To add this code:

1. **Open the frame set in DESIGNER.**

   This is the page that includes all the other pages in it. Even if you've deselected the border option, DESIGNER still shows your Web pages with a border to make them easier to edit.

2. **Choose View⇨Document Source.**

   The HTML text editor opens and displays the codes that create the grids of your frames. Remember that the individual pages that are loaded in the frame set each have their own HTML code files — what's displayed here just defines how the frames align with each other.

3. Add the following codes to the <FRAMESET> **code:**

```
FRAMEBORDER="NO" FRAMESPACING="0"
```

Other codes will also be within the <FRAMESET> code. Just make sure that the codes you type are inside the < and > brackets.

4. Click the Keep Changes button.

The DESIGNER window reappears, where everything looks the same as you left it. Go ahead and preview the page in Internet Explorer to see that the changes were made.

Part III
Creating Your Own Graphics

The 5th Wave   By Rich Tennant

MIDTOWN P

WHERE'S THE
DANG DOOR?!

Website Design Co.

C'mon in!

OUR AWARDS

In this part . . .

One of the things that makes WebMaster Suite such
a great value is the huge number of additional
programs, beyond SiteManager and DESIGNER, that Corel
puts at your disposal. Probably the most useful among
these are the graphics programs: PhotoPaint, DRAW,
MOVIE, and WORLD.

This part shows you how to use each of these programs
to create totally rad graphics and multimedia visuals for
your Web site.

Chapter 14

Get Pixelated with PhotoPaint

A mystery surrounds PhotoPaint, and I haven't quite figured it out yet. PhotoPaint is essentially identical to Corel PhotoPaint 7 Plus, though it does lack some of the really high-end bells and whistles. Yet PhotoPaint comes packaged with WebMaster Suite, which sells for significantly less than PhotoPaint 7 costs by itself.

You can do just about everything with PhotoPaint, from scanning photographs to editing clip art to adding text. The only thing you can't do is print.

If you've never used an image editing program, you may be a little intimidated by all the unfamiliar terms that you encounter. Never fear: I explain everything you need to know in this chapter. One thing you will notice about this chapter, however, is that I don't include a lot of step-by-step instructions: I show you what the tools are and how to use them, but you really have to roll up your sleeves and practice with this program to get good at it.

Chapter 7 contains a lot of information about the images that you can use in Web pages. I recommend that you look over that chapter before you do too much with PhotoPaint. PhotoPaint is so rich with features that I can't cover them all in the space I have. This chapter introduces you to the tools that you use the most when you create Web pages, but if you really want to put PhotoPaint through its paces, pick up *CorelDRAW 7 For Dummies,* by Deke McClelland (IDG Books Worldwide, Inc.) and read Chapters 15, 16, and 17. (PhotoPaint is also packaged with CorelDRAW 7.)

Getting Started

As with every program in WebMaster Suite (except for SiteManager), you can start PhotoPaint a few different ways:

- ✔ Choose Start➪Programs➪Corel WebMaster Suite➪Corel PhotoPaint.
- ✔ Click the PhotoPaint button in the DESIGNER Applications toolbar.
- ✔ Double-click an image file in SiteManager's left-side file list to automatically loads the image in PhotoPaint.
- ✔ Double-click an image in DESIGNER and, when the Image Properties dialog box appears, click the Edit Image button to automatically load the image into PhotoPaint.

If you opened PhotoPaint through the Start menu or by clicking the PhotoPaint button in DESIGNER, the friendly Welcome to Corel PhotoPaint dialog box greets you. From there, you can create a brand-new image, open the last image you worked with, open a different image, or scan a new image (if you set up a scanner when you installed WebMaster Suite).

The screening room

After you load an image into PhotoPaint, which I explain in the next section, "Open sesame," the screen looks fairly similar to the view in every other Windows program. You have menus, a status bar, and gobs of toolbars (see Figure 14-1). Table 14-1 describes what each of these screen elements does.

Table 14-1	The PhotoPaint Screen
Screen Part	**What It Does**
Image	Edit your images here. (Of course, your images probably won't be the logo for Bob's Virtual Video Emporium.)
Menu bar	As in other Windows programs, you make menu selections here.
Minimize, Restore/ Maximize, and Close buttons	As in other Windows programs, these buttons control the size of the PhotoPaint window and allow you to close the program.
Toolbar	You can open files, use the Clipboard, access help, control the zoom level, and do many other things by using the buttons in the toolbar.

Toolbar   Open roll-up menu   Tool properties

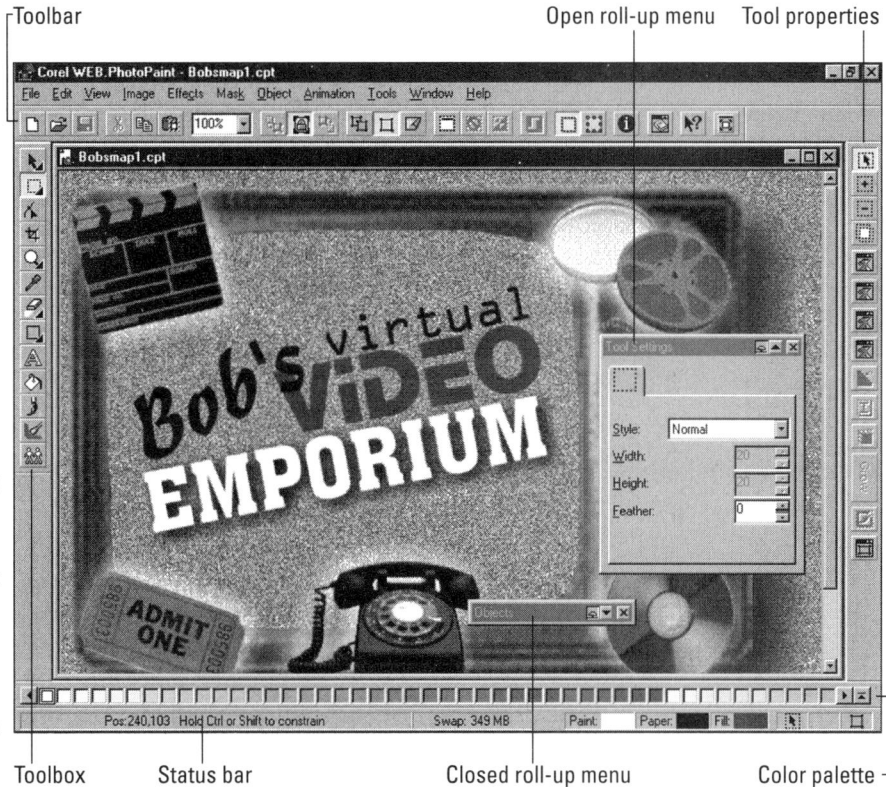

Figure 14-1:
The
PhotoPaint
screen and
all its
myriad
parts.

Toolbox   Status bar   Closed roll-up menu   Color palette

Screen Part	*What It Does*
Toolbox	Select the different tools for painting, erasing, working with masks and objects, and applying special effects.
Property Bar	This toolbar changes to display settings that you can make for a specific paint tool.
Status bar	Look here for information about the current image and your system.
Roll-up menu	Different roll-up menus perform different functions. This may be a new feature to you. A roll-up menu is like a toolbar that you can hide away when you don't need it. But it reappears at a touch of the down-arrow button in its title bar.

Open sesame

With the 547 kajillion buttons, photographs, bars, and other images that come with WebMaster Suite, you may never create a new image from scratch. You can spend years just working with the ones that already exist. You do, however, become *extremely* skilled at opening existing images.

Opening an image in PhotoPaint is basically like opening a file in any other Windows program. But Corel has added a couple of nice features to make your life easier. To open an image:

1. **If you want to open an image from the WebMaster Suite CD#2, put the CD in your drive.**

   If the image you want is on the CD that came with this book, put that disc in your drive instead. The CD-ROM that comes with this book contains two clipart libraries with tons of images that you can open in PhotoPaint — see "Celine Chamberlin's Clipart" and "Jelane's Free Web Graphics" in Appendix B for a short description of the clipart.

2. **Choose File⇨Open, press Ctrl+O, or click the Open button in the PhotoPaint toolbar.**

   The Open an Image dialog box appears.

3. **Locate the image you want to open.**

   Select drives from the Look in drop-down menu and double-click folders in the central file area to open them.

4. **Click the image you want to select it.**

   This is the point where you get the benefit of one of PhotoPaint's special file-opening features: When you highlight an image, PhotoPaint displays a thumbnail sketch of the image in the preview window at the right edge of the dialog box (so long as the Preview check box is selected). Near the bottom of the dialog box, it also displays the size and format of the image. This information can be very helpful because the files on the CD have bizarre names, like b2anlg01.gif, which tells you absolutely nothing about the image.

5. **Click Open, press Enter, or double-click the icon next to the image name.**

   The image opens in PhotoPaint.

What's new?

Using existing images is great, but even with all the images that come with WebMaster Suite and the CD that accompanies this book, you probably still want to create your own images with PhotoPaint. Being faced with a totally blank image window may feel a little intimidating, but with a little practice using all the tools, you'll be cranking out Web-ready images that'll make you proud.

To create a new image:

1. **Choose File⇨New, press Ctrl+N, or click the New button in the PhotoPaint toolbar.**

   The Create a New Image dialog box appears.

   You can also open this dialog box by clicking the Create a New Image button in the Welcome to Corel PhotoPaint dialog box that appears when you start the program.

2. **Select the color depth from the Color Mode drop-down list.**

   Although you have four choices here for Web images, you only need to concern yourself with two: Paletted and 24-Bit RGB color. Use Paletted when you're creating GIF images and 24-Bit when you're creating JPG images. Chapter 7 has an explanation of these two file formats and some tips on which one to use for different types of images.

3. **Pick a background color for the image from the Paper color drop-down list.**

   This is the color of the "canvas" that you'll be painting on. Typically, you want to pick the same color as the background of the Web page to which you'll be adding the image.

4. **Specify a size for your image.**

   Select pixels from the drop-down list to the right of Width, if it isn't already selected. Then type the number of pixels wide and high that you want the image in the Width and Height text boxes.

   - If you're creating icons, typical sizes are 24, 36, or 48 pixels square (both width and height are the same).

   - If you're creating a banner ad (like the ones you see in Web sites that advertise other Web sites or products), the standard size is 468 pixels wide by 60 pixels high.

   - For logos and other images, set the height and width to whatever you want. Remember that the larger the image is, the longer it takes to load.

5. **Specify the image's resolution.**

   The *resolution* is the number of pixels (or dots) that equals one inch when the image is printed. You may think that specifying a resolution is unnecessary, but remember that people will probably print your Web pages, and you want the images to look good when they do. Both 72 dpi (dots per inch) and 96 dpi work well for images printed from the Web.

Type the desired resolution in either the Horizontal or Vertical text box. Do not deselect the Identical values check box! You may create some screwy problems for your visitors' printers if the Horizontal and Vertical resolutions are not the same.

6. Click OK.

If you selected 24-Bit RGB Color for your color mode, the dialog box closes and a new, blank image window appears.

If you selected Paletted, the Create a New Image dialog box is replaced by the Color Table dialog box.

7. Select a color table from the <u>T</u>able drop-down list.

Select either Microsoft Internet Explorer or Netscape Navigator, depending on which browser you think most visitors will use to view your site. Currently, Netscape Navigator still holds the lead in market share, but Microsoft Internet Explorer is gaining fast. I wish I could give you a hard-and-fast rule about which color table to use, but with the Browser Wars still going strong, it's a little too early for that.

8. Click OK.

The dialog box closes, and a new, blank image window appears. Now you can begin painting to your heart's content.

Those three important words: Save, save, save

Well, it doesn't do you much good to edit or create an image if you don't save it, now does it? Saving an image from PhotoPaint is pretty much the same as saving any other file from any other program. You do need to keep a few things in mind, though, so that DESIGNER can use the image in your Web site.

The vast majority of Web browsers only understand two types of images: GIF files and JPG files. Be sure to save your images in one of these formats. For more information about GIF and JPG images, see Chapter 7.

If you opened an existing image from your hard drive, choose <u>F</u>ile⇨<u>S</u>ave. Depending on the type of image you're saving (GIF or JPG), you see one of two dialog boxes that ask for more information:

✔ If your image is a GIF file, the GIF89a options dialog box opens. Here, you can specify whether you want the image to be *interlaced* — that is, to first appear fuzzy in the browser window and then to get progressively sharper.

You can also set a transparent color, if you want one, from this dialog box. Your options for transparency are None, Masked area, and Image color. (*Transparency* in a GIF image means that the area or color doesn't show up when the image appears in a Web browser, allowing the background image or color to show through.)

- **If you select Masked area:** Everything outside the image's mask is transparent. If the image doesn't include a mask, this option is grayed. *Masks* are the electronic equivalent of masking tape: They let you paint in some parts of your image without having to worry about harming an area that's perfect. (See "Masks," later in this chapter.)

- **If you select Image color:** You can specify the transparent color. Click the small crosshair on the color in the thumbnail of the image or select the color from the color table to the right of the image. (Clicking the image is generally easier.)

Click OK when you're done setting the options to save the file.

✔ If the image is a JPG file, the JPEG Export dialog box appears. Here you specify the quality factor you want to use. The higher the number, the smaller the file size, but the worse the image looks. For the best appearance, set the quality factor no higher than 6. Selecting the Progressive check box is similar to the interlaced option for a GIF image.

Your hard drive whirs for a moment as it saves the image.

If you created a new image, opened an image from WebMaster CD#2, or want to save an altered image under a different name:

1. **Choose File⇨Save As or click the Save button.**

    The Save an Image to Disk dialog box appears.

2. **Navigate your hard drive to find the folder in which you want to save your image.**

    If you plan to use the image you're saving in your Web site, make sure that you save it in the Web root folder (see Chapter 3 for more information). If you took my advice in Chapter 3 and created a separate Image folder within your Web root, save this image in that folder.

3. **Specify a name for the file in the File name text box.**

    If you loaded this image from the WebMaster Suite CD and don't mind the sometimes-bizarre names they give, just leave the name as is.

4. **Select the image format in the Save as Type drop-down list.**

    If the image is paletted, select CompuServe Bitmap (GIF). If it's 24-bit RGB, select JPEG Bitmap (JPG).

   5. Click Save.

   The Save an Image to Disk dialog box closes.

   - If you selected CompuServe Bitmap for the file type, the GIF89a options dialog box opens. Set the Transparency and Interlace options, and then click OK. The image is saved to disk.

   - If you selected JPEG for the file type, the JPEG Export dialog box opens. Set the Quality Factor and Progressive options, and then click OK. The image is saved to disk.

Vroom-a-zoom-zoom

Most of the images that you're likely to edit for your Web pages are fairly small — a button or a small icon, for example. Trying to work with an image like that at its actual size can be a real bear. Luckily, you can zoom in and out so that you can see and work with the image better.

Because being able to see your work is so important, PhotoPaint provides you with a lot of tools to precisely zoom in and out (see Figure 14-2). Before you start zooming in and out with small images, you want to make the image window much larger so that you can see more. To do this, either drag the lower-right corner of the image window down and to the right, click the Maximize button, or press Alt+– (minus sign) and then press X.

To zoom in to a specific area of the image:

1. **Select the Zoom tool from the toolbox.**

2. **Click-and-drag a box around the area.**

   When you release the mouse button, the image expands to show the area.

Zoom levels below 100 make the image appear smaller; levels above 100 make it appear larger. To zoom to a standard zoom level, do either of the following:

- Choose View⇨Zoom and then select a zoom percentage.
- Click the down arrow next to the Zoom Level drop-down list (see Figure 14-2) and then pick a percentage.

To zoom in to the next standard zoom level, do any of the following:

- Press F2. The image expands from the center of the screen.
- Select the Zoom tool and click it anywhere in the image. The image expands, centered on where you clicked.
- Select the Zoom tool and then click the Zoom In button on the Tool Properties toolbar. The image expands from the center of the screen.

View menu   Zoom level   Image window   100% scale   Zoom out
                                           1:1 scale   Zoom in
                                           Zoom to fit   Zoom tool

Figure 14-2:
PhotoPaint
provides
many
tools for
changing
the view of
the image.

Zoom tool   Navigator pop-up button

To zoom out to the next standard zoom level, do any of the following:

- Press F3.
- Select the Zoom tool and either right-click or Shift+click.
- Select the Zoom tool and click the Zoom Out button on the Tool Properties toolbar.

To view the image at its normal size (100% scale), do either of the following:

- Press Ctrl+1.
- Choose View⇨Zoom 100%.

To have the image fill the entire image window, do any of the following:

- ✔ Press F4.
- ✔ Choose View⇨Zoom to Fit.
- ✔ Select the Zoom tool and click the Zoom to Fit button on the Tool Properties toolbar.

When you're zoomed in and editing an image, make sure that you are using a zoom level that's in the even 100s (100, 200, 300, and so on). If you don't, you won't get an accurate view of the image.

When you zoom in very close, you often can't see the entire image. In this case, you have a number of ways to move around the image so that you can see different areas. Here are two of my favorites:

- ✔ Drag the scroll bars at the bottom or right sides of the image window.
- ✔ Click and hold the Zoom tool until the Hand tool appears. Select the Hand tool and then click-and-drag in the image window to change your view.

A Fresh Coat of Paint

Here's what you've been waiting for — actually painting, drawing, and working with images! If you're unfamiliar with paint programs (Windows Paint, PhotoShop, and so on), working with PhotoPaint may seem a little daunting. You may find the mouse hard to control while you're painting, and you won't get exactly what you want. Patience, dear reader.

You really need to work with a paint program to get good at it. The PhotoPaint tools are very similar to those that actual painters use. You wouldn't expect to start churning out DaVinci-esque masterpieces the first time you picked up a paintbrush. So take your time, fiddle around with all the tool adjustments, and you'll soon be an electronic artist.

Color me blue

Before you can start using the PhotoPaint tools, you need to be able to pick the colors you want to paint with. You can pick the colors from two main places: the Color roll-up (shown in Figure 14-3), and the Color palette (refer to Figure 14-1). Don't confuse the Color palette with a paletted image. The *Color palette* is like a painter's palette, from which you pick your colors. A *paletted image* uses 256 specific colors.

To pick a paint color from the Palette, just click the color you want to draw with. You can also pick the fill color — just by right-clicking on a color. The section "Tastes great, more filling," later in this chapter, goes into more depth on how to set the fill color and use really spiffy custom fills.

To pick a color from the Color roll-up, choose View⇨Roll-Ups⇨Colors to open the roll-up (see Figure 14-3), and then click a color from the group at the bottom of the roll-up. You can see at a glance which colors are currently set by looking at the Paint color box in the upper-left corner of the roll-up. The lower-right box shows the paint color, and the upper-left box shows you the paper color (more about the paper color in the upcoming section, "The erasers").

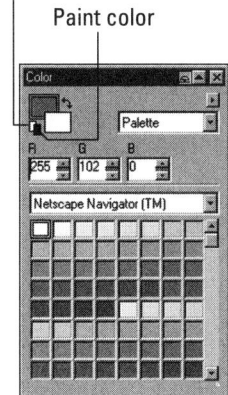

Figure 14-3:
Pick your colors with ease from the Color roll-up.

 If you want the paint color to be the same as a color that's already in the image, select the Eyedropper tool from the toolbox and then click within the image on the color you want. Notice that the paint color box at the bottom of the PhotoPaint screen changes to the color you clicked.

To reset the colors to their original settings (black paint, white paper, and black fill), choose Edit⇨Reset Colors.

Tools of the trade

PhotoPaint comes with a wide variety of painting tools to choose from. Pick the tool you want from the toolbox (see Figure 14-4), and then begin to draw. Each of these tools is explained in this section.

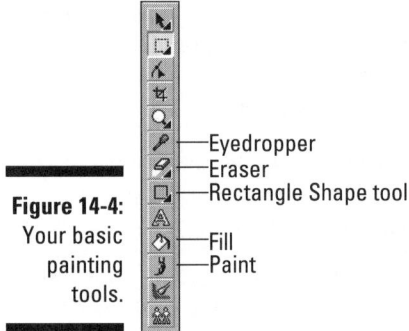

—Eyedropper
—Eraser
—Rectangle Shape tool

—Fill
—Paint

Figure 14-4:
Your basic
painting
tools.

Brush up on painting

 You may think that the Paint tool is a simple little thing — you just click the tool and start drawing. Sure, you can do that, but the Paint tool is really a sophisticated *collection* of tools that you can use for a variety of effects.

Double-clicking the Paint tool opens the Tool Settings roll-up (see Figure 14-5). From this roll-up, you can pick a different brush and change the size, shape, and other attributes for the brush.

┌Brushes

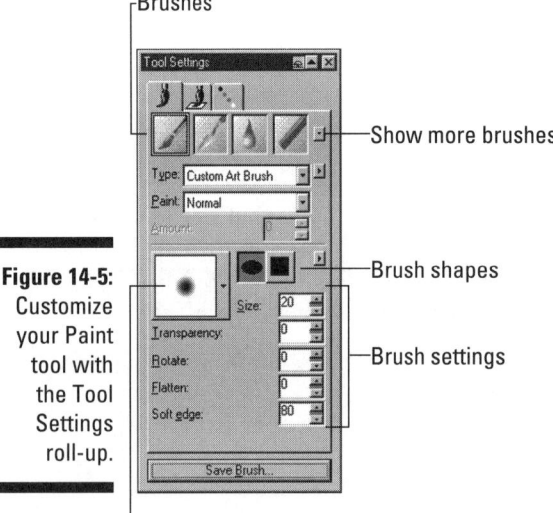

—Show more brushes

—Brush shapes

Figure 14-5:
Customize
your Paint
tool with
the Tool
Settings
roll-up.

—Brush settings

└Preset brushes

To see all the brushes at your disposal, click the small Show More Brushes button. The Brushes list expands to fill the roll-up. You then click the brush you want to use to pick it. Each brush has a number of variations that are listed in the Type drop-down list.

To draw using the Paint tool, just select the tool and then click-and-drag it in the image window. The Graffiti and Power Sprayer brushes are *speed sensitive*. That is, the faster you drag the mouse, the less "paint" they deposit on the image.

The shape of things to come

The Shape tools let you create different shapes: rectangles, ellipses, polygons, and straight lines.

One thing you notice right off the bat about the Shape tool's button in the toolbox is that it has a little triangle in the lower-right corner. This means that more tools are packed into the Shape tool than just the rectangle. To display the other tools, click and hold the Shape tool button. A pop-up menu appears and displays the other available shapes (see Figure 14-6). To pick one of these Shape tools, click it. The pop-up menu closes, and the tool you picked now appears as the Shape tool button.

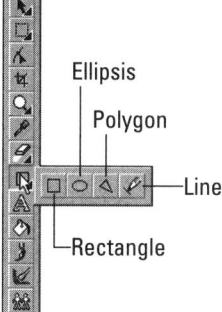

Figure 14-6: The Shape tool button hides a pop-up menu with other shapes.

Ellipsis

Polygon

Line

Rectangle

The Line tool lets you draw straight lines quickly and easily. To draw a line:

1. **Select the Line tool from the toolbox.**
2. **Click the point in the image where you want the line to start.**

   A line extends from where you clicked the mouse pointer.

3. **Move the pointer and click where you want the line to end.**
4. **If you want to add another line from this ending point to somewhere else, just click again somewhere else.**

   If you are done drawing the line, double-click at the ending point.

When you're drawing with the Line tool, you press the Ctrl key to force the line that you're working on to be vertically or horizontally straight, with no angle.

The Rectangle, Ellipsis, and Polygon Shape tools let you create outlines or filled objects in the shape of, well, rectangles, ellipses, and polygons. The Rectangle and Ellipsis tools work very similarly: You select the tool and then click-and-drag to create a shape:

- ✔ If you don't press any buttons while you make the shape, you start from a corner of the rectangle or the corner of an invisible box around the ellipsis.

- ✔ Press the Ctrl key while you drag with the tool to make your shape a perfect square or circle, for the Rectangle and Ellipsis tools, respectively.

- ✔ Press the Shift key while you drag to create your shape from its center.

- ✔ Press both Ctrl and Shift while you drag, and your shape is a perfect square or circle, built from the center.

The Polygon tool lets you make many-sided shapes. To use the Polygon tool:

1. **Select the Polygon tool from the toolbox.**

2. **Click where you want one point of your shape.**

   A line goes from this point to the tool pointer.

3. **Click where you want another point.**

   The line becomes a triangle with one vertex on your starting point, another on your second point, and the third at the tool pointer.

4. **Add more points to define the shape.**

5. **Double-click when you add the final point to your shape.**

   A line now runs from the final point to the first one you added, completing the shape.

When drawing with the Polygon tool, press the Ctrl key to force the line that you're working on to be vertically or horizontally straight, with no angle.

The properties of the shape or line that you draw (line thickness, color, and so on) aren't etched in stone. You have nearly complete control over the appearance of your shape. Double-click the Shape tool button in the toolbox to open the Tool Properties roll-up, shown in Figure 14-7. Note that this figure shows how the roll-up looks when the Rectangle tool is selected — selecting one of the other shape tools changes some of the options available:

- ✔ **Fill:** Specifies the color or pattern that fills the shape you draw. *Fills* are explained in complete detail next in this chapter under "Tastes great, more filling." (The four buttons that control this option aren't available if you're using the Line tool.)

Uniform fill

Fountain fill

Bitmap fill

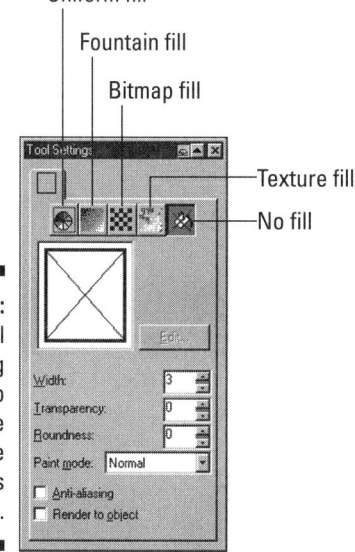

Texture fill

No fill

Figure 14-7:
The Tool
Setting
roll-up
when the
Rectangle
tool is
selected.

- ✔ **Width:** Specifies how wide, in pixels, you want the outline of the shape to be.

- ✔ **Transparency:** Sets the shape's opacity. A setting of 0 (zero) means that the outline is totally opaque. A setting of 99 means that the line is almost totally transparent.

- ✔ **Joints:** Specifies how two line segments join together (see Figure 14-8). Select from Butt, Filled, Round, and Point. For wide lines, I suggest you don't use the Butt option because of the "V" that's chopped out between the two line segments. (This option isn't available for the Rectangle or Ellipse tool.)

- ✔ **Roundness:** Sets the radius, in pixels, for rounded corners of a rectangle (this option isn't available for Ellipsis, Line, or Polygon tools).

- ✔ **Paint mode:** Determines how the color you're drawing your line with interacts with the colors you draw over. This is a super-technical setting that you'll probably never use.

- ✔ **Anti-aliasing check box:** When you select this option, the edge of your shape is softened a little to avoid a hard, jagged appearance.

- ✔ **Render to object check box:** Turns the shape into an object, so that it does not affect what you're painting over (more about objects later in this chapter, under "Objectivity Is in the Eye of the Beholder").

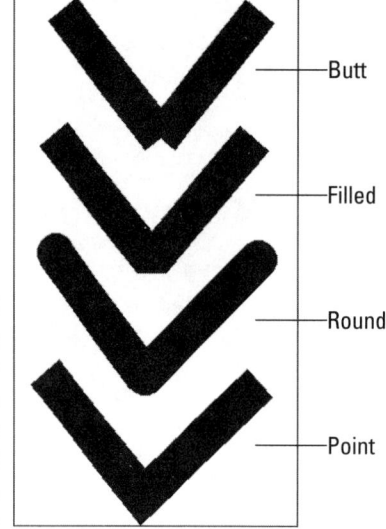

——Butt

——Filled

——Round

——Point

Figure 14-8:
The four
Joints
options
for the
Line tool.

Tastes great, more filling

 The Paint and Shape tools are great if you want to paint in small areas of the image. If you have a large area you want to fill in, you really need the Fill tool. When you click an image area with the Fill tool, the entire color patch that you clicked is replaced with the new color or pattern.

Remember the old Saturday morning cartoons (the good ones from Warner Brothers, not the current crop of merchandising tie-ins for *Genetically Altered Lizard Warriors*)? When the anthropomorphic rabbits and ducks needed to paint a room, they grabbed a roller and paint. The paint looked like wallpaper with patterns, colors, and the whole nine yards. The Fill tool lets you do the same thing. When you select the Fill tool, the Tool Settings roll-up shows you its options (see Figure 14-9).

In the Tool Settings roll-up, you have the following options:

✔ Select your fill type from the four buttons at the top of the roll-up. Each type has an almost infinite number of variations:

- **Uniform Fill:** Creates a fill that is a solid color.

- **Fountain Fill:** Adds a fill that changes from one color to another.

- **Bitmap Fill:** Uses a small image as a tile that is repeated in the fill area. This is similar to Windows desktop wallpaper, and a Web page background image.

- **Texture Fill:** Creates a new fill on the fly, based on settings you make.

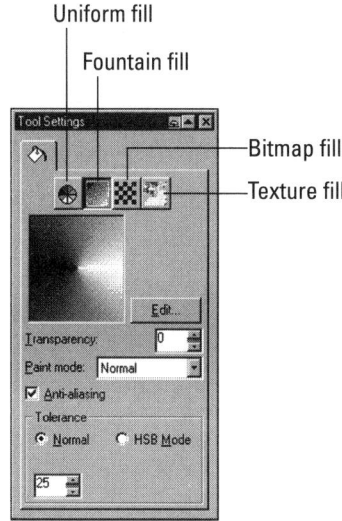

Uniform fill

Fountain fill

Bitmap fill

Texture fill

Figure 14-9:
Set your fill
in the Tool
Settings
roll-up.

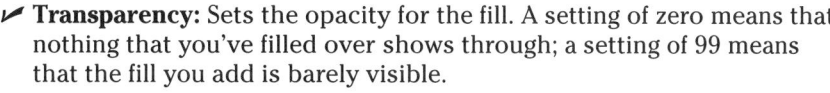

✔ **Transparency:** Sets the opacity for the fill. A setting of zero means that nothing that you've filled over shows through; a setting of 99 means that the fill you add is barely visible.

✔ **Paint Mode:** Determines how the colors in your fill interact with what you're filling over. This is super-technical, and I'd advise against using these options.

✔ **Anti-aliasing check box:** When you select this option, the edge of your fill is softened a little, to avoid a hard edge look.

✔ **Tolerance:** Controls how many colors you fill when you use the Fill tool. A setting of zero means that only the exact color you click is changed. In a 24-bit RGB image, you may find that this doesn't give you a whole heck of a lot of filled space. A setting of 100 means that every color gets filled. Depending on the image, you may have to fiddle around with this setting to get the proper amount of filled area.

Figure 14-10 shows an example of the four fills.

When you pick a fill type, you're not done yet. Click the Edit button to open a dialog box specifically for the type you selected. When you're done setting up your fill, click OK to return to the Tool Settings roll-up. You can then use the tool you selected.

Uniform Fill

Pick your color in the same way as you would using the Color roll-up (explained earlier in this chapter under "Color me blue"). Before you pick your color, you need to set your color mode:

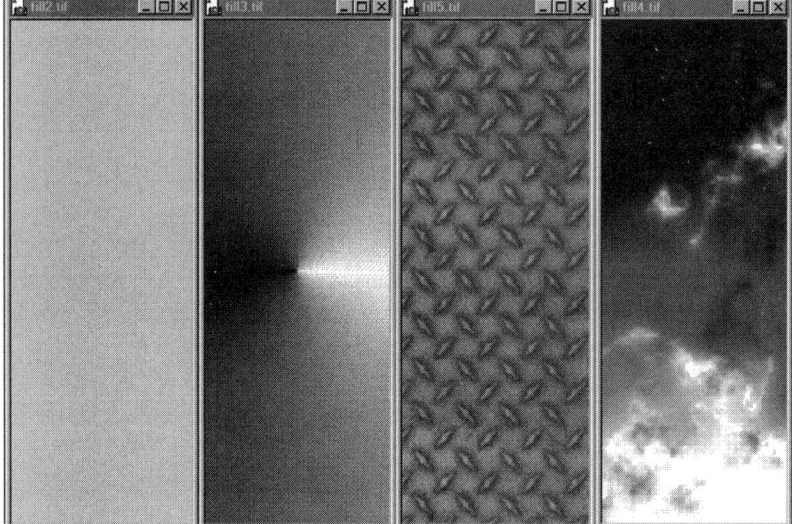

Figure 14-10:
A sample
of the
four fills:
Uniform,
Fountain,
Bitmap, and
Texture fills
(from left to
right).

✔ If you're working in 24-bit RGB, select the Color Models button on the right and then select RGB from the Model drop-down list.

✔ If you're working on a paletted image, select the Palettes button (second from the top, on the right), and then select the palette you're using in the image from the Type drop-down list.

Fountain Fill

Select a type of fountain fill (linear, conical, radial, square, or rectangular) from the Type drop-down list. When you pick a type, a preview of it appears in the window at the right of the dialog box.

✔ Set the colors you want for your fountain in the From: and To: drop-down lists.

✔ Interactively set the center point and/or angle of your fill by clicking or clicking-and-dragging in the preview window.

✔ The Edge Pad setting specifies how much of the ending colors appear at the ends of the fill. A number greater than zero makes a band of solid color.

Bitmap Fill

Click in the preview window at the top of the dialog box to display a list of preset bitmaps that you can use.

Texture Fill

Select one of the Texture libraries from the drop-down list and then pick a specific texture from the Texture list. You can mess around with the settings and colors at the bottom of the dialog box, but you'll probably find that the settings are okay as they are.

Don't cry over spilled milk

It happens to the best of us: You make a mistake somewhere along the line and have to erase it or undo it. That's just life, and you don't have to beat yourself up over it. Use the tools that PhotoPaint gives you, and you'll be right as rain.

Undo

Undo is your easiest way to correct a mistake. Just choose Edit➪Undo, (or press Ctrl-Z), and the last action you took in PhotoPaint is instantly wiped away. If you're like me, you don't notice your mistakes until a couple of minutes after you've made them. Don't worry: You can tell PhotoPaint that you want to be able to undo more than one thing:

1. **Choose Tools➪Options or press Ctrl+J.**

   The Options dialog box appears.

2. **Click the Memory tab.**

   The memory options appear.

3. **Make sure that the Enable undo check box is selected.**

   If this check box is deselected, you can't undo anything!

4. **Set the number of actions you want to be able to undo in the Undo levels text box.**

   Because PhotoPaint has to store all the information about what you've done, the higher this number is set, the more memory it takes. I have no hard-and-fast rules for the number of undo levels that you should use. I usually keep it between five and ten. If you're working on a large RGB image, set the number lower to conserve memory. If you're working on a fairly small paletted image, you can set the number higher.

5. **Click OK.**

   The dialog box closes.

   Note: The little warning about having to restart PhotoPaint for the options to take effect refers to the memory setting options, not the number of undo levels you've set. However, you can't suddenly undo ten things if you've increased the setting from five. PhotoPaint has only stored five actions, so you have to do five more things before you can undo all ten.

With more than one undo level set, you can choose Edit⇨Undo as many times as the number of levels you've set.

The erasers

Just like the name says, the Eraser tool erases what you've painted. But with a powerful program like PhotoPaint, you know that there has to be more to it than that. . . .

 Actually, PhotoPaint has three erasers, and each has its own particular specialty. To pick the different erasers, click and hold the Eraser tool in the toolbox, and select the tool you want from the pop-up menu (see Figure 14-11).

Figure 14-11:
The PhotoPaint Eraser tools give you more options than the little piece of rubber on the end of your pencil.

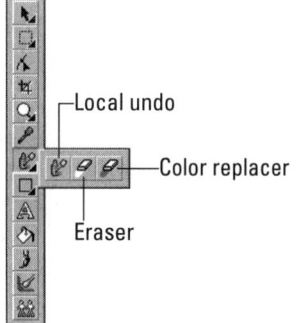

Local undo

Color replacer

Eraser

 Do *not* double-click any Eraser tool in the toolbox. Doing so does *not* open the Tool Settings roll-up. If you double-click the Eraser tool, the eraser effect takes over your entire page. This can be as minor as replacing every pixel of one color with another up to the really horrible action of erasing your entire image. If you should happen to do this by mistake (which I've done on many occasions), use PhotoPaint's handy-dandy Undo feature.

If you want to open the Tool Settings roll-up and adjust the eraser, choose View⇨Roll-Ups⇨Tool Settings. The settings for the erasers are very similar to those for the Paint tool, detailed earlier in the chapter in "Brush up on painting."

So what do these different erasers do, anyway?

✓ **Erase:** Erases everything that's painted in a certain area. Note, however, that if you've changed the paper color, what you erase to is the new paper color, not what you originally set.

✓ **Local Undo:** Erases the last thing you did, but in a small area. This is particularly useful if you slipped with one of your tools and painted over something you didn't want to.

✔ **Color Replacer:** Replaces one color with another. Specifically, it replaces whatever the paint color is with whatever the paper color is. You can set the paper and paint colors as detailed earlier in this chapter in "Color me blue." This is a really nice tool to use when you want to change the color of something.

Masks

If you've ever painted your walls, you know how important masking tape can be. Without it, that nice wood trim around your doorways would be the same color as your walls. Similarly, PhotoPaint lets you mask areas around your image so that you don't mess them up. After you create a mask, everything contained in it can be painted, while everything outside it is protected from errant brush strokes.

I think that masked areas work a little backwards. You may want to think about them this way: Unlike a piece of masking tape that prevents paint from going where the tape is, a PhotoPaint mask *allows paint only in the masked area*.

PhotoPaint puts seven masking tools at your disposal so that you can create and manipulate your masks. These tools are all available from the Mask pop-up menu, shown in Figure 14-12. Each one works a little differently and has its own particular usefulness.

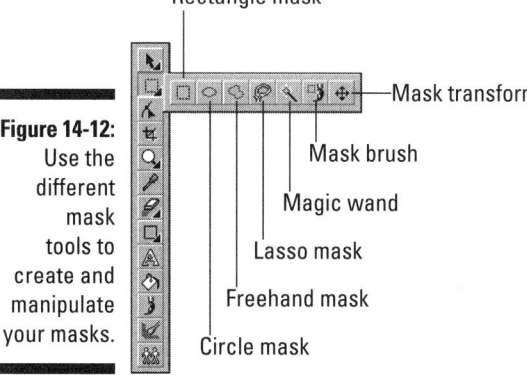

Figure 14-12: Use the different mask tools to create and manipulate your masks.

Rectangle mask — Mask transform — Mask brush — Magic wand — Lasso mask — Freehand mask — Circle mask

You can use these seven tools to create and alter masks:

- **Rectangle Mask tool:** This tool creates a mask in the shape of (surprise) a rectangle. This tool works exactly the same way as the Rectangle Shape tool I discussed earlier in this chapter in "The shape of things to come." To create a mask, select the Rectangle Mask tool and then click-and-drag the cursor in the image to create the mask size you want. When you release the mouse button, the mask appears.

- **Circle Mask tool:** You guessed it! This one makes a mask in the shape of a circle. Actually, it makes one in the shape of an oval, but if you hold down the Ctrl key while you drag, you get a circle.

- **Freehand Mask tool:** Operates the same way as the Polygon Shape tool. Click at one point in your shape and then click at another point. Keep doing this until you have a mask outlined in the shape you want. Then double-click a point to finish.

- **Lasso Mask tool:** This one is really just a version of the Freehand Mask on steroids. You create your mask the same way as with the Freehand Mask tool, but the Lasso gives you more control over your mask. It only includes the background color. This is similar to the way the Color Replacer works. You can specify how close the masked colors have to be to the background color. Just specify a tolerance in the Tool Settings roll-up.

- **Magic Wand tool:** This tool is particularly useful if you have a large area of mostly the same color that you want to mask. Just click the cursor anywhere in the area to select the entire area as a mask. You can also specify how close the masked colors have to be to the background color by specifying a tolerance in the Tool Settings roll-up.

- **Mask Brush tool:** This one works like the Paint tool and lets you paint a mask onto an image.

- **Mask Transform tool:** With the Mask Transform tool you can change the size of your mask.

One thing to keep in mind is that you can only have one mask at a time. However, a mask can have more than one area. To work with masks like this, you have to set the Additive option in the Tool Properties toolbar. You can choose among four ways to create multiple mask areas:

 - **Normal:** When you create a new mask, the old mask is removed. This is the default setting.

 - **Additive:** When you create a new mask, you add its area to the old one.

- **Subtractive:** When you create a new mask, you subtract its area from the old one.

 - **XOR:** When you create a new mask, you add its area to the old one, _except_ where the two masks overlap. In the overlapping area, the mask is removed.

When you want to mask a very large area, you may want to mask a small area and then swap the mask so that the originally unmasked area is now masked, and vice versa. To do this, create a mask and then choose Mask⇨Invert. This is similar to using the Subtractive option but gives you more control.

If you already created an object in the image, as explained in the following section, "Objectivity Is in the Eye of the Beholder," you can use its shape as a mask. To do this, choose Mask⇨Create from Object. To remove your mask, choose Mask⇨Remove.

When you have your mask in place, you can use the final tool on the Mask pop-up, the Mask Transform tool, to make it larger, smaller, or move it.

✔ **To make the masked area larger or smaller:** Select the Mask Transform tool (eight square *scaling handles* appear around your mask). Click and drag one of the scaling handles to make the mask larger or smaller.

- Use any of the four corner handles to make the mask larger or smaller by the same vertical and horizontal amounts.

- Use one of the side or top handles to make the mask larger or smaller, but only in that direction.

- Press the Shift key while you drag a scaling handle to make the mask larger or smaller from its center rather than from the opposite side or corner.

- Press the Ctrl key while you drag a scaling handle to make the mask larger in 100 percent increments: twice as big, three times as big, and so on. You can use both the Ctrl and Shift keys in combination to make the mask larger in 100 percent increments from its center.

✔ **To move the mask itself (not the painted area inside the mask):** Select the Mask Transform tool, then click inside the masked area, and drag the mask to its new location. When you release the mouse button, the mask drops into place.

Objectivity Is in the Eye of the Beholder

Objects are amazingly useful things. With them, you can move a section of an image, rotate the section, or even use the object as the clickable area in an image map (you can learn more about image maps in Chapter 7). You can do even more things with objects, but these are the basic ones that you use the most when you create Web graphics.

Here are two main ways to create an object:

- Mask an area and then choose Object⇨Create from Mask.

- Press Ctrl+C to copy a masked area or entire picture into the Clipboard. Then choose Edit⇨Paste⇨As New Object (or press Ctrl+V). If you want, you can paste the object into a totally different image.

Move to the beat

 To move an object, select the Object Picker tool, click inside the object (eight square scaling handles appear around the object), and drag it to its new location.

If you want to *scale* the object (make it look larger or smaller):

1. Select the Object Picker tool.

2. Click the object you want to scale.

The eight scaling handles appear around the object.

3. Click-and-drag one of the scaling handles to make the object larger or smaller.

Scaling an object works the same as scaling a mask, which is described in the earlier section, "Masks."

4. Press the Spacebar.

The tool that you most recently selected is reselected, and your object is now at its new size.

If you want to rotate an object:

1. Select the Object Picker tool.

2. Click the object you want to rotate.

The eight scaling handles appear around the object.

3. Click the object again.

Rounded arrow-headed lines replace the scaling handles.

4. Click-and-drag one of the rounded arrow lines to rotate the object.

Holding down the Ctrl key while you rotate the object limits the angles that you can rotate the object to 15-degree increments.

5. Press the Spacebar.

The tool that you most recently selected is reselected, and your object is now at its new angle.

Scaling and rotating an object, especially one that's fairly small or is in a paletted image, can have some pretty homely results — sharp edges looking really fuzzy and the possibility of your object becoming unrecognizable. Don't forget our old friend Undo.

A clickable object

As I discuss in Chapter 7, an *image map* is an image that links to different locations, depending on where within the image you click. You can use objects to easily create an image map. To do this:

1. **Select an object.**

   The eight scaling handles appear around the object. (This assumes that you already have an object in the image. If you don't have an object, create one as outlined earlier in "Objectivity Is in the Eye of the Be-holder.")

2. **Choose Object⇨Tag WWW URL.**

   The Tag WWW URL dialog box appears (see Figure 14-13). The object you selected is highlighted in the Object list, and a thumbnail is shown next to the list.

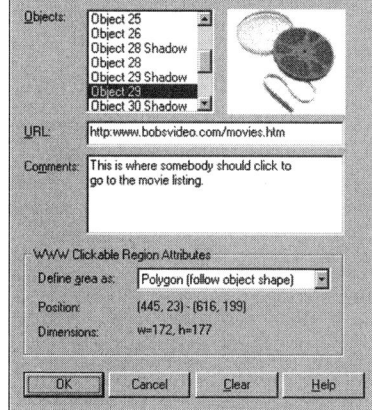

Figure 14-13: Use this dialog box to build an image map by using an image's objects.

3. **Type the URL that you want the object to link to in the URL text box.**

   See Chapter 6 for a discussion of links and URLs. If you don't know where you want the object to link to, type a fake URL, like http://www.fakelink.com, to fill the space. You can then go back and edit the image map when you add the image to a Web page (see Chapter 7).

4. **Select the type of region you want as the border of the object from the Define area as drop-down list.**

   Unless the object is rectangular, circular, or oval, I suggest using the Polygon option. This makes a region that closely hugs the object.

5. **Add a comment in the Comments text box to remind yourself what this link is supposed to do.**

6. **Select another object from the Objects list and specify its URL (as noted in Steps 3, 4, and 5).**

   You can add as many clickable objects as you want.

7. **When you're done, click OK.**

   The dialog box closes, and the objects have URLs associated with them.

8. **Save the image in your Web site folder in either GIF or JPG format, as detailed earlier in this chapter under "Those three important words: Save, save, save."**

   If you plan to edit the image again later, save the image in PhotoPaint CPT format first and then save it in GIF or JPG format.

PhotoPaint Isn't a Word Processor, But . . .

You use the Text tool a great deal when you're making Web graphics — adding labels to buttons, inserting names in company logos, and so on. Any text you add to your image is an *editable object* (meaning that you can go back and change the text later), unless you combine the text with the background or with another object, or unless you save your image in a format other than standard PhotoPaint format (PhotoPaint format images have an extension of .cpt).

1. **Double-click the Text tool in the toolbox.**

   The cursor changes to an I-beam shape, and the Tool Settings dialog box appears (see Figure 14-14). If you don't want to open the Tool Settings dialog box, or if it's already open, you can just single-click the Text tool button.

2. **Click the cursor where you want to start the text.**

   A vertical blinking bar appears in the image, showing you the approximate height that your text will be.

3. **Type in the text.**

   You can type anything you want. Press Enter to add another line of text.

Figure 14-14:
Set your
text
properties
in the Tool
Settings
dialog box.

Text object   Text cursor

4. Set the properties for your text in the Tool Settings dialog box.

The text properties are *sticky:* That is, they stay as whatever you set them, even if you exit and then restart PhotoPaint. You can also make these adjustments before you type your text, but I like to do it afterward, so I can see the changes take effect as I make them.

You can select the font you want, its size, even the alignment (left, right, or center), by using standard word processor-like controls.

• **The Character Spacing:** Specifies how close or far apart you want your letters. Character spacing is normally zero, but you can make the letters closer or farther apart. Set the number as less than or greater than zero, respectively.

• **Line Spacing:** Specifies how far apart lines of text are. Normally, this setting is 100 percent. A setting of less than 100 makes the lines closer together, and greater than 100 makes them farther apart.

• **Anti-aliasing:** Smoothes the edges of your text so that it doesn't look as harsh and computer generated.

• **Render to Mask:** Makes the text a mask instead of an object when you do Step 5. Note that you can't edit your text later if you select this option.

5. When you're done, select the Object Picker tool.

The eight object scaling handles appear around the text. You can now work with the text as you would any object. Note that if you selected the Render to Mask option, your text now appears as a mask marquee, not as an object.

If you want to go back and edit your text later, select the Text tool from the toolbox, and then click the text object. A box appears around the text object (it may take a few tries to get the text selected). The text editing features are fairly limited: You can type new text and use the Backspace and Delete keys to get rid of text, and that's about it.

If you scaled or rotated the text object by using the Object Picker tool, the text is returned to its originally created form. Also, when you edit text, its color changes to whatever the current paint color is.

Image Is Everything

You may find that an image just isn't the right size, color depth, or angle, and you know you just have to switch things around. PhotoPaint makes adjusting your entire image easy.

Cropping

Cropping reduces the size of an image. Just like if you cut the edges off a photograph, cropping reduces the size of the image, but what's shown remains the same size (unlike resampling, which is discussed later in this chapter under "Resampling"). You can crop an image two ways: crop to the mask (if you have one) or use the Crop tool.

If you want to crop your image to a mask, choose Image➪To Mask. Everything outside the smallest rectangle that holds your mask is deleted from the image. If you want to crop to an object, choose Mask➪Create from Object before you crop.

To use the Crop tool:

1. **Select the Crop tool.**

   The cursor changes to a funky kind of double-X thing.

2. **Click-and-drag a box around the area that you want to crop to.**

   A rectangle follows the Crop tool while you drag.

3. **Release the mouse button when the rectangle is the size you want it.**

   Eight scaling handles appear around the rectangle.

4. **Fine-tune the shape of the cropping rectangle.**

   Use the scaling handles the same as you would for an object or a mask (the Ctrl and Shift key combinations don't work for this).

5. **When the cropping rectangle is the right size, double-click within the rectangle.**

   Everything outside the smallest rectangle that holds your mask is deleted from the image.

Resizing

Resizing is similar to cropping, with one major exception: In addition to making your image smaller, you can also make it larger.

When you resize an image, everything you already painted stays the same size, but you make the overall image larger or smaller. If you make the image larger, all the new space is the current paper color. If you make the image smaller, you end up with less image, just like when you crop.

To change the paper size:

1. **Choose Image➪Paper Size.**

   The Paper Size dialog box appears. Notice the preview window at the top of the dialog box. It shows you how the image will look after you accept any settings you make.

2. **Adjust the placement of the original portion of your image in the Placement drop-down list.**

   The options in the Placement drop-down list determine where the original portion of the image is located in the newly resized image. The options that you are provided are fairly self-explanatory.

3. **If you're going to make the image larger, select the color for the new area from the Paper color drop-down list.**

   You can select any color you want, no matter what the paper color was.

4. **Specify the new size of your image.**

   Set the height and width to whatever number you want (typically, you want to use pixels as the unit of measure). If you want to set the height and width independently, deselect the Maintain aspect ratio check box.

5. **Click OK.**

   The dialog box closes, and the image is now bigger or smaller than it was before, depending on what numbers you entered for the height and width. If the image is now bigger than the image window, scroll bars appear at the bottom and right edges of the window.

Resampling

Resampling is like cropping or resizing an image, with one major exception: The image still has the same overall look, but it uses a different number of pixels than it did before. Figure 14-15 shows the same image, twice resampled. The largest version was resampled to 300 percent of the original size, and the smaller version was resampled to 25 percent of the original size.

Resampling can make a big difference in the appearance of an image. Making the image smaller can eliminate fine details; making an image bigger can accentuate the pixels (notice the blockiness of the 300 percent resampling in Figure 14-15).

To resample an image:

1. **Choose Image⇨Resample.**

   The Resample dialog box appears.

2. **Set the new size of the image.**

   Specify the size in pixels in the Width and Height text boxes or as a percentage of the original image size in the text boxes to the right of Width and Height.

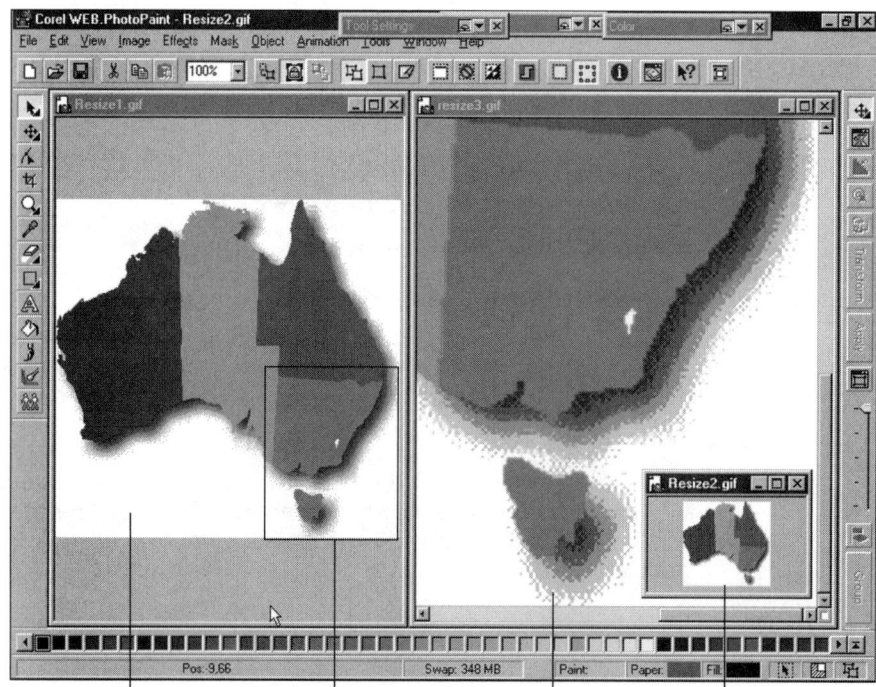

Figure 14-15: The two images on the right are resamples of the image on the left.

Original image   Area of 300% resample   300% resample   25% resample

Although you'll probably never want to do this, you can change the width and height amounts independently if you deselect the Maintain aspect ratio check box.

3. Select the resizing Process.

If you're creating an image that will be a transparent GIF, use the Stretch/Truncate option. This leaves your edges sharp. Otherwise, use the Anti-alias option, to help the image maintain a smooth appearance.

4. Click OK.

The dialog box closes, and PhotoPaint reworks the image to its new size.

Converting colors

Say you have a 24-bit RGB image that you want to save as a GIF. When you try to do this, a little dialog box says. "No, no, no! You can't do that!" When you click OK, you're right back where you started. Before you can save a 24-bit RGB image as a GIF, you need to convert it to 8-bit paletted format. You may also have cases when you want to convert an 8-bit image to 24-bit.

To change a 24-bit image to 8-bit paletted format:

1. Combine all objects with the background and remove all masks.

Leaving the masks in place can really mess up your converted image.

2. Choose Image⇨Convert To⇨Paletted (8-bit).

The Convert to Paletted Image dialog box appears.

3. Under Palette type, select Custom.

This allows you to use the Netscape Navigator palette or Microsoft Internet Explorer palette for the image.

4. Select the Dithering type.

Dithering lets the image simulate more colors than it has by placing pixels of different colors near each other — you generally can't see the individual pixels unless you look closely at the image. However, dithering can make an image look fuzzy.

I suggest leaving the Dither Type option set to None in most cases, especially if you're going to be making an image into a transparent GIF. Dithering can wreak havoc with the border between the transparent and visible parts of the image.

The Error Diffusion option produces a more natural looking image, whereas Ordered looks, well, more orderly. If you must dither, I suggest using the Error Diffusion method.

5. **Click OK.**

The Convert to Paletted Image dialog box closes. Assuming you se-lected the Custom Palette type option, the Color Table dialog box opens. (If you didn't select Custom, then you're all done.)

6. **Select the palette you want to apply to your image from the Table drop-down list.**

Select either Netscape Navigator or Microsoft Internet Explorer. You have to make the same judgment call I talk about throughout this chapter to decide which one. Sorry I can't be more helpful about this.

7. **Click OK.**

The Color Table dialog box closes, and the image updates as the number of available colors is reduced. The colors may change a little on your screen. This is perfectly natural, and there's nothing you can do about it. Because fewer potential colors are available to make up the image, PhotoPaint chooses the ones in the new palette that most closely match the ones in the original image.

You can also use the preceding technique to change the palette being used by an image. For example, if the image uses the Microsoft Internet Explorer palette and you would rather it used Netscape Navigator instead, just go through the preceding procedure and select Netscape Navigator in Step 6. *Voilà!*

You can also convert a paletted image to RGB if you want to add some fancier painting to it, for example. To convert a paletted image to RGB, choose Image⇨Convert To⇨RGB Color (24-bit). That's all there is to it.

The image may not look any different, but there are two differences: The image takes up a lot more space, and your painting looks a lot nicer when any of your tools is set to anti-alias. Also, note that you can't save the image in GIF format.

You may also hear converting an RGB image to a paletted image referred to as *color reduction.* This is another one of those terms that really isn't that important but makes you sound knowledgeable when you drop it around the water cooler.

Flipping out

If you would prefer the image to be upside down, sideways, or some other way, PhotoPaint makes doing this easy.

To rotate an image:

1. Choose one of the following options:

- **Image⇨Rotate⇨90° Clockwise:** The entire image rotates ¹/₄ turn in the clockwise direction, and you're all done. The overall image size remains the same.

- **Image⇨Rotate⇨90° Counterclockwise:** The entire image rotates ¹/₄ turn in the counterclockwise direction, and you're all done. The overall image size remains the same.

- **Image⇨Rotate⇨180°:** The entire image rotates through ¹/₂ a rotation, and you're all done. The overall image size remains the same.

- **Image⇨Rotate⇨Custom:** You specify an exact rotation angle in the Custom Rotate dialog box that opens.

2. Set the rotation angle in the Angle text box.

Set the angle in degrees and select the Clockwise or Counterclockwise radio button to set the direction.

3. Check Maintain Original Image Size to force the rotated image to retain the same height and width.

You may clip off portions of the image if you use this option. Also, portions of the paper by now visible. Select the paper color are using the Paper Color drop-down list.

4. Check the Anti-aliasing check box to smooth the rotated image.

If you're going to use this image as a transparent GIF, I advise that you don't check this box because the edge between the transparent and opaque parts of the image won't be sharp and you can get a fuzzy halo around the opaque area of your image when it appears in a Web browser.

5. Click OK.

The dialog box closes, and the image rotates through the angle that you specified.

Note: You lose some image quality when you rotate an image by any angle other than 90 degrees or 180 degrees.

To flip an image side-to-side, choose Image⇨Flip⇨Horizontally. To flip an image top-to-bottom, choose Image⇨Flip⇨Vertically.

Chapter 15

What's Your Vector, Victor?

*I*n Chapter 14, I introduce Corel PhotoPaint — the powerful bitmap editing program that comes with WebMaster Suite. One of the limitations of bitmap objects is that they are exactly one size. If you make them bigger or smaller, you lose image detail.

Also included with Corel WebMaster Suite is WEB.DRAW, a *vector-based* editing program. Whereas a bitmap image is based on a *pixel* (the tiny dots that make up an image on your computer screen), a vector image uses mathematical formulas to detail the sizes and shapes of objects. When you resize a vector image, it looks exactly the same as it did, except that the image is bigger or smaller.

Unfortunately, Web browsers can't display vector images. To add a DRAW picture to your Web page, you have to export it as a bitmap (in GIF or JPG format). The real advantage of DRAW is that you can export your image in any number of sizes, and each one is just as sharp and clear as the next. As with PhotoPaint, however, you may have a steep learning curve with DRAW, so you have to practice, practice, practice.

WEB.DRAW (DRAW for short) is essentially the same as CorelDRAW Version 5, though WEB.DRAW has been altered to make Web publishing easy. Its bitmap export feature is superb, and you can use DRAW to create image maps (for more about image maps, see Chapter 7). Entire books have been written about CorelDRAW, and this chapter introduces you to its most commonly used features — for a more in-depth look at CorelDRAW 5, check out *CorelDRAW 5 For Dummies* by Deke McClelland (published by IDG Books Worldwide, Inc.).

Gentlemen, Start Your Engines

Before you can use DRAW, you have to start the program. Like most WebMaster Suite programs, you have a couple of different ways to do this:

✔ Choose Start➪Programs➪WebMaster➪Corel DRAW.

✔ Click the Corel DRAW button in DESIGNER's Application toolbar.

When DRAW starts, you are greeted by a blank screen with a little rectangle showing where your page is (see Figure 15-1).

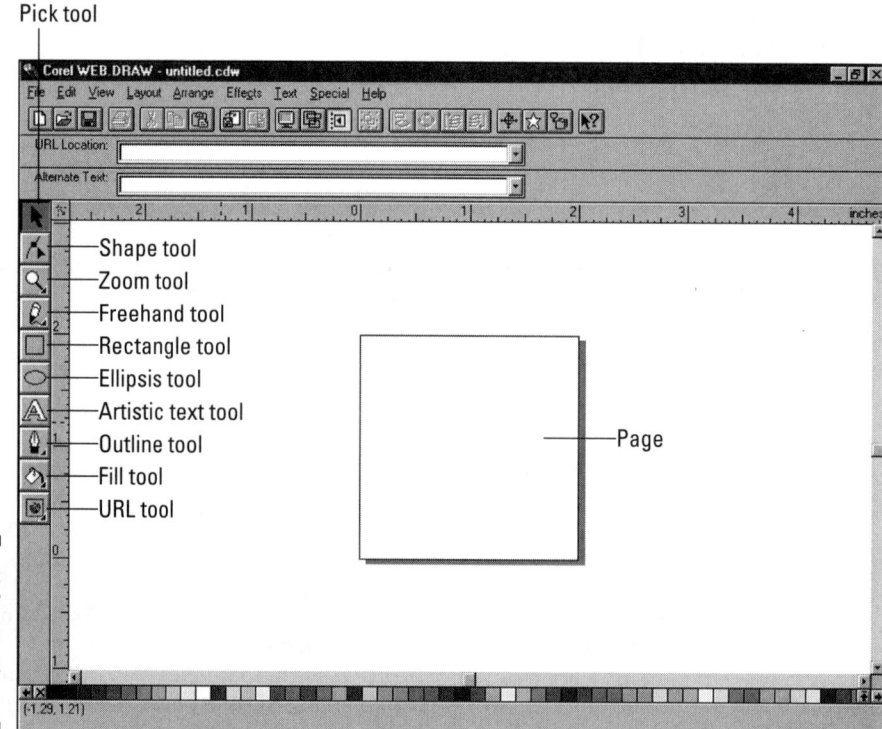

Pick tool

Shape tool
Zoom tool
Freehand tool
Rectangle tool
Ellipsis tool
Artistic text tool
Outline tool
Fill tool
URL tool

Page

Figure 15-1:
DRAW
opens to a
blank
screen.

Opening an image

You're sure to create tons and tons of images using DRAW, so you have to know how to open an image:

1. **Choose File⇨Open, or press Ctrl+O, or click the Open button on the tool bar.**

   The Open Drawing dialog box appears. If you haven't saved a currently open drawing, you'll be prompted to do so before this dialog box opens.

2. **Specify the type of file you're looking for in the List Files of Type drop-down list.**

   You can open DRAW (CDW) and CorelDRAW 5 (CDR) files. You can also open Pattern Files (PWG), but you probably will never use this option.

   If you have any drawings that were made in CorelDRAW versions later than 5, you need to save them in Version 5 format before you can open them in DRAW.

3. **Locate the drawing you want to open.**

   Select a hard or floppy disk drive from the Drives menu and then double-click folders in the Directories list to open folders.

4. **Select the image.**

   Just click the drawing once to highlight it. When you highlight an image, DRAW displays a thumbnail sketch of the image in the preview window at the right edge of the dialog box. This thumbnail can be really helpful if you have a drawing with a Windows 95 long filename, because DRAW automatically truncates filenames. For example, if the filename is bobs_logo_version_1.cdw, DRAW only displays the name as bob_lo~1.cdw.

   You can turn the preview of the drawing on and off by checking and unchecking the Preview check box.

5. **Click OK, or press Enter, or double-click the image's name.**

   The drawing opens in DRAW, and you're ready to do with it what you want.

Saving an image

It wouldn't do you much good to spend time creating a drawing if you couldn't save it, now would it?

Even if you publish your image (as I outline in the next section, "Publishing an image"), you still want to save a DRAW version of it so that you can edit it later in its best quality.

To save a DRAW image:

1. **Choose File⇨Save (Ctrl+S) or File⇨Save As.**

   The Save Drawing dialog box appears. Use the Save As command if you want to save an existing drawing under a new name.

2. **Type a name for your drawing in the File Name text box.**

   Remember that this name has to use the old Windows 3.1 naming scheme: You can have a maximum of eight letters before the period.

3. **If you plan to open the drawing in a standard version of CorelDRAW, select CorelDRAW! File (*.cdr) (not the limited version that comes with WebMaster Suite) the List Files of Type drop-down list.**

   Otherwise, leave this setting as Corel DRAW File (*.cdw), because a normal CorelDRAW file won't contain any image-map information that you add. (I explain image maps in Chapter 7 and later in this chapter.)

4. **Locate the folder in which you want to save your drawing.**

   Select a hard or floppy disk drive from the Drives menu and double-click folders in the Directories list to open folders.

5. **Click OK to save your drawing.**

   The dialog box closes, your hard drive spins for a moment, and you're all done!

Publishing an image

When you're ready to use your drawing in a Web page, you have to make sure that it's in a *format* that Web browsers can understand. It has to be a GIF or a JPG image for anyone else on the Web to see it.

You can save your drawing directly to a GIF or JPG image, though you should only do this if you haven't added any image map information (more about this in "Your Image Map to the Stars," later in this chapter). To turn your vector drawing into a bitmap, GIF, or JPG image:

1. **Choose File⇨Publish⇨to GIF or JPEG.**

   The Publish to an Image dialog box opens. This dialog box is essentially the same as the DRAW Open and Save dialog boxes.

2. **Specify a name for your image in the File Name text box.**

   Remember that this name has to use the old Windows 3.1 naming scheme: The name can be a maximum of eight letters before the period.

3. Select CompuServe Bitmap (GIF) or JPEG Bitmap from the List Files of Type drop-down list.

Chapter 7 discusses the difference between these two file types. Sometimes, exporting an image in GIF format can result in similar colors *blending* together, causing you to lose some definition.

4. Locate the folder in which you want to save your image.

Select a hard or floppy disk drive from the Drives menu and double-click folders in the Directories list to open folders. I suggest that you save the image in you Web root folder or, if you organized your site as I outline in Chapters 3 and 4, save it in your Images folder.

5. Click OK.

If you selected CompuServe format, the dialog box closes and is replaced by the Bitmap Export dialog box (see Figure 15-2). The remaining steps show you how to select your settings for a GIF image.

If you selected JPEG, the Export JPEG dialog box opens. Click OK to save your JPG file, and you're done.

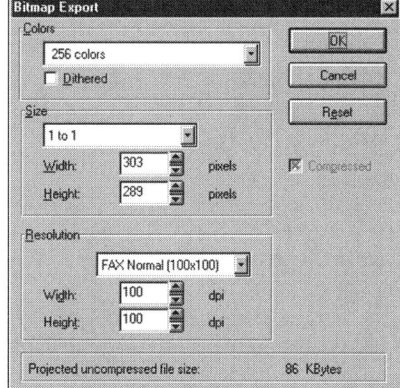

Figure 15-2: Enter the information for your image here.

6. Specify the attributes for your image

- Select 256 colors from the Colors drop-down list. If you plan to use this image as a transparent GIF, don't check the Dithered check box (I explain dithering in Chapter 14).

- Select 1 to 1 from the Size drop-down list. This enables you to specify the size of your image in the Resolution area of the dialog box (see the next bullet point).

• Either select a standard resolution from the Resolution drop-down list or specify custom width and height resolutions. If you enter custom amounts, you must keep the width and height settings the same, or your image will look stretched when it is displayed on a Web page. Also notice the overall size of your image in the Width and Height text boxes.

7. Click OK.

The dialog box closes, and the Transparent Color dialog box opens.

8. If you want to create a transparent GIF, check the Transparent Color check box.

The preview window and a color palette become visible.

9. In the left window, click the color that you want to be transparent in your image.

The small box next to the Transparent Color check box changes to the color you clicked.

10. Click OK.

The dialog box closes, your hard drive spins for a moment, and you're all done.

You can publish only portions of your image by selecting some of your image's objects before you start publishing it, and then checking the Selected Only check box in the Publish to an Image dialog box.

You should not publish your image directly to GIF or JPG format if you included image map information with your objects. In this case, you must publish either to a new HTML file or directly into DESIGNER. Which option you choose depends on how you started DRAW:

 ✔ If you started DRAW via the Start menu, publish your drawing to a new HTML page.

 ✔ If you started DRAW by clicking the DRAW button in DESIGNER, you can publish directly to the page that was open.

To publish your drawing to a new HTML page:

1. Choose File⇨Publish⇨to HTML.

The Publish to HTML dialog box that opens works the same as the standard Open and Save dialog boxes, with the addition of the Image File Type section.

2. Specify your HTML filename and location.

In the File Name text box, enter the name of the Web page that will contain your image and specify the drive and folder in the Dri̲ves and D̲irectories lists.

3. Select whether you want to save your image in G̲IF or JPEG (J̲pg) format in the Image F̲ile Type area.

4. Click OK to close the dialog box.

The same Bitmap Export or Export JPEG dialog box that I describe in Step 5 of the preceding set of instructions opens. Follow the same procedure as I note in Steps 6 through 10 of those instructions to set the options for the image.

5. Open the HTML page in DESIGNER and either edit the page or copy the image to an existing page.

To copy the image to an existing page, use the E̲dit⇨C̲opy and E̲dit⇨P̲aste commands.

To publish your drawing to your current DESIGNER page, choose F̲ile⇨ Pub̲lish⇨to W̲EB.DESIGNER. DRAW closes, and your image now appears in DESIGNER. If you haven't saved the changes to your drawing, a dialog box pops up to ask whether you want to save your changes.

When you publish your image to HTML or to an existing Web page, only a client-side image map is included, not a server-side image map. Client-side image maps are used by newer browsers, whereas server-side image maps are required by older browsers. If you want to include a server-side image map, follow these instructions (you can find out more about image maps and this procedure in Chapter 7):

1. Double-click the image in DESIGNER.

The Image Properties dialog box opens.

2. Click the Image Map tab.

3. Click the E̲dit Map button.

The Image Map Editor opens.

4. Click S̲ave.

5. When the Save Image Map File As dialog box opens, type a name in the File N̲ame text box and then click S̲ave.

You return to the Image Properties dialog box.

6. Click OK.

The Image Properties dialog box closes, and you return to DESIGNER.

Drawing Objects

Objects are the whole point behind DRAW. If objects didn't exist, you could get by with bitmap images. Adding objects is fairly easy and becomes second nature after you do it a few times.

Adding lines

When you were in school, you were taught that a line is the shortest distance between two points. In other words, a line is straight. Okay, that's the geometric definition, but the artistic definition says that a line can also be curved.

First, I talk about drawing a straight line, then I go on to curved lines, and then (this is the really powerful part) I talk about changing a line all around.

You use the Freehand tool to add straight lines to your image. To add a straight line:

1. Click the Freehand tool in the toolbox.

The cursor changes to an X (or crosshair).

2. Click the cursor in your drawing where you want the line to start.

A line now runs from this point and follows the cursor as you move it (see Figure 15-3).

3. Click the cursor again where you want the line to end.

The line locks into this position. To force the line to be vertical or horizontal, press the Ctrl key while you move the cursor.

You can also add on to an existing line. Click the ending point again and draw more stuff. No matter which way you made the first line (straight or curved), you can add a straight or curved section to it.

To draw a curved line with the Freehand tool:

1. Click the Freehand tool in the toolbox.

The cursor changes to a crosshair.

2. Click the cursor in your drawing where you want the line to start and drag the cursor as if you're using a pencil.

A curved line follows the cursor as you move it.

3. Release the mouse button after you're done.

The line locks into this position.

Start of line   Cursor

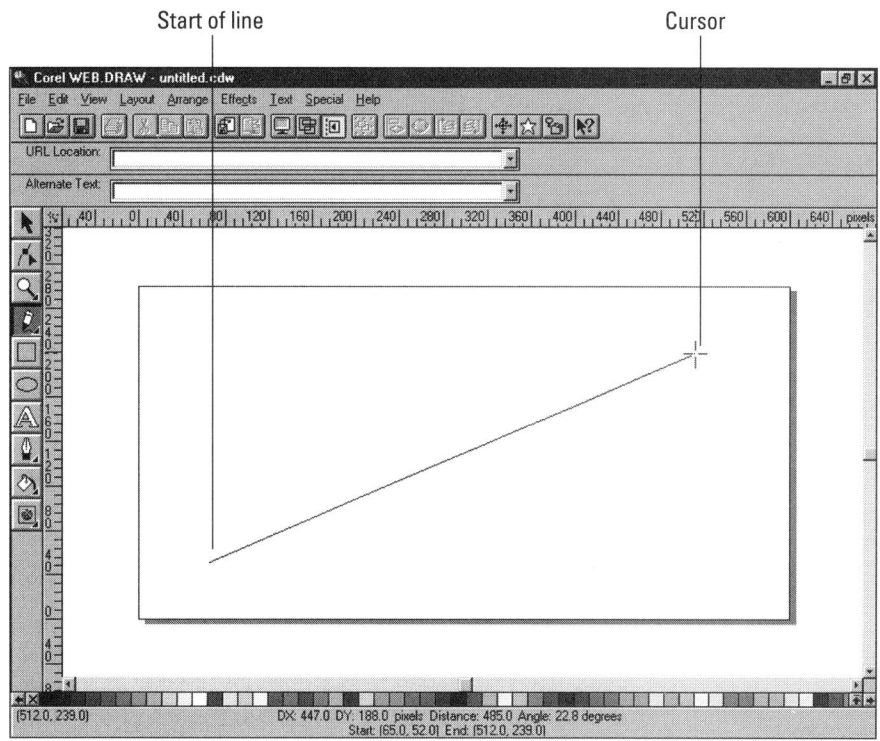

Figure 15-3:
Drawing a
line is as
easy as
1, 2, 3.

When you finish your line, you see a bunch of bumps at various points. If the line is straight, the bumps are at every corner. If it's a curve, the bumps appear at irregular intervals (see Figure 15-4). If you select the Pick tool, the bumps seem to disappear. These bumps are called *nodes,* and you can use them to edit the shape of your line with the Shape tool. The pieces of line between the nodes are called *segments*.

 If you want to make any major changes to your lines, open the Node Edit roll-up (see Figure 15-5). Double-click the Shape tool in the toolbox to both select the Shape tool and open the roll-up.

To edit a node, a node segment, or a couple of nodes:

- ✔ **To move a node:** Click the bump and drag it to its new location. If the bump is at the end of a curved segment, two dashed lines come out of the node and the nodes nearest it (see Figure 15-6). These dashed lines represent the shape of the curve — notice that they are tangent to the curve and the longer the lines, the broader the curve.

- ✔ **To change a segment from a straight line to a curve or vice versa:** Click the line segment and select To Curve or To Line, respectively.

Node

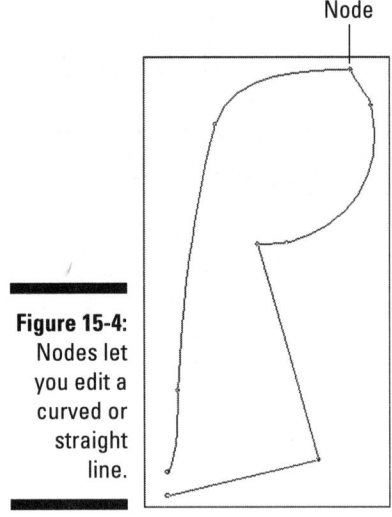

Figure 15-4:
Nodes let
you edit a
curved or
straight
line.

Add node

Remove node

Join nodes

Figure 15-5:
Exercise
complete
control over
your lines.

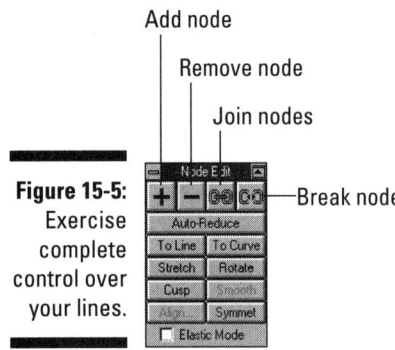

Break node

✔ **To join two nodes together:** Use the Shape tool to select both nodes (using the same techniques that I outline later in "Selecting objects") and click the Join Nodes button in the roll-up.

✔ **To break a node into two separate nodes:** Click the node to select it and then click the Break Node button in the roll-up.

✔ **To reshape curves in a line:** Drag the ends of the dashed lines coming out from the nodes (the ends of these lines are called the *control points*).

✔ **To change a node type:** You can have three types of nodes between line segments: cusp, smooth, and symmetrical. A *cusp* is a sharp corner, whereas *smooth* and *symmetrical* are rounded. (The curvature is identical on both sides of a symmetrical node, but the curvature doesn't have to be identical on both sides of the smooth node.) Figure 15-6 shows these different types of nodes. To change a node type select the node, and then click the appropriate button in the roll-up. You can only have a cusp or smooth node between a straight and curved segment.

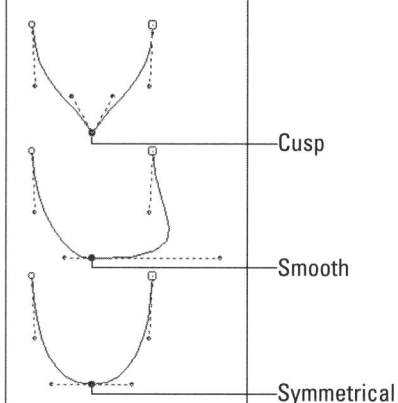

Figure 15-6: The three types of nodes.

—Cusp

—Smooth

—Symmetrical

Rectangles and ovals

You can draw rectangles and ellipses easily, using the aptly named Rectangle and Ellipsis tools. To draw a rectangle or ellipse, simply select the tool and then click and drag to create your shape, releasing the mouse button after you're done. The Ctrl+drag, Shift+drag, and Ctrl+Shift+drag options work exactly the same as they do in PhotoPaint. To find out more about these tools, see Chapter 14.

Text

Adding and editing text in DRAW works similarly to PhotoPaint. Select the Text tool, click where you want to begin your text, and then type something. After you're done, click the Pick tool, and you're all set. You have more flexibility in what you can do with that text after you type it, however.

To alter an entire piece of text's type style:

1. **Select the Pick tool.**

2. **Click the text object that you want to alter.**

3. **Choose Text⇨Text Roll-Up or press Ctrl+F2.**

   The Text roll-up menu appears (see Figure 15-7).

Font

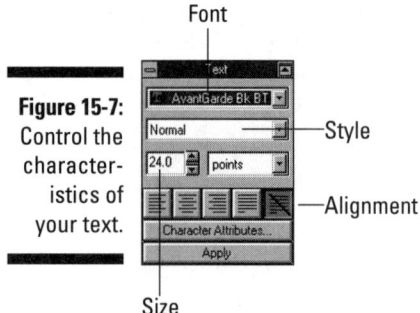

Figure 15-7:
Control the
character-
istics of
your text.

—Style

—Alignment

Size

4. **Select the text characteristics that you want and then click Apply.**

The entire text object updates to contain the new characteristics.

Manipulating Objects

Objects are the bread and butter of DRAW. You create all kinds of objects by using the Rectangle, Ellipse, Freehand, and Text tools, but what happens if you don't draw your new objects exactly where you want them? What if one object overlaps another so that you can't see it? This section shows you how to make objects bend to your will.

Selecting objects

To manipulate an object, you first have to select it. There are two ways to select an object: Select the Pick tool and click on the object, or select the Pick tool and draw a box, called a *marquee,* around the object (click and drag the cursor just as you do with the rectangle tool that I outline in "Rectangles and ovals," earlier in this chapter). When you select an object, eight small black boxes, called *scaling handles,* appear around it (one at each corner and one on each side).

To select more than one object, select one object and then hold down the shift key and click another. You can select as many objects as you like this way. Note that when you select an object by using the marquee, any object that falls within the marquee is selected, so this makes the marquee especially useful when you want to select a number of objects.

To select an object using a marquee, you must draw the box around the entire object — because DRAW thinks that the overall object size includes its control points (see Figure 15-8). Therefore, the task of selecting an object by dragging a box around it with the Pick tool can be difficult. Often, you may find that clicking the object is easier than dragging a marquee around it.

The object's size

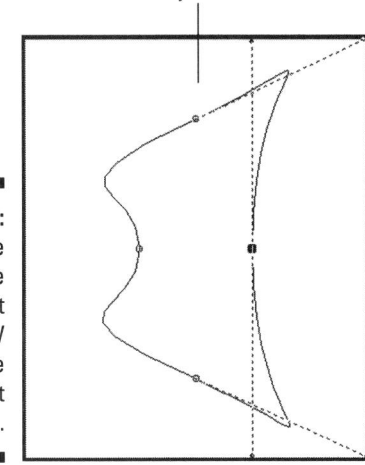

Figure 15-8:
The
rectangle
shows what
DRAW
thinks the
object
size is.

Often, you group a number of objects together and then find that you want
to change something about the group: its size, color, or shape, for example.
If you press the Ctrl key while you click the object you want, circular scaling
handles (rather than the standard square scaling handles) surround your
object. These circular scaling handles let you know that you've selected an
object that's part of a group. You can now do just about anything you want
with the object, except delete it.

Ordering objects

No, this section isn't about ordering objects around by yelling things like
"Drop and give me 20 pushups!" This section is about changing the objects'
order on the page to change the way they overlap.

By changing the object order, you can change the way objects look against
one another. When you have more than two objects, the program places
these objects in intermediate levels between the front and back object (see
Figure 15-9). Even when objects don't overlap, they still have front to back
order.

To change an object's place in the order, select the object and then:

   ✔ Choose Arrange➪Order➪To Front or press Shift+Page Up to make the
     object the farthest forward object.

   ✔ Choose Arrange➪Order➪To Back or press Shift+Page Down to make the
     object the farthest back object.

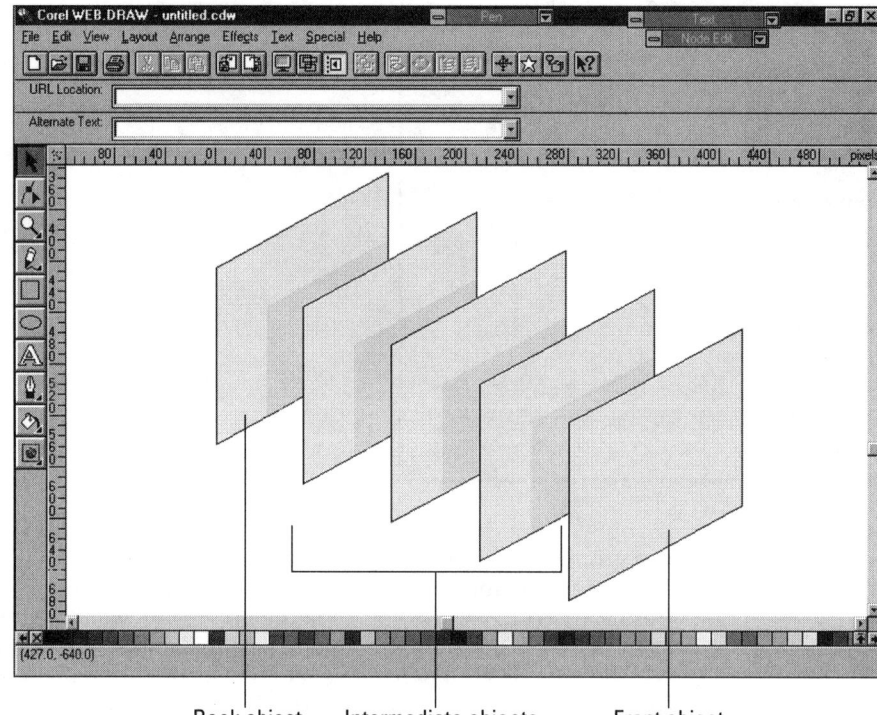

Figure 15-9:
Many
overlapping
objects.

Back object   Intermediate objects   Front object

 ✔ Choose Arrange⇨Order⇨Forward One or press Ctrl+Page Up to move
   the object one place forward in order.

 ✔ Choose Arrange⇨Order⇨Back One or press Ctrl+Page Down to move
   the object one place back in order.

If you select more than one object, you can swap the order of the objects by
choosing Arrange⇨Order⇨Reverse Order.

Your Image Map to the Stars

In addition to being able to output crisp bitmap images in almost any size,
DRAW lets you assign Uniform Resource Locators (URLs) and alternate text
to objects so that you can use your bitmap images as image maps. If you
make your images in DRAW, this is the easiest way to create an image map.

Every object in your DRAW image can have its own special URL.

To add a URL to an object:

1. **Select the object with the Pick tool.**

   The scaling boxes appear around the object.

2. **Click the URL Location text box at the top of the DRAW window.**

   An insertion point begins to blink.

3. **Type the URL (Web address) that you want the object to link to.**

   If you know that you previously made a link to the address by using DRAW, click the down arrow next to the text box and select the address from the list that opens.

   Chapter 6 contains a full description of URLs and how to use URLs when linking Web pages together.

   If you don't know the address, you can put in a fake address for now (something like `http://fakeaddress.htm`). You can put in the correct address later by using the Image Map Editor.

4. **Click the Alternate Text text box.**

   An insertion point begins to blink and a crosshatch pattern appears over your object, indicating that a URL is associated with it.

5. **Type the text that you want your site's visitors to see when they place the mouse pointer over the object.**

   This text appears at the bottom of your visitors' Web browser screens. Note that this text only appears in Netscape browsers — if your page is viewed in Microsoft Internet Explorer, the filename of the page that's linked to the object appears at the bottom of the page.

   You can also pick text that you've already used. Click the down arrow next to the text box and select the text from the drop-down list that opens.

6. **Click the Pick tool anywhere in your drawing.**

   The two text boxes clear.

The URL fly-out menu at the bottom of the toolbar (see Figure 15-10) provides you with three tools that you can use to make *transparent* URL objects. These objects aren't visible in your published bitmaps, but they do set up the locations for an image map.

Use the URL tools exactly the same way you do their visible cousins, the Rectangle, Ellipsis, and Freehand tools — see "Drawing Objects," earlier in this chapter, for more information. After you draw the URL object, add URL and Alternate Text values the same as you do for a "normal" object.

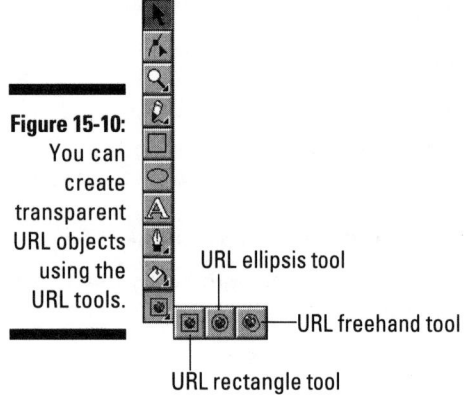

Figure 15-10:
You can
create
transparent
URL objects
using the
URL tools.

URL ellipsis tool

URL freehand tool

URL rectangle tool

If the crosshatch pattern is driving you crazy while you're editing your
drawing, choose View➪URL Fill. The check mark next to URL Fill disappears
in the menu. The crosshatch pattern is no longer visible, but the URL
information is still there — just click an object to find out. If you want to see
the crosshatch pattern again, choose View➪URL Fill.

When you create a bitmap of your DRAW image, the URL information is not
stored in the bitmap itself. You have to either publish to DESIGNER or to an
HTML page. Refer to "Publishing an image," earlier in this chapter.

In many ways, you may find that creating image maps in DRAW is much
easier than dealing with the Image Map Editor in DESIGNER. To make an
image map for an existing bitmap image, import it into DRAW and then use
the transparent URL tools to create your image map. Then publish your
DRAW page to DESIGNER or as a new HTML file.

Chapter 16

Be the Next Walt Disney with MOVE

. . . .

In This Chapter

▶ Opening and saving MOVE animations

▶ Creating a new animation

▶ Hiring actors

▶ Building your own actors

▶ Adding a background

▶ Using sound

▶ Publishing your animation

. . . .

*I*n Chapter 11, you find out how to add existing multimedia files to your Web pages. What do you do when the animation you want to include doesn't exist? Why, you make it yourself, of course.

Don't panic. MOVE is a basic animation program that lets you quickly and easily create all sorts of animated files to include in your Web pages. Even if you've never done any sort of multimedia creation before, you can make your page come alive in a very short time with the simple-to-use tools that MOVE puts at your disposal.

In this chapter, you discover how to create smooth, interesting animated files to include in your Web pages and which publishing method is best for a project.

Dealing with MOVE Files

Before you can begin to create or edit an animation file, you have to start MOVE. That makes sense, right? Corel makes starting MOVE easy, no matter what else you're doing:

- ✔ If you're already running DESIGNER, you click the Corel MOVE button in the Applications toolbar to start MOVE. When you start MOVE this way, you have the option to publish your animation directly to the Web page you're editing. (I tell you exactly how to publish your animations at the end of this chapter in "Publishing Your Animation.")

- ✔ Choose Start⇨Programs⇨Corel WebMaster Suite⇨Accessories⇨ WEB.MOVE.

When MOVE opens, a blank animation window greets you (see Figure 16-1). Don't worry, it's not as intimidating as it looks.

Animation window

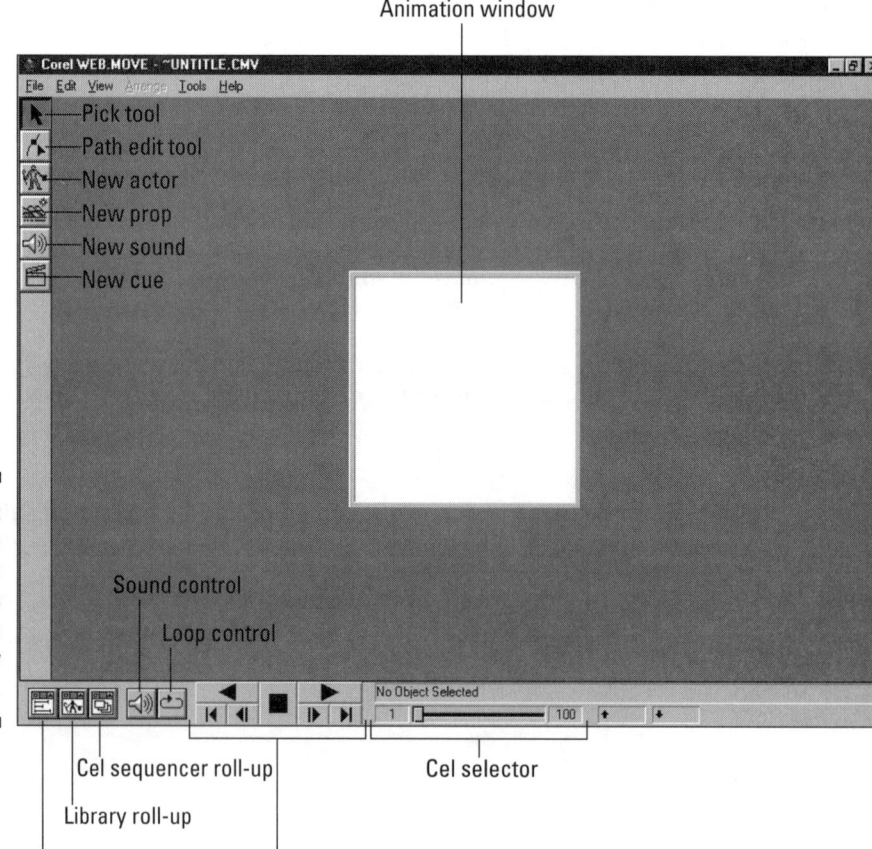

Figure 16-1:
Filling the Animation window is easier than you may think.

Sound control

Loop control

Cel selector

Cel sequencer roll-up

Library roll-up

Timeline roll-up   Preview controls

Opening and saving animation files

You open and save MOVE files the same way you do in any other kind of program. The one thing you need to keep in mind is that MOVE is a Windows 3.1 program, so you can't use Windows 95 long filenames. The Open and Save dialog boxes are also a little bit different than most of the WebMaster Suite programs.

To open an existing MOVE animation:

1. Choose File⇨Open.

The Open Animation File dialog box appears (see Figure 16-2).

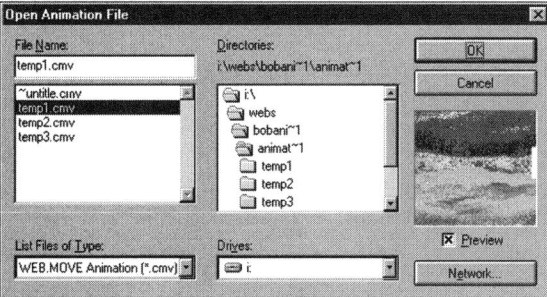

Figure 16-2:
MOVE uses
Windows
3.1-style
Open and
Save dialog
boxes.

2. Select the drive containing the file from the Drives drop-down list.

3. Select the folder containing the file from the Directories list.

Double-click a folder to open it.

4. Select the file you want from the File Name list.

You can also type the name into the File Name text box. If you pick the file from the list and the Preview check box is selected, the preview window at the right of the dialog box shows the first frame of the selected animation.

5. Click OK.

The dialog box closes, and your file loads into MOVE.

To save your animation file:

1. Choose File⇨Save or choose File⇨Save As.

- Whether this is the first time that you're saving your animation or you chose Save As, the Save Animation As dialog box opens. This dialog box is identical to the Open Animation File dialog box shown in Figure 16-2, except that it does not include a preview window.

- If you're working with an existing animation and you selected Save, the hourglass appears briefly, the file is saved, and you're all done.

2. **Select the drive where you want to store the file from the Drives drop-down list.**

3. **Select the folder where you want to store the file from the Directories list.**

   Double-click a folder to open it.

4. **Type the name you want to give the file in the File Name list.**

   Be sure to type the full filename including the three-letter extension (the part after the period), or MOVE creates a new folder using the name you typed.

5. **Click OK.**

   The dialog box closes, and your file is saved.

The files you save in MOVE can't be placed in a Web page. You need to publish your animations for them to be Web-compatible. "Publishing Your Animation," later in this chapter, details how to publish your animations in a variety of Web-compatible formats.

Previewing an animation

While you build your animation, you don't want to keep publishing it, starting your browser, loading a page, and watching your animation. That process takes too long. You want to be able to see your animation quickly and easily so that you can figure out whether you like your changes.

The Preview Controls at the bottom of the MOVE window (see Figure 16-3) let you see your animation as it will appear in your Web page.

Figure 16-3:
The Preview Controls should seem familiar to you.

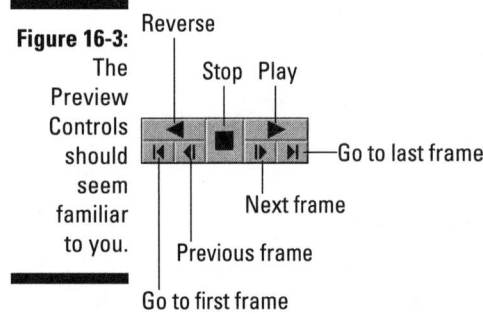

The Preview Controls should seem familiar to you. These controls work just like those on a VCR:

- **Play:** Previews your animation.

- **Reverse:** Previews your animation backwards.

- **Previous frame:** Shows the frame just before the one that is currently displayed.

- **Next frame:** Shows the frame just after the one that is currently displayed.

- **Go to last frame:** Displays the last frame of your animation.

- **Go to first frame:** Displays the first frame of your animation. If you're playing an animation that doesn't repeat, click this button before you start playing it. Otherwise, the animation picks up from your current frame rather than showing the whole thing.

Casting Call

You work with three types of visible objects in an animation: actors, props, and backgrounds. You also work with the sound track, but that isn't really visible, now is it?

Props and backgrounds are static images that you use to create your set (I talk about these in the next section, "Building Your Set"). Actors, on the other hand, are *moving* pictures that add life to your animation. A baby actor may be crawling, an airplane actor may spin its propeller, or a flag actor may wave in the breeze. After you add an actor to your animation, you can move it around by setting up a path.

Don't think of actors as people (actors in MOVE, not actors in general). Actors in MOVE can be anything from a toaster to your company's logo, so don't limit your thinking.

Adding actors

MOVE comes with a lot of premade actors for you to include in your animations. The easiest way to add these premade actors is with the Library roll-up menu:

1. **Insert Corel WebMaster Suite CD #2 into your CD-ROM drive.**

2. **Choose Tools⇨Library Roll-Up or click the Library Roll-Up button.**

   The Library roll-up window appears (see Figure 16-4).

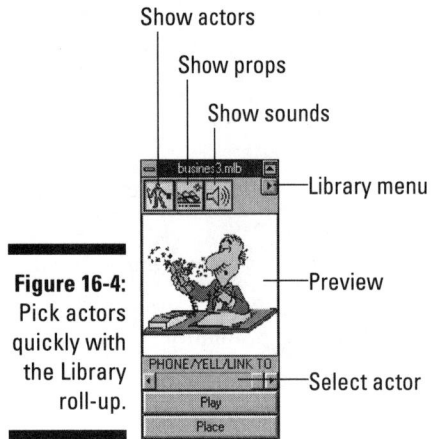

Show actors

Show props

Show sounds

Library menu

Preview

Figure 16-4:
Pick actors
quickly with
the Library
roll-up.

Select actor

3. Click the Library Menu button.

A menu pops up next to the dialog box. If the library you want already appears in this roll-up, you can skip this step and go to Step 7.

4. Select Open Library.

The Open Library dialog box appears. This dialog box already shows the \Webmove\Library folder of WebMaster Suite CD #2. (If it doesn't, or if you want to open a library that's in another folder, select drives from the Drives drop-down list and double-click folders to select them in the Directories list.)

5. Select the library file you want to open from the File Name list.

The animations shown in the 2-D Animations and 3-D Animations sections of the WebMaster Suite's *Clipart* book correspond to the library files that you see. Check out the clipart available to you to save a lot of time rather than open each library and check out each actor separately.

6. Click OK.

The Open Library dialog box closes, your CD-ROM drive spins for a moment, and then the first actor of this library appears in the preview window.

7. Select an actor.

Move the slider underneath the preview window to display other actors. You can preview the actors in motion by clicking the Play button. While the actor is playing, the Play button changes to a Stop button. You click the Stop button when the actor's motions begin to annoy you.

8. **Click the Place button.**

The actor you selected is now in your animation. Click the Play button at the bottom of the MOVE screen to see your actor move in your animation. Click Stop when you've had enough.

Creating your own actors

If you can't find just the right actor, you can create one from scratch using the built-in paint editor for DRAW or MOVE.

Using DRAW

DRAW lets you create actors fairly painlessly, using the familiar tools that I explain in Chapter 15. Here are two interesting twists to creating an actor in DRAW:

- ✔ You need to create your actor at twice the size that you want it to appear in MOVE. In other words, if you want your actor to be 40 pixels high in MOVE, create it 80 pixels high in DRAW.

- ✔ The Cel Select roll-up menu lets you control the individual frames (also called *cels*) of your DRAW animation.

To create a new actor using DRAW:

1. **Choose Edit➪Insert New➪Actor or click the New Actor button.**

The New Actor dialog box appears.

2. **Type a name for the actor in the Object Name text box.**

3. **Select CorelDraw 1.0 Graphic from the Object Type list.**

4. **Click OK.**

The dialog box closes, and DRAW opens to a blank page. The Cel Select roll-up menu is also open.

5. **Use the standard DRAW tools to create an image.**

Later in this section, I tell you how to use the Cel Select roll-up menu to work with frames.

6. **After you're done editing your actor, choose File➪Exit & Return.**

DRAW closes, and you return to MOVE, where your new actor is sitting smack dab in the middle of your frame.

If you didn't save your DRAW image before returning to MOVE, a dialog box appears and asks if you want to save your image. Click Yes to save your image so that you can go back and edit it later.

The Cel Select roll-up makes creating multiframe actors a cinch. Using the Cel Select roll-up, you can add and delete frames, copy and move objects between frames, and access a preview of your *actor in progress*. The Cel Select roll-up opens automatically when you start DRAW to create a new actor. See Figure 16-5 for a view of the Cel Select roll-up and its menu.

Frames   Menu button

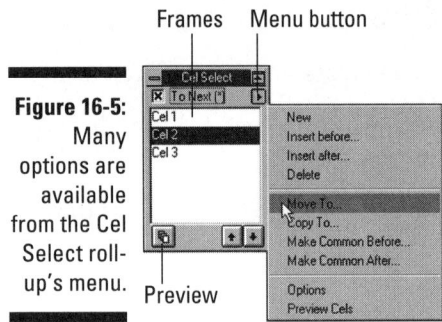

Figure 16-5:
Many
options are
available
from the Cel
Select roll-
up's menu.

Preview

The To Next check box offers an extremely easy way to create a multiframe actor. When you select this check box, any action you perform on objects creates a new frame containing the result of the action. These actions can include scaling an object, changing its size, or moving it around your page. Be careful, though, because selecting this check box can lead to the creation of a lot of extra frames that you aren't expecting.

For more control over your frames, you can use the menu from the Cel Select roll-up.

To add a new frame:

1. **Select a frame in the Cel Select roll-up.**

   The name of the frame is highlighted.

2. **Click the menu button and select New.**

   The Append New Cels dialog box appears.

3. **Set the number of cells you want to add in the text box.**

4. **Click OK.**

   The dialog box closes, and the number of frames you entered in Step 3 are added after the last cel.

To copy or move objects from one frame to another:

1. **Select the frame containing the objects you want in the Cel Select roll-up.**

2. **Select the objects you want to copy or move.**

   Use standard DRAW selection techniques, which I outline in Chapter 15.

3. **Click the menu button and select Copy To or Move To.**

   Select the action you want to perform. The menu closes, and the cursor changes to a large black arrow with the word To? in it.

4. **Click the arrow cursor on the frame that you want to move or copy the objects to.**

   The cursor changes back to normal, and the objects are copied or moved.

To delete a frame or a number of frames:

1. **Select the first frame that you want to delete.**

   This is the frame that is highest on the list (the lowest cel number).

2. **Click the menu button and select Delete.**

   The Delete Cel dialog box appears.

3. **Set the number of frames that you want to delete in the text box.**

   If you set the number to more than 1, the other higher numbered cels that are deleted are located after the one you selected.

4. **Click OK.**

   The dialog box closes, and the cels are deleted.

Using the MOVE Paint Editor

If you prefer to paint your actors, you can use MOVE's built-in Paint Editor. If you're familiar with PhotoPaint, you'll be right at home with the Paint Editor (see Figure 16-6), even though it's a much more limited program. Chapter 14 details the use of PhotoPaint.

If you want more control over the creation of your actors, I suggest that you use PhotoPaint to create a multiframe image, save your actor as a QuickTime or AutoCAD animation, and then import it. You can still edit your actor using Paint Editor. Just double-click your actor to open Paint Editor — you're actor is displayed, ready for you to edit it.

Paint tools   Paint Editor

Figure 16-6:
Paint Editor
is a simple-
to-use paint
program
that you
can use to
create and
edit actors.

With all that said, now you can find out how to use Paint Editor.

To create a new actor:

1. Click the New Actor button on the toolbar.

The New Actor dialog box appears.

2. Type a name for your actor in the Object Name dialog box.

3. Select Corel MOVE 1.0 from the Object Type list.

4. Click OK.

The New Actor dialog box closes, and Paint Editor and its toolbox open.

5. Use the painting tools to draw a single cel of your actor.

These paint tools work almost identically to those in PhotoPaint.

6. Add more frames to give your actor motion.

I discuss this procedure in the next set of instructions.

7. Paint these other cels.

8. After you're finished, choose File⇨Apply and Exit.

Your actor appears in your frame.

To add more cels to your animation:

1. Choose Edit⇨Insert Cels (or press Ctrl+T).

The Insert Cels dialog box appears.

2. Set the number of new frames you want in the Number of Cels to Insert text box.

3. **Set where you want the new frames to be inserted.**

   • The Before Current Cel radio button adds the new frames before the currently selected one.

   • The After Current Cel radio button adds the frames after the currently selected one.

4. **If you want to keep the same image for all the new frames, select the Duplicate Contents check box.**

   You can repaint these new cels to incorporate any changes you want to make.

5. **Click OK.**

   The dialog box closes, and the new frames are added to your animation.

To delete frames from your animation:

1. **Select the first frame that you want to delete.**

   This is the lowest number cel.

2. **Choose Edit⇨Delete Cels.**

   The Delete Cels dialog box appears.

3. **Set the number of frames you want to delete in the text box.**

4. **Click OK.**

   The dialog box closes, and the cels are deleted.

Building Your Set

If you just use actors in your animations, you're not going to get your best results. Imagine a movie with only actors prancing around on an empty sound stage. *Boring!*

You need to build a set for your actors to perform in. For an animation, you build your set by using backdrops and props.

Adding props

Props are similar to actors except for one minor difference: Props don't move.

Adding props is almost identical to adding an actor:

1. **Insert Corel WebMaster Suite CD #2 into your CD-ROM drive.**

2. **Choose Tools⇨Library Roll-Up.**

   The Library roll-up window appears.

3. **Click the Library Menu button.**

   A menu pops up next to the dialog box. If the library you want already appears in this roll-up, you can skip this step and go to Step 7.

4. **Select Open Library.**

   The Open Library dialog box appears. This dialog box already shows the \Webmove\Library folder of WebMaster Suite CD #2. If it doesn't appear or if you want to open a library that's in another folder, select drives from the Drives drop-down list and double-click folders in the Directories list to select them.

5. **Select the library file you want to open from the File Name list.**

   Five prop libraries (PROPS1 through PROPS5) are contained in the 2-D folder. The contents of these libraries are shown in the 2-D Animations section of the WebMaster Suite's *Clipart* book.

6. **Click OK.**

   The Open Library dialog box closes, your CD-ROM drive spins for a moment, and the first prop of this library appears in the preview window.

7. **Select a prop.**

   Move the slider underneath the preview window to display different props.

8. **Click Place.**

   The prop you selected is now in your animation. If the prop is bigger than your animation window, you are asked if you want to resize the object to fit in the window (that is, make the object smaller), resize the animation window to fit the prop (that is, make the animation larger), or leave both the prop and the animation window at their original sizes. Answer this question however you want.

Adding a background

An animation background is very similar to a background that you use in a Web page. It stays behind the actors and props in your animation and gives them a pretty backing to work against.

To make a prop into a background:

1. **Select the prop that you want to use as a background.**

   Click the prop once so that a dashed outline surrounds it.

2. **Choose Edit⇨Object Properties.**

   The Prop Information dialog box appears.

3. **Click the Background check box.**

4. **Click OK.**

   The dialog box closes, and your prop is now locked as a background. If your prop did not fill your animation window, it's now tiled (just like a Web page background image) to fill the window.

 Before you convert a prop into a background, make sure that you set its timing with the Timeline (which I explain later in this chapter in the "Timeline" section). After you make your prop into a background, it's locked, and you can't make any changes to it.

To delete a background:

1. **Click the Timeline roll-up button.**

   The Timeline roll-up appears (see the later section "Directing Your Picture" for more information about using the Timeline).

2. **Double-click the name of your background.**

   The Prop Information dialog box appears.

3. **Deselect the Background check box.**

4. **Click OK.**

   The Prop Information dialog box closes. If your background was tiled, it no longer is tiled. It is once again a normal, everyday prop.

5. **Click the prop that was once the background to select it.**

   A blinking outline appears around it.

6. **Press Delete.**

   The Delete dialog box appears and asks whether you're sure that you want to delete the background.

7. **Click OK.**

   The dialog box closes, and the background disappears.

Adding a Soundtrack

Just like with a movie, sound can add a great deal to your animations. Unfortunately, another thing they can add is download time. A simple animation can become huge if you add too much sound to it.

To add a sound to your animation:

1. **Insert Corel WebMaster Suite CD #2 into your CD-ROM drive.**

2. **Choose Tools⇨Library Roll-Up or click the Library roll-up button.**

   The Library roll-up window appears.

3. **Click the Library Menu button.**

   A menu pops up next to the dialog box. If the library you want already appears in this roll-up, you can skip this step and go to Step 7.

4. **Select Open Library.**

   The Open Library dialog box appears. The \WebMove\Library folder of WebMaster Suite CD #2 already appears. The Corel sound files are contained in the \Webmove\Library\Sounds folder.

   To open the Sounds folder or to open a library that's in another folder, select drives from the Drives drop-down list and then double-click folders to select them in the Directories list.

5. **Select the library file you want to open from the File Name list.**

6. **Click OK.**

   The Open Library dialog box closes, your CD-ROM drive spins for a moment, and the name of the first sound of this library appears just below the preview window. A bunch of dots representing the sound appear in the preview window.

7. **Select a sound.**

   Move the slider underneath the preview window to display other sounds. You can click the Play button to preview the sound. While the sound plays, the Play button changes to a Stop button. You can click the Stop button when the repeating sound begins to annoy you.

8. **Click Place.**

   The sound you selected is now in your animation — it will begin playing when the currently selected frame is displayed.

Directing Your Picture

This section is where everything comes together. Everything up to this point in the chapter has been about adding actors and props — where they go and how they move has been completely left out . . . until now. This section reveals the true power of MOVE.

Placing props and actors

When you add actors and props to your animation window, they just plop in place. Chances are, this isn't where you really want them, however. You may be asking yourself, "How do I move them around and place them where I want?"

I'm glad you asked. To rearrange your actors and props, click and drag them to whatever position you want them to be. If you want to select more than one object, click the first object and press the Shift key while you click the second, or third, or fourth — you get the idea.

Sometimes you can't see one of the actors behind another, or the actors look odd (note that props are always behind actors). To change the order of your actors or props:

1. **Select the object whose order you want to change.**

2. **Open the Arrange menu.**

3. **Select one of the four order options (To Front, To Back, Forward One, or Back One).**

   You can also use the Timeline to change object order, which I discuss in the next section, "Timeline."

 A lengthier discussion of object order is in Chapter 15. Even though MOVE is a different program than DRAW, object order works exactly the same way, so you may find Chapter 15 to be helpful.

Timeline

The Timeline lets you determine when your actors, props, and backgrounds appear during your animation. The Timeline roll-up (see Figure 16-7) provides you with complete control over your actors, props, backgrounds, and sounds.

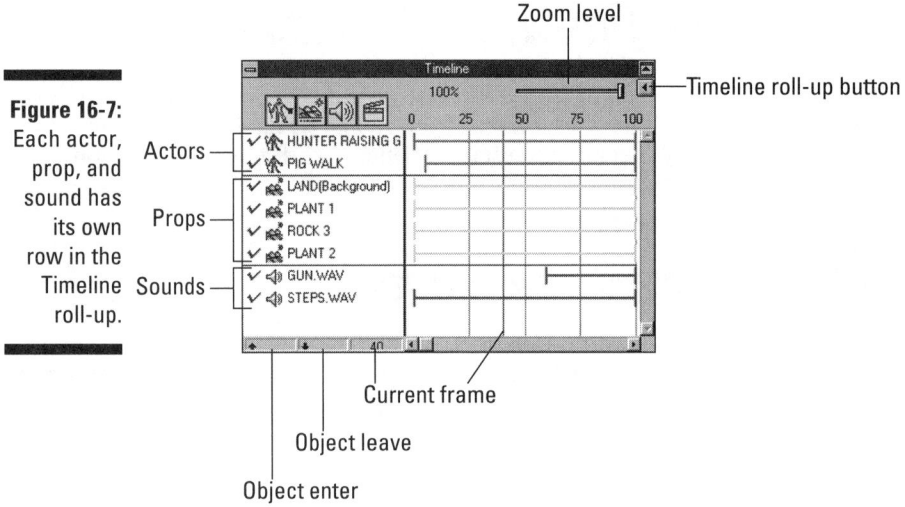

Figure 16-7:
Each actor,
prop, and
sound has
its own
row in the
Timeline
roll-up.

 To open the Timeline roll-up, click the Timeline roll-up button at the bottom of the MOVE window. When the Timeline initially appears, it just gives you a list of the various objects in your animation. To view the full timeline, click the right-arrow button in the upper-right part of the dialog box.

Now you can see your whole animation laid out for you — big whoop, right? What can you do with the Timeline?

✔ **Use the I-beam lines on the right side of the Timeline to set when your actors, props, and sounds enter and leave your animation.**

To set when an object shows up in your animation: Place the cursor over the left end of the object's I-beam. The cursor changes to a vertical bar with a left arrow. Drag the vertical line of the I-beam to the left or right. Notice that the number next to the small up arrow at the bottom of the roll-up changes to show you the frame in which the object enters.

To set when an object leaves your animation: Place the cursor over the right end of the object's I-beam. The cursor changes to a vertical beam with a right arrow. Drag the vertical line of the I-beam to the left or right. Notice that the number next to the small down arrow at the bottom of the roll-up changes to show you the frame in which the object leaves.

To leave the object's duration (the time between when it enters and exits) the same but change *when* it comes and goes: Place the cursor anywhere in the middle of the I-beam and drag it to the left or right. While the cursor is over the I-beam, it changes to show two vertical lines with arrows pointing both ways.

✥ ▮ ✔ **To change an object's order:** Use the object's names (see "Placing props and actors," earlier in this chapter, and object ordering information in Chapter 15 for more information on object order). To change an object's order, click its name at the left side of the roll-up and drag it up or down (the cursor changes to two horizontal lines with an up and a down arrow). The higher an object is on the list, the farther back it is. You probably want to have your background as the highest object in the prop section.

✔ **To see a more detailed view of the right timeline window:** Drag the slider at the top of the roll-up to the left (if you drag it to the right, you get a less detailed view). You can then use the scroll bar at the bottom of the roll-up to see different sections of the timeline.

Making your actors move

Making the objects move is the whole point behind animation, isn't it? An actor that looks like a walking pig that just sits there in the middle of your frame looks kind of silly. You want to be able to have it walk around and move as the animation is playing. (Props can move, too, not just actors.)

To make the objects move, you give them a path. Just like a walking path, an animation path is something that the objects follow. To create a path:

1. Click the Path Edit Tool on the toolbar.

A small black dot appears near the object, the cursor changes to a big, black arrow, and the Path Edit roll-up appears (see Figure 16-8).

The black dot is a *path node* — a marker where the object is to be at a specific time. When you first add an object, only one node exists, so the object doesn't move.

Set number of nodes

Figure 16-8:
Create and edit a path using the Path Edit roll-up.

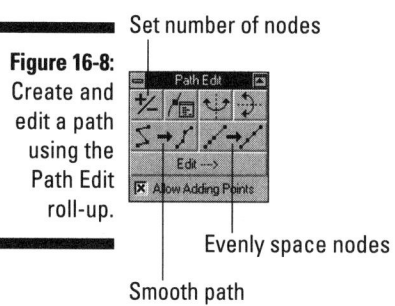

Evenly space nodes

Smooth path

2. Click the Allow Adding Points check box in the Path Edit roll-up.

3. **Click the cursor a number of times to create a path for the object to follow.**

   Each time you click the cursor, a new black dot appears, and a line runs from the previous node to your new one. The previous node changes to a black outlined square. Each node you add shows where the object will be one frame after the previous one. Don't get too detailed about the path just yet. You can use the roll-up's various tools to add more nodes automatically.

4. **After you establish the basic shape of the path, you can begin to edit it using the cursor and the controls in the Path Edit roll-up (see Figure 16-9).**

   You can click the cursor on the line between two nodes to add new nodes. If you click off the line, a new node appears, and a line connects it to the last path node.

First node   Last node

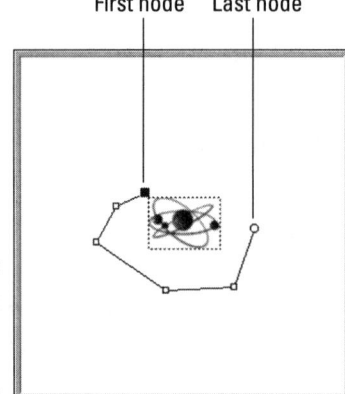

Figure 16-9:
A typical
path.

To move a node, place the cursor over the node (the cursor changes to a small crosshair) and then click-and-drag the node to its new location. After you're finished, release the mouse button.

You use the Path Edit roll-up to make automatic changes to the path.

✔ Each node on the path represents a single frame. If the path has seven nodes, including the start and end nodes, the object only moves for seven frames. After the motion ends, the object just sits there where the end node is located.

To add more nodes, click the Set Number of Nodes button in the Path Edit roll-up (the upper-left button). The Scale Path dialog box appears. Type the number of frames you want the path to run in the Desired text box and then click OK. The path is updated to include the number of nodes that you indicate.

If your new number is higher than the original number of nodes, the new nodes are placed roughly equally throughout the path.

If the number is lower than the original number, the nodes are removed from the path. MOVE *tries* to keep the shape of the path the same.

✔ Big changes in distance or direction between two nodes makes the motion of your actor look jerky. To smooth out the path, click the Smooth Path button (the wide, left button in the Path Edit roll-up). MOVE shifts the paths around to make the path run more smoothly, instead of being jerky. This works best when you have a larger number of nodes.

✔ The speed in which the object moves along its path is based on the distance between the nodes. The farther apart two nodes are, the *faster* the object moves between them.

Think of it this way: An object takes one frame to move from one node to the next, so the farther apart the nodes are, the faster the object has to move. To use a quick analogy, imagine that your car always takes one hour to get between two exits on the highway, regardless of how far apart the exits are. If the exits are 10 miles apart, you travel 10 miles in one hour, or 10 miles per hour. If the exits are 100 miles apart, though, you travel 100 miles per hour to move between the exits.

To make the distance between each node the same, click the Evenly Space Nodes button (the wide right button in the Path Edit roll-up). Your nodes move so that the lines between them are all the same length.

To make the path the smoothest it can be, I suggest that you work in the following order:

1. **Create your basic path.**

2. **Set the total number of nodes that you want, as I outline in the first bullet in the preceding bulleted list.**

3. **Smooth out the path using the Smooth Path button.**

4. **Finally, make all your nodes the same distance apart, using the Evenly Space Nodes button.**

   This button makes the actor "run" at the same speed throughout your animation by making the distance between each of the nodes the same.

Publishing Your Animation

Your animation is exactly what you hoped it would be, and you're ready to put it in your Web page. As with DRAW, you publish your animations. For more information on the various types of multimedia files that you can include in your Web pages, refer to Chapter 11.

Which publishing method you use depends on your animation and who will be viewing it. To publish your animation, use one of the following commands:

- ✔ **File⇨Publish⇨to Animated GIF:** This option is great if your animation doesn't include any sound and is fairly small and short. When you pick this option, the Export To Animated GIF dialog box appears. Use this dialog box as you would any standard Save dialog box. (I tell you how to use the Save Animation As dialog box earlier in this chapter in "Opening and saving animation files.")

- ✔ **File⇨Publish⇨to Movie:** You can publish to a movie file in Video for Windows, MPEG, or QuickTime format. These options let you include sound in your movie, but most browsers can't view them directly. When you pick this option, the Export to Movie dialog box opens. Use this dialog box as you would a standard Save dialog box.

- ✔ **File⇨Publish⇨to Individual Files:** This option lets you save each individual frame as one in a series of images on your hard drive. When you pick this option, the Export to Individual Files dialog box appears. This dialog box works like a normal Save dialog box, with a couple of exceptions:

    - Because a number is added to the end of your filename (one number for each frame), keep your filename short. For example, if your animation is 100 frames long, you need to leave space for the three digits in the frame number. Your filename (to the left of the period), therefore, can only be five letters rather than the standard eight.

    - You have the option to save the images in a number of different formats. Pick the format you want to use from the List Files of Type drop-down list.

    - You can choose which frames you want to export to images and the number in the name of the first file. Use the three Export Options text boxes at the bottom of the dialog box.

- ✔ **File⇨Publish⇨to Java:** This option creates a new Web page with your animation already included in it in the form of a Java applet (I discuss Java applets in Chapter 11). This option is excellent if your animation is larger than 500K when published in GIF format. The reason for this limit is that your visitors have to download 500K of Java files needed to view an animation. Visitors to your Web site who don't have Java-capable browsers, however, will not be able to see the animation.

- ✔ **File⇨Publish⇨to DESIGNER:** Your animation is saved as a Java applet and placed in your current Web page. You can only access this option if you started MOVE from DESIGNER.

- ✔ **File⇨Publish⇨to Sound:** This option saves just the soundtrack that you created for your animation.

Chapter 17

Your Site in Three Dimensions

*T*hese days, only a handful of Web sites offer VRML (Virtual Reality Modeling Language) as an alternative to their standard Web pages. Although the VRML in these sites may be pretty cool, the people who create these sites still publish their important stuff in standard, everyday Web pages (the ones that I detail throughout the rest of this book). Why hasn't VRML taken over the Web like everyone said it would?

It's not that VRML isn't a cool technology. It's not that VRML doesn't work. The reasons that VRML hasn't caught on are very simple:

✔ Building a VRML site is painfully difficult.

✔ Viewing a VRML site can take eons because a visitor's system has to download an enormous amount of information.

✔ People are comfortable with the Web — they don't want to learn an entirely new way of using the Internet.

In this chapter, I introduce you to some tools available for creating 3-D worlds by using WORLD. Reading this chapter takes you halfway to becoming a fledgling rookie of VRML authoring. Unfortunately, becoming really good at creating VRML can take weeks or months of practice — and you're likely to use words that would cause your mother to wash your mouth out with soap.

Believe me when I say that I'm not trying to dissuade you from using WORLD. But because VRML sites haven't really caught on with Web users, I treat VRML as more of a toy for right now: fun to play with, but not the way to spend your time when you're under a tight deadline for getting a Web site out the door.

The Universe of WORLD

Starting WORLD is as easy as starting all the other WebMaster Suite programs. How you start WORLD depends on where you are at the time:

  ✔ Choose Start➪Programs➪Corel WebMaster Suite➪Accessories➪Corel WEB.WORLD.

  ✔ Click the WEB.WORLD button on the DESIGNER Applications toolbar.

When you first start WORLD, a confusing mishmash of windows greets you (see Figure 17-1). The windows really aren't that confusing when you take a moment to look at them. The following bulleted list tells you a little bit about each part of the WORLD program screen and the windows that make it up. However, to really get a good feel for each part of the program, check out the rest of this section.

Decorator window   3-D Space window   Plane Builder   Object Height control

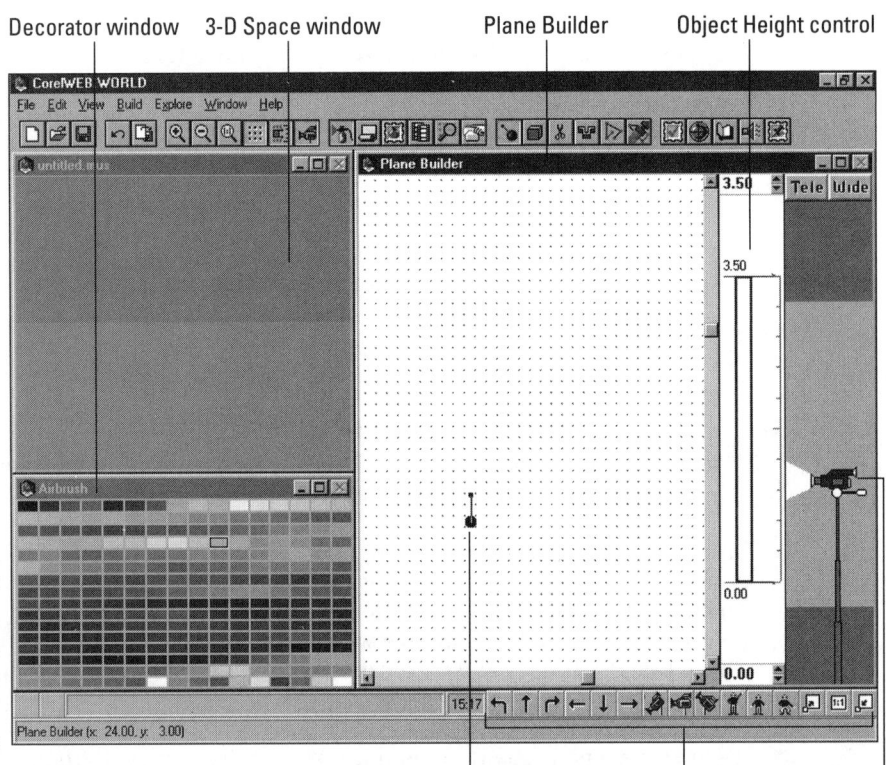

Figure 17-1: What does all this mean?

Pinocchio tool   Preview controls   Camera control

Here are the different parts of the WORLD program screen:

- ✔ **3-D Space window:** Shows you what your VRML site looks like, complete with colors, textures, pictures, videos, and so on.

- ✔ **Plane Builder:** Shows a plan view of your site. You can think of this window as a set of blueprints for your world. This is where you create your objects, which are then shown in all their 3-D splendor, in the 3-D Space window. Use the Pinocchio tool, Camera control, and the Preview Control tools to set the viewpoint for the 3-D Space window.

- ✔ **Decorator window:** Pick paints, textures, and images from this window to include in your virtual world. The contents of the Decorator window change depending on which tool you select.

Save the world

If you're familiar with opening and closing files in the other Windows 3.1 compatible programs in WebMaster Suite, you'll feel right at home with WORLD.

To open an existing virtual world:

1. **Choose File⇨Open.**

   The Open 3-D Space File dialog box appears.

2. **Select the file that you want to open.**

   Select a drive from the Drives drop-down list. In the Directories list, double-click folders to open them.

3. **After you open the folder containing the file you want to open, click the file once to highlight it.**

   WebMaster CD #2 has a bunch of very impressive WORLD samples and templates. Check out the listing in the Samples and Templates sections toward the end of the WebMaster Suite Clipart book. You can find them in the Webworld\Samples folder.

4. **Click OK.**

   The dialog box closes, and the world you selected is loaded into WORLD, ready for you to mess around with.

Saving an VRML world is just as easy. Whether you've already saved your world or you opened an existing world, just choose File⇨Save (if you've opened a virtual world from the WebMaster Clipart CD, you have to use the following instructions the first time you save the world to your hard drive). Your hard drive spins for a moment, and then you're all done.

If you want to save a new world or save your world with a new name, follow these steps:

1. **Choose File⇨Save As.**

   The Save 3-D Space File dialog box appears.

2. **Select the folder you want to save your world in.**

   Select drives from the Drives drop-down list and double-click folders to select them in the Directories list.

3. **Type a name for your world in the File Name text box.**

   WORLD is a Windows 3.1 compatible program, so you can't use long file-names. You're restricted to a name that's no longer than 8 letters. Okay, 11 letters, if you include the extension MUS at the end (`filename.mus`). All right, 12 letters if you count the extension *and* the period.

4. **If you want to include notes about your world, click the 3-D Space Attached Text Box check box to select that option and type your notes in the large text box that appears.**

5. **Click OK.**

   The dialog box closes, your drive spins for a while, and then you're done.

Stepping out in the world

You want to go take a look around a world? Okay. Just make sure to look both ways before you cross the street.

The controls you use to view a VRML world in Corel WORLD are really quite simple to use after you get the hang of them. The Preview controls on the bottom right are listed in the following table, and the Camera controls appear in Figure 17-2.

Preview Control	*What It Does*
↰	Turn left
↑	Move forward
↱	Turn right
←	Move left
↓	Move backward
→	Move right

Preview Control	What It Does
	Look down
	Look straight ahead
	Look up
	Raise camera
	Default camera height
	Lower camera
	Zoom in
	Zoom normal
	Zoom out

The Preview Control buttons at the bottom of the screen are fairly self-explanatory. Click a button, and your view changes. The Pinocchio and Camera tools, however, work together and are a little more difficult to get a handle on. (The Pinocchio and Camera tools are explained in the next two paragraphs.)

 The Pinocchio tool shows a really big-nosed person (hence the name Pinocchio) standing in the Plane Builder window. The little block represents the tip of Pinocchio's nose, and the circle is his head. Pinocchio's nose shows you which direction the 3-D Space window's preview is looking. To move your viewpoint in the 3-D Space window without changing the direction you're looking, click Pinocchio's head and drag it around the Plane Builder. To change the preview direction, click-and-drag Pinocchio's nose. Your preview also shows the direction that Pinocchio's nose is pointing. You can also take a walk around your virtual world by dragging Pinocchio's nose forward and back. Before you can use the Pinocchio tool, you have to choose Build➪Pinocchio.

The camera tool lets you set the height and angle (up and down) of the preview. To move the camera up or down, click and drag the white circle just under the camera. To tilt the camera, click and drag the handle at the rear of the camera.

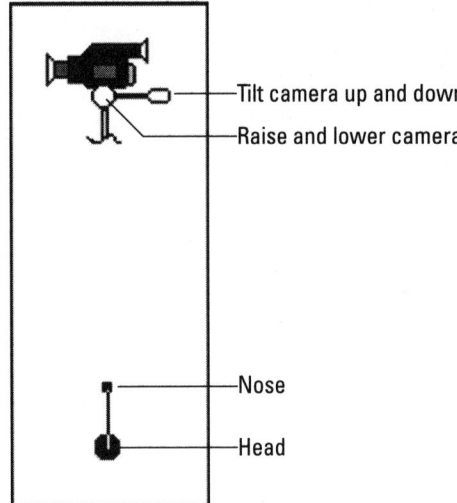

Figure 17-2:
In addition to the Preview controls, the Pinocchio and Camera tools let you position your viewpoint in the 3-D Space window.

Tilt camera up and down

Raise and lower camera

Nose

Head

Building a Better World

You use three types of objects to build your world: boxes, walls, and faces. These three objects may seem limiting if you've spent time with DRAW or PhotoPaint, which have tons of different shapes to work with. You're really not limited, though. Just look at the beautiful samples and templates that come on WebMaster CD#2 if you think that you can't create cool stuff with WORLD.

These boxes aren't for shipping

The most basic objects in WORLD are boxes. As the name implies, a box is — well — box shaped. You have complete control over the height, width, and length of the box while you create it.

To create a box:

1. Choose Build⇨Add Box.

The Box button in the toolbar is now pressed in.

2. Set the bottom and top heights for your box.

Set the heights by dragging the top and bottom arrows in the Object Height control area of the Plane Builder window. I describe height adjustments at more length in the next section, "Going to new heights."

3. **In the Plane Builder window, click where you want one of the corners of the box.**

   As you move your mouse away from where you clicked, a rectangle follows the cursor. Nothing appears in the 3-D Space window yet.

4. **Click where you want the other corner of the box.**

   The box now appears in the 3D Space window (assuming that Pinocchio is pointing at it). WORLD adds fairly random colors to the sides of your box. To find out how to make your box look the way you want it to, check out "Decorator to the Stars," later in this chapter.

Editing a box you've added is a little more involved than it is in DRAW. WORLD has no picker tool, so you can't just click the box and drag it around. If you placed a box in the wrong location, you have two choices:

- ✔ **Undo adding the box (choose** <u>E</u>dit⇨<u>U</u>ndo**).** You can undo more than one thing by selecting the Undo command a number of times until you reach the action you want undone. You can remove a box that you added several actions ago, as long as you don't mind removing everything else that you've done since you added the box.

- ✔ **Use the Cutout Box tool (choose** <u>B</u>uild⇨<u>C</u>utout Box**).** This tool works just like the Box tool, except that instead of adding a box, it removes some or all of a box. The Cutout Box tool also uses the height controls (which I outline in the next section, "Going to new heights") so that you can remove thin slices of a box, as well. Figure 17-3 shows two different cutouts — one that removed a hunk the entire height of the box and another that removed only a thin slice. The Cutout Box tool works with both boxes and walls — don't try to use it to remove portions of faces, though, or you could get some really funky results. (Faces are explained later in this chapter in "The face that launched a thousand ships.")

   Here's one drawback to using the Cutout Box tool to remove an entire box: If you have several objects lined up on top of each other, you can accidentally remove part of a box that you don't want to remove if the height adjustments aren't set properly.

Going to new heights

Your world would be fairly boring if everything were the same height. You wouldn't be able to add ceilings and floors or cut windows out of walls. Setting the height adjustments takes a little getting used to, but when you see how it works, you won't have any trouble working with the controls.

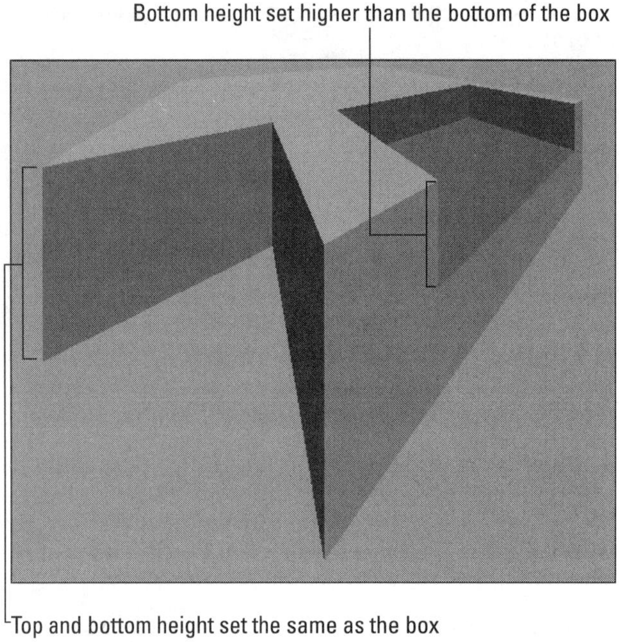

Bottom height set higher than the bottom of the box

Figure 17-3:
These two
cutouts
show the
power of
the Cutout
Box tool.

Top and bottom height set the same as the box

Use the Height Control tool (see Figure 17-4) to set the heights at which you draw your objects (or remove areas from them, if you're using the Cutout Box tool).

Using the Height Control tool is easy:

- ✔ **To set the top height for an object you want to create:** Drag the top arrow line up or down. The number just above the line changes to tell what the height is set to. Both the arrow and the number are labeled as Draw Top in Figure 17-4.

- ✔ **To set the bottom height for an object you want to create:** Drag the bottom arrow line up or down. The number just below the line changes to tell what the height is set to. Both the arrow and the number are labeled as Draw Bottom in Figure 17-4.

- ✔ **To change the Maximum Top and Minimum Bottom (both the top and bottom heights can only be between the Maximum Top and Minimum Bottom settings):** Click inside the text box of the number you want to change and type the new number. You can also use the up and down arrows on the right side of the text boxes to change these settings.

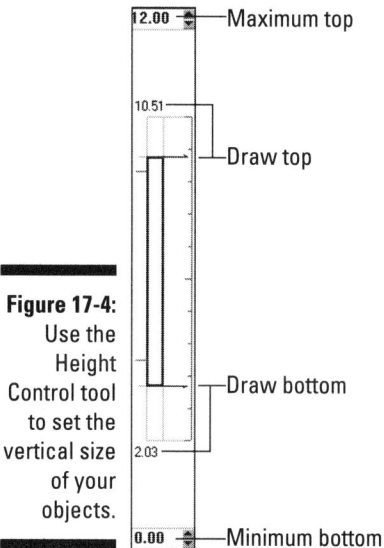

Figure 17-4:
Use the
Height
Control tool
to set the
vertical size
of your
objects.

Good walls make good neighbors

Walls are like boxes because they have height and width, but they're a little different to draw because you only have to specify the beginning and ending of the wall, not the corners. This difference makes walls particularly useful because you can draw a series of walls that are all linked together without having to draw a bunch of individual objects, so you can save some time.

To draw a wall:

1. **Choose <u>B</u>uild⇨Add <u>W</u>all.**

   The Wall Tool button on the toolbar is pressed in.

2. **In the Plane Builder window, click where you want the wall to begin.**

   As you move the cursor, a line goes from the starting point of the wall to the cursor. Even though the line following the cursor may run at an angle, the wall that you build only goes vertically or horizontally (as you can see in the Plane Builder window).

3. **Click where you want the wall to end.**

   The line becomes much fatter, though the wall doesn't yet show up in the 3-D Space window. If you want to add another wall, just click a new ending point.

4. **After you're done building walls, select the Pinocchio tool.**

   The walls now appear in the 3-D Space window (assuming that Pinocchio is pointing at them).

By default, walls are 0.25 wide. You may ask, "Zero point two five *what?*" Well, it can be feet, meters, microns, or light-years. The units in which distances are measured in WORLD really don't matter. If you feel more comfortable, though, you can just imagine them to be feet (or meters, if you're from anywhere but the United States).

The default wall width (0.25) is equal to the default distance between the grid dots that are shown in the Plane Builder window. You can change both the width of walls and the distance between the grid dots very easily, using the Builder Settings dialog box. To open the Builder Settings dialog box, choose Build⇨Builder Settings.

In the Builder Settings dialog box, you can make the following settings:

- **Grid Size:** Type the distance between the grid dots in the Plane Builder (and the distance that your walls, boxes, and faces snap to) in the Grid X text box. The Grid Y number changes to match it.

  If you want to have different grid settings for the X and Y (horizontal and vertical axes, which you can see in the Plane Builder window), then deselect the Isotropic check box. You can now type different numbers in the Grid X and Grid Y text boxes.

- **Wall Width:** In the Wall Width text box, type the width that you want your walls to be drawn at. This doesn't change the width of any walls that you've already drawn — only walls that you draw after you set this number.

- **Levels:** By default, the Plan Builder window shows all the objects in your world. This can get really confusing, however, if you're building a multilevel world. To see only the level that you're working on, select the Show Only Current Level radio button. Then only those objects that are between the Maximum Top and Minimum Bottom settings are shown.

The face that launched a thousand ships

At their most basic, *faces* are just walls that have no width — think of a face as a wall that's as thin as a piece of paper. They have one big advantage over walls, though: You can draw them at any angle you want.

To add faces:

1. Choose Build⇨Face⇨Draw Face.

The Draw Face button on the toolbar is now pressed in.

2. **In the Plane Builder window, click where you want the face to begin.**

   As you move the cursor, a line goes from the starting point of the face to the cursor.

3. **Click where you want the face to end.**

   The line is locked in place in the Plane Builder window, and the face appears in the 3-D Space window (assuming that Pinocchio is looking at it). If you want to add another face, just click a new ending point.

4. **After you're done building faces, select the Pinocchio tool to finish.**

As I mention earlier in the section "These boxes aren't for shipping," you can't use the Cutout Box tool to work with faces. If you want to erase a face:

1. **Choose Build▷Face▷Erase Face.**

   The Erase Face button in the toolbar is now pressed in.

2. **Click just past the end of the face that you want to erase.**

   A box now goes from the point where you clicked to the cursor.

3. **Move the cursor so that the box completely surrounds the face.**

   You can't erase part of a face.

4. **Click the cursor.**

   The face contained inside the box now disappears.

Decorator to the Stars

As you've built objects, you probably thought to yourself, "Gee, this is neat and all, but I really hate the colors. How can I repaint my world?" Well, even if you didn't think that — between you and me — the random colors that WORLD uses when it creates objects can be fairly ugly.

The reason for these random colors is that, by using contrasting colors, you can more easily recognize different objects in the 3-D Space window. Figure 17-5 uses no color differences — as a result, you can't tell one object from another. Compare this world to the one in Figure 17-6, which is exactly the same except that Figure 17-6 *does* use random colors.

Your world would still be fairly boring if all you could do was change colors. In the real world, objects are more than just painted. You can add just about any kind of effect you want to your virtual objects: wallpaper, pictures on walls, movies, and so on. Yes, you can even paint your objects different colors.

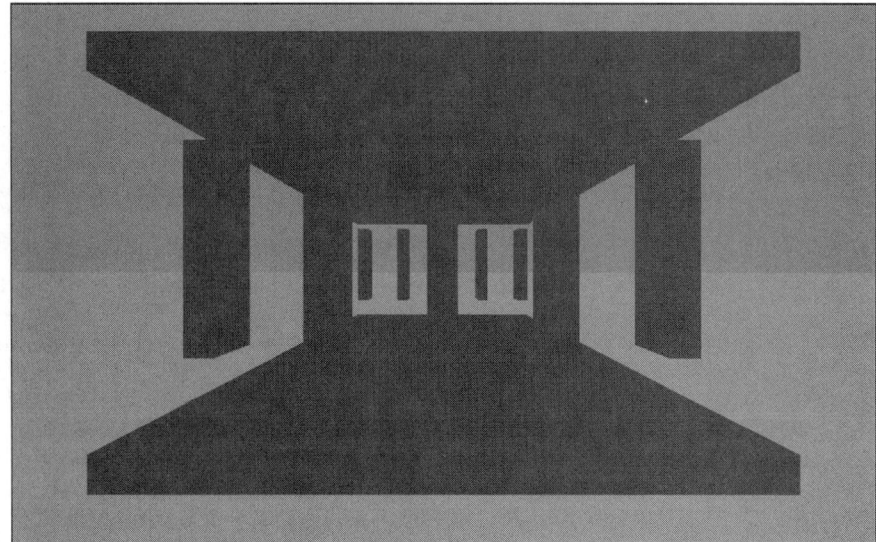

Figure 17-5:
All the object colors in this world are the same, making it much harder to figure out than Figure 17-6.

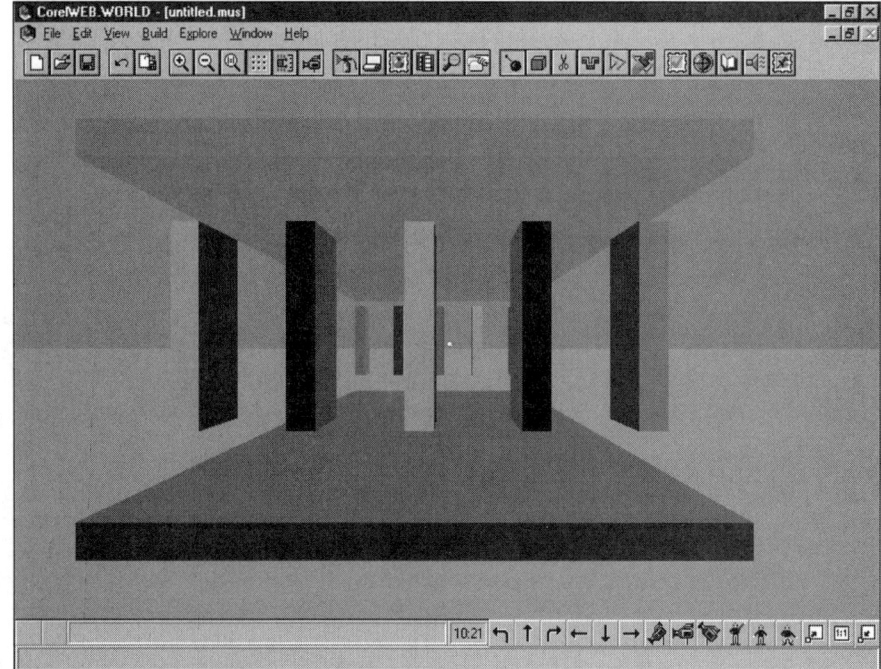

Figure 17-6:
Contrasting colors make the floor, pillars, and ceiling distinct.

Color my world

Painting objects is the easiest way to change their appearance, mainly because the Airbrush tool is already selected.

To paint an object:

1. **Choose View⇨Decorator⇨Airbrush.**

   If the Airbrush tool wasn't already selected, the Airbrush button on the toolbar is now pushed in, and the Decorator window now displays a palette of colors.

2. **Pick a color from the palette.**

   Just click the color that you want to paint an object.

3. **In the 3-D Space window, right-click the object whose color you want to change and choose Apply Color from the pop-up menu that appears.**

   Only one face of the object will be painted. To paint an entire object the same color, you have to right-click each face of the object and select Apply Color. Don't forget the top and bottom! (You can also click the color in the palette and drag it onto the object.)

Hanging wallpaper

Wallpaper. The word conjures up images of Saturdays shot to heck while you stand knee-deep in paste, and every strip that you put up peels off 10 minutes later. Luckily, adding wallpaper to objects in WORLD is infinitely easier.

In its simplest form, adding wallpaper is exactly like painting an object: You click the Wallpaper tool (or choose View⇨Decorator⇨Wallpapers), pick a wallpaper from the Decorator window, shown in Figure 17-7, and apply the paper to an object by right-clicking a face and selecting Apply Wallpaper. Boom, you're done.

Figure 17-7:
This Decorator window shows the images available to hang as wallpaper.

Hang a picture on the wall

In addition to covering an entire object with an image, you can include small pictures in various places throughout your world. You can even add moving pictures.

To add a picture or movie to your world:

1. **Insert Corel WebMaster Suite CD #2 in your drive.**

2. **Choose <u>V</u>iew⇨<u>D</u>ecorator⇨<u>P</u>ictures or <u>V</u>iew⇨<u>D</u>ecorator⇨<u>M</u>ovies.**

   The Pictures or Movies button is now pressed in (depending on which menu item you selected), and the Decorator window shows a selection of pictures. These pictures are on the WebMaster Suite CD #2. Only the first frame of each movie is shown.

3. **Select a picture from the Decorator window.**

   Just click the picture once.

4. **Right-click where you want to place your picture.**

   A pop-up menu appears.

5. **Select Apply Picture or Apply Movie, as appropriate.**

   The image or movie now appears on your object.

To move or resize a picture or movie:

1. **Right-click the picture or movie and select Move/Resize from the pop-up menu.**

   When you place the cursor over the picture or movie, the cursor now looks like a painting with two arrows on it.

2. **Click and drag the image to move it.**

3. **Click the image or movie in the upper-right corner and drag to resize it.**

Just like in a regular Web page, images can act as hyperlinks. To make an image into a hyperlink:

1. **Right-click the image or movie and choose <u>E</u>dit Attachment.**

   Either the Movie Attachment Editor or the Picture Attachment Editor dialog box appears (depending on whether you selected a movie or a picture).

2. **Select Link to URL from the Function drop-down list.**

   The Input URL dialog box appears.

3. **Type the URL of the link in the Universal Resource Locator text box.**

   The URL is the Web address that you type in your browser to go to a page.

4. **Click OK.**

   The Input URL dialog box closes, and your URL now appears in the Parameters text box.

5. **Click OK.**

   The Movie or Picture Attachment Editor dialog box closes, and your image or movie responds as a link when your visitors click it.

To delete a picture or movie, click the image in the 3-D Space window and then choose Edit⇨Delete.

The World Belongs to Everyone

After you go through all the trouble to create a world, keeping all that information to yourself would be a shame — you have to publish it!

If you started WORLD through DESIGNER, here's how to publish your world:

1. **Choose File⇨Publish to WEB.DESIGNER.**

   The Publish dialog box appears, asking if you want to save your world before continuing.

2. **I suggest clicking Yes, even if you've saved your world recently — just to be on the safe side.**

   The Save 3-D Space File dialog box appears.

3. **Click OK to save to the same name.**

   A dialog box appears and asks whether you really want to replace the file.

4. **Click Yes.**

   Your world saves to the same location. Your hard drive spins for a moment, copying the image and movie files you used, and then WORLD closes. Your world now appears in DESIGNER.

   Your world is saved to a folder called WORLD# inside the folder that contains your Web page. (The pound sign represents any number, depending on how many worlds you published.) This folder also contains a copy of the WORLD file (the one that ends in .mus) and a graphic that is included in your Web pages to show your visitors what your virtual world looks like.

If you started WORLD from the Start menu, here's how to publish your world:

1. Choose File⇨Publish to VRML.

The Select Destination Path and File Name dialog box appears. Note that if you haven't yet saved your WORLD file, the dialog box includes the File Name text box in which you need to enter a name for your world.

2. Select the location for your world.

Pick a drive from the Drives drop-down list and double-click folders in the Directories list to open them.

3. Click OK.

Your world is saved to a file with the extension .wrl. Any images, movies, or wallpapers that you added to your world are copied to the same location.

4. Create a link to your world in a Web page.

Create the link as you would any other hyperlink (refer to Chapter 6). When your visitors click on the link, your world appears in their browsers.

Part IV
Publishing Your Site

The 5th Wave   By Rich Tennant

@RICHTENNANT

NO HOME PAGE

PLEASE

In this part . . .

Creating your Web site is about 99.9 percent of the battle, but the war's not won yet. You still have to post your site to a server so that other people can visit it; otherwise, why create the site in the first place?

In this part, you find out how to publish your site to a Web server and also how to let Web surfers know that your site exists so they visit it.

Chapter 18

Using the Instant Publisher Wizard

● ●

In This Chapter

▶ Publishing to PageDepot

▶ Updating your PageDepot Web site

● ●

*C*orel and MicroCrafts have teamed up to make publishing your Web site extremely easy and relatively inexpensive. You can use the MicroCrafts Web servers to store your site and make it available to anyone in the world. This is a great option if your Internet service provider (ISP) charges extra for hosting a Web site or if you want to keep your maintenance tasks to a minimum. The team of MicroCrafts and Corel have come up with the Instant Publishing Wizard to help you easily copy your files to MicroCrafts PageDepot Web server computers — copying your files to a Web server is called *publishing*.

To entice you to publish your site to the PageDepot server, MicroCrafts lets you publish your site free for 30 days. After that time, you have the option of paying MicroCrafts a very reasonable price for continuing to be your Web server (this is called *hosting* your Web site) or having your files deleted from their computer. Don't worry, though, you still have all your files on your own computer and you can publish them to another server if you want to.

The Instant Publisher Wizard makes short work of getting your Web site up and running and keeping all your remote files up-to-date. If you make changes to your site after you've published it, you don't have to worry about what changes you made (the way you do when you publish via File Transfer Protocol (FTP), as outlined in Chapter 19). You just start the Wizard, tell it to update your site, and sit back while it does the work for you by publishing only your new and changed files to PageDepot.

This chapter includes all the steps necessary to publish your site to the PageDepot server and to update your site after it's on the server.

Another great advantage of the MicroCrafts PageDepot service is that you can incorporate MicroCrafts' built-in Common Gateway Interface (CGI) scripts into your Web site. CGI scripts are programs that run on a Web server that can add extra functions to your pages. Chapter 10 contains information about CGI scripts and the e-mail form, guest book, and Web site search capabilities that PageDepot puts at your disposal. In addition, PageDepot has a spiffy counter that you can use to keep a running total of the number of visitors to your Web site.

Publishing to PageDepot

The first time you publish your Web site to PageDepot, you have to answer some simple questions about yourself and your site. As with everything else you do to maintain your Web site on PageDepot, you work through the Instant Publisher Wizard. This Wizard makes your job extremely quick and easy. You just answer the questions that the Wizard asks and *voilà!* Your Web site is open for business. Note that if you want to sign up for one of MicroCrafts' hosting plans (beyond the 30-day free trial of its Basic Plan), you need to have a credit card handy.

To upload your Web site to PageDepot server for the first time:

1. **Start your connection to the Internet.**

2. **Start SiteManager and load your Web site as I describe in Chapter 3.**

3. **Choose File⇨Publish to the Internet.**

   The PageDepot Instant Publisher dialog box appears (see Figure 18-1).

4. **Select the Publish a New Web Site radio button and then click Next.**

   The Wizard now asks for the location of the Web site you want to publish. The site that you currently have open in SiteManager is automatically listed here, so if that's the site you want to publish, you're set.

   If you want to publish a different site, you can type its location in the text box, or you can click Browse, locate the folder holding the site you want, and then click OK.

5. **Click Next.**

   The Wizard now displays a description of all the services available from PageDepot.

6. **Click the appropriate tab to select the PageDepot service plan that you want to use.**

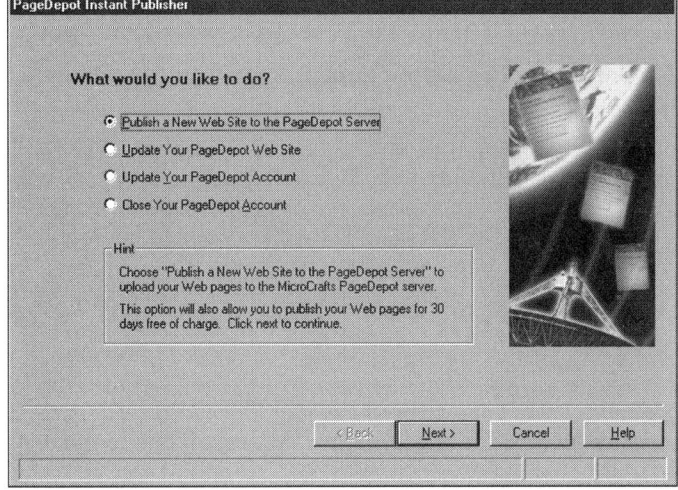

Figure 18-1:
Publishing
your new
Web site is
a breeze
with the
PageDepot
Instant
Publisher
Wizard.

PageDepot offers three plans:

- **The Basic Plan:** Provides 5MB (megabytes) of storage space for your Web site, accommodates up to 250 visitors a day, and includes automatic submission to three search indexes. (See Chapter 20 for more information about the search indexes.) This plan is the least expensive option — when you publish your site for the 30-day free trial, you are limited to the Basic Plan.

- **The Standard Plan:** Provides 10MB of storage space, accommodates up to 1,000 visitors per day, includes submission to ten search indexes, and offers telephone technical support.

- **The Deluxe Plan:** Gives you 50MB of storage space, accommodates up to 2,500 visitors per day, includes submission to 100 search indexes, provides telephone technical support, and gives you the option of listing your Web site with its very own domain name (like www.your_company.com, for example) for an additional fee of $75 per year. This plan is the most expensive option.

7. **Click Next.**

   The Wizard now asks you for the name you want to use as your Web address. This name can be anything you want and doesn't need to be the same as the name of the Web root folder on your computer.

8. **Type a name for the folder in which your Web site will appear on the PageDepot server.**

   This name can be anything you like and is added to PageDepot's domain name. Your Web site URL becomes www.PageDepot.com/ your_folder/ (where your_folder is the name that you type in this step).

Write down the URL that you create in this step (or in Step 10) so that you know where to point a browser to in order to find your site.

9. **Pick one of the PageDepot domain names under which to list your Web site.**

   You can select from `www.PageDepot.com` and `www.Designer.com`. Your Web site URL then becomes `www.PageDepot.com/your_folder/` or `www.Designer.com/your_folder/`, respectively. There's no difference in service between these two domain names. Just pick the one that sounds better to you.

10. **If you want a custom domain name, select the radio button under Custom Domain.**

    Choosing a custom domain means that your Web site URL is simply `www.any_name.com`, without the PageDepot domain name. To adjust your custom domain name, type a different name in the text box at the top of the dialog box.

    After you've clicked the radio button, the options in the Custom Domain area of the dialog box become available so that you can choose any of those options. Enter the following information:

    • Type the name of your company or organization (or your own name if this is a personal Web site) in the Organization Name text box.

    • If you already have a domain name, you can transfer its registration to PageDepot by selecting the Transfer Domain Name check box.

    • This custom domain name service has an additional cost of $75 per year. You may also have to pay an initial setup charge.

    The Custom Domain option is only available if you choose the Deluxe Plan in Step 6.

11. **Click Next.**

    The Wizard now requests a password.

12. **Type a password in both the Password and Verify Password dialog boxes.**

    Enter a password that you know you'll remember. This password is used to make sure than an unauthorized person doesn't start making changes to your Web site. If you want the Wizard to remember your password so that you don't have to type it every time you update your system, select the Save Password check box. This is an excellent option so that you don't have to remember your password, especially because you can't update your site later without your password.

13. Click Next.

The Wizard contacts PageDepot and, after a few moments, displays a request for your personal information.

14. Type the requested information.

Only your name and street address are required (including the city, state, zip or postal code, and country); the remaining information is optional. This information is used to contact you about your site and also is generally required for billing.

15. Click Next.

The Wizard now requests your credit card information. This transaction is secure, which means that nobody but MicroCrafts can read this information — it won't be stolen by some marauding hacker.

16. Choose the method you want to use to pay for your PageDepot Web site.

If you want the 30-day free trial, select the Free 30 Days Web Site radio button. If you have selected one of the options requiring payment (which Step 6 outlines) or you want PageDepot to continue hosting your site after the 30-day free trial, then click either the Credit Card via Modem or Credit Card via Fax radio button.

If you select the Credit Card via Modem option, then you must click the button showing the type of credit card you're using and enter its number and expiration date in the appropriate text boxes (as well as the card holder's name, if it's different from the name you entered when asked for your personal information).

If you select the Credit Card via Fax option, the text boxes disappear and are replaced by the Print Fax Form button. Click this button to print out a form that you need to fill out and fax to MicroCrafts.

17. Click Next.

The Wizard displays your information again. If you need to make any changes, click the Back button, make your changes, and then click Next.

18. Click Finish.

The progress of your upload is displayed on-screen. When the update is complete, a Congratulations screen appears.

19. Click Done.

The Instant Publisher Wizard closes, and you return to SiteManager.

20. After about 20 minutes, you can start your browser and check out your new Web site.

The URL that you enter in your browser is the one you entered in Steps 8, 9, and 10.

Updating Your Site

One of the great truisms of the Web is that it's always changing. This is true of your own Web site as well. You add new pages and images or decide that a page has outlived its usefulness and should be removed. If you've published your site to PageDepot, the Instant Publisher Wizard takes away all the guesswork of updating your site by checking for any differences between the files on your hard drive and the files stored on the PageDepot servers. If, on the other hand, you've published your site to your own Web server or an ISP, you need to use the FTP client that I describe in Chapter 19.

To update your Web site by using the Instant Publisher Wizard:

1. **Start your connection to the Internet.**

2. **Start SiteManager and load your Web site as I describe in Chapter 3.**

3. **Choose File⇨Publish to the Internet.**

   The Page Depot Instant Publisher Wizard dialog box appears (refer to Figure 18-1).

4. **Select the Update Your PageDepot Web Site radio button and then click Next.**

   The Wizard now asks you to select the Web site you want to update.

5. **Select the Web site you want to update from the Site Name drop-down list.**

   If you've only published one Web site to PageDepot, the site is already selected.

6. **Type your password in the Password text box.**

   This is the password that you created in Step 12 when you first published your site. If you elected to have the Wizard save your password, it is already entered.

7. **Click Next.**

   You now get two options for updating your Web site: Upload your entire site, or upload only the changes.

8. **Select the Upload Changes Since Last Upload radio button and then click Next.**

   The progress of your upload is displayed on-screen. When the update is complete, the Congratulations screen appears.

9. **Click Done.**

   The Instant Publisher Wizard closes, and you return to SiteManager. After about ten minutes, you can start your browser and check out your updates.

Chapter 19

Publishing Your Web Site
Manually Using FTP

● ●

In This Chapter

▶ Configuring the SiteManager FTP client

▶ Publishing your Web site to a server

▶ Updating your Web site

▶ Downloading files from your Web site

● ●

A s I explain in Chapter 18, the Instant Publishing Wizard lets you publish your Web site to the MicroCrafts PageDepot server. But what if you don't want to use MicroCrafts? Using SiteManager's built-in File Transfer Protocol (FTP) system, you can publish anywhere on the Internet, assuming that you have the right to publish at a particular location.

FTP is a series of standard commands — called *protocols* — that are used to move files from one computer to another over the Internet. Don't freak out! Gone are the bad old days of having to remember a kajillion weird commands to use FTP. These days, you can use any one of the large number of FTP programs (called *clients*) to publish your Web site to the Web. So many FTP clients exist that deciding which one to use may be the hardest decision you have to make.

Luckily, WebMaster Suite has an excellent FTP client built right into SiteManager that you can use to get your Web site up and running. Even if you (for some bizarre reason) choose to *not* use SiteManager's FTP client, everything in this chapter is going to be fairly similar to what you'll do with any client you choose.

Client is another one of those terms to throw out when you're standing around the water cooler and want to impress your coworkers. For example, a *client program* works on your computer and accesses another computer's server. Your *e-mail client* accesses your mail provider's mail server and enables you to send and receive e-mail. An *FTP client* gives you access to an FTP server so that you can send and receive files (called *uploading* and *downloading,* respectively). To push the topic a bit, a *Web browser* is a *Web client.*

Configuring the FTP Client

Unfortunately, you can't just jump in and publish your Web site. You have to provide your FTP client with some information about the Web site that you're publishing to before you can get down to the nitty-gritty details of moving your files.

This is another place where the information on the Cheat Sheet at the beginning of this book comes in handy. If your server administrator hasn't yet filled out the form, I suggest that you take the time to have it done. If you're in a big hurry, try a quick telephone call.

After you have the information, you can configure your FTP client:

1. **Start your connection to your Web server.**

   If you're publishing to an Internet Service Provider (ISP), start your connection to the Internet. If you're publishing your Web site to a local or corporate server, you're probably already connected (check with your system administrator).

2. **Start SiteManager and load your Web site.**

   Of course, if SiteManager is already running, you can ignore this step and go directly to Step 3.

3. **Choose File⇨FTP.**

   The FTP dialog box appears (see Figure 19-1).

Your local files   Your Web server files

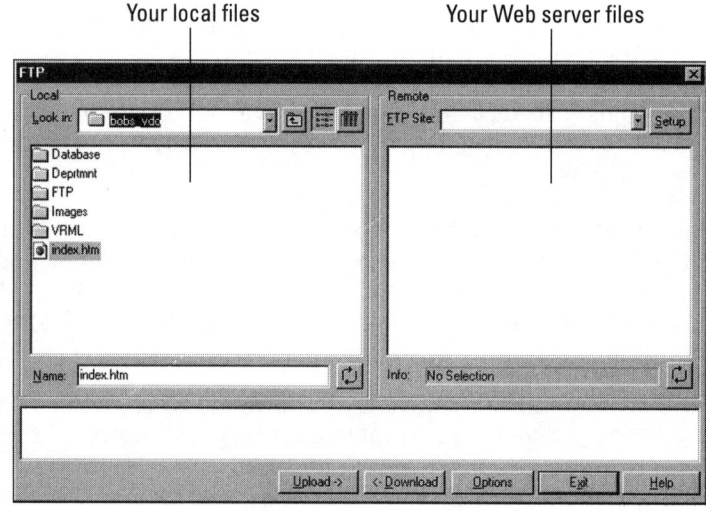

Figure 19-1:
The FTP
dialog box
looks
similar to
Windows
Explorer.

4. Click the Setup button.

The FTP Site Properties dialog box appears (see Figure 19-2).

Figure 19-2:
Tell
WebMaster
where your
Web site
will be
located.

5. Type a name for your Web site in the Description text box.

This process doesn't alter your Web site — it's just a way for you to identify this site configuration from others in case you work on more than one Web site. Even if you only work on one Web site, you have to type a description.

6. Type the name of the FTP root in the FTP Site text box.

Typically, this name is written as `ftp.domain.com`. You can find this information in the File Transfer Protocol area of the Cheat Sheet at the front of this book (assuming that you had your server administrator fill it out). Do not include any slashes (/) or folder names here.

7. Type the port number of your server's FTP service in the Port# text box.

Set this number to `21` unless your server administrator specifically tells you otherwise. A *port* is kind of like a telephone line that the server listens to — each type of request to the server (FTP, Web page, e-mail, and so on) goes to a different port.

8. Type your access name in the User name text box.

The name you type is your user name for accessing the Web server, and it may be different from your computer login name. If you're publishing your Web site to an Internet Service Provider (ISP), your access name is generally the name you enter in the Dialup Networking dialog box.

9. Type your password in the — you guessed it — Password dialog box.

I promise that I won't peek. Your password appears as a bunch of asterisks.

10. **Type the name of the File Transfer Protocol folder in which your Web site will be located in the <u>W</u>orking Folder text box.**

    Note that this name is usually slightly different from your site's URL. You can find the FTP address of your Web root on the Cheat Sheet at the front of this book (assuming that you had your server administrator or ISP fill the sheet out).

11. **Click OK.**

    The FTP Site Properties dialog box closes, and a bunch of text shoots through the bottom window of the FTP dialog box. After a few moments, the name of your FTP root appears in the window to the right (see Figure 19-3). You're now ready to publish!

    If you get the dreaded ! No FTP connection established message in the window to the right, click the Setup button to find out where you may have made a mistake. Also, double-check with your system administrator to make sure that you have the rights to connect to the site via FTP and that the site has been set up. Even though you can access the system using a Web browser, you may not have permission to add or remove files by using FTP.

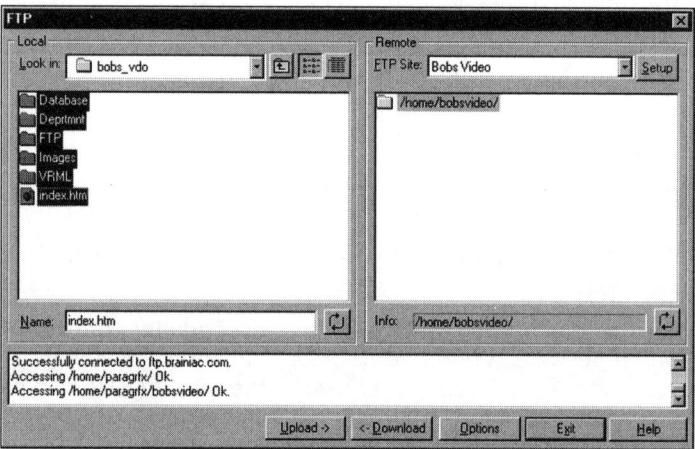

Figure 19-3: Your empty site, just waiting for you to fill it.

If you publish more than one site, you can add additional FTP locations. Click Setup again and open the FTP Site Properties dialog box. Then click New and type the information noted in the preceding steps for a different site.

Publishing Your Web Site

After your FTP location has been configured (see the earlier section "Configuring the FTP Client"), you're ready to publish (also called *upload*) your files so that anyone with a browser can visit them.

To publish your files:

1. Start your connection to your Web server.

If you just configured the FTP client and haven't left the program, you're already connected to your server. You can skip directly to Step 5.

If you're publishing to an Internet Service Provider (ISP), start your connection to the Internet. If you're publishing your Web site to a local or corporate server, you're probably already connected (check with your system administrator if you're unsure).

2. Start SiteManager and load your Web site.

3. Choose File⇨FTP.

The FTP dialog box appears.

4. From the FTP Site drop-down list, select the site you want to upload files to.

This drop-down list contains any sites that you configured in the previous section.

5. Select the files and folders you want to publish from the Local list.

You can select a number of files and folders at one time. Just use the standard Ctrl+click and Shift+click methods: Ctrl+click selects only those files or folders that you click; Shift+click selects everything between the two files or folders that you click.

When you select a folder, every file and folder contained within it is selected as well.

If you want to select your entire site, click the top-most item in the Local list and then Shift+click the bottom-most item. I strongly suggest that you publish your Web site this way, especially to a UNIX computer, so that you can make sure that the capitalization of your filenames remains correct. On a UNIX computer, the file Bob.htm is not the same as BOB.htm, so incorrect capitalization can break links in your Web site.

6. Click the Upload button.

The text box at the bottom of the dialog box spouts a bunch of gibberish. Your files are now being uploaded to your Web site.

Every few seconds, the text changes to say something along the lines of `Uploading such-and-such file` or `Creating such-and-such directory`. A small progress bar appears at the bottom of the dialog box and gives you the status of each operation. FTP only sends one file at a time, so uploading your entire site may take a while — depending on how large your Web site is and how fast your connection is. Hey, try to be patient.

Eventually, the scrolling text stops, and the line `Accessing filename OK` appears (the name of one of your files takes the place of `filename`). You now see a listing of all the files you chose to upload in the Remote list to the right (see Figure 19-4).

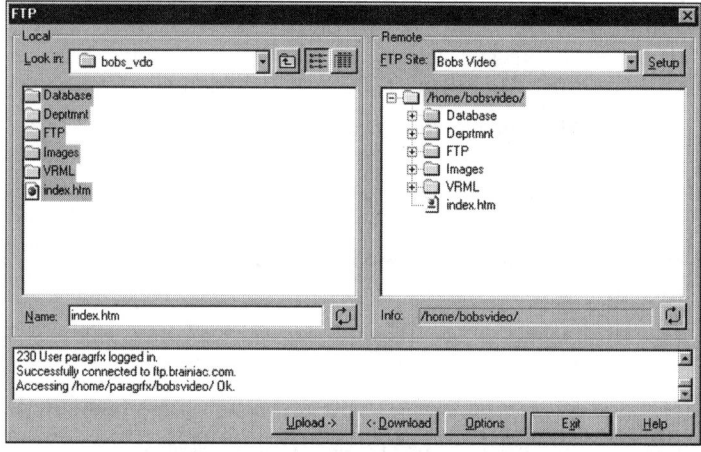

Figure 19-4: Your files are ready to be accessed by your visitors.

7. Click Exit.

The FTP dialog box closes.

8. Start your browser and view your Web site.

You should test your Web site after you upload it to make sure that all your links work as you intended.

9. Shut down your browser and close your connection to the Internet.

You're done!

Updating Your Web Site

Change. It's one of the things that makes the Web so darned exciting. Your Web site will probably never be truly finished — you'll always be updating text to announce the latest widget your company offers or to show off the cute picture your kid brought home from school. Web authors are forever changing images to make their sites look better, adding whole new pages, and removing stuff that's outlived its usefulness.

Updating existing files

You can update existing files one by one if you know which files have changed since your last upload. This process, known as *refreshing* files, can be time-consuming because you have to select each file, open the proper folder in your server, and upload the file.

To refresh files on your server:

1. **Start your connection to your Web server.**

2. **Start SiteManager and load your Web site.**

3. **Choose File⇨FTP.**

   The FTP dialog box appears.

4. **From the FTP Site drop-down list, select the site you want to upload files to.**

5. **Select the files you want to refresh from the Local list.**

    To open a folder, double-click it. If you want to move up to a higher level folder, click the Up One Level button.

6. **In the Remote list, open the folder containing the files you want to refresh.**

   To open a folder, click the + sign next to it. The folder you open must be the same one that you opened in the Local list.

7. **Click the Upload button.**

   A dialog box appears to tell you that the file already exists and asks if you really want to replace it.

8. **Click the Yes button.**

   The dialog box closes, some text scrolls by in the text box at the bottom of the dialog box, and your file is updated.

9. **Repeat Steps 5 through 8 for each file you want to update and then click Exit.**

   The FTP dialog box closes.

If you have a lot of files to update, this job can be pretty tedious and time-consuming. Here are some tips to make this job a little easier:

✔ Update your changed files right after you make the changes. Don't wait for a time when you have to upload a lot of changes.

✔ Organize your Web site using folders as I discuss in Chapters 3 and 5. Instead of updating individual files, update an entire folder and click the Yes button every time a dialog box asks you if you want to replace the existing file on the server.

Deleting files from your Web site

Sometimes, you have to delete files and folders from your server. Maybe a page is out-of-date, or an image is particularly ugly — whatever the reason, you will, eventually, end up having to remove files from your Web site.

To delete files and folders:

1. **Start the FTP dialog box and select your Web site from the FTP drop-down list.**

2. **Select the file or folder that you want to delete from the Remote list.**

   You can only select one file or folder at a time. Keep in mind that if you select a folder, everything inside of it is selected as well.

3. **Press Delete on your keyboard.**

   A dialog box appears, asking if you really want to delete the file or folder.

4. **Click the Yes button.**

   The file or folder is deleted. You may attempt to delete a folder several times before it is actually deleted because the FTP client has to find all the files and folders it contains. Just press the Delete key again if your folder is still there after the text stops moving in the progress bar at the bottom of the dialog box. (You may have to select the folder again before you delete it.)

If you ever need to retrieve files from your Web site, just select them individually from the Remote list and click the Download button. The file is copied to your local site.

Chapter 20

Hey! Check Out My Web Site

● ●

In This Chapter

▶ Finding out about search engines

▶ Posting to search engines

● ●

*S*o you've used WebMaster Suite's advanced tools to create a gorgeous, feature-filled, and yet quick-to-download Web site. You've uploaded your site to a Web server, and it's sitting there waiting for visits (called *hits* in Web parlance). Now you're just waiting for all those messages saying "Hey, I found your site on the Internet, I liked the information you gave me, and I want to do business with you."

The e-mail message never comes. What happened? Maybe nobody knows that your Web site is out there! You have to advertise the fact that your Web site exists — that's where search engines come in.

Search engines are huge databases that store a little information about a ton of Web sites. When people want to find a Web site about a particular subject, they point their browsers to a search engine page, type a few words about the subject, and the search engine gives them a bunch of possible Web sites to visit.

Unfortunately, search engines don't know that your Web site exists unless you tell them. In this chapter, I explain posting (adding a Uniform Resource Locator) to the most popular search engines so that your Web site gets maximum exposure. As with most Web tasks, posting your URL is much easier than it used to be. In the past, you had to enter a bunch of keywords about your Web site (for example, a dentist may have included the words *dentist, cavity, tooth, teeth,* and so on). Today, you typically just have to type the URL of your Web site's home page, and the search engines do the rest.

As an added bonus in this chapter, I include the URLs for a Web page (aptly labeled *Post page*) that you can use to post your Web site and a page you can use to search for information (also appropriately labeled *Search page*).

 When you type your Web site URL in any of the search engines, make sure that you include the `http://` part of the address. You may not be familiar with typing in `http://` at the beginning of a Web address because all modern browsers insert it for you. The Cheat Sheet at the beginning of this book lists your site's URL (assuming that your server administrator filled it out) in the first three lines: the domain (the `www.domain.com` part), the root directory (if your home page isn't in the root folder of the server), and the home-page filename. You can find out more about URLs in Chapter 6.

AltaVista

At the very bottom of the post page is a small text box. Simply type the URL of your Web site's home page (the `index.htm` or `default.htm` file) and click the Submit URL button. AltaVista is fairly quick about adding your Web site to its database.

- ✔ **Search page:** `altavista.digital.com`
- ✔ **Post page:** `altavista.digital.com/av/content/addurl.htm`

Advertise your Web site

In addition to just posting your Web site to the search engines, you can also include your Web site URL on your business cards, company stationery, and even advertisements you publish. Doing so can greatly increase your Web site's exposure and hit rate.

Also, you may want to consider joining with a number of other Web sites that trade links — you add a link to their Web site if they add one to yours. Typically you want to trade links with sites that are related to your own so that you know that the people visiting the other sites are interested in what you have to offer.

Here's another idea: A loosely organized group called the Internet Link Exchange uses banner advertisements in its members' pages. The banner advertisement you add to your pages constantly changes without any intervention from you. To find out about the Internet Link Exchange, point your browser to:

`www.linkexchange.com`

AOL NetFind

Part-way down the post page is a form where you type the URL of your Web site home page (the `index.htm` or `default.htm` file) and your e-mail address. Then click the Send button. You may need to wait for up to two weeks before NetFind scans your Web site and adds the URL to its database, so be patient.

- ✔ **Search page:** `www.aol.com/netfind/`
- ✔ **Post page:** `www.aol.com/info/addurl.html`

Excite

Type the URL of your Web site home page (the `index.htm` or `default.htm` file) and your e-mail address in the post. Then click the Send button. The Excite scanning process may take up to two weeks.

- ✔ **Search page:** `www.excite.com`
- ✔ **Post page:** `www.excite.com/info/add_url.html`

Infoseek

Type the URL of your Web site in the provided text box and click the Add/Update URL button. Infoseek is generally fairly quick about adding your Web site.

- ✔ **Search page:** `www.infoseek.com`
- ✔ **Post page:** `www.infoseek.com/AddUrl?pg=DCaddurl.html`

WebCrawler

Type your URL in the small text box and click the Add URL button. WebCrawler lists your Web site fairly quickly.

- ✔ **Search page:** `www.webcrawler.com`
- ✔ **Post page:** `www.webcrawler.com/Help/GetListed/AddURLS.html`

Check out the page at `www.webcrawler.com/Help/GetListed/HelpAddURL.html` for more information about helping the search engines really understand your Web site and provide the best summary of the it.

Part V
The Part of Tens

The 5th Wave   By Rich Tennant

"HONEY! OUR WEB BROWSER GOT OUT LAST NIGHT AND DUMPED THE TRASH ALL OVER MR. BELCHER'S HOME PAGE!"

In this part . . .

The previous parts of this book are devoted to making you one with Corel WebMaster Suite, but what about content? What about the words and graphics that go into making your site a place that people will want to visit? Just what the heck are you going to put on your Web site, anyway?

This part helps you answer some of those nagging questions. Here, I introduce ideas (in convenient groups of ten) to help get your creative juices flowing, show you how other people are designing and using their sites, and suggest some of the extra tools you can use to get the effects you want.

Chapter 21

Ten Ways to Use Your Site

● ●

*T*he World Wide Web has been called the most important development in communications since Johannes Gutenberg invented movable type. I'm not sure that I would go quite that far, but it certainly is a big change from the way things used to work.

Gutenberg's invention of movable type in the 15th century made it possible to mass produce books and moved the world into a new age of literacy and advancement. Previously, only the extremely wealthy could afford books, but after the invention of movable type, books became within the reach of the middle class. Books, newspapers, and magazines began to thrive, although the means to print them was still controlled by a relatively small number of people.

With the advent of the Web, everybody can be a publisher — with a world-wide market. Any idea you have, any product you want to sell, any service you want to provide is instantly accessible to anyone with a computer. You have power. So what do you do with it?

In this chapter, I discuss ten different ways that you can use your Web site. Hundreds of other ways exist, but I picked ten ways that have a lot of range. Some of these ways are best suited to personal Web sites, others to corporate Web sites, and others to academic Web sites. The great thing about a Web site is that you can incorporate any or all these ideas into a single Web site. Now sit back, skim the next few pages, and let your creative juices flow.

Corporate Web Sites

Many kinds of companies can benefit from having a Web site. From advertising to sales to public relations, here are just a few ways that your company can use its Web site.

Do you publish a catalog?

Consider creating a Web catalog. A Web catalog increases your catalog budget by a mere pittance and reaches a far larger audience than you could probably afford using conventional publishing.

Consider the following ideas to help you keep your costs down and make your online catalog of greater benefit to your visitors:

- Use the same photographs that your printed catalog uses.
- Link thumbnail-sized copies of your photographs to larger, more detailed ones.
- Include more information about each product than you can afford (in space and money) to include in a printed catalog.
- Put the Uniform Resource Locator (URL) of your catalog and your company home page in your printed catalog.
- Include an order form that your visitors can print and mail.
- Consider adding an interactive Web purchasing system. This adds greatly to the cost and required technical expertise, however.

Tired of answering the same old questions?

Post a Frequently Asked Questions (FAQ) page. Include answers to all those nagging questions like, "Where are your offices located?" and "When is your business open?" I'm sure that, given five minutes, you can think of hundreds of questions.

Looking for the perfect employee?

In addition to putting ads in the classified section of your local newspaper, put job postings on your Web site. You'll increase the number of people that may read your job listing from a couple hundred thousand to millions. Your chances of finding just the right person will increase as well.

Does your company send out press releases?

Most press releases are buried on page 10 of the business section and are chopped to a couple small paragraphs. Make sure that your entire message gets through by posting your press releases to your Web site.

Do you have downloadable product updates?

Save your company the expense and hassle of sending out diskettes with software updates on them. Post the updates to your Web site. (Your company may need to keep some diskettes or CDs on hand for customers with slow Internet access, but can save a bundle overall.)

Personal Web Sites

Almost every Internet Service Provider (ISP) gives you space to create your own Web site as part of your monthly fee. Many corporations also provide space on their servers for their employees to create Web sites. Here are a couple suggestions for what to put on your Web site.

Looking for work?

Why not post a page on your Web site that includes your resume? Though you can post a pure text version of your paper resume, remember that you have all the hyperlink and graphics capabilities of the Web at your disposal:

- ✔ Make links to any companies that you worked for.
- ✔ Provide short descriptions of your work experience with links to more detailed descriptions.
- ✔ Include examples of your work (if they're appropriate to show on a Web page).
- ✔ Make sure that you post your page to all the search engines (you can find out more about search engines in Chapter 20). Also, track down the Web sites of the human resources departments where you'd like to work and e-mail them your URL.
- ✔ If you're still working for someone else, remember that your current boss may see this, so be careful! Don't publish your resume on your company's Web site — not only is this unethical, but it darned well may be illegal.
- ✔ Because you mastered WebMaster Suite with this book, don't forget to add the title *Whiz-bang Web Producer* to your resume!

Interested in tracking down your roots?

Consider posting a genealogy page that includes your family tree (at least as much of it as you know). To make adding to your family tree easier, add a form that potential relatives can fill out to give you information about themselves and their ancestry. Don't forget to post your page to the search engines so that others can find it easily.

Academic Web Sites

Students, professors, and staff can use a school, college, or university Web site to foster communication and avoid problems.

Do your students interrupt you during your private time?

Post your class and office schedule to your Web page. You can easily add updates when your schedule changes unexpectedly.

Do your students lose their handbooks?

Publish an electronic copy of your student handbook to your Web site, and you'll never again hear, "I didn't know I could only miss two classes before I fail." Remember that you can use the Net Transit Wizard in DESIGNER to import word processor documents to save yourself a lot of typing! See Chapter 5 for instructions on how to use Net Transit.

Do your parents always bug you for your grades?

Include a Mom and Dad page that you can use to keep them up-to-date on your latest test scores and sports achievements. This won't stop the "Why don't you ever call?" complaints, but it can cut down on the "Why didn't you tell us?" questions.

Chapter 22

Ten Way-Cool Tools You Must Have

• •

*Y*ou're probably thinking to yourself, "Hey, WebMaster Suite is absolutely packed with tons of useful tools and utilities. Why do I need anything else?" Well, you do.

Color Picker

When you edit your Hypertext Markup Language (HTML) code by hand (as discussed in Chapter 13), you need the Color Picker by Professional Web Design. This handy-dandy online utility ensures that you specify colors that match your image palette and are browser-compatible. (See Chapter 7 for a discussion of image palettes.) Whereas all of the other utilities in this chapter are actual programs that you install on your computer, Color Picker is a Web page with some sophisticated programming added in — you don't need to install it on your computer, just point your browser to the Color Picker Web page.

One of the great things about this Web page is that it provides you with all the HTML code you need to use the colors you create. The Color Picker only creates colors for the Netscape palette. If you use this utility, make sure that your GIF images are based on the Netscape palette, not the Microsoft palette. You can find Color Picker at the following URL:

```
junior.apk.net/~jbarta/weblinks/color_picker
```

DUNCE

No, I'm not calling *you* a dunce. The Dial-Up Networking Connection Enhancement (DUNCE) from Vector Development is a great utility that makes connecting to your Internet Service Provider (ISP) via a modem fast and easy ("dial-up" comes from your modem dialing-up your ISP). DUNCE remembers your dial-up password, lets you schedule programs to run, and even redials your ISP if you get disconnected. You can find DUNCE at the following address:

```
www.vecdev.com/dunce.html
```

FormMail

You want to include a form in your Web page but don't want to write the CGI script to make it work? Matt Wright's CGI script, FormMail, is an excellent way to retrieve information from your visitors in the form of an e-mail message. Lucky for you, this program is included on the CD-ROM that comes with this book. Chapter 10 explains how to create forms and use CGI scripts. Check out the following URL for even more great CGI scripts available for your downloading pleasure:

```
worldwidemart.com/scripts
```

GIF Construction Set

Alchemy Mindworks' GIF Construction Set is a great utility for constructing GIF animations. Sure, you can use MOVE to animate actors and props as I explain in Chapter 16, but GIF Construction Set lets you assemble wildly different images as individual frames of an animation. You can find GIF Construction Set at the following URL:

```
www.mindworkshop.com
```

Microsoft Dial-Up Networking 1.2 Upgrade

Although the old version of the Microsoft Dial-Up Networking upgrade was called the ISDN Accelerator Pack, this upgrade does a whole lot more than deal with ISDN (*Integrated Services Digital Network,* a really fancy and high-speed modem that makes 56Kbps modems seem like snails). This is an upgrade to the dial-up networking that comes with Windows 95. You can find this upgrade at the following URL:

```
www.microsoft.com/ntserver/info/PPTPdownload.htm
```

Microsoft Web Fonts

In Chapter 6, you can find out how to incorporate different fonts in your Web pages. In that chapter, I recommend that you stick to a couple basic fonts because not everyone viewing your Web site has the same fonts that you do. Microsoft has put together a bunch of free fonts that you can use in your Web site and that you can make available to your visitors. You can find these fonts at the following URL:

```
www.microsoft.com/typography
```

To save space on your Web server, make links to these fonts on the Microsoft site rather than store them yourself.

Palette Express

When you create your own GIF images for your Web site, you make sure that they all use the same palette (see Chapter 15). What happens, though, when you download images or incorporate screen shots? Rhode Island Soft Systems' Palette Express updates your images so that they all use the same palette, and your site avoids the funky colors you sometimes see. You can find Palette Express on the CD-ROM that comes with this book, or you can find the program at the following URL:

```
www.risoftsystems.com
```

WinGate

If you have two or more computers networked and only one data telephone line, you need WinGate proxy from Deerfield Communications. This fantastic utility lets any computer on your network access the Internet through a single modem. You can find this utility at the following URL:

```
www.wingate.net
```

WinZip

Want to include large files on your site for your visitors to download? You can compress the files using the number one Windows-based compression utility: WinZip from Nico Mak Computing. WinZip lets you compress (and decompress) files in the standard .zip format making most files about half their original size. You can find WinZip on the CD-ROM that accompanies this book and at the following URL:

```
www.winzip.com
```

WS_FTP

The File Transfer Protocol (FTP) dialog box in SiteManager is an excellent limited-use FTP client that you can use for the relatively simple task of publishing your Web site (as explained in Chapter 19). When you really need control over how you move your files, use WS_FTP from Ipswitch, Inc. You can find WS_FTP on the CD-ROM that comes with this book and at the following URL:

```
www.ipswitch.com
```

Chapter 23

Ten Web Sites to Give You Ideas

*P*robably the best way to decide how to organize your site and get ideas for content and appearance is to study existing Web sites. But where do you start? I've chosen the ten sites in this chapter to help you get moving on your voyage of discovery — some are technical sites with raw information about building Web pages, some just look cool, and others are set up extremely well.

Corel Corporation

The Corel Corporation Web site (`www.corel.com`) has two great things going for it:

- ✔ It's a well-laid-out site that loads very quickly in spite of the fact that it tends to use a lot of graphics.
- ✔ It was created with WebMaster Suite — just look at all the exciting ways that you can use this powerful program!

Also check out `www.corel.com/corelweb/webmaster/` for more information and upgrades for WebMaster Suite.

...For Dummies

Another site that uses graphics sparingly but still manages to look great is the *...For Dummies* site (`www.dummies.com`). This site is organized extremely well; surf around this site and see how everything dovetails nicely. Also notice that the page is designed for a 640-pixel-wide screen but still looks excellent on an 800-pixel-wide screen because of the centered table — notice the blank area on both sides of the text. Check out Chapter 8 for information about creating tables.

iGOLF

Check out the great way that the iGOLF site (`www.igolf.com`) uses tables to organize information into columns. This site is extremely easy to navigate and easy to read — it looks more like a magazine than your normal, every-day Web site. In addition to the tables, look at the unobtrusive icons that give you quick access to everything on the site. Also, check out the iGOLF sister site, Tour Golf Club, at `www.tourgolfclub.com` for more imagination-sparking ideas.

Infoseek Web Kit

Here's a way to bring some more traffic into your site: Add a premade search engine form to your page. Adding this form is easy with Infoseek's Web Kit. You don't even have to have Infoseek's database on your site; the Web Kit forms access Infoseek directly and take care of all the work for you. Visit the Infoseek Web Kit site (`www.infoseek.com/Webkit?pg=webkit_intro.html`) and Chapter 20 for more information.

Microsoft Site Builder Network

The Microsoft Site Builder Network (`www.microsoft.com/sitebuilder`) is an excellent resource for finding out the latest information about new Web developments, downloading utilities, and just plain keeping on top of things. By adding the Internet Explorer logo to your site, you can join Site Builder Network (SBN) and get an e-mail update and access to its download area. Keep in mind that the information you get on this page is skewed almost totally toward Microsoft's products or products it has licensed, so you also want to check out the site that I mention in the next section.

Netscape DevEdge Online

To get the nonMicrosoft side of the Web technology story, join Netscape's DevEdge program (`developer.netscape.com`). This Web site contains tons of resources, examples, and programs to download.

Shameless Self-Promotion

What would the world be without shameless self-promotion? Pretty boring. So to do my part in making the world a more interesting place, I'm pushing my own company's Web site (www.paragrafix.com). On the practical side, though, check out my use of frames and forms that keep the site organized and easy to navigate. Also, notice that the site looks exactly the same whether you have a frames-capable browser or not — I used the trick that I outline in Chapter 9 to keep my development work to a minimum.

Titleist & Footjoy Worldwide

The Titleist Web site (www.titleist.com) is an excellent example of an online store that's easy to navigate. The Titleist site also provides its visitors with a choice of high-bandwidth (for visitors with fast Web connections) or low-bandwidth (for visitors with slow Web connections) sites that work very well. In the high-bandwidth site (select blue tees on the home page), notice the nice use of frames and easy navigation techniques. In the low-band width site (select white tees on the home page), check out how neat the site looks because of the tables. Both high- and low-bandwidth sites also provide a lot of information about golf that isn't directly related to sales of Titleist equipment — adding information that isn't directly related to something you're trying to sell is a great way to ensure that people visit your site.

Windows95.com

The Windows95.com site (www.windows95.com), has two interesting features that can really help you with your Web site construction:

✔ An innovative look based on its subject matter

✔ A host of tools, utilities, and applications that are indispensable

World Wide Web Consortium

Contrary to what Microsoft and Netscape may think, the World Wide Web Consortium (www.w3.org) sets the standards for just about everything on the Web. Its site is one of the best resources available for all the technical issues involved in producing Web pages. Note that some of what you find here is a little high end, so keep your head screwed on tight while you search for information.

Appendix A
Installing WebMaster Suite

*I*n a moment of ambition and inspiration, you bought Corel WebMaster Suite so that you could create your own Web site, but the program is still sitting in its unopened box. Well, before you even attempt to begin building your site, you have to install the software. Don't worry — the installation is a breeze. The Installation Wizard walks you through a bunch of questions and then goes to work copying the required files to your hard drive.

No matter how simple the installation process, though, working through an installation cold can be a little daunting. I suggest that you quickly skim the following procedure so that you're familiar with what the Installation Wizard will ask you before you begin.

To install WebMaster Suite:

1. **Start your computer.**

   If your computer is already running, shut down all your open applications.

2. **Insert WebMaster Suite CD-ROM #1 in your CD-ROM drive.**

   This CD has an autorun feature — just wait a few moments for the installation program to start, and you see the WebMaster Suite screen (see Figure A-1).

   If the program doesn't begin to run after a short while, choose Start⇨Run to open the Run dialog box. Then type **d:/intro.exe** in the text box and click OK. (If your CD-ROM drive is not named d, substitute the letter of your CD-ROM drive.)

3. **Click the text that reads Corel WebMaster Suite Setup.**

   The installation program begins and displays the Corel Setup Wizard dialog box. If you want to install Netscape Navigator or the O'Reilly Personal Web Server, consult the WebMaster Suite documentation.

4. **Click Next.**

   The WebMaster Suite license agreement appears. Read the license agreement before proceeding.

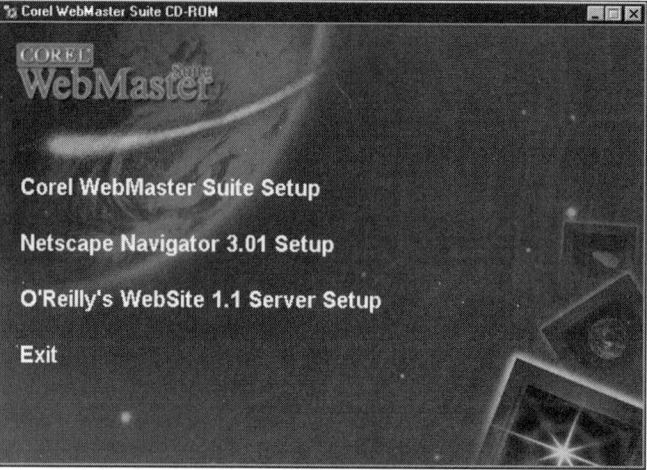

Figure A-1:
The kickin'
music and
this dialog
box begin
your
journey of
installing
WebMaster
Suite.

5. Click Accept.

The Wizard now asks for your personal information and displays
information it has gleaned from your system (see Figure A-2). If you
don't agree with the conditions detailed in the license agreement, click
the Decline button to end this installation.

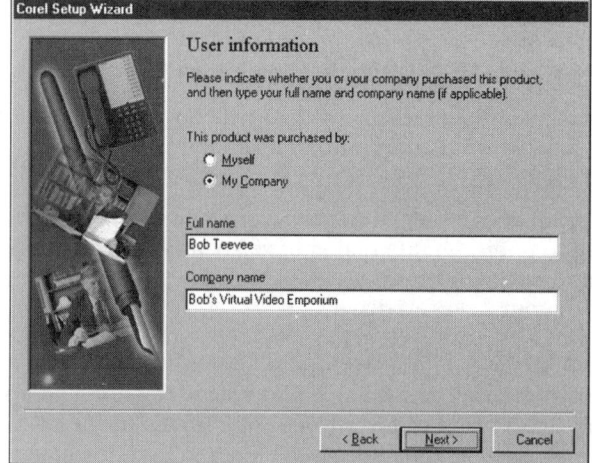

Figure A-2:
Your
personal
information.

6. If the information is correct, click Next.

If the information about you is not correct, make the necessary changes
and then click Next. The Wizard now displays your personal information
again.

7. Click Next.

The Wizard now asks you for your WebMaster Suite serial number.

8. Enter your serial number in the two dialog boxes.

You can find this number on your registration card. After you fill out the registration card and send it to Corel, keep the serial number portion for your own records — I like to tape these sheets to the inside cover of my manuals so that they're always handy if I ever need to call Customer Service or Technical Support.

9. Click Next.

The Wizard now wants to know what type of installation you want to perform — Typical or Custom.

10. Select the Typical radio button and click Next.

You are now asked about your scanner — if you have one.

11. If you have a scanner click the check box.

Selecting this check box enables you to scan photographs directly into PhotoPaint. Select your scanner manufacturer from the list that appears. Note that you have to set up your scanner later — follow the WebMaster Suite documentation to do this.

12. Click Next.

You are now asked to specify the locations where the setup program will store WebMaster Suite and the typefaces that it installs.

13. To accept these folders, click Next.

I suggest that you leave the Fonts folder location as it is — the default location is where Windows 95 stores all your other fonts.

If you have more than one hard drive, I suggest changing the drive letter name under Destination Directory because the C drive of a computer running Windows 95 can get full very quickly. When you finish making this change, click Next. The Wizard now displays a list of your shortcut folders.

14. To accept the default folder (Corel WebMaster Suite) as your shortcut folder, click Next.

You are now ready to install. The Wizard displays your folder choices. If you want to go back and make any changes to the information you've already entered, click Back to work your way backward through the Wizard.

After you've finished installing WebMaster Suite and when you want to run one of its programs, choose Start⇨Programs⇨Corel WebMaster Suite and then select the program you want.

15. Click Install.

The Wizard dialog box closes, and a small status bar opens to show the progress of your installation. The installation can take a while, depending on the speed of your computer and your CD-ROM drive. If at any time you want to halt the installation of WebMaster Suite, click Cancel.

Be sure to keep your hands away from the keyboard during the installation because the Cancel button is highlighted — if you happen to hit the Space bar or the Enter key, the installation is canceled and you have to start over again. Nothing happens to your computer, but you waste time getting to this point.

When the installation is complete, a new dialog box opens and asks if you want to register WebMaster Suite online.

16. Click No.

This is just my personal preference. I prefer to fill out the little product registration cards with a good old-fashioned pen and send them in the mail.

This dialog box closes, and another dialog box tells you that your installation is complete!

17. Click OK.

The install system closes, and a bunch of new folders are open.

18. Close the folders.

Corel WebMaster Suite is now installed and ready to run. Congratulations!

Appendix B

About the CD

· ·

Corel WebMaster Suite is an almost perfect product. Using its countless programs, utilities, and pieces of clipart, you can build an entire Web site without ever starting another program or creating a piece of art on your own. There are a couple of extras, though, that can make your site more exciting, useful, and easier to create. For your convenience, I've assembled a bunch of these goodies on the CD-ROM that accompanies this book.

Here's a taste of what you can find on the *Corel WebMaster Suite For Dummies* CD-ROM:

- ✔ **Microsoft Internet Explorer Version 4.0:** The absolute latest version of the Microsoft Web browser

- ✔ **Palette Express:** The shareware version of Rhode Island Soft Systems image palette utility

- ✔ **Sound Forge:** A fantastic sound-recording and -editing program

- ✔ **Corel WebMaster Suite trial:** A 30-day trial version of Corel WebMaster Suite — the subject of this book.

System Requirements

Make sure that your computer meets the minimum system requirements in the following list. If your computer doesn't match up to most of these requirements, you may have problems in using the contents of the CD.

- ✔ A PC with a 486 or faster processor. (The processor can be from any of the major companies like Intel, AMD, or Cyrix.)

- ✔ Microsoft Windows 95 or later, or Windows NT 4.0 or later.

- ✔ At least 8MB of total RAM installed on your computer. For best performance, I recommend that PCs have at least 16MB of RAM installed. 16MB is required if you install all the features of Internet Explorer for Windows 95; 24MB is required if you install Internet Explorer on a computer running Windows NT.

✔ At least 125MB of hard drive space available to install all the software from this CD. (You don't need as much space if you don't install every program.)

✔ A CD-ROM drive — double-speed (2x) or faster.

✔ A sound card and speakers.

✔ A monitor and display card capable of displaying at least 256 colors (8-bit color) — 16-bit or 24-bit color is best if you'll be creating new images with CorelDRAW 7.

✔ A mouse or other pointing device.

✔ A modem with a speed of at least 14,400 bps.

If you need more information on the basics, check out *PCs For Dummies,* 4th Edition, by Dan Gookin, or *Windows 95 For Dummies* by Andy Rathbone (both published by IDG Books Worldwide, Inc.).

How to Use the CD

To install the items from the CD to your hard drive, follow these steps:

1. **Insert the CD into your computer's CD-ROM drive.**

2. **Click the Windows Start button and select Run.**

3. **In the dialog box that appears, type** D:\SETUP.EXE.

   Odds are, your CD-ROM drive is listed as drive D under My Computer. Type in the proper drive letter if your CD-ROM drive uses a different letter.

4. **Click OK.**

   A license agreement window appears.

5. **Because you're sure to want to use the CD, read through the license agreement, nod your head, and then click Accept.**

   After you click Accept, you'll never be bothered by the License Agreement window again.

6. **Click OK to acknowledge that you're ready to view the contents of the CD.**

   From here, the CD interface appears. The CD interface enables you to install the programs on the CD without typing in cryptic commands or using yet another finger-twisting hot key in Windows. The software on the interface is divided into categories whose names you see on the screen.

7. **To view the items within a category, just click the category's name.**

   A list of programs in the category appears.

8. **For more information about a program, click on the program's name.**

   Be sure to read the information that appears. Sometimes, a program may require you to do a few tricks on your computer first, and this screen tells you where to go for that information, if necessary.

9. **To install the program, click the appropriate Install button; if you don't want to install the program, click on the Go Back button to return to the previous category screen.**

   After you click the Install button, the CD interface drops to the background while the CD begins installation of the program you chose.

   When installation is complete, the interface usually reappears in front of other open windows. Sometimes, the installation confuses Windows and leaves the interface in the background. To bring the interface forward, just click once anywhere in the interface's window.

   Note: To save space on your hard drive, you don't need to install the clipart that comes on this CD-ROM. Instead, just use the browse feature in DESIGNER's Image Properties dialog box to find the image you want and load only the particular images you're going to use. (Remember that DESIGNER automatically copies images to your Web root folder for you.) For more about adding images to your Web pages, see Chapter 7.

10. **To install other items, repeat Steps 6, 7, and 8.**

    You can use the Go Back button at any time to return to the previous screen.

11. **When you're done installing programs, click Quit to close the interface.**

    You can now eject the CD-ROM. Carefully place it back in the plastic jacket of the book for safekeeping.

What You'll Find

The following is a summary of the software on this CD-ROM. The CD interface helps you install software easily. (If you have no idea what I'm talking about when I say *CD interface,* flip back a page or two to find the section "How to Use the CD.")

Celine's Original GIFs

This collection of images, borders, and buttons is an excellent addition to the clipart that comes with WebMaster Suite.

You can see other examples of Celine's work and pick up new art at her Web site:

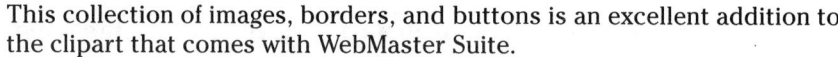

```
www.specialweb.com/original
```

Corel WebMaster Suite Trial

Still trying to decide whether Corel WebMaster Suite is right for you? This 30-day trial of the powerful Corel WebMaster Suite lets you take the programs out for a test drive. You get WEB.DESIGNER, for authoring web pages; WEB.PhotoPaint image editor; WEB.SiteManager, for creating and managing your site; and WEB.DATA, for translating database information into HTML. To find out more about this amazing set of Web-authoring tools, visit the Corel Corporation on the Web at `www.corel.com`.

FormMail

FormMail is a Common Gateway Interface (CGI) program that runs on your Web server. It takes the contents of a form in one of your Web pages (see Chapter 10) and e-mails it to you. For FormMail to work, it must be installed on your Web server, typically in the `/cgi-bin` folder. Placing FormMail on your server is something that your server administrator has to do.

To use FormMail to handle your Internet form, create a form as explained in Chapter 10 and set your form fields' names to those required by FormMail. Complete instructions for FormMail are included in the `readme.txt` file.

Jelane's Free Web Graphics

Another excellent collection of Web graphics. I hand-selected this group of 30 families from Jelane's vast assortment of graphics sets.

To see more, visit Jelane's Web site at:

```
www.erinet.com/jelane/families
```

Please note that these graphics are licensed for personal and nonprofit use. If you want to use any of them on a commercial site, go to `www.erinet` `.com/jelane/families/copy.html` and read the copyright notice for instructions on using these images.

Microsoft Internet Explorer 4

If you're still slogging through the Web using Internet Explorer 3.02 or lower (or, even worse, you don't have the browser at all), here's your chance to upgrade to Version 4.0.

Palette Express

Palette Express is a shareware program from Rhode Island Soft Systems, the twisted geniuses behind the "Hey, Macaroni" screen saver. This program automatically updates your paletted images so that they all share the same palette — an invaluable feature if you include GIFs in your Web site (and who doesn't!).

You can see more of Rhode Island Soft Systems' shareware programs at:

```
www.risoftsystems.com
```

Sound Forge

In Chapter 11, I show you how to make a very primitive recording by using the Windows 95 Sound Recorder. Although Sound Recorder does the job of recording sound, if you *really* want to work with sound, you need a top-notch editor like Sound Forge.

WinZip 6.3

Zipping is a cute way to describe the process of condensing one or more files into a single teeny, tiny package that is useless until you unzip it. (Think of sitting on an overstuffed suitcase and zipping it shut; you can't get at all the goodies inside until you unzip it.) You really need an unzipping program to deal with compressed files that you download, specifically those files with the file extension .zip (these files are called, unsurprisingly, *zip files*). Zip files are especially useful on the Internet because they files take up less space and require less time to download. You can send and receive zip files as e-mail attachments, or you can download them from Web pages, particularly shareware sites.

A Connecticut programmer named Nico Mak wrote a nice little Windows shareware program called WinZip. WinZip can both zip (compress) and unzip (decompress) files for you. To find out more ingenius program, visit `www.winzip.com` on the World Wide Web.

WS_FTP LE 4.5

After you've finished designing your Web site and are ready to publish it, you need to use a File Transfer Protocol (FTP) program to copy your files to your Web server. The FTP module in DESIGNER is an excellent light-duty FTP client, but if you really have some major work to do, WS_FTP is the program you need.

If You Have Problems (Of the CD Kind)

I tried my best to compile programs that work on most computers with the minimum system requirements. Alas, your computer may differ, and some programs may not work properly for some reason.

The two likeliest problems are that you don't have enough memory (RAM) for the programs you want to use, or you have other programs running that are affecting the installation or running of a program. If you get error messages like `Not enough memory` or `Setup cannot continue`, try one or more of these methods and then try using the software again:

- Turn off any antivirus software that you have on your computer. Installers sometimes mimic virus activity and may make your computer incorrectly believe that it's being infected by a virus.

- Close all running programs. The more programs you're running, the less memory is available to other programs. Installers also typically update files and programs. So if you keep other programs running, installation may not work properly.

- Have your local computer store add more RAM to your computer. This is, admittedly, a drastic and somewhat expensive step. However, if you have a Windows 95 PC or a Mac OS computer with a PowerPC chip, adding more memory can really help the speed of your computer and enable more programs to run at the same time.

If you still have trouble with installing the items from the CD, please call the IDG Books Worldwide Customer Service phone number: 800-762-2974 (outside the U.S.: 317-596-5430).

Index

IDG Books Worldwide, Inc., End-User License Agreement

READ THIS. You should carefully read these terms and conditions before opening the software packet(s) included with this book ("Book"). This is a license agreement ("Agreement") between you and IDG Books Worldwide, Inc. ("IDGB"). By opening the accompanying software packet(s), you acknowledge that you have read and accept the following terms and conditions. If you do not agree and do not want to be bound by such terms and conditions, promptly return the Book and the unopened software packet(s) to the place you obtained them for a full refund.

1. **License Grant.** IDGB grants to you (either an individual or entity) a nonexclusive license to use one copy of the enclosed software program(s) (collectively, the "Software") solely for your own personal or business purposes on a single computer (whether a standard computer or a workstation component of a multiuser network). The Software is in use on a computer when it is loaded into temporary memory (RAM) or installed into permanent memory (hard disk, CD-ROM, or other storage device). IDGB reserves all rights not expressly granted herein.

2. **Ownership.** IDGB is the owner of all right, title, and interest, including copyright, in and to the compilation of the Software recorded on the CD-ROM ("Software Media"). Copyright to the individual programs recorded on the Software Media is owned by the author or other authorized copyright owner of each program. Ownership of the Software and all proprietary rights relating thereto remain with IDGB and its licensers.

3. **Restrictions on Use and Transfer.**

   (a) You may only (i) make one copy of the Software for backup or archival purposes, or (ii) transfer the Software to a single hard disk, provided that you keep the original for backup or archival purposes. You may not (i) rent or lease the Software, (ii) copy or reproduce the Software through a LAN or other network system or through any computer subscriber system or bulletin-board system, or (iii) modify, adapt, or create derivative works based on the Software.

   (b) You may not reverse engineer, decompile, or disassemble the Software. You may transfer the Software and user documentation on a permanent basis, provided that the transferee agrees to accept the terms and conditions of this Agreement and you retain no copies. If the Software is an update or has been updated, any transfer must include the most recent update and all prior versions.

4. **Restrictions on Use of Individual Programs.** You must follow the individual requirements and restrictions detailed for each individual program in Appendix B of this Book. These limitations are also contained in the individual license agreements recorded on the Software Media. These limitations may include a requirement that after using the program for a specified period of time, the user must pay a registration fee or discontinue use. By opening the Software packet(s), you will be agreeing to abide by the licenses and restrictions for these individual programs that are detailed in Appendix B and on the Software Media. None of the material on this Software Media or listed in this Book may ever be redistributed, in original or modified form, for commercial purposes.

5. **Limited Warranty.**

   (a) IDGB warrants that the Software and Software Media are free from defects in materials and workmanship under normal use for a period of sixty (60) days from the date of purchase of this Book. If IDGB receives notification within the warranty period of defects in materials or workmanship, IDGB will replace the defective Software Media.

   (b) IDGB AND THE AUTHOR OF THE BOOK DISCLAIM ALL OTHER WARRANTIES, EXPRESS OR IMPLIED, INCLUDING WITHOUT LIMITATION IMPLIED WARRANTIES OF MER-CHANTABILITY AND FITNESS FOR A PARTICULAR PURPOSE, WITH RESPECT TO THE SOFTWARE, THE PROGRAMS, THE SOURCE CODE CONTAINED THEREIN, AND/OR THE TECHNIQUES DESCRIBED IN THIS BOOK. IDGB DOES NOT WARRANT THAT THE FUNCTIONS CONTAINED IN THE SOFTWARE WILL MEET YOUR REQUIREMENTS OR THAT THE OPERATION OF THE SOFTWARE WILL BE ERROR FREE.

   (c) This limited warranty gives you specific legal rights, and you may have other rights that vary from jurisdiction to jurisdiction.

6. **Remedies.**

   (a) IDGB's entire liability and your exclusive remedy for defects in materials and workmanship shall be limited to replacement of the Software Media, which may be returned to IDGB with a copy of your receipt at the following address: Software Media Fulfillment Department, Attn.: *Corel WebMaster Suite For Dummies*, IDG Books Worldwide, Inc., 7260 Shadeland Station, Ste. 100, Indianapolis, IN 46256, or call 800-762-2974. Please allow three to four weeks for delivery. This Limited Warranty is void if failure of the Software Media has resulted from accident, abuse, or misapplication. Any replacement Software Media will be warranted for the remainder of the original warranty period or thirty (30) days, whichever is longer.

   (b) In no event shall IDGB or the author be liable for any damages whatsoever (including without limitation damages for loss of business profits, business interruption, loss of business information, or any other pecuniary loss) arising from the use of or inability to use the Book or the Software, even if IDGB has been advised of the possibility of such damages.

   (c) Because some jurisdictions do not allow the exclusion or limitation of liability for consequential or incidental damages, the above limitation or exclusion may not apply to you.

7. **U.S. Government Restricted Rights.** Use, duplication, or disclosure of the Software by the U.S. Government is subject to restrictions stated in paragraph (c)(1)(ii) of the Rights in Technical Data and Computer Software clause of DFARS 252.227-7013, and in subparagraphs (a) through (d) of the Commercial Computer-Restricted Rights clause at FAR 52.227-19, and in similar clauses in the NASA FAR supplement, when applicable.

8. **General.** This Agreement constitutes the entire understanding of the parties and revokes and supersedes all prior agreements, oral or written, between them and may not be modified or amended except in a writing signed by both parties hereto that specifically refers to this Agreement. This Agreement shall take precedence over any other documents that may be in conflict herewith. If any one or more provisions contained in this Agreement are held by any court or tribunal to be invalid, illegal, or otherwise unenforceable, each and every other provision shall remain in full force and effect.

Installing the CD-ROM

To install the items from this book's CD-ROM onto your computer, follow these steps:

1. **Insert the CD into your computer's CD-ROM drive and close the drive door.**

2. **Click the Windows Start button and select Run.**

3. **In the dialog box that appears, type** D:\SETUP.EXE.

   Odds are, your CD-ROM drive is listed as drive D under My Computer. Type in the proper drive letter if your CD-ROM drive uses a different letter.

4. **Click OK.**

   A license agreement window appears.

5. **Read through the license agreement and then click Accept if you agree to its terms.**

   After you click Accept, you'll never be bothered by the License.

6. **Click OK to indicate that you're ready to view the contents of the CD.**

   In a moment, the CD interface appears. The software on the interface is divided into categories whose names you see on the screen.

7. **To view the items within a category, just click the category's name.**

   A list of programs in the category appears.

8. **For more information about a program, click on the program's name.**

   Be sure to read the information that's displayed. Sometimes, a program may require you to make adjustments to your computer first, and this screen tells you where to go for that information, if necessary.

9. **To install the program, click the appropriate Install button; if you don't want to install the program, click on the Don't Install button to return to the previous category screen.**

For more information about the CD that comes with this book, see Appendix B.

Discover Dummies Online!

The Dummies Web Site is your fun and friendly online resource for the latest information about ...*For Dummies*® books and your favorite topics. The Web site is the place to communicate with us, exchange ideas with other ...*For Dummies* readers, chat with authors, and have fun!

Ten Fun and Useful Things You Can Do at www.dummies.com

1. Win free ...*For Dummies* books and more!
2. Register your book and be entered in a prize drawing.
3. Meet your favorite authors through the IDG Books Author Chat Series.
4. Exchange helpful information with other ...*For Dummies* readers.
5. Discover other great ...*For Dummies* books you must have!
6. Purchase Dummieswear™ exclusively from our Web site.
7. Buy ...*For Dummies* books online.
8. Talk to us. Make comments, ask questions, get answers!
9. Download free software.
10. Find additional useful resources from authors.

Link directly to these ten fun and useful things at
http://www.dummies.com/10useful

For other technology titles from IDG Books Worldwide, go to
www.idgbooks.com

Not on the Web yet? It's easy to get started with *Dummies 101*®: *The Internet For Windows*® *95* or *The Internet For Dummies*®, 4th Edition, at local retailers everywhere.

Find other ...*For Dummies* books on these topics:
Business • Career • Databases • Food & Beverage • Games • Gardening • Graphics
Hardware • Health & Fitness • Internet and the World Wide Web • Networking
Office Suites • Operating Systems • Personal Finance • Pets • Programming • Recreation
Sports • Spreadsheets • Teacher Resources • Test Prep • Word Processing

IDG BOOKS WORLDWIDE
BOOK REGISTRATION

Register This Book and Win!

We want to hear from you!

Visit **http://my2cents.dummies.com** to register this book and tell us how you liked it!

- ✔ Get entered in our monthly prize giveaway.

- ✔ Give us feedback about this book — tell us what you like best, what you like least, or maybe what you'd like to ask the author and us to change!

- ✔ Let us know any other ...*For Dummies* topics that interest you.

Your feedback helps us determine what books to publish, tells us what coverage to add as we revise our books, and lets us know whether we're meeting your needs as a ...*For Dummies* reader. You're our most valuable resource, and what you have to say is important to us!

Not on the Web yet? It's easy to get started with *Dummies 101®: The Internet For Windows® 95* or *The Internet For Dummies,®* 4th Edition, at local retailers everywhere.

Or let us know what you think by sending us a letter at the following address:

...*For Dummies* Book Registration
Dummies Press
7260 Shadeland Station, Suite 100
Indianapolis, IN 46256
Fax 317-596-5498

BUSINESS AND
GENERAL
REFERENCE
BOOK SERIES
FROM IDG

COMPUTER
BOOK SERIES
FROM IDG